GPS

Land Navigation

GPS Land Navigation

A Complete Guidebook for Backcountry Users of the NAVSTAR Satellite System

Michael Ferguson

illustrations by Leah Tucker

A practical guide to effective use of the Global Positioning System. Written for hikers, backpackers, cross-country skiers, mountain bikers, fishermen, hunters, equestrians, snowmobilers, 4-wheelers and other land-based outdoor recreation enthusiasts (and the good folks who occasionally have to rescue them).

Glassford Publishing
Boise, Idaho

Fifth Printing, December 1999

Library of Congress Catalog Card Number: 96-78541

Ferguson, Michael H., 1950-
  GPS Land Navigation
1. Global Positioning System. 2. Orienteering. 3. Navigation, Inland.
  4. Outdoor Recreation. 5. Hiking

ISBN 0-9652202-5-7

Printed in the United States of America
10 9

DISCLAIMER: The information provided in this book is accurate to the best knowledge of the author and publisher. However, much of it is taken from materials supplied by various GPS receiver manufacturers and government agencies. There is no warranty, therefore, express or implied, as to the accuracy of any material contained herein.

Table Of Contents

Preface

This book is a practical guidebook for anyone who uses, or wants to use, the Global Positioning System —GPS— for backcountry and off-road land navigation. It doesn't presume or require that you have any prior knowledge of GPS, cartography, orienteering, or any other traditional route-finding skills.

You'll find a wide range of topics covered in these pages. From GPS hardware (receivers, compasses, altimeters, etc.) to GPS software (maps, coordinates, bearings, etc.) to GPS skills (trip planning, route finding, map reading, etc.), this book gives you the information you need to get the maximum benefit and pleasure from owning and using the U.S. global positioning system.

That's right, **you** own the global positioning system. The NAVSTAR satellite system was originally developed for the U.S. military and is now operated by the U.S. Department of Defense. This resource is available world-wide to any person with the necessary technology (a receiver) in hand, but the American taxpayer is the ultimate owner of this system.

This book covers an extensive array of GPS-related equipment and information that will allow you to achieve the maximum potential from the GPS system. It is also possible, however, to use a GPS receiver quite effectively by itself. You can decide how you want to use your GPS receiver based on your specific needs. This book will help make your options clear.

In addition to the "how-to" elements of GPS receiver use, you'll also find several useful appendices. They're packed (literally) with actual coordinate data that you can enter into your GPS receiver and use to navigate to specific locations. The highest peak in every county, every state capitol, and all U.S. Interstate/U.S. Highway intersections are listed for easy entry into your GPS receiver's waypoint database.

These precise coordinates have both fun and practical applications. Among other things, they can help you get your GPS receiver locked-in fast, thereby avoiding lengthy "initialization" procedures. All you need to do is select a coordinate you know is within one or two hundred miles of your actual position. They can also make it easy to identify and verify the location of significant landmarks you may encounter during your travels.

Finally, if you don't own a GPS receiver but you are considering buying one, the section on GPS receivers in Chapter 2 and Appendix 4 are for you. They will help you identify relevant GPS receiver features as they relate to your requirements. They will also assist you in selecting the best unit to fit your particular needs.

How To Use This Book

This book is intended to provide you with everything you need to know in order to fully utilize your GPS receiver. All you need to add is a receiver and its operating manual. While it would be flattering to hear that you had read this book cover to cover, only a few readers are likely to be that absorbed by this topic and material. This is a reference book, and you should read the parts that appeal to you.

Every effort has been made to make each chapter a complete stand-alone unit. Some are more important than others. The most important chapters are Chapter 2 and Chapter 6.

Chapter 2 (GPS Hardware) is important because it gives the straight scoop on both the capabilities and the limitations of GPS receivers. Sometimes the manuals that are supplied with GPS receivers fail to acknowledge the shortcomings of this phenomenal technology. The most critical element of this chapter is knowing how and why 2D mode can get you in trouble.

Chapter 6 (GPS Skills) gives you a thorough description of how to get the most value from your GPS receiver by using it wisely and effectively. It also should save you from a considerable amount of trial and error in getting up to speed with GPS. You may need to read all or parts of Chapters 2 to 5 before digging into Chapter 6. If you encounter too many unfamiliar terms and concepts in Chapter 6, then save it for last.

Generous amounts of cross-referencing, a thorough index, and careful organization are intended to make it easy for you to find specific information quickly and easily. Start with the Table of Contents, then try the Index when you need to search for information on a specific topic.

Don't let GPS terminology get in your way — an extensive Glossary of Terms is included at the end of this book. There you'll find definitions for many of the terms that appear in the main text. That's another way to help you deal with the problem of encountering so much new material and terminology. Be aware that the Index does not point to the Glossary of Terms, so if you're looking up a concept, it's probably a good idea to look in both places.

While the side margins help make this an attractive book, they're really there so you can make ample notes to yourself about the topics covered in the text and figures. Remember, this is a reference book. You should be making notes as you go for your own later reference.

The three-level numbering system used for section headings is included to give a clear notion of how the topics are organized *while you're reading the book*. The first level corresponds to the chapter title, which is also shown on the upper left page header. The second level corresponds to major sections, which are also shown on the upper right page header. The third level corresponds to sub-sections. You can easily see the context for a sub-section by noting the chapter and major section that are printed on the page headers.

A Few Words About Terminology

The advent of GPS for personal navigation has brought with it a baffling array of new terms. Unfortunately, the terminology can quickly become confusing and sometimes is just plain wrong. Among other things, it makes it difficult to communicate some of the concepts presented in this book. In order to eliminate as much potential confusion as possible, the material presented throughout this book conforms to certain semantic "rules." These semantic rules are explained under the next two headings, and they should be considered a framework for the chapters that follow. But please recognize that they only apply to this book, and you can't rely on them beyond these pages.

Locations, Position Fixes, Landmarks, and Waypoints

Coordinates are a fundamental underpinning of the GPS system. Your location on the earth is defined by a pair of coordinates (plus an associated datum). The coordinates that are displayed when your receiver is tracking at least 3 satellites are known as your "position fix." The distinction between your location and your position fix is that your location is the actual physical place that you occupy, while your position fix is the place your GPS receiver says you are at. Under normal circumstances your position fix will most likely be within 100 meters of your actual location. Just remember it this way: location refers to an actual place, position fix refers to coordinates reported by the GPS receiver. They should be close, but only rarely are they identical.

When a position fix is assigned a name and stored in a GPS receiver's memory it is called a "waypoint." A waypoint can also be created by entering coordinate values obtained from a map or some other source (such as the appendices in the back of this book).

Some (but not all) Magellan receivers use the term "landmark" in the place of "waypoint." This book, however, only uses the term waypoint. If your receiver calls a stored position a landmark, just substitute that term in your mind every time you see the term waypoint in this book. They mean the same thing. Remember, a waypoint (or Magellan's landmark) is not a physical location on the ground, but rather the coordinates that approximate that location. This is a subtle, but important, distinction.

Directions, Bearings, Headings, and Azimuths

Directions are among the most important navigational "outputs" of the GPS system. The way you find a location with your GPS receiver is to follow the direction information the receiver provides you. You must first have a waypoint stored that represents the coordinates for the location you wish to find. The receiver then reports the direction from your current position fix to the waypoint you want to find.

Semantic problems arise due to the various terms that are used to describe directions. First the bottom line: In this book (and in most GPS receivers) the term "bearing" is used to describe either the direction from your position to a waypoint, or the direction from one waypoint to another. Bearings are either reported by the GPS receiver or obtained with a protractor and a map. The term "heading" is used to describe the direction you are actually traveling (or if you're standing still, the direction you are facing). Headings are most often obtained with a compass, but they can be obtained with a GPS receiver that is in motion. Again, a somewhat subtle distinction but ever so important.

The use of the term "bearing" in the manner just described is technically incorrect for reasons that are fully explained on page 145. In a nutshell, the correct term for a direction (as reported by a GPS receiver) is an "azimuth." However, this semantic infraction is relatively minor. Since virtually every GPS receiver produced uses the term bearing, it's what we'll use in this book.

Datums

Finally, a few words about a very important concept in the world of GPS — datum. This term is very important to land navigators using GPS for reasons explained beginning on page 44 under the heading "setup parameters." A datum specifies the earth-model (the ellipsoid) and the origin associated with a particular set of coordinates. A datum is needed to properly describe a specific location on earth. *Without a datum, coordinates are absolutely worthless.*

Even though the datum is often omitted, it is always implied. As you'll see later in this book, it pays to understand which datum (of the many available) you need to use.

Acknowledgments

This book would not have been possible without the help of many great people. First and foremost, thanks go to Diana for supplying the inspiration (and the long weeknights of solitude) that got this project off the ground in the beginning. And to Jack & Penny for occasionally dragging me away from the computer long enough to keep my sanity (and a little color in my cheeks). And certainly to Claire and Maria, for both unintentionally showing me the real value in this technology, and helping me unlock the mystery of 2D mode. A special thanks to Glenn for sharing his knowledge, his GPS World magazines, his surveyor training material, and not one but two rounds of proofing. Steve Stuebner deserves thanks and credit for both his multi-faceted assistance and his inspiration. Steve showed me that writing a book truly is within reach of the little guy.

There are some wonderful folks in the highly competitive world of consumer GPS receiver manufacturing. Jim White at Magellan, Leann McNabb at Trimble, Bill Wright at Silva Marine, Chad Warford at Lowrance and Steve Featherstone at Garmin were all very helpful and patient. Their generous contribution of their time, the use of their products, and the review of critical sections in this book was of immeasurable value. Thanks also go to their many associates (too many to name) in their respective companies who helped this project along the way.

The technical information and many of the images used throughout this book came from a wide variety of sources. Special thanks to Troy Bunch of the Bureau of Land Management, Alan Gunderson of the U.S. Geological Survey, Dennis Milbert of the National Geodetic Survey, Sheldon Bluestein of the Ada County Assessor's Office, Tom Damiani of Rockwell International, Pirjo Talka of Suunto USA, and Carol Brandt of the U.S. Transportation Department for information they generously supplied. Matthew Heller of Wildflower Productions was kind enough to provide a copy of TOPO! for review.

Proofing books is probably one of the more thankless assignments that anyone can accept, but my deepest thanks go to the many friends and associates who willingly took on that burden. Glenn Bennett, George Brogdan, Doug Colwell, Diana Douglas, Sandy Elliott, Eric Haff, Jack Harrison, Claire Lowrie, Mike Lyons, Bob Meredith, Steve Stuebner, and Scott Williams gave a ton of useful advice and made this a much better product. Nonetheless, it goes without saying that any remaining errors (or fog) are the full responsibility of the author.

And to anyone I overlooked, my sincere apology and heartfelt thanks.

Chapter 1:

Introduction to GPS

The Global Positioning System is easily the most significant development in navigation since the compass. As you'll soon see, GPS is not just about navigation. In just a few years, virtually everyone will rely on this technology in both subtle and dramatic ways.

GPS is not a brand new system. *GPS World*, a monthly magazine devoted exclusively to this amazing technology, is in its ninth year of publication. The first GPS satellites were launched almost 20 years ago, in 1978.

Trimble, a major manufacturer of handheld GPS receivers, has called GPS "the next utility," suggesting that it will eventually become as commonplace in everyday life as the telephone is today.

Already, GPS is used to keep urban buses on schedule, navigate ships and airplanes, and perform precision surveying. Exciting new uses are emerging in farming, mining, forestry, shipyard operations, inventory control, land management, and many other fields. GPS is being introduced in a vast array of new commercial applications for several simple reasons: it saves time, it saves money, and it even saves lives.

Personal use of GPS on land is just beginning. It won't be long before a GPS receiver is standard equipment for anyone heading into the backcountry for work or play. Again, the reasons are simple: with GPS you can go farther, enjoy your surroundings more, and widen your margin of safety.

The Global Positioning System is the most significant development in land navigation since the compass.

1.1 A World Full Of Uses

You probably had very specific uses in mind when you purchased your GPS receiver. Nevertheless, the breadth of potential outdoor recreation uses for GPS is astonishing.

Hunters and fishermen can log their favorite spots then later navigate a successful return trip with ease. Hikers and mountain bikers can explore and "map" new trails, and share their discoveries with other GPS users without resorting to complicated route instructions. River runners can check their location relative to a campsite or a major rapid. Skiers and snowmobilers can venture out into the stark beauty of the winter landscape confident that storms and whiteouts cannot "blind" them and thwart a safe return home. Search and rescue personnel can quickly and accurately identify and locate isolated and remote locations. Whatever your particular outdoor interest, GPS can probably make it safer and more fun than ever before.

The first group to make widespread personal use of GPS were mariners. Magellan introduced the first handheld GPS receivers for nautical use in 1989. They sold for $3,000. In early 1997 a fully functional GPS receiver with interface capabilities (for linking it to auto pilots and other marine electronics) could be obtained for under $200! More sophisticated units that contain extensive map data and color displays are priced under $1,000 and are becoming common in consumer marine applications. Today it's hard to imagine anyone venturing into the open seas (or coastal waters) without a GPS receiver aboard.

Photo Courtesy Rockwell International

Figure 1-1: *A GPS Satellite Closeup*

GPS is starting to show up in some relatively new areas. Automobile manufacturers are moving toward integrating GPS into the electronics of passenger cars. One recent development is a marriage of GPS and cellular telephone technology that gives the driver one-button emergency transmission capability. The driver simply pushes a "panic" button on the overhead console, and the integrated cellular phone sends an emergency telephone message complete with precise vehicle location information.

Another emerging automotive application is the integration of GPS capabilities with on-board electronic maps. A display panel in the dashboard gives the driver a constantly updated, zoomable map of the vehicle's vicinity, with the position of the vehicle highlighted on the map. When linked with broadcasts of traffic congestion data, the map display will also be able to show the least congested route to a specific destination.

The really good news is you don't have to buy a new GPS equipped car to take immediate advantage of this technology while driving. Most handheld GPS units that are currently available have a cigarette lighter power cord option, making it practical to use your backcountry GPS receiver in your car. In fact, you may find that getting you to the trailhead is one of the most useful secondary applications for your GPS receiver!

Golfers are even finding GPS in use on the links. Recently several golf courses have equipped their golf carts with GPS receivers that give the golfers information on distance to the next hole, and give the course's management real-time information on the flow of golfers through the course. The end result is more golfers are able to use the fairways on a busy day.

...this book can show you why GPS is such a valuable piece of equipment for the outdoor enthusiast.

But let's get back to <u>your</u> use of GPS. This book will provide you with a clear understanding of how to get the most out of this fantastic new navigation tool. If you don't yet have a GPS receiver, this book can show you why it is such a valuable piece of equipment in the outdoors, and assist you in deciding which of the many available receivers is right for you.

A word of caution: This book is *not* meant to replace the manual that comes with your GPS receiver. In fact, it is important that you study your manual carefully and learn how to operate the features and functions of your particular GPS receiver. You can do this as you work through the information contained in this book. This book will help you learn how to use your receiver to its fullest, without the need to discover the many and varied capabilities of GPS by yourself.

Besides thoroughly covering how to use GPS technology, this book also provides an extensive amount of actual coordinate data in several appendices. You can use this coordinate data in a variety of different ways. It gives you information that can help you avoid the slow process of "initializing" your GPS receiver when you're in a new location. It can help you identify distant peaks when you're traveling in unfamiliar territory. It can also help you keep track of your progress when your travels extend across the Interstate highways of this land.

So without further ado, let's dig into the workings of the Global Positioning System and see just what it can do for you!

1.2 NAVSTAR — The Satellite System

NAVSTAR is the name of the U.S. government's global positioning system. It is also what your GPS receiver depends on for its operation. GPS receivers are just one part of a three-part system that uses the timing of radio signals to measure distance, velocity, and time. The complete system consists of a **control segment** (the satellite ground stations), a **space segment** (the satellites in orbit), and a **user segment** (the receiver in your hand). Although legend has it that NAVSTAR stands for <u>Nav</u>igation <u>S</u>atellite <u>T</u>iming <u>A</u>nd <u>R</u>anging, it's really just a word that sounded good to the developers of the system.

The **control segment** is the foundation of the NAVSTAR system. It is a network of ground stations that serve as the central nervous system of the GPS system, constantly providing control information to the individual satellites within the system. The responsibilities of the control segment include tracking satellite positions, keeping the satellites in their proper orbits, and telling the satellites their exact positions and the exact time.

The **space segment** of the NAVSTAR system consists of 24 satellites (plus two spares) in high orbit above the earth. Each satellite orbits the earth once every 12 hours. These

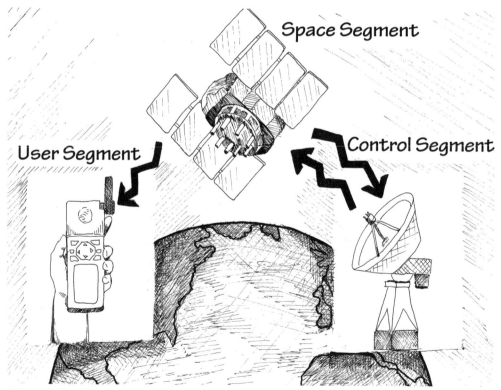

Figure 1-2:   GPS System Segments

satellites are located approximately 12,000 miles above the earth's surface, and they each follow one of six orbital paths. Each satellite contains four atomic clocks, and continuously sends radio signals that are used by the GPS receiver to calculate its position.

The **user segment** of the NAVSTAR system is the part you hold in your hand — the receiver. This is where your position is determined. The GPS receiver includes a radio receiver, quartz clock, memory, and a CPU that performs a wide variety of calculations.

The NAVSTAR global positioning system originated in 1973 as the Defense Navigation Satellite System. In 1978 the NAVSTAR 1 through NAVSTAR 4 satellites were launched and became operational. By December 1993 a full constellation of 24 satellites was in orbit and the NAVSTAR system was declared to have reached Initial Operational Capability (IOC). At that point the NAVSTAR system was no longer considered an experimental system.

The satellites used for GPS fall into three categories that relate to their capabilities. Block I satellites were the early models and have all been replaced. Block II and IIR satellites are newer and more advanced. Block II satellites add the means for restricting signals supplied to civilian GPS users, and Block IIR satellites add more accurate atomic clocks and improved orbiting capabilities. Once the satellite constellation consisted entirely of 24 Block II and IIR satellites (i.e., all Block I satellites had been replaced) the system was declared to have reached Full Operational Capability (FOC). That occurred in July 1995.

The NAVSTAR system is designed so that any location on earth will have line of sight access to a minimum of six satellites at all times, as long as there is an unobstructed view of the sky from horizon to horizon. It

Fig 1-3: Deployment Of GPS Satellite 009

Photo Courtesy Rockwell International

takes at least four satellites for a GPS receiver to obtain a three-dimensional (3D mode) position fix. A 3D mode position fix provides horizontal coordinates *plus* elevation. Most GPS receivers can also provide a two-dimensional (2D mode) position fix when only three satellites are being tracked. A 2D mode position fix only provides horizontal coordinates. ***See page 41 for important warnings about using 2D mode***.

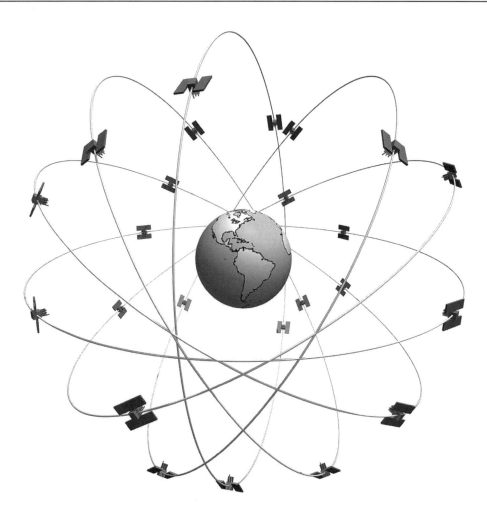

Figure 1-4: *GPS Satellite Constellation - The Space Segment*

The process of providing a position fix, receiver velocity, and UTC time is the extent of the satellite system's role in GPS technology. Everything else (heading, distance and direction to waypoints, estimated time of arrival, etc.) are calculations performed solely by the GPS receiver using a combination of **[1]** position fixes obtained using the satellites, **[2]** software permanently stored in the receiver, and **[3]** waypoint data that you loaded into the receiver's memory.

1.2.1 How GPS Works

A GPS receiver determines its position by measuring the time it takes radio signals, moving at the speed of light, to travel from each of four GPS satellites to the GPS receiver. This provides the GPS receiver with the data to determine its distance from each of the satellites. A simplified 2-dimensional illustration of this process is shown in Figure 1-5.

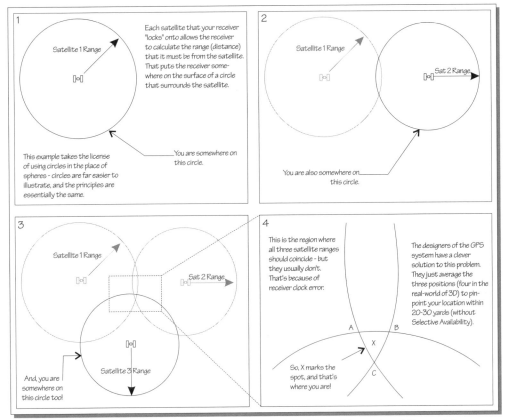

Figure 1-5: *How GPS Finds Your Position (A Simplified Two-Dimensional Example)*

By knowing the precise location of each satellite (from ephemeris data each satellite sends), the receiver can compute the location of a spherical surface that it must be on. That sphere is centered on the satellite and has a radius equal to the distance from the satellite to the receiver. Add a second satellite and the intersection of these two spheres identifies a circle the receiver must be on. Add a third satellite and the intersection of the circle and the third sphere identifies two points, one of which is the receiver's location. This process is similar to, but slightly different than, triangulation with a compass.

A fourth satellite is required to achieve the level of accuracy offered by the NAVSTAR GPS system. That's because the clock in the handheld GPS receiver is not accurate enough to measure the receiver's distance from each satellite to within a few meters. The fourth satellite provides three more redundant "triangulation" measurements that are averaged and thereby cancel your receiver's time related errors.

To see that the fourth satellite gives three more redundant positions, consider the possible three-way combinations of satellites. Satellites 1-2-3, 1-2-4, 1-3-4, and 2-3-4 each yield a pair of points. One point from each of the four pairs should be the location of the receiver, and therefore the same. Measurement errors related to the receiver's clock, however, result in differences. Fortunately, the receiver's clock error affects all four positions in the same way. This makes it possible to use averaging to eliminate most of the effect of the receiver's clock error. This is the key to how a 10 ounce GPS receiver achieves accuracy (without Selective Availability) of better than 30 meters at least 95 percent of the time.

An interesting by-product of the GPS system is its accurate time... you can't get more clock accuracy than you'll find in your GPS receiver.

Most GPS receivers can operate in 2D mode when they receive signals from only three satellites. Two-dimension mode works by using elevation in place of the fourth satellite. Two-dimension mode requires elevation as an input rather than providing it as an output. This feature has its roots in the marine side of GPS applications, where elevation is not a significant variable. On land it is very risky to rely on a 2D mode position fix because inaccurate elevation data can cause very substantial horizontal position errors. Unfortunately, most GPS receiver manuals don't provide adequate warnings about the hazards of using 2D mode position fixes. AS A PRACTICAL MATTER YOU SHOULD AVOID USING 2D MODE. You need to be very familiar with your receiver so that you know when it is in 2D mode. For more information about this important topic see page 41.

An interesting by-product of the GPS system is its extremely accurate time. The time it takes the GPS radio signals to travel from a satellite to the GPS receiver is measured (by the GPS receiver) in nanoseconds! Although the clock in the GPS receiver is not as accurate as the atomic clocks in the GPS satellites, it is constantly being updated with precise UTC time (Universal Time Coordinated, also known as Greenwich Mean Time) when it is locked onto the satellites. From a practical standpoint, you can't get more accurate time than the time provided by your GPS receiver. Just think, you'll never miss the bus again!

1.2.2 GPS Position Accuracy

An important aspect of the NAVSTAR system is the accuracy of the position fixes it supplies. The primary factors influencing the position accuracy you obtain from your GPS receiver are [1] operator error, [2] Selective Availability, [3] the number and geometry of the satellites being received, [4] multipath interference, and [5] atmospheric conditions.

GPS error sources are independent of one another and they are cumulative. This means that any reduction in one error source (for example, operator error) improves the overall accuracy of position fixes. Consequently, when you obtain waypoint coordinates from a map, it is definitely worthwhile to be as accurate as possible.

When considering issues of GPS position accuracy, be careful to recognize the distinction between accuracy and precision. They are not the same. Precision means a fine level of measurement, or high resolution. Accuracy means measuring something close to its true value. A GPS receiver typically shows very precise coordinates, usually to the nearest tenth of a second or thousandth of a minute. That's within 10 feet in terms of ground distance. But the accuracy of civilian GPS receivers is limited to about 100 meters — over 300 feet — when Selective Availability is in use. Without Selective Availability, the accuracy of a typical civilian receiver is within 30 meters — about 100 feet — at least 95 percent of the time. Either way, a GPS receiver usually provides much more precision than accuracy. Now let's take a closer look at the factors behind GPS accuracy.

Operator Error

Mistakes that you make as the operator of a GPS receiver are among the most severe <u>and</u> the most avoidable of the GPS errors. Fortunately, operator errors are not normally a problem when it comes to position fixes. The really big operator errors tend to be related to manual waypoint entry. A good example of this kind of error occurs when you simply enter the wrong coordinates.

The primary mistakes to watch out for when entering coordinate values are having the wrong datum specified, using the wrong zone in the UTM coordinate system, and using the wrong hemisphere (either north/south or east/west) in the latitude/longitude coordinate system. Of course outright keypunch errors can also be quite serious. A good way to prevent really gross errors is to check the distance and direction from a newly entered waypoint to another waypoint or your current position. If the distance is off by hundreds or even thousands of miles (don't laugh, it happens), you probably entered the wrong zone or hemisphere. If it's off by a smaller distance, you probably keyed the wrong numbers.

An easily preventable source of operator error can occur when you read coordinates from a map. Any inaccuracy that occurs when you read coordinate values becomes an addition to the natural and man-made inaccuracy inherent in the receiver itself. Again, it is worthwhile to be as accurate as possible when you obtain coordinate values from a map.

A way that operator errors <u>can</u> affect position fixes is through the display of coordinates. If you haven't set the correct datum for a map you're using, the coordinate values on your receiver's display will not match those of the map. How much error occurs because of using the wrong datum depends on the difference between the datum you are using, and the datum you should be using.

A common datum error in the continental United States is using NAD27 (North American Datum of 1927) in place of NAD83, or vice versa. The amount of error this introduces varies by location, but it is never more than 200 meters in the lower 48 states. Other "wrong" datums can lead to much greater errors, some in excess of a mile.

The only sure way to eliminate operator error is to understand your GPS receiver very thoroughly, be very careful when entering coordinate data and selecting a datum, and check your entered coordinates for reasonableness right after you enter them.

Selective Availability

Selective Availability, or SA, is a man-made form of GPS error that is intentionally introduced by the military operators of the NAVSTAR system. It is intended to deny military adversaries the level of GPS accuracy available to U.S. and allied forces. That goal is accomplished by dithering, or "lying" about, the time and/or location information sent out by each satellite.

Selective Availability is intentionally introduced by the military operators of the NAVSTAR system...to increase the error for civilian users.

The effects of SA impact personal navigation in two ways. One is reduced accuracy of position fixes. The other is distortion in the *speed over ground* and *direction of travel* information displayed by the receiver when it is moving at relatively slow speeds.

The presence of SA increases the horizontal position error of civilian GPS receivers to over 100 meters no more than five percent of the time, and to over 300 meters no more than one-tenth of one percent of the time. Put differently, GPS positioning error from natural and SA sources combined should not exceed 100 meters more than one out of twenty position fixes, and that error should not exceed 300 meters more than one out of one thousand position fixes. In practice, GPS users should experience horizontal accuracy to within 50 meters over half the time, *even when Selective Availability is turned on*.

Here's how SA impacts speed and direction: If you're walking south at 5 mph, but SA is "going north" at 3 mph, your receiver will erroneously tell you you're going 2 mph. If SA switches to south at 3 mph, your receiver will say you're going 8 mph. If the direction SA is "going" relative to your true direction is lateral, then the direction of travel indicated by your receiver will also be inaccurate. If you are going north at 3 mph, but SA is "going west" at 3 mph, your receiver will tell you it's going northwest at 4.2 mph.

While the presence of Selective Availability is unfortunate, it is not a serious problem for the typical backcountry GPS user. Having a position fix to within 100 meters most of the time (and usually much better than that) is adequate to identify and locate trail junctions, campsites, or other geographic features. The direction of travel distortion caused by SA is not usually a problem, because you should be using a magnetic compass for ground directions.

Selective Availability really impacts civilian GPS use in aviation, marine, ground transportation, and other commercial applications. Precise landings of aircraft in adverse weather, piloting boats and ships through treacherous passages, and locating cars and trucks in urban street grids requires greater accuracy than Selective Availability provides.

Fortunately for these civilian GPS applications, a system known as DGPS (Differential Global Positioning System) has been developed that recaptures the undithered accuracy of the GPS system — and then some. Through the use of ground or satellite based radio beacons, a differential compensated GPS receiver can achieve a level of accuracy **with SA on** that far exceeds the accuracy of the same receiver by itself **with SA off**.

Differential GPS is presently available in most coastal areas of the U.S., but it is not currently relevant to the typical recreational or backcountry GPS land navigator. Although it will work with most handheld personal navigation receivers, differential GPS equipment involves a separate radio receiver that must be electronically connected to the GPS receiver. This adds considerable expense, weight, and bulk. Again, backcountry GPS users can generally get by reasonably well with accuracy at the 100 meter level.

Backcountry users may, however, find a way around Selective Availability in the future as the Wide Area Augmentation System (WAAS) is implemented for aviation users. This system is being implemented by the FAA and will provide differential corrections from a network of geostationary satellites. The beauty of WAAS is that it can work through the same channels used for receiving NAVSTAR signals, effectively eliminating the need for separate radio beacon receivers. With luck the system and equipment will be be available by late 1998.

3D Mode

One of the most basic requirements for GPS position accuracy is *having a lock on at least 4 satellites*. This puts your receiver in 3D mode. Even though the elevation component of a 3D GPS position fix is subject to a large amount of error (about 150 percent of the horizontal error), 3D mode is essential for obtaining a reliable horizontal position fix.

Receiver manuals usually explain 2D mode by saying that when only three satellites are being tracked, the vertical (elevation) component of position is not provided. This implies that 2D horizontal coordinates are reasonably accurate. What the manuals don't tell you is that without very accurate elevation data, the horizontal coordinates provided in 2D mode can be extremely unreliable. In fact, a 2D position fix can easily be off by a distance in excess of a mile!

Knowing when your receiver is (and isn't) operating in 3D mode is crucial to safe use of the GPS system... inadvertently using 2D mode can put a position fix off by miles.

This issue is of critical importance to backcountry GPS users, and is also discussed on page 41. The good news is that as long as your receiver is tracking at least 4 satellites, its position fixes should be very reliable. In 3D mode you can count on very good accuracy — within the limits discussed elsewhere in this section.

Satellite Geometry

Satellite geometry refers to the position (in the sky) of the satellites your receiver uses to calculate a position fix. This is an important factor in achieving an accurate position fix. Poor satellite geometry can add hundreds of feet to the receiver's position error. The full constellation of 24 satellites generally provides good potential geometry most of the time. Local obstructions (mountains, cliffs, large buildings, trees, etc.) that block satellite signals are much more likely to be causes of poor satellite geometry.

The ideal "geometry" for the satellites your receiver uses to calculate its position is one satellite directly overhead and three other satellites equally spaced around the horizon. Less than ideal geometry occurs when the satellites used to calculate a position fix are clustered overhead, aligned in a straight line, or both. Because of the constantly changing position of the satellites in their orbits and unavoidable obstructions on the ground, it is rare that you will experience ideal geometry. If you experience geometry related problems (or a mysterious inability to get a satellite lock within a few minutes), try waiting for the satellites to change position. That may solve the problem. On some occasions it seems that simply turning the receiver off then right back on can cure a case of "blindness."

How far you are away from ideal geometry is often indicated by a measurement known as Dilution of Precision, or DOP. There are DOP's for the vertical position (elevation), horizontal position (including the north-south and east-west components of horizontal position), time, and various combinations of these components.

PDOP, or Position Dilution of Precision, has all the separate components combined into a single measurement. Larger values indicate reduced accuracy. If your receiver reports DOPs, its manual should indicate acceptable levels of DOP.

Sometimes GPS receiver manufacturers substitute their own indicator of position error (in feet, meters, or an error index) in place of DOP's. The details of these accuracy indicators (and how you interpret them) vary widely depending on the manufacturer and model of receiver. Refer to your receiver's user manual to determine how your receiver supplies satellite geometry related accuracy information.

Multipath Interference

Multipath interference occurs when the radio signal from the satellite bounces off of some object (a building, cliff, etc.) before being "heard" by your receiver. This can lead to errors in the distance the receiver calculates from the satellite(s) whose signal "bounced."

To avoid multipath error stay away from large buildings or cliffs when taking a position fix. Unfortunately, it is very difficult to know when multipath interference is "interfering" with your position fix.

Atmospheric Conditions

Radio signals such as those transmitted by GPS satellites travel at 186,000 miles per second (the speed of light) through space, but they actually slow down as they pass through the earth's atmosphere. An "average" amount of slowing is built into the ranging calculations performed by GPS receivers. Variations in atmospheric conditions (and hence the amount of slowing) are another source of reduced accuracy. Fortunately, the error introduced by variations in atmospheric conditions is only in the range of 5-10 meters.

Nonetheless, this source of reduced accuracy can be minimized by the simultaneous use of a second signal at a different frequency. This is exactly what dual channel "L1/L2" receivers do. Unfortunately, the availability of receivers that process the second signal, known as the P-Code, is limited to U.S. and allied military forces and a few authorized civilian GPS users. The second frequency is also subject to encryption, turning it into what is known as the Y-Code. This encryption is the foundation of anti-spoofing (A-S), a method of securing the precise positioning service (PPS) for military users.

With the "natural" sources of inaccuracy considered (clock error, satellite geometry, and atmospheric conditions), a typical civilian GPS receiver with a good view of the sky should be able to regularly achieve an accuracy of about 30 horizontal meters, and 45 vertical meters. Vertical accuracy is less than horizontal accuracy because of the geometry of the system (all the satellites are limited to a hemisphere). However, this level of system accuracy is before considering the effects of 2D mode, multipath interference, and SA.

1.2.3 GPS Policy Directions

The U.S. Congress commissioned a major study of the NAVSTAR system in 1994. That study was performed by two separate working groups — the National Academy of Public Administration (NAPA) and the National Research Council (NRC) — that examined different aspects of the NAVSTAR system. The study was completed in 1995, and the two separate work groups issued a joint report entitled "The Global Positioning System — Charting The Future."

The NAPA/NRC report made a number of recommendations for improvements to the NAVSTAR system. One of those recommendations was that Selective Availability be permanently turned off, and that another method (known as anti-spoofing) be used to accomplish military security

Figure 1-6: *NAPA/NRC GPS Study*

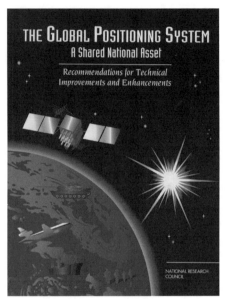

Figure 1-7: NRC GPS Study

objectives. The basis of this recommendation was the ineffectiveness of Selective Availability in meeting military objectives, and the constraint that Selective Availability imposes on full commercial development of GPS technology. Interestingly, the NAPA work group was headed by James Schlesinger, former U.S. Secretary of Defense.

The NRC issued a second report in 1995 that reinforced the findings and recommendations in its joint report with NAPA. Both studies recognize the military issues associated with GPS, but emphasize the overwhelming civilian adoption of this technology.

A study by the RAND Corporation issued in early 1996 ("The Global Positioning System—Assessing National Policies") took an opposite approach on the issue of Selective Availability. It recommended that it be left on until political and diplomatic agreements can be put in place to resolve military security concerns. This report appears to be the basis for a White House policy proclamation issued on March 29, 1996 that said, among other things, Selective Availability will be kept active for the next 4 to 10 years.

It remains to be seen how the issue of Selective Availability will actually play out in the near term. Considerable pressure remains to eliminate Selective Availability, and that pressure is mounting. International standards for commercial radio navigation are teetering on the basis of U.S. military policies concerning GPS. Selective Availability and lack of assured access to the basic GPS signals are proving to be stumbling blocks in adopting GPS as the global standard for commercial systems of air, land, and water navigation. Indeed, both Japan and the European Community are exploring development of their own commercial GPS systems.

Another recommendation that came out of both the NAPA/NRC and the RAND GPS studies may be of greater interest to you as a GPS owner. Both studies recommended that basic access to the GPS satellite radio signals should continue to

Figure 1-8: RAND Corp. GPS Study

be provided free of charge to the public. Already, commercial vendors are emerging in the area of differential GPS services. For a fee, these vendors provide radio signals from reference ground stations that enable GPS receivers to reach accuracy levels below one meter. It is technically feasible for the government to implement a fee system for access to the basic GPS satellite signals themselves. As you can imagine, the commercial GPS industry does not favor such fees.

1.3 GLONASS - Russia's GPS

The United States is not the only country with a functioning GPS system. Russia also has a satellite system similar to the NAVSTAR system. The Russian system is known as GLONASS (Global'naya Navigatsionnaya Sputnikovaya Sistema).

While similar to the NAVSTAR system, GLONASS uses slightly different technology that makes it incompatible with NAVSTAR GPS receivers. There are some specialty GPS receivers on the market, however, that work with both NAVSTAR and GLONASS signals. No handheld receivers that use GLONASS are presently (as of early 1997) sold in the U.S.

An interesting aspect of the GLONASS GPS system is that it does not employ any signal degradation techniques such as NAVSTAR's Selective Availability. Nonetheless, GLONASS is not capable of the level of positioning accuracy offered by NAVSTAR's P-code signal (the second signal that overcomes much of the NAVSTAR system's atmospheric-related inaccuracy). GLONASS does, however, achieve approximately the level of accuracy obtained with NAVSTAR's C/A-code signal without Selective Availability (i.e., if NAVSTAR's SA feature was turned off). In fact, the level of accuracy obtainable today with GLONASS was cited in the aforementioned NAPA/NRC study as one of the reasons that Selective Availability serves no useful purpose and should be turned off.

Chapter 2:

GPS Hardware

Today, one small instrument is all you need to answer that age-old question: Where in the world am I? That instrument is, of course, a GPS receiver. Two other instruments that go hand-in-hand with a GPS receiver are a compass and an altimeter. When combined with a map, these instruments can keep you from ever getting lost again.

Anyone planning to use GPS for backcountry navigation should be familiar with more than just GPS receivers and their readouts. As you'll see, GPS does not eliminate the need for traditional navigation instruments (such as compasses and altimeters) if you want to safely navigate the backcountry. GPS will, however, make backcountry navigation much easier and far more certain. With GPS you'll always know exactly where you are. That adds up to greater peace of mind and more time to spend on the reasons that brought you to the backcountry in the first place.

GPS does not eliminate the need for traditional navigation instruments... but it does make backcountry navigation much easier and safer.

This chapter deals primarily with GPS related hardware. It provides the information you need to select and operate the basic equipment used in satellite-based land navigation. Later chapters explain the fundamentals of GPS related "software" (maps, coordinates, bearings, etc.) in much greater detail.

By dividing the basic tools used for GPS land navigation into "hardware" and "software," this book tries to simplify the process of explaining the various parts of the overall system. The term "hardware" refers to the instruments (GPS receiver, compass, altimeter, etc.) that are used to obtain position fixes, directions, distances, and elevations. The term "software" refers to the information that is processed (maps, coordinates, bearings, etc.) by these instruments. It is not software in the literal (computer program) sense, although computer programs for use with GPS receivers are available and discussed on page 44.

As you can see, GPS related tools include a number of traditional navigation instruments. They are important because they both complement your GPS receiver when it is the centerpiece of your route finding toolkit, and they provide an important backup in the event that the GPS system or your receiver stops functioning.

Additional items of hardware, in the form of map measurement devices and instruments, are very helpful when you work with maps. These map reading aids do on maps what GPS receivers do in the real world — they provide you with precise coordinates.

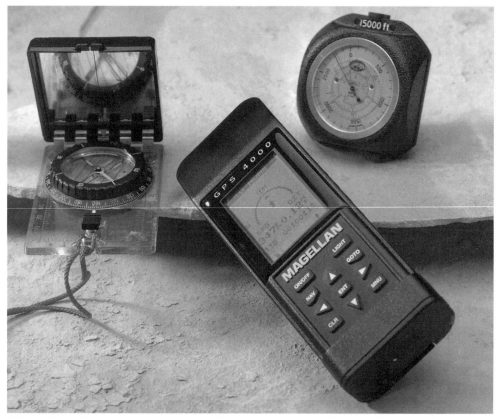

Figure 2-1: *Three Basic Instruments Of Land Navigation*

2.1 GPS Receivers

Like many newly emerging technologies, GPS is undergoing rapid change. The full satellite constellation (24 orbiting satellites plus 2 spares, all maintained by the U.S. Department of Defense) has only been in place since late 1993, and only became fully operational in 1995. This "space segment" of the NAVSTAR GPS system is likely to remain fairly stable for the foreseeable future.

The "user segment" of the system (the GPS receiver you hold in your hand) is likely to undergo continued rapid change and improvement. New models are being introduced every year. Although ease of use and convenience options are being added, the basic navigation information provided by all GPS receivers remains the same:

[1] Your position in terms of coordinates and elevation,

[2] The direction to any waypoint you specify (or between any two waypoints),

[3] The distance to any waypoint you specify (or between any two waypoints),

[4] Your speed of travel, and

[5] Your direction of travel.

Your *position,* the *direction to a waypoint* (see page *xiii* in the Preface for the definition of a waypoint), and the *distance to a waypoint* are the essential GPS outputs for backcountry land navigators. These outputs can be obtained either while you are standing still or while you are in motion. Your *speed of travel* and *direction of travel* are non-essential GPS outputs. To obtain them you must be in motion. At low speeds, such as when traveling on foot, horseback, bike, etc., Selective Availability seriously degrades the accuracy of both speed and direction of travel readouts (see page 10 for information about Selective Availability).

The last point is particularly important. *It is not possible to receive accurate direction of travel information from your GPS receiver if you're not in motion, or if your speed is relatively slow (under 10-15 mph).* That is why a compass is an invaluable accessory to your GPS receiver.

Besides, using a GPS receiver as a compass consumes a large amount of battery power. Why use your receiver's precious "juice" when a simple magnetic compass can do the job better to begin with?

GPS receivers also provide a wide variety of miscellaneous information that is of limited use to land navigators. Most of this additional information is fairly standard, such as *estimated time of arrival* (the time you would arrive at a specified waypoint based on your progress from the last waypoint), *velocity made good* (the rate at which you're closing in on a selected waypoint), and ***cross track error*** (the amount of lateral distance you are off of a straight line course between two waypoints).

To a large extent this additional information is a carryover from the nautical origins of today's handheld GPS receivers. While this information can be interesting (and even helpful at times), it is important to recognize its limitations. One limitation, already mentioned, is the inherent imprecision of speed measurements when traveling on foot, horseback, or bike. Another is the fact that land courses, unlike sea or air courses, usually involve uneven terrain that makes it undesirable to rigidly stick to a straight line course. This limits the usefulness of ***cross track error***, and it also casts doubt on the accuracy of ***estimated time of arrival***. Nonetheless, these features are described later in this chapter.

Other more specialized information is found only in particular models or brands of GPS receivers. Examples include the direction and/or time of sunrise and sunset for any date and location you specify; the position of the sun and/or moon (direction and height above the horizon) for any date, time, and location you specify; coordinates expressed as a measurement offset relative to the corner of a map; steering adjustments; and various kinds of graphical displays. Your GPS receiver's manual should indicate the full set of features and information offered by your particular receiver model. Again, many of these

Figure 2-2: *Popular Handheld GPS Receivers*

specialized features have nautical origins. Some, such as sun and moon positions, can be of occasional use to land navigators. Many, such as steering adjustments, anchor drift alarms, and Man Over Board keys, have little practical use in land navigation.

2.1.1 Features of GPS Receivers

For land-based navigators the big GPS changes are small — as in how small GPS receivers are becoming. Popular models are well under 1 pound, and the lightest units are approaching ½ pound. These weights include operating batteries, but exclude a protective case and a spare set of batteries. Another major development is a new generation of parallel channel receivers that offer remarkable sensitivity yet are among the smallest available.

Other changes of benefit to land navigators are in the GPS receiver's internal software and user interface. New and expanded features such as graphic line plots of the user's track, built-in digital maps, one-button route marking on the fly, route inversion capabilities, and multiple route storage capacity extend GPS functionality well beyond simply providing position fixes. You can even make a real-time connection between a GPS receiver and a lap-top or palm-sized computer, thereby giving the GPS receiver a practically unlimited supply of memory. All this is available today in GPS receivers that weigh under 10 ounces!

Each GPS receiver on the market has a unique set of features and characteristics. If you already have a receiver, hopefully it has the right set of features for you. If you are considering buying a receiver, the following feature descriptions should help you identify the inevitable tradeoffs that you'll face when you make your purchase decision.

Above all, the best GPS receiver for your use depends on how you will use it. You'll need to "weigh" the relative importance of the various considerations that apply to your use. A backpacker will probably put a lot of emphasis on weight. A hunter might be more concerned about how rugged a receiver is. A skier may want a receiver that has a low minimum operating temperature and works well with lithium or ni-cad batteries for cold-weather performance. The main issues are laid out in the following paragraphs. You'll find a detailed comparison of various brands and models of GPS receivers in Appendix 4.

Weight

Less is better. It's that simple. Typical weights for handheld receivers range from just over one-half pound to over two pounds. When comparing different units, be sure to factor in a spare set (or sets) of batteries and a protective case. You should allow an average of five minutes of operation for each "fix" you expect to take in the field. Relate this to the rated battery life of the unit to calculate how many sets of batteries you think you'll need. Then add one more set. Don't use "battery-saver mode" run-time specifications to calculate estimated operating time. This mode only saves battery life during continuous operation, not the "on-and-off" operation that is typical during actual field use.

Channels

There are two types of GPS receivers for personal navigation. Multiplexing receivers have 1 to 3 channels, and rapidly cycle through the satellites that are being used to obtain a position fix. Parallel receivers have 5 to 12 channels, so that each satellite that is being used for a position fix has its own separate channel that is continuously being read. Parallel channel receivers can be designed to "over solve" a position, meaning that more than 4 satellites can be used to calculate a position fix. This can provide marginal improvements in position accuracy. The primary benefit of parallel channel receivers is their improved sensitivity and ability to obtain and hold a satellite lock in difficult situations, such as forests or urban environments, where signal obstruction is a problem. Be careful not to confuse the number of satellites that can be tracked at one time with the number of parallel channels. Even one and two channel receivers can track as many as 12 satellites at a time. They just don't track then simultaneously.

Antennas

External antennas (usually quadrifilar helix) are vulnerable to breakage, but are relatively easy and inexpensive to extend for short distances using coaxial cable — say to the windshield of a car or truck. Internal antennas (usually microstrip patch) are protected by the receiver's outer case, but cannot be extended with just a coaxial cable. Most (but not all) models with internal antennas have a connector for adding a remote antenna. This is more costly than a simple external antenna extension cable, but this option does permit much longer extensions of the remote antenna. An extended or remote antenna can make it much easier and more reliable to use your GPS receiver in a vehicle.

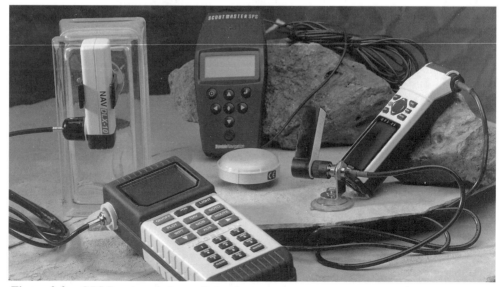

Figure 2-3: *GPS Receiver Antenna Extensions*

Power Supply

You may want to use an external power supply (camcorder battery, car, etc) to supplement the receiver's internal batteries. A wider range of operating voltage will give you greater flexibility in hooking up your own power supply (such as a video camera battery). Ni-cad or lithium battery capability can be important if the GPS receiver will be used in conditions of extreme cold. It is also important to be aware of how long the unit will operate on a set of batteries. Short battery life means extra batteries and extra weight.

Operating Environment

Two characteristics are important. One is the degree of water resistance. Some units are completely water-proof (they even float), others are water resistant (i.e., they shouldn't be submerged), and others shouldn't be allowed to even get wet. Most personal navigation receivers are at least water resistant (thanks to their nautical origins). The other operating environment characteristic that can be very important is operating temperature range. This is not a limitation of the battery system (although batteries are relevant for low temperature operation), but rather the LCD (liquid crystal display) that provides visual output from the GPS receiver. LCDs have real limits that apply to both their operating range (i.e., a temperature below which the display fades out) and their storage range (i.e., a temperature below which the display can be damaged). If you intend to use a GPS receiver in extreme cold, make sure that it can handle very low temperatures. And try using it with gloves.

Memory

More is better. Unfortunately, there's no standard measurement available. A receiver's memory is reflected in how many waypoints and routes can be stored, the length of descriptive name and memo fields associated with routes and waypoints, and how much track plot data can be stored. In all likelihood you will probably want to supplement any receiver's internal memory with hard copy notes, and possibly a personal computer waypoint management program.

Coordinate Systems

Latitude/longitude is the most common coordinate system. All GPS receivers utilize this system. UTM (Universal Transverse Mercator) is a metric coordinate system that's designed to be easy to use. UTM is a desirable feature, but not all receivers offer this capability. The UPS (Universal Polar Stereographic) coordinate system is a complement to UTM and provides coverage of the polar regions (above latitude 84 north and below latitude 80 south). MGRS (Military Grid Reference System) is a subset of UTM. It is important only if you want to use military maps. A variety of foreign coordinate systems are used in Britain, Ireland, Switzerland, etc. These coordinate systems match the maps

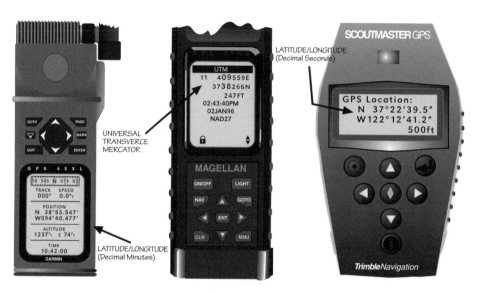

Figure 2-4: *Examples Of GPS Coordinate Systems*

produced in those countries. One company, Trimble Navigation, uses an "Over and Up™" system that gives coordinates in terms of distance from the lower right corner of any map. An enhanced Over and Up™ system from Trimble is referenced to the full set of almost 54,000 USGS 7.5-minute topographic maps. After all is said and done, for North American use latitude/longitude and UTM are the most useful grid systems — all others are "specialized" in one way or another, and relate to special needs.

Map Datums

A datum is part of the reference system that ties the GPS receiver's readouts to a specific map. Some GPS receivers contain well over a hundred different datums to choose from. Most GPS receivers cover the handful of standard North American datums quite well. The need for special datums is mainly an issue for overseas use. Being able to select the correct foreign datum can be important because use of the wrong datum can lead to coordinate "errors" that are quite large — over a mile! A user-defined datum option is a nice feature offered on some models. It can make up for the absence of a specific datum that you may need overseas, but using this feature requires considerable knowledge.

Measurement Units

Metric (meters, kilometers, kilometers per hour), statute (feet, miles, miles per hour), and nautical (nautical miles, knots) are the basic distance-related measurement options. All GPS receivers have these basic measurement systems. Some receivers allow only one universal setting (pick one system, it applies to everything) while other receivers allow mixing units (distance in kilometers, speed in knots, elevation in feet). Another area of measurement choice is declination offset options — true north, grid north, magnetic north, or a user-specified offset. Measurement options may vary by model and brand of receiver.

Accessories

Remote antennas, antenna extension cables, power and data cables, differential GPS capability, computer interface software, and mounting brackets make up some of the more useful (and specialized) accessories available for lightweight, handheld GPS receivers. Finding a convenient way to mount your GPS receiver on the dashboard of your car can greatly extend its usefulness, and connecting the receiver to your vehicle's power supply can be economical. When selecting a GPS receiver, be sure to compare the availability and cost of any optional accessories you think you may need.

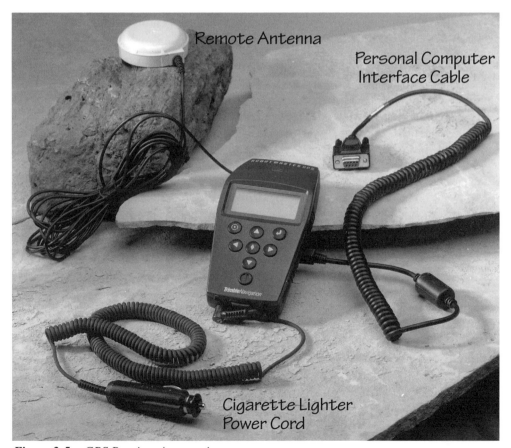

Figure 2-5: *GPS Receiver Accessories*

Bells & Whistles

This area of GPS receiver design is wide-open. Graphic displays, built-in maps, sunset/sunrise time, sunset/sunrise azimuth, satellite signal strength indicators, satellite position maps, battery strength meters, audible alarms, course deviation indicators, anchor drift, and man-over-board buttons are some of the more common "bells and whistles" features. Some of these are carry-over nautical concepts and have little or no practical use for land navigation. Some of the more useful of these miscellaneous features for land navigation include automatic route reversal, a satellite position map, a battery strength meter, and one key waypoint logging. You should identify the features that are important to you and make sure they're available in the receiver you select.

2.1.2 Basic Functions of GPS Receivers

This section's purpose is twofold. First, it is intended to give you an understanding of what the various GPS functions mean to an actual GPS user — you. Second, it is intended to "decode" the various dialects — GPS-speak — that are used by different manufacturers of GPS hardware.

The operating manuals that are supplied with GPS receivers have varying degrees of user friendliness, but none of them really provides a solid underpinning on the topic of *why* you use the various functions of GPS receivers. By dividing basic GPS functions into three general categories, you will be able to get a better perspective on how the various features and display screens in your receiver relate to one another.

The terminology used in the world of GPS can get confusing in a hurry. Different manufacturers (and sometimes different models from the same manufacturer) use different terminology for identical features. You need to recognize this variability to avoid becoming confused. It is a good idea to be familiar with the various names used for a particular feature so that you won't be thrown off course (so to speak) by your friend's Brand X receiver. Think of it as being multilingual.

Let's start by separating the basic functions of GPS receivers into three distinct groups. The main categories of information supplied by GPS receivers are:

[1] Position and waypoint coordinates,

[2] The distance and direction between your position and/or stored waypoints, and

[3] Travel progress reports.

If we divide the items shown on the various display screens of a GPS receiver into these three categories, it will provide you with a better perspective on what your receiver is telling you.

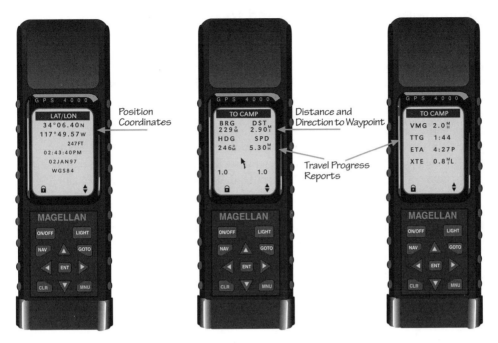

Figure 2-6: *Examples Of The Three Basic Kinds Of Information Supplied By GPS Receivers*

Position and waypoint coordinates refer to the pairs of numbers that represent real-world locations. Coordinates define your current position and coordinates define the stored waypoints that represent all the "memorized" locations that are important to you. Coordinates are what your GPS receiver relies on for virtually everything it does for you.

The distance and direction from your position to a waypoint is the information that you will usually be most interested in — as in: Where am I relative to where I want to be? For example, you may ask your receiver how far and what direction it is to your camp. To use your receiver's distance and direction functions, you must have previously stored the coordinates for the waypoint you are seeking (in this case, your camp).

Travel progress reports tell you how you're doing relative to your travel objectives. Your GPS receiver can give you "travel progress reports" that indicate everything from your speed, to what time you'll arrive at your destination based on your current rate of progress. To use progress report functions you must be in motion, and for some (such as ETA) you must also have a stored waypoint.

There are a variety of other features that various models of GPS receivers have that are of more limited use, especially for backcountry land navigation. "Auxiliary" functions such as anchor drift alarms, sunrise/sunset calculations, moon phase, and track plots are described at the end of this section.

Coordinates (Position Fixes and Waypoints)

Determining your exact position is the most basic function of the GPS system. Your current position can be reported in terms of either angular coordinates (latitude and longitude) or rectangular coordinates (UTM or one of several other rectangular grid systems). All it takes to obtain your current position fix is to be able to "track" at least three or four satellites.

Coordinates can also be associated with locations that you have stored in the memory of your GPS receiver. Stored locations are usually called waypoints or landmarks — it depends on the GPS manufacturer. For simplicity the rest of this book will only refer to waypoints, but you can substitute the term landmark because it means the same thing.

Waypoints are stored coordinates that represent real-world locations that you care about for some reason. One difference between a position fix and a waypoint is the waypoint will have a name. Another is that the coordinate values of a position fix constantly change as you move about (or as Selective Availability "moves" you about), whereas a waypoint's coordinate value remains fixed until you erase it, edit it, or change datums.

A waypoint can be a location you were at 30 seconds ago, or it can be a location on the other side of the earth that you (and your GPS receiver) have never visited. Which leads us straight into the next topic, how to store waypoints.

You can use one of two methods to store a waypoint in your receiver's memory. Waypoints can be stored by using "keystrokes" to enter the coordinate numbers as if you were using a typewriter or a calculator. Waypoints may also be stored by pushing a button (or sequence of buttons) to automatically record the coordinates associated with your current position fix. There are some very important differences between these two methods of entering a waypoint's coordinates.

If you enter a waypoint automatically (that is, you store your current position fix) it does not matter what datum you've specified in the receiver's setup menu. That's because storing your current position fix automatically puts it into the receiver's memory in the WGS84 (World Geodetic System of 1984) datum. WGS84 is the datum that the NAVSTAR satellite system (and your receiver) use for internal processing. When you select a different datum the receiver simply translates the displayed coordinate value from WGS84 to the datum you selected.

Let's say you have selected NAD27 (North American Datum of 1927) as the datum used by your receiver — this is the datum used on most USGS topographic maps. Your current position will be calculated internally based on WGS84, then converted to NAD27 for display. If you change the datum selection to WGS84, the coordinate values that are displayed will change, but the position calculated (or stored) inside the receiver will remain the same. In fact, any time you change the datum that is "active" all you're really doing is shifting the coordinate values that will be displayed for a given position. The position stored in memory will not change.

Position Fix	Stored Waypoint
Based On Real-Time Satellite Tracking	Based On Coordinate Values Entered Into The Receiver's Memory
Represents An Approximation Of The Receiver's Actual Position	Represents Either A Snapshot Of A Position Fix Or User-Supplied Coordinates
Has No Name	Must Have Either A User-Supplied Name Or A Receiver-Generated Name
Constantly Changes As The User's Position Changes (May Change Even When Receiver Is Stationary If Selective Availability Is On)	Once Created, Waypoint Coordinates Do Not Change Unless Edited By User
Is Limited To Locations Actually Occupied By The Receiver	Can Be Specified For Any Location On Earth

Figure 2-7: *Position Fix Vs. Stored Waypoint*

Coordinate systems are handled in a similar way. The receiver's internal coordinate system is ECEF, which is a three-dimensional cartesian coordinate system whose origin is the center of the earth. You never see coordinates displayed in the ECEF system because it is impractical for humans to use. But machines (computers) like it. For more information on the ECEF coordinate system see page 134.

Whenever you see coordinate values displayed on the screen of a GPS receiver they are converted from the ECEF system. Likewise, when you store a position fix its coordinates are displayed in whatever coordinate system you've selected, but it is stored as ECEF coordinates. The receiver uses the appropriate mathematical formula to convert between ECEF and the coordinate values shown on the display.

The bottom line is that a waypoint that was created by storing a position fix will always be accurate (within the limitations associated with satellite geometry, multipath interference, atmospheric conditions, and Selective Availability) at the time it was created.

Now let's look at what happens when you input waypoints manually. This is where you key in the actual numbers that represent the coordinates. When you enter a pair of coordinates the receiver converts the values you enter into WGS84 and ECEF. If you've selected WGS84 as the datum, no datum conversion is done. That's fine if the coordinates are taken from a map (or some other source) that was prepared using WGS84. It is not fine if the coordinates are taken from a map that was prepared using another datum — say NAD27. In this case the coordinate values you enter should be converted inside the receiver, but because you selected WGS84 the receiver thinks they need no datum conversion. The stored waypoint will be "off" by whatever amount of conversion should have been, but was not, applied.

Turning A Position Fix Into A Stored Waypoint

1. Position Receiver In Desired Location

2. Ensure Receiver Is "Locked" Onto Satellites In 3D Mode

3. Perform Keystroke Sequence Required By Your GPS Receiver Model To Store Coordinates That Are Being Displayed

4. Assign Name To Stored Waypoint (Or Let Receiver Assign A Default Name Automatically)

Note: The Current Datum And Coordinate System Settings DO NOT Affect The Stored Waypoint, But They Do Impact The Coordinate Values That Are Displayed

Figure 2-8: Storing Waypoints: Using Your Current Position Fix

That's why it is very important that you have the correct datum specified when you enter a waypoint manually. The wrong datum can yield significant position errors (hundreds of meters), so it pays to be very careful.

Coordinate systems are less likely to be a problem since their differences are usually much more obvious. Generally, it is not too difficult to tell the difference between latitude/longitude and UTM when you're working with coordinates. The important thing to recognize is that regardless of the coordinate system that was active when a waypoint was stored, it is always converted and stored as ECEF. Later, any coordinate system you select for displaying the waypoint will be just as "accurate" as any other coordinate system.

Once you store a waypoint it consists of a name (either the default name your receiver automatically assigned or the one you chose), a coordinate value (stored as ECEF, but displayed according to the coordinate system currently selected), and various other fields of information that vary by model of receiver. Most GPS receivers allow you to edit some or all of the fields associated with a particular waypoint. The other fields of information can include the elevation of the waypoint, the time and date the waypoint was stored, a memo field, etc.

Most GPS receivers also display elevation, but this information is of limited use to backcountry users. That's because the elevation provided by a GPS receiver is considerably less accurate than the horizontal coordinates. In fact, with Selective Availability activated the elevation error range is plus or minus 156 meters. A good barometric altimeter is a far better instrument for obtaining accurate elevation information (see page 55).

Storing A Waypoint Using Coordinates You Supply

1. Obtain Coordinate Values (Latitude/Longitude, Easting/Northing, Etc.) From An External Source (Read From A Map, Appendix Of This Book, Etc.)

2. Set The Receiver's Datum And Coordinate System To Match Those Associated With The Source Of The Coordinates

3. Select Your Receiver's Waypoint Entry Mode, Then Enter The Name And Coordinate Values In The Sequence Required By Your Receiver

   Note: The Datum And Coordinate System Settings DO Affect The Stored Waypoint. They Must Be Set Correctly WHEN THE COORDINATE VALUES ARE ENTERED. After That They Can Be Changed Without Impacting The Stored Waypoint, But They Will Impact The Coordinate Values That Are Displayed

Figure 2-9: *Storing Waypoints: Using Coordinates You Supply (Keypad Entry)*

Now for the bottom line of this section. Without a doubt two of the most important skills you need to develop for backcountry GPS use are:

[1] **Being able to quickly and easily store waypoints based on your current position fix (see Figure 2-8), and**

[2] **Being able to quickly, easily, and accurately store waypoints from coordinate values that you obtain from maps or other sources (see Figure 2-9).**

Consult your receiver's users manual to learn the exact procedures involved, then practice these skills until they are second nature.

In summary, coordinates (both your current position fix and stored waypoints) are the heart of the GPS system. You must understand and be aware of certain parameter settings (the datum and the coordinate system) when working with coordinates. Again, the only exception to this is when you automatically store your current position fix as a waypoint. In this case the datum and coordinate system settings are irrelevant.

Important Note From The Author: As this book was about to go to press, the author encountered a newly-released GPS receiver that did not convert the coordinate values of stored waypoints when different datums were selected. This appears to be a logic error and has been brought to the manufacturer's attention. You may want to verify that your receiver handles waypoints and datums correctly. A check can be performed by comparing the coordinate values of a stored waypoint when different datums are selected. If the values don't change, you may have a logic error in your receiver's firmware.

Distance and Direction (GoTo, Routes, Etc.)

Once you have at least one waypoint stored in your GPS receiver it becomes possible to utilize the functions that give you the distance and direction to stored waypoints. These are the most valuable features of GPS for backcountry land navigators. Distance is a very straightforward item of information, since all you need to worry about are the units of measurement (metric, statute, nautical). Direction, on the other hand, can be quite confusing.

The direction between two locations is usually called a bearing, although it is sometimes called a course, especially in the case of the legs of a route. Just to keep things confusing, some GPS manufacturers call the direction you are actually traveling course over ground. Your actual direction of travel may also be called your heading or your track. The direction you are actually traveling is a much different concept than the direction between waypoints. This will be covered in the next section on travel progress reports (see Figure 2-13).

Usually distance and direction will pertain to the distance and direction from your current position to a stored waypoint. This can be obtained using your receiver's "GoTo" function. Some receivers also have a feature that shows you a list of waypoints along with their distances and directions from your current position fix. It is also possible to select a specific waypoint from among all stored waypoints and see its distance and direction from your current position fix. There are probably a number of different ways your receiver can be "asked" for this information. Consult your receiver's manual for the particular methods available to you.

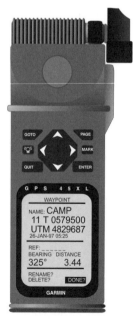

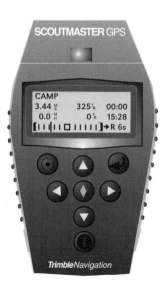

Figure 2-10: *Examples Of The Basic "GoTo" Screens On Various GPS Receiver Models*

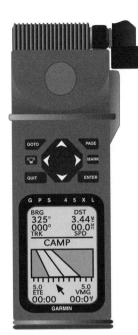

...tions Of "GoTo" Screens

GPS receiver give you the distance and direction
...re in camp, but you want to see how far it is from
...g (where you stored a waypoint) to the peak you
...so stored a waypoint). This is accomplished by
...ints in the particular manner required by your
...ion that does just this, or you may need to specify
..."ax" this information out of your receiver. There
.../pe of information. Whatever the method(s), you
...nformation from your particular GPS receiver.

You also need to be aware that the distances your receiver calculates between waypoints
are straight lines on the surface of the WGS84 ellipsoid — approximately mean sea level.
This means you must allow for any extra distance caused by winding trails, plus the extra
distance caused by the slope between locations at different elevations. On a 10 degree
slope the actual straight-line ground distance will be less than 2 percent more than the GPS
receiver indicates. On a 45 degree slope the actual straight-line ground distance will be
over 40 percent more than the receiver indicates.

Obtaining distance and direction measurements between stored waypoints can be handy
for comparing alternative routes, planning a trip in advance, or just answering interesting
trivia questions. In essence, with this function you can obtain the distance and direction
between any two points on earth as long as you know their coordinates. Just be aware that
the direction provided is along a great circle path (beginning at the "from" waypoint) and
not along a rhumb line. See page 146 for an explanation of these terms.

As long as the initial data entry for a particular waypoint was done using the correct datum and coordinate system, it doesn't matter what these parameters are set to when you read the distance and direction information. That's because all position fixes are stored internally as WGS84 ECEF coordinates. You will usually have a choice between metric, statute, and nautical distance measurement units. The one to choose is strictly a matter of your preference.

The direction between two waypoints is a little more tricky, because there are setup parameters that impact the way directions are displayed by your GPS receiver. The most important parameter to be aware of when working with direction is the declination setting. Options can include some or all of the following:

[1] True direction (no offset, 0° referenced to true north),

[2] Grid direction (grid declination as the offset, exact offset value provided by the receiver, 0° referenced to grid north),

[3] Magnetic direction (magnetic declination as the offset, approximate value provided by the receiver, 0° referenced to magnetic north), and

[4] User selected offset (any amount of offset, as specified by the user).

Try not to let all of your receiver's parameter options confuse you. Think of them as providing the flexibility to customize the way your receiver works for you. Some

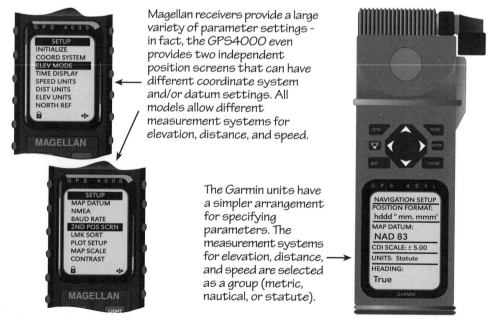

Magellan receivers provide a large variety of parameter settings - in fact, the GPS4000 even provides two independent position screens that can have different coordinate system and/or datum settings. All models allow different measurement systems for elevation, distance, and speed.

The Garmin units have a simpler arrangement for specifying parameters. The measurement systems for elevation, distance, and speed are selected as a group (metric, nautical, or statute).

Figure 2-12: *Setting The Basic Parameters Used By GPS Receivers*

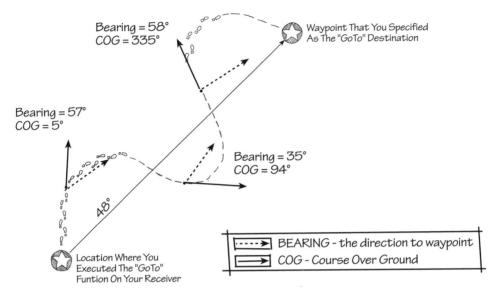

Bearing = 58°
COG = 335°

Waypoint That You Specified
As The "GoTo" Destination

Bearing = 57°
COG = 5°

Bearing = 35°
COG = 94°

48°

Location Where You
Executed The "GoTo"
Funtion On Your Receiver

BEARING - the direction to waypoint
COG - Course Over Ground

Figure 2-13: *COG (Course Over Ground) And Bearing — Two Different Concepts*

parameter settings, notably the datum and to a lesser degree the coordinate system, are dictated by the map you're using. Others, such as the declination mode and distance units, should probably be left at a basic setting that works for you, at least until you move up the GPS learning curve.

Try this as a good starting point for the "discretionary" setup parameters: UTM for the coordinate system (unless you prefer to work with a latitude/longitude scale), magnetic headings (unless you have declination adjustment on your compass and prefer true headings), and distance in feet and statute miles (unless you prefer the metric system).

Almost everything mentioned above about distance and direction also applies to routes. Routes are a standard feature of most handheld GPS receivers. A route is a group of waypoints that have been linked into a sequence known as "legs." Legs are just two waypoints (a "from" waypoint and a "to" waypoint) along with the distance and direction between them. Each successive leg in a route starts "from" the prior leg's "to" waypoint. This means a route consisting of "n" legs will have "n+1" waypoints.

Routes are handy because they can simplify the use of GPS. One way they do this is by automatically switching to the next leg as you pass through successive waypoints. Another convenience feature of routes is you can usually reverse them, meaning that you don't need to re-enter waypoints when you want a route that simply backtracks. Not all receivers with routes offer a reverse route feature.

Another feature related to distance and direction found in most handheld GPS receivers is *cross track error* (XTE). It tells you how far you are to the left or right of a course you've set to a waypoint. This function is a carryover from the nautical roots of most handheld GPS receivers. In some receivers it is called *course deviation indicator* (CDI). They're basically the same.

XTE indicates how far and in what direction you have "wandered" away from a straight-line course between two waypoints. That straight-line course is either the current leg of an active route, or it is the course line formed when you last performed a "GoTo" function. In the latter case, each time you perform a "GoTo" function the course line is re-established from the position you are at when you re-execute the "GoTo."

Another feature sometimes associated with XTE is a suggested heading that will get you back to your original straight line course. This suggested heading is usually a compromise between your current straight-line course to the destination waypoint and the shortest distance to the line of the original course.

The purpose of XTE is to keep track of how far you have "wandered" from a straight-line course. The question land navigators must ask themselves is: So what? — does XTE have any relevance? In most cases XTE doesn't really tell you anything particularly useful. It's rare that the course for a backcountry route would be a straight line. If it is, say over featureless plains or tundra, then XTE could be useful (except that once you're off course, you would need a good reason to go back to the original course instead of heading straight for the destination).

In short, the value of XTE to land-based users of GPS is limited. If you are an aviator needing to fly a particular air traffic lane, it matters. If you are a mariner needing to keep

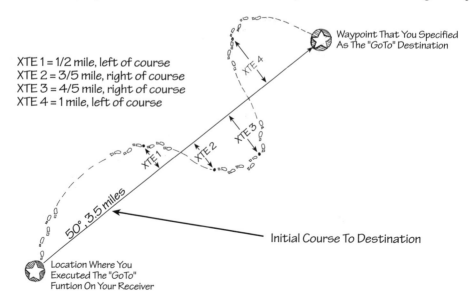

Figure 2-14: XTE (Cross Track Error); Also Known As CDI (Course Deviation Indicator)

your boat in a particular shipping lane, it matters. But most overland travel is not through terrain as featureless (or collision-prone) as airspace or the seas. If you're traveling by road or trail, this feature doesn't usually provide much benefit. Even if you're traveling overland off-trail, there will probably be terrain features that make it sensible to intentionally go "off-course."

In the final analysis, there is not much value in XTE for most land applications of GPS. It is a part of the GPS display, however, and you should understand what it is telling you so that it doesn't distract you from the truly beneficial aspects of using GPS for land navigation.

In summary, using the distance and direction capabilities of your GPS receiver can be boiled down to knowing how to do two things. One is knowing how to obtain the distance and direction from your current position to a specified waypoint or list of waypoints. The other is knowing how to obtain the distance and direction between two (or more) stored waypoints.

Progress Reports (SOG, COG, VMG, ETA, TTG, etc)

The final category of basic GPS receiver functions should be called alphabet soup. It includes various indications of your dynamic, or motion related, progress. These functions are of limited value to backcountry land navigators because of both Selective Availability (which ruins the accuracy of motion-related functions at slow speeds) and battery drain (GPS receivers consume a considerable amount of power when operated continuously). These functions can be useful, however, if your GPS receiver is mounted to the handlebar or dashboard of a motorized vehicle and it is hooked up to the vehicle's power supply.

The display of motion-related functions is usually scattered among the static functions described in the previous two sections. Because these dynamic progress indicators are not usually separated (in a display sense) from the coordinate and distance/direction displays, they can make your initial encounter with GPS quite confusing.

There are a wide variety of dynamic-progress related features in today's handheld GPS receivers. Perhaps the most universal, and least confusing, is the "speed" indicator, which is an almost instantaneous readout of your velocity of travel. This measurement is often called *speed over ground* (SOG) for reasons that will soon be clear.

Another motion-related progress indicator is your direction of travel, often called *course over ground* (COG), or heading. It is very important to recognize the difference between this motion-related concept and the direction to a waypoint. If you're not careful, you can mistake one for the other and find yourself off course. See Figure 2-13.

A measure related to both your speed over ground and your destination waypoint is called *velocity made good* (VMG). This is the rate you are "closing" on a destination waypoint (you must have either a route or a "GoTo" active). If you are heading directly toward the waypoint your speed and your VMG will be the same. If you are not headed directly at the waypoint, but your course is within plus or minus 90 degrees of the course straight to the waypoint, then you are getting closer to the waypoint as you move forward. You should recognize that if you stay on a course that doesn't point directly at the destination waypoint you will never actually arrive there. This function is popular among racing sailboat captains, since they usually can't sail straight at an upwind mark. Instead, they tack back and forth. VMG indicates the best combination of boat speed and angle of attack. See Figure 2-15.

Another kind of progress report provided by GPS receivers is the estimated time it will take to reach a particular destination at your current speed and direction of travel. It may be called *estimated time enroute* (ETE), *time to go* (TTG), or some other phrase. This is simply a conversion of the VMG (*velocity made good*) measurement to a time measurement. It is calculated by multiplying VMG times the distance to the destination waypoint. Some receivers give the information as *estimated time of arrival* (ETA), which is just the current time plus ETE. Some receivers even have a screen that gives this information for all remaining legs of the current route.

One characteristic of dynamic progress reports is that you must be moving before there is anything to report. In the case of goal oriented items (such as VMG, ETA, ETE, etc.), you must have a goal (usually established with the "GoTo" function or by activating a route) and you must be moving toward the goal, otherwise the display will be blank. If you find that some or all of the progress report items report a value when you're motionless, that's just Selective Availability making the receiver think it is in motion.

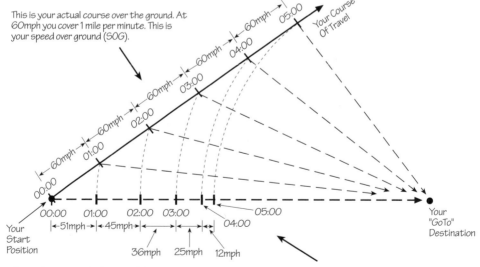

This is the rate at which you are "closing" on your destination waypoint during each minute of travel. It's your velocity made good (VMG). As the angle between your course and the direction to the waypoint increases, your VMG diminishes.

Figure 2-15: *Velocity Made Good (VMG) Is The Rate At Which You "Close" On Your Destination*

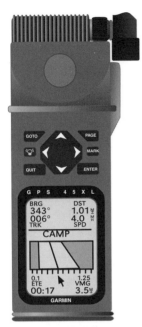

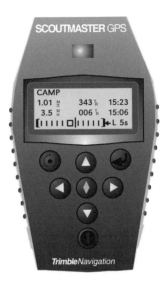

Figure 2-16: *Examples Of ETE/TTG And ETA Displays*

Selective Availability also limits the accuracy of velocity related measurements at slow speeds. In general, speeds over 10-15 mph are needed to overcome the effects of Selective Availability. Some receivers have the ability to average the position data used to calculate velocity related values. The result is a more stable (but sluggish) display of velocity related items. At slower speeds you need to watch your display for unstable readouts — a sure sign of Selective Availability related problems.

In summary, all GPS receivers provide a variety of travel progress indicators, but those indicators are of limited benefit to backcountry land navigators. One reason is that Selective Availability ruins their accuracy at slow speeds, and the other is the battery drain that accompanies continuous receiver operation.

Miscellaneous GPS Receiver Functions

There are a wide variety of auxiliary functions available with the various models and brands of handheld GPS receivers. Projections of certain events over space and time (sunrise, sunset, moon phase, even satellite positions) allow you to find the status of these events at a particular place and future date of your choice. This can be useful for planning purposes. Graphic plotter screens can show you visually where you've been or where you need to go (to stay on course).

A common auxiliary feature is a display of the exact time of sunrise and sunset for any waypoint and any date you specify. A less common auxiliary feature tells you the exact position (elevation and azimuth) of the sun or moon at any location, date, and time you specify.

Real-time satellite status information (elevation, azimuth, signal strength) can be used to optimize reception in difficult environments such as forests, mountain valleys, urban valleys, etc. Most receivers provide either a table or a graph that shows the position of the satellites currently in the sky and the signal strength of the satellites being tracked.

Graphic plots of waypoints and your track can help you visualize the course you've taken or that you need to take. Graphic "highways" can give you a visual indication of your position relative to a destination waypoint and the course to it. The trouble with these features is that you either need to have your receiver on continuously to use them, or you need to be traveling relatively fast for them to be accurate, or both. This is not likely to be the case unless you are traveling in or on a motor vehicle and the receiver is mounted to the handlebar or dashboard.

Some receivers can average a position reading taken at a fixed position over time, thereby overcoming the effects of Selective Availability. By averaging for at least one hour, the horizontal error range of a position fix can be reduced from 100 meters to 10 meters. This feature overcomes Selective Availability and provides differential GPS accuracy without a differential beacon, but it requires time and patience.

In summary, these miscellaneous features are nice, but they're not essential for backcountry navigation. This is especially true if you are limited to operating on battery power.

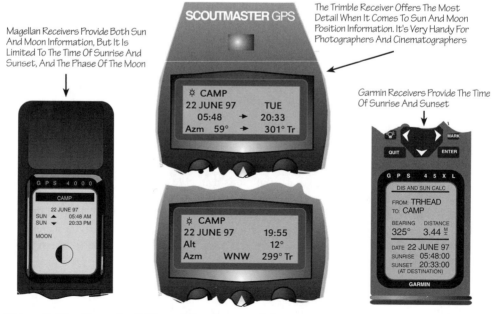

Figure 2-17: Examples Of Some Miscellaneous Information Supplied By GPS Receivers

2.1.3 Limitations of GPS Receivers

When you use a GPS receiver for personal navigation it is important that you understand its limitations and idiosyncrasies.

Line of Sight

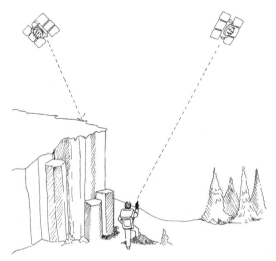

A GPS receiver must have a direct line of sight to a satellite in order to receive the satellite's signal. While GPS satellite signals will penetrate glass and light-weight barriers (such as canvas), they will not usually penetrate buildings, forest canopies, or other dense obstacles. This means that you need to be aware of obstructions that may limit the number of satellites you can receive.

Some GPS receivers have a feature that gives the position of the satellite constellation (azimuth and elevation) in real time. You can use this feature to help you find the best

Figure 2-18: Line Of Sight Is Essential

reception location in your vicinity. Since the satellites are in constant motion, sometimes just waiting for their positions to change can improve your reception.

Stale Data

You need to know if the data being displayed on your GPS receiver's screen is based on a current position fix or an old position fix. Receivers indicate this information in a variety of ways. Some receivers show the current satellite lock status on all position and navigation screens. Other receivers require that you either go to a particular screen or decode "hints" to figure this out. It is very important that you understand how your particular receiver indicates whether or not it has a current position fix.

2-D Operating Mode

You need to be aware if your receiver is operating in two-dimensional mode. This happens when your receiver can only track 3 satellites. See page 6 for an explanation of how GPS receivers use satellites to obtain position fixes.

A receiver operating in 2D mode uses the center of the earth as a substitute for a satellite, and it uses elevation in the place of a satellite range. The problem with 2D mode lies in the elevation value.

A GPS receiver not only doesn't calculate elevation in 2D mode, it requires elevation as an input. In most cases if you don't supply an elevation value, the receiver assumes one. Serious position inaccuracies (as in <u>miles</u> of error) can result if the elevation "assumed" by your receiver is wrong. Some receivers default to an elevation of zero. Others may use the last elevation that was actually calculated by the receiver. If the last time you used the receiver was one hour and 2,000 vertical feet ago, you could have a serious problem getting an accurate position fix in 2D mode. As a general rule, two-dimensional position fixes should be avoided.

You may be able to put elevation data into your receiver if you absolutely need a 2D position fix. Try to be as accurate as possible with the elevation you supply the receiver. And be aware that all GPS receivers calculate elevation as height above the ellipsoid, although some use an internal table to convert their elevation readouts to height above the geoid. USGS maps, on the other hand, always give elevation as height above mean sea level, which is height above the geoid.

The geoid is a physical phenomenon that is measured. It is a surface of constant gravity. Where there is ocean it is the surface of the ocean. Where there is land it is where the ocean would be if the land weren't in the way. It is not a "smooth" surface. In a given location, the vertical difference between the surface of the geoid and the surface of the ellipsoid is called geoid/ellipsoid separation. This difference can be substantial—up to 52 meters in the continental United States. Figure 2-20 shows a simulated image of the surface of the geoid across the United States. The ellipsoid, on the other hand, would look like a smooth, featureless beach ball. That means the difference between the surface of the ellipsoid and the surface of the geoid is highly irregular. Receivers that use a table to convert from ellipsoid elevation to geoid elevation are able to get within about 5 meters of the true geoid elevation.

The additional horizontal error that results from inaccurate elevation values in 2D mode can be as much as 5 times the amount of elevation error. This is caused by the geometry of 2D mode (the "4th" pseudo-satellite at the center of the earth, in the opposite hemisphere)

The ellipsoid is a flattened sphere (it bulges at the equator) that is used to model the shape of the earth at sea level. It represents zero elevation in the GPS system.

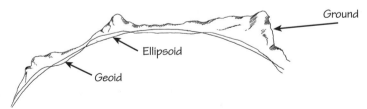

The geoid is the surface of constant gravity that coincides with the average level of the earth's oceans - mean sea level. On the oceans it is the surface of the ocean. On the continents it is where the surface of the ocean would be if the continent were not in the way. It represents zero elevation in the USGS topographic map series.

Figure 2-19: *The Vertical Distance Between The Geoid And The Ellipsoid Is Variable*

Image Courtesy U.S. National Geodetic Survey

Figure 2-20: *A Simulation Of The Surface Of The Geoid — Continental U.S.*

and the fact that elevation error does not "average out" with the range errors from the actual satellites. 2D elevation error is from a different source than receiver clock error.

It's Not A Compass

A GPS receiver is not a compass. A GPS receiver cannot tell you the direction it is pointed. It can only tell you the direction it is moving. This capability can be used to simulate a compass in a pinch, but Selective Availability seriously reduces the accuracy at walking speeds. Also, using a GPS receiver as a compass will rapidly deplete its batteries.

This means that you should plan to use a magnetic compass as a part of your GPS tool kit. Only use your GPS receiver as a compass when you need a backup for a lost or broken magnetic compass. (Note: if you use your GPS receiver in a motor vehicle or with some outside source of "unlimited" power, it can serve very effectively as an accurate compass—as long as it is moving at over 10-15 mph.)

Slow Startup

It takes a long time (up to 15 minutes) for a GPS receiver to figure out where it is if it has been moved a long distance (over several hundred miles) since it was last used. You can shorten the process, however, by telling the receiver approximately where it is. This is called initialization. It may also be necessary to enter the date and approximate time if they have been lost from the receiver's memory. Many newer receivers have a list of locations (such as major cities) built-in so that you can initialize the receiver without entering actual coordinate data.

Setup Parameters

It is important that you properly enter certain "critical" parameter settings, especially if you use your GPS receiver with external information derived from maps, compasses, or even coordinate listings (such as those found in the appendices of this book). Without proper settings a GPS receiver cannot give you accurate navigation information.

The most important of these "critical" parameters is the datum associated with the map or coordinate data you're using. Setting the wrong datum can lead to a position error in excess of one mile! See page 78 for more information on datums.

Matching the declination mode setting, or consciously adjusting for it, between the GPS receiver, your compass, and your map is also very important. See page 52 for more information. A failure to match compass and GPS receiver declination modes can lead to heading errors of over 20° in the continental United States. Traveling at 20° off course will put you 1,800 feet (over 1/3 of a mile) wide of an objective that is just one mile away. Even with an error of only 5° you'd get no closer than 460 feet to that objective.

If you used the wrong declination direction (say, east instead of west) the error would be twice the amount of actual declination. A 40° direction error means you would miss an objective that is one mile away by 3,400 feet (almost 2/3 of a mile). In other words, you wouldn't even get close.

The time of day given by the GPS receiver, while very accurate, is stored inside the receiver as *Universal Time Coordinated*, or UTC. To display the correct local time you must set your location's offset from UTC. It's easy to tell if you've done this correctly when you're in civilization — either the local time shown on your receiver is correct, or it is off by exactly one or more hours. In the backcountry it may not be so obvious. By the way, setting the wrong local time offset does not impact position accuracy.

There are other optional parameters you will want to set as a matter of convenience. These convenience settings have no right or wrong values, you just need to be aware of how they are set. The type of coordinate system (usually latitude/longitude or UTM), distance units (metric, statute, nautical), and speed units (km/h, mph, knots) are examples of optional parameters. There may be other optional parameters that apply to your particular GPS receiver.

2.1.4 GPS & Computer Programs

Connecting your GPS receiver to a computer can be a very handy and timesaving feature. GPS receivers designed for personal navigation have two basic types of "links" to personal computers. One is a real-time link that sends a continuous stream of position data from the receiver to the computer. That data is then stored and/or displayed on the computer's screen. If it is displayed, it is done so as points or a path on an electronic map of the surrounding area. This type of computer link is like an extension of the receiver's display screen and display software. It is similar to the kinds of systems that are starting to appear in the dashboards of cars that are equipped with GPS. It is not likely to be of much use to backcountry GPS users, since it is quite bulky and consumes considerable power.

A second type of link between a GPS receiver and a computer involves using the computer to enter, manage, and store waypoint, route, track, and other data that is used in the GPS receiver. This type of link involves uploading and downloading between the GPS receiver and a PC. The PC becomes an extension of the GPS receiver's keypad and memory. This type of computer link can be very useful for backcountry GPS users, since it allows data entry and storage to be done on a personal computer. That can be much more efficient than using the four scroll keys and limited memory of a typical handheld GPS receiver.

Most current GPS receiver models offer both of these features. Some older receivers can only output data. That means they can be linked to a moving map display, but you can't store waypoints and routes outside the receiver, then upload them at some later time.

You can purchase GPS/PC interface software from the receiver's manufacturer or, in some cases, one of several third-party sources. Delorme Mapping Company and Chicago Precision Mapping both offer GPS mapping software, and even sell a bundled kit that includes a GPS receiver. Wildflower Productions has developed electronic map software (TOPO!) that doesn't yet, but eventually will, communicate directly with GPS receivers. With any 3rd party software, you need to make sure it's compatible with your receiver.

For simple waypoint and route management, it's hard to beat WAYPOINT+, available free on the Internet. This program's main screen and its waypoint list/editing screen are shown in Figure 2-21. As of this writing, it only works with Garmin GPS receivers.

The bottom line for anyone interested in using a personal computer with a GPS receiver is to make sure that the receiver has the interface capabilities you desire (download only or upload and download), and then select a software package that performs the necessary functions. Unless you have a need to do GIS (geographic information systems) or mapping type applications, waypoint/route data management is probably all you really need from the computer interface. Digital maps can also be quite valuable, and they don't need to be linked to the GPS receiver to be of value. See page 103 for more information on digital maps and related software.

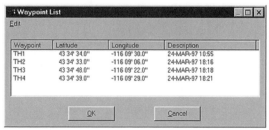

Figure 2-21:   *Waypoint Management Software Allows You To Upload And Download Waypoints To A PC — This Is WAYPOINT+ (A Freeware Program Available On The Internet)*

2.2 Compasses

Although a GPS receiver is very good at giving the bearing to a waypoint, it cannot easily give actual directions on the ground. That's because unlike a compass, a GPS receiver doesn't know which way it is pointed. A GPS receiver can only give you an indication of ground direction if it is actually moving over the ground. As you can imagine, this is a cumbersome way to find an actual direction — although it can work in a pinch.

This means that a compass is an important companion to your GPS receiver in most field applications. Together they are unbeatable for getting you where you want to go.

One manufacturer (Silva) does offer an actual electronic compass bundled into a GPS receiver. As handheld GPS receiver technology advances, this combination may become more common. But for now most GPS receivers don't have this capability. Even if your receiver has a built-in electronic compass, it is a good idea to have a mechanical compass along as a backup.

Figure 2-22: *Different Types Of Compasses*

2.2.1 Compass Types

There are literally dozens of different handheld compasses available for outdoor recreationists. Popular brands that offer a wide selection of models suitable for use in the backcountry include Brunton (USA), Silva (Sweden), and Suunto (Finland). The types of compasses suitable for backcountry recreation fall into three basic categories:

[1] Baseplate compasses,

[2] Mirror compasses, and

[3] Sighting compasses.

The first two types usually are available in versions that have declination adjustability, an option well worth the few extra dollars it usually costs. Other options, such as a built in clinometer (for measuring slopes), are less important. The third type of compass usually doesn't offer declination adjustability, but does provide <u>very</u> accurate direction read-outs.

Baseplate Compasses

The most basic type of compass covered here is known as a "baseplate compass." They are fine for obtaining general directions, and they have been used quite successfully for serious orienteering for many years. The base of a baseplate compass usually has English and/or metric distance scales built-in. Because the base is transparent, the degree dial can also be used as a crude protractor.

The weakness of baseplate compasses is they don't offer the level of precision commensurate with that obtained from a GPS receiver (i.e., to within one degree). This is due to the absence of a precise sighting mechanism. Nonetheless, if you can accept accuracy that is only to within plus or minus several degrees, such a compass is more than adequate for basic land navigation (with or without a GPS receiver). Some people may find the overall simplicity of a baseplate compass a virtue, and intentionally forego the higher accuracy obtainable with a mirror or sighting compass. There's nothing wrong with making that choice.

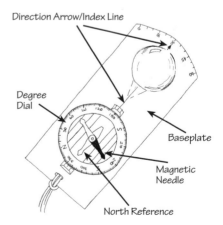

Figure 2-23: *Baseplate Compass Parts*

Mirror Compasses

A mirror compass represents a step up from the baseplate compass in terms of precision. It adds a hinged mirror that can be used to simultaneously sight the compass on a distant location and align the magnetic needle with the north reference on the dial. A good mirror compass is marked in two degree increments and provides bearings to a precision of one degree. When sighted, the compass' index line will either be on a degree mark—an even degree—or between two marks—an odd degree.

Besides offering higher precision, a mirror compass comes with a "built-in" case. The hinged sighting mirror typically folds down over the dial, serving as a protective cover. A mirror compass can also be opened wide, effectively turning it into a baseplate compass. The sighting notch becomes the equivalent of a direction arrow.

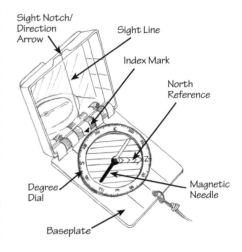

Figure 2-24: *Mirror Compass Parts*

Sighting Compasses

An even higher level of precision (in some models to within a quarter degree) is offered by true sighting compasses, where the compass card is viewed through a lens and a lubber line is aligned with the target. This type of compass can also be very easy to use, because it has fewer moving parts. Instead of a separate magnetic needle and degree dial, these two components are combined into what is known as the "compass card." In effect, the dial always automatically aligns itself with magnetic north.

There are, however, downsides to this type of instrument. Their design is usually such that they can't serve as a ruler or protractor. They also don't usually offer declination adjustment capability as an option. But they do have an exceptional ability to obtain bearings, and they also make it easy to follow a bearing.

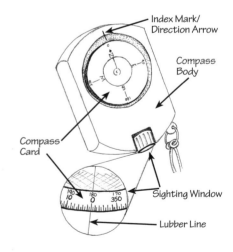

Figure 2-25: *Sighting Compass Parts*

Other Types Of Compasses

There are other types of compasses available, but most are not well-suited for backcountry use with a GPS receiver. Some, however, will nonetheless serve a backcountry direction-finding role if pressed into service. At the inexpensive end of the spectrum is the simple dial compass that is nothing more than a magnetic needle enclosed in a clear dial. The needle is the only moving part, and the direction scale is fixed in place around the needle. This is the type of compass you might attach to the zipper of your jacket and have along as an inexpensive backup.

On the other end of the spectrum are high precision compasses such as military lensatic compasses or the Brunton Pocket Transit. These compasses tend to be heavy in both price and weight, but they will obviously do a more than adequate job of giving accurate directions — some offer precision measured in minutes (or mils) as opposed to degrees. Let your back and your wallet decide.

Marine equipment suppliers offer additional lines and types of compasses, including completely electronic models. Many of these compasses will work for backcountry travelers, but they tend to be overkill for typical land navigation purposes. The bottom line is that a simple baseplate, mirror, or sighting compass will do the job accurately and reliably for very little cost.

2.2.2 Using A Compass (With Or Without GPS)

Using a compass involves performing one of two basic procedures. One is setting a bearing (the direction you want to travel) on the compass and following it over the ground. The other is sighting on a distant target and obtaining the bearing to that target from your current location. You can think of these two procedures as either inputting a direction (the former) or outputting a direction (the latter).

Following A Bearing

Following a bearing usually starts with reading the value for the bearing from your GPS receiver. Typically you'll find the bearing either by using the route menu of your receiver or by performing a "GoTo" function. It really simplifies the process to use magnetic directions. All currently available handheld GPS receivers are capable of displaying magnetic directions.

If you're using a baseplate or mirror compass, rotate the dial of the compass until the bearing you want to follow is aligned with the direction arrow on the baseplate of your compass. Hold the compass in front of you with the direction arrow pointing forward. Rotate your body until the compass needle is aligned with the north reference in the compass dial. At this point the direction arrow is pointing in the direction of the bearing you "dialed in," and all you need to do is proceed in that direction.

Baseplate or Mirror Compass

1. Dial-in the bearing you want to follow (example bearing is 256°).

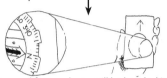

2. Holding compass so the direction arrow is in front of you, rotate your body so that the magnetic needle is aligned with the north reference in the compass dial.

3. Proceed forward; you will be headed in the direction you dialed-in to the compass.

Sighting Compass

1. Hold the compass in front of you with the direction/index mark pointing forward, then rotate your body so the desired bearing is aligned with the direction/index mark (example bearing is 256°).

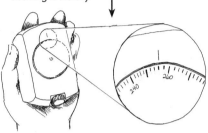

2. Proceed forward; you will be headed in the direction that appears at the direction/index mark.

Figure 2-26: *Using A Compass To Follow A Bearing*

This procedure is the same whether you are using a baseplate compass or a mirror compass. In the case of a mirror compass, you unfold it and use the mirror sight notch as though it is a direction arrow.

The important thing to remember when using either a baseplate or mirror compass is that following a bearing requires just two steps. First, "dial in" the bearing you want to follow by aligning it with the baseplate's index line/direction arrow. Then, rotate the whole compass so that the needle is aligned with the north reference in the dial. Your compass will now be pointing in the direction you "dialed in."

If you're using a sighting compass to follow a bearing the process is even simpler. There's no "dial" to set, so you just hold the compass in front of you at about chest height. With the index mark pointing ahead of you, rotate your whole body until the desired bearing appears at the index mark. That's the magnetic direction you are now facing. If you need more precision, you can view the compass card through the sighting window.

A neat trick that really simplifies the process of following a bearing involves finding a distinct feature ahead of you that is on the bearing you want to follow. Instead of constantly following the compass bearing, just head for the feature. Once you arrive at the feature repeat the process. If you lose sight of the feature, revert to your compass for heading information. Just make sure that the feature is a location you can actually attain. That way it doesn't matter what your course is when traveling to the feature.

Baseplate or Mirror Compass

1. Aim your compass so the direction arrow is pointing at the distant object.

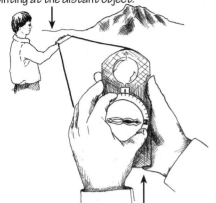

2. Rotate the compass dial so that the magnetic needle is aligned with the north reference.

3. Read the direction to the distant object from the index mark next to your compass dial.

Sighting Compass

1. Look at the distant object while simultaneously viewing the compass card through the sighting window.

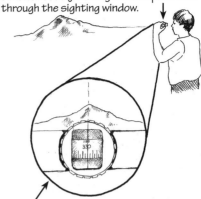

2. Read the direction to the distant object from the compass card in the sighting window. Most sighting compasses also show the back-bearing in smaller numbers above or below the bearing.

Figure 2-27: *Using A Compass To Obtain A Bearing*

Obtaining A Bearing

The process for obtaining the bearing from your location to some distant target (or just reading the direction you are facing) is very similar to following a bearing, just in reverse. First you point the compass direction arrow at the target (or direction) for which you want to obtain the bearing. If you're using a baseplate or mirror compass, rotate the dial until the north reference in the dial is aligned with the magnetic needle. Now you can read the bearing to the distant target from the dial (i.e., where the dial is aligned with the direction arrow/index mark on the compass baseplate).

If you want to "sight" with your mirror compass the process is basically the same, except you must simultaneously "aim" the compass using the sighting mechanism and rotate the dial to align the north reference with the compass needle. You'll need to have the mirror at about a 45° angle in order to both sight and align at the same time.

If you're using a sighting compass, just point the compass at the target you're interested in and read the direction from the index mark. If you want a more precise bearing look through the sighting window, align the lubber line with the target, and read the bearing from the edge of the compass card.

Sometimes you want to find the direction from the target to your position. This is called a "back-bearing." To obtain a back-bearing, first obtain the bearing in the normal way, then add or subtract 180° to determine the back-bearing. Since angular directions fall into a range from 0° to 360°, add 180° if the original bearing is under 180°, subtract 180° if the original bearing is over 180°. Most sighting compasses have back-bearings marked on the compass card in small characters above or below the bearing scale.

2.2.3 Magnetic Declination

One of the important options to consider when you buy a compass is a feature known as *declination adjustment*. This feature allows you to shift the alignment of the north reference in the compass dial by the amount needed to offset the magnetic declination in the area where you are operating. With the declination adjustment set, your compass will display true, not magnetic, directions. This makes it very convenient when you use your compass with a map, since map grids are usually aligned with (or close to) true north.

The way that declination adjustment works is by rotating the north reference within your compass dial while holding the degree scale in place, thereby shifting the direction readout by the desired amount. The compass needle itself still points to magnetic north, but the north reference no longer points to north on the compass dial (see Figure 2-28).

GPS receivers can also be adjusted for magnetic declination, but it works in the opposite way. Instead of giving bearing and heading readouts in terms of true directions, the GPS receiver can be set to shift its readouts east or west by a specified number of degrees that correspond to the amount of magnetic declination in the area of use.

By Rotating This Adjustment Screw You Can "Shift" The North Reference By The Desired Number Of Degrees East Or West Of True North.

Of Course, The Amount Of Shift You Apply To The North Reference Depends On The Amount Of Magnetic Declination In The Area Where You Will Be Using The Compass.

Figure 2-28: *Setting The Declination Adjustment On A Compass*

In fact, many GPS receivers have an automatic declination adjustment option built-in. This feature automatically sets the amount of magnetic declination adjustment according to the location of the receiver. As you change locations the amount of declination adjustment automatically changes to match your location. Remember, declination adjustment should be set on either your compass (magnetic converted to true) or your GPS receiver (true converted to magnetic), but not both. The ability to set a magnetic declination offset in the GPS receiver makes it convenient to work with an unadjusted compass.

If you anticipate using a map in the field, then it is best to set the appropriate magnetic declination adjustment on the compass and use the GPS receiver in true north mode. Then the readings taken from any of the three tools (map, compass, GPS receiver) will be true bearings, with no need for any further manual adjustment. This is certainly the least confusing option, and it minimizes the probability of making declination mistakes.

If your compass doesn't have declination adjustment capability then you should probably set your GPS receiver to operate in magnetic direction mode. Then all you need to remember is your compass and GPS directions won't match the true directions on your map. That's usually not a problem, though, since you'll mostly use your map for coordinates, and let your receiver handle directions. It is more important that your receiver's directions be consistent with your compass.

2.2.4 Magnetic Interference

Whenever you use a magnetic compass, <u>any</u> magnetic compass, another important rule needs to be understood: *Stay clear of any potential sources of magnetic interference*. This means buildings (electrical currents), autos (steel, electrical motors), fences (wire, nails), even hand tools. The needle of any compass is highly susceptible to being deflected away from magnetic north by proximity to such objects.

Table 2-1 provides suggested minimum distances to ensure the most accurate compass readings possible. Even metal framed eyeglasses can throw off a compass that is being sighted against your cheek!

Incidentally, magnetic interference is not a problem when it comes to GPS receivers. GPS receivers do not rely on magnetic fields for their inputs, therefore they are not affected by magnetic fields.

Suggested Distances To Avoid Magnetic Interference	
High Tension Power Lines, Buildings, Etc.	55-60 meters
Large Trucks, Buses, Cars Etc.	18-20 meters
Telephone Lines, Wire Fences, Etc.	8-10 meters
Rifles, Shotguns, Axe, Shovel, Hand-tools, Etc.	2-3 meters
Pocket Knife, Transistor Radio, Binoculars, Etc.	½-1 meter

Table 2-1: *Magnetic Interference Chart*

2.2.5 Magnetic Inclination

One last concept worth mentioning briefly is magnetic inclination—the "dip" associated with the earth's magnetic field at various locations. Inclination occurs because the earth's magnetic field is not parallel with the earth's surface in the vicinity of the poles. In essence, a magnetic compass needle is pulled "down" away from horizontal at locations nearer to the poles. This means that compass needles need to be counter-balanced for this dip, and hence they are designed for specific inclination zones.

A compass balanced for use in northern latitudes wouldn't work well in southern latitudes because of this dip. The north end of the needle dips down in northern latitudes, while the south end of the needle dips down in southern latitudes. Figure 2-29 shows a map of inclination "zones" used in the manufacturing of Suunto compasses. These are just regions that have similar amounts of magnetic dip. Compasses are generally balanced for the zone where they will be sold. Other manufacturers may use fewer or greater numbers of inclination zones.

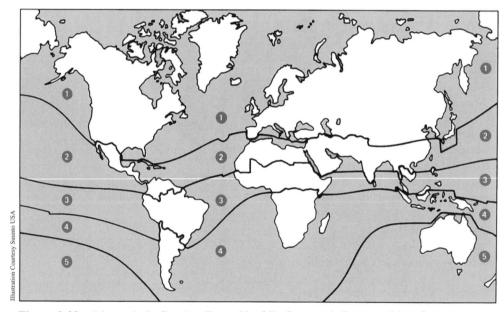

Figure 2-29: *Magnetic Inclination Zones Used By Suunto, A Compass Manufacturer*

2.3 Altimeters

Although most GPS receivers display altitude along with a position fix, they are not very useful as altimeters. That's because a GPS receiver's vertical error is over 50% larger than its horizontal error — in other words, ±500 feet with Selective Availability turned on. In fact, when a GPS receiver is operating in 2D mode *you* may need to supply it with elevation in order for the position reading to be reasonably accurate. That's one reason it is worthwhile to add an altimeter to your GPS toolkit.

Altimeters are just very accurate barometers. They have simply been scaled to reflect altitude differences associated with barometric pressure differences. An altimeter doesn't actually measure feet or meters. It measures the weight of the air above it.

Altimeters have traditionally been very useful additions to the map and compass when used in field work. This was especially true if the user was not able to obtain one or both visual fixes required for triangulation with a compass - say, in a snowstorm.

GPS receivers make this backup function of altimeters less important, but there may be places (such as a narrow canyon, or a dense forest) where the GPS receiver won't function

Figure 2-30: *Various Kinds Of Altimeters*

in 3D mode, or perhaps it won't function at all. At times like this, it is nice to have a handy back-up — your trusty altimeter!

2.3.1 Resetting Your Altimeter

An altimeter left in one place can show elevation changes of hundreds of feet in just a few hours. That's because weather systems have a habit of changing the air pressure around us. Strong wind is usually a good indication that rapid atmospheric pressure changes are occurring.

To be used successfully, your altimeter should be reset frequently. That doesn't mean sending it back to the manufacturer. Resetting an altimeter just means periodically adjusting its elevation reading at locations where you know the actual elevation. That's where your GPS receiver comes in. By giving precise position fixes at points of known elevation, your GPS receiver and topographic map can help you reset your altimeter. Later, when GPS satellite signals can't be located, your altimeter will be ready to serve as a backup.

*A **note of caution:*** do not use the altitude reading taken directly from your GPS receiver to reset your altimeter. Vertical (elevation) errors associated with the GPS system are over 50% greater than horizontal (coordinate) errors, and can easily

Locate your position on the map.

Enter the elevation for your position from the map.

Figure 2-31: *Altimeter Adjustment*

measure in the hundreds of feet. Either read the elevation for your location from a topographic map, or pre-record elevations for known waypoints in a notepad (some GPS receivers have memo fields where you can enter this information). Then reset your altimeter to those actual values when you are at each waypoint.

By keeping your altimeter adjusted its services will be available when you need to take a GPS position fix and all you can obtain is two-dimensional mode. Remember this: the reliability of a 2D position fix is directly related to the accuracy of the elevation used for the position fix. Your horizontal error range is increased by a factor of up to five times the elevation error.

2.3.2 Elevation Change & Temperature

The relationship between elevation change and barometric pressure change is not fixed. The barometric pressure difference between two points at different elevations will vary depending on the air's temperature. Cold air is more dense, so the pressure difference will be greater when it is cold. Warm air is less dense, so the pressure difference will be smaller when it is warm. Altimeters are calibrated so that the elevation difference shown will be accurate if the column of air being weighed is at the "standard" temperature. Even the best altimeters are subject to measurement errors if the temperature in the column of air being measured (i.e., the air directly above the altimeter) is not at the "standard" temperature.

Figure 2-32 shows the international standard temperature chart. This will give you an idea of what constitutes "standard" temperature. As you can see, it depends on the elevation. However, for a particular temperature variance from standard, the percentage elevation error is constant. It is approximately 0.22 percent for each Fahrenheit degree of difference.

Here's an example: At a temperature 5° Fahrenheit above standard, an actual elevation difference of 1000 feet would show up as 989 feet of elevation difference on your altimeter. The warmer than standard air is less dense, so the barometric pressure difference over the 1000 feet of elevation difference is less than normal.

At 50° above standard temperature the altimeter would show a change of 890 feet. Again, the warmer than standard temperature leads the altimeter to understate the true amount of elevation difference. In fact, here's an easy way to remember the relationship: for every 5 degrees above the standard temperature, the elevation difference will be 1.1 percent low. Conversely, for every 5 degrees below the standard temperature, the elevation reading will be 1.1 percent high.

Since these temperature-induced errors are cumulative, frequently resetting your altimeter is a good way to minimize the error due to both non-standard temperatures and fluctuating barometric pressure.

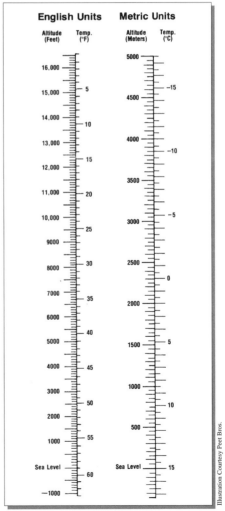

Figure 2-32: Standard Temperature Chart

2.3.3 Temperature & Altimeter Error

Elevation measurement errors associated with non-standard air temperatures should not be confused with measurement errors that are associated with changes in the temperature of the altimeter itself. High quality altimeters are temperature compensated in the sense that their readings do not change if only the temperature of the altimeter itself changes (that is, if there is no actual pressure change).

Inexpensive altimeters that *are not temperature compensated* will show elevation changes in situations where the only physical change is in the temperature of the instrument itself. An uncompensated altimeter can show a 200 foot elevation change in cases where it has not moved, the atmospheric pressure has not changed, but the temperature of the altimeter has gone up (or down) by only 20 degrees Fahrenheit!

Temperature compensation is an important feature for any altimeter that will be used for backcountry navigation. You should definitely try to obtain an altimeter that is temperature compensated.

2.3.4 Choosing An Altimeter

If you don't already have an altimeter, and are considering purchasing one, there are several good options available.

The best altimeter for backcountry use is still a strictly mechanical unit made in Switzerland by Thommen. Besides being exceptionally accurate, Thommen altimeters work without batteries or a power source of any kind. Their downside is that they are expensive.

A convenient option that is less expensive is the new breed of wristwatch altimeters. Avocet's Vertech is a good choice, at a considerably lower price than the all mechanical Thommen. The Vertech offers sophisticated data storage and processing capabilities, but it comes at a price: the battery. As with all things that are electronic, no power, no altimeter.

Several budget-minded altimeter options are available in the form of bike computers. Yes, there are bike computers that give elevation readouts. Perhaps the most widely used model is made by, you guessed it, Avocet. This option is typically less expensive than the wristwatch version, but you get fewer frills. You do, however, get a very nice bike computer in the bargain.

2.4 Map Reading Aids

This section introduces you to the tools that are used to move information (usually coordinates) to and from maps. When using GPS with maps you will find that you need to:

[1] Read coordinates from the map and enter them into the GPS receiver, and/or

[2] Read coordinates from the GPS receiver and locate their position on the map.

When and why you perform these functions is covered in Chapter 6 on GPS skills. How you perform them is covered in this section.

Much of this section is focused on tools for working with USGS 7.5-minute topographic maps. These maps are widely available and they are ideally suited to meeting backcountry land navigation needs. Some of the tools discussed are specifically designed for use with maps of this series. In other cases the tools are generic in nature and can be used with virtually any map. Tools that only work with specific map series will be clearly identified as such.

The USGS topographic maps are well-marked with both latitude/longitude and Universal Transverse Mercator (UTM) coordinates. Either coordinate system can be used with good results. It can, however, take a bit of effort to extract the information needed for GPS purposes. The tools discussed here make that task much simpler.

In the past, locating positions on a map primarily involved reading directions and distances from the map. GPS receivers have rendered those functions mostly obsolete. Now you read the coordinates for the points you are interested in, and your GPS receiver will compute the precise direction and distance between them. The only thing you need to do is obtain the coordinate information.

There are actually four basic coordinate systems shown on USGS topographic maps, but only two that readily work with GPS — latitude/longitude, and

Figure 2-33: *The "Instruments" For Working With Maps*

UTM. As you gain experience in working with topographic maps you may find that you prefer one over the other. It is useful, nonetheless, to be familiar with both these systems. They are described in detail in Chapter 4. What follows in this chapter are some devices that make working with coordinates and maps easier. You can usually find these tools in blueprint stores, nautical supply stores, and other places where maps and map supplies are sold.

2.4.1 Laminates

One of the first things you'll want to consider with any map is whether or not to have it laminated. Basically, this boils down to a matter of personal preference.

A laminated map is impervious to rain, snow, and other sources of moisture. However, a laminated map will need to be rolled (instead of folded) to prevent delamination. This can be a pain. A non-laminated map can be folded and placed inside a zip-lock bag for protection, but it is ultimately more vulnerable to the elements than a laminated map. There are also sprays that can be applied to paper maps to make them more water resistant

Some vendors of USGS topographic maps can also laminate them for you. If your map supplier is unable to do lamination, or you already own unlaminated maps, a blueprint supply company can usually provide this service.

You will probably want to use a different type of marking device depending on whether the map you're working with is laminated or not. If it is not laminated, mechanical pencils with a relatively fine lead are a good choice. They provide a good degree of smudge resistance, yet can be erased if necessary. After your map is laminated, there are special waterproof pens available from blueprint supply companies that resist smudging from moisture and fingers, yet erase completely with a special eraser pen. Staedtler is a brand that offers a wide selection of colors and point thicknesses.

Figure 2-34: *USGS Topo Map Being Laminated*

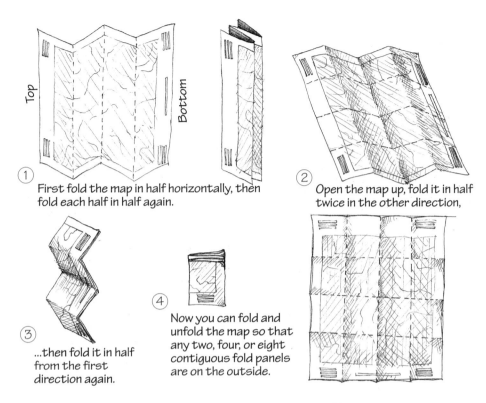

(1) First fold the map in half horizontally, then fold each half in half again.

(2) Open the map up, fold it in half twice in the other direction,

(3) ...then fold it in half from the first direction again.

(4) Now you can fold and unfold the map so that any two, four, or eight contiguous fold panels are on the outside.

Figure 2-35: *Folding A Map For Convenient Use In The Field*

You may want to put certain markings (grids, graticules, declination ruling lines, specific waypoints, etc.) on your map before having it laminated. This provides maximum permanence for those markings. Just be careful — once a map has been laminated you can't change your mind about those markings.

If you don't laminate and roll your map, you'll probably want to fold it and protect it in a clear plastic map case. How you fold your map is a matter of personal preference, but an accordion-style method is very convenient and works well. This method is illustrated in Figure 2-35.

2.4.2 Straight-Edge Ruler

A good straight-edge ruler is essential for preparing most topographic maps for land navigation. Depending on your preferences, you can use the straight-edge to apply either latitude/longitude graticules, UTM grid lines, or magnetic declination ruling lines. Some of the newer USGS topographic maps come with fine-line UTM grids already printed on the face of the map. None come with graticules or declination ruling lines.

If the map you're using doesn't have UTM gridlines, and you don't want to add them, a straight-edge still comes in handy when reading UTM coordinates from the map, and when applying coordinates to the map. This process is discussed in the next section on roamers and dividers.

When selecting a straight-edge you should get one that is long enough to cover the entire paper surface of the maps you'll be using. In the case of USGS 7.5-minute topographic maps it should be at least 26 inches long, but not more than about 36 inches. It should be fairly heavy and skid resistant if possible, so you can draw perfectly straight full length lines in a single stroke. A thin layer of cork on the bottom of the straightedge is nice.

A beveled edge on the top of your straightedge allows greater precision when you draw lines. A slight bevel on the bottom (or a thin backing of cork) will prevent ink bleeding if you use an ink pen for drawing your lines. A bevel (or cork) on the bottom will also make it easier to pick up the straight-edge.

The primary lines you *may* want to draw on your maps with a straightedge are:

[1] 2.5-minute latitude/longitude graticules and extensions of the neatline graticules (for use with the latitude/longitude coordinate system), or

[2] 1,000 meter UTM grids (for use with the UTM coordinate system).

If you plan to use a latitude/longitude ruler, the latitude/longitude graticules should be extended to the physical edge of the map sheet (i.e., all the way across the border region of the map). You'll also need to add new graticules (two horizontal and two vertical) at the 2.5-minute tick marks. See Figure 3-31 on page 101 for an example.

UTM grid lines only need to be drawn between the neatlines (that is, they don't need to be extended into the border area). Although a few of the newer USGS topographic maps come with UTM grid lines already printed on the face of the map, most do not. All USGS topographic maps have UTM tick marks on the neatlines. See Figure 3-30 on page 99.

If you decide to draw both latitude/longitude graticules and UTM gridlines on the same map, you may want to use different colors to avoid confusion. The UTM ticks are printed in blue on the margins of USGS maps. Latitude/longitude ticks are printed in black.

It used to be fairly standard procedure to apply declination ruling lines to topographic maps. These lines "tilt" by the amount of magnetic declination in the area covered by the map, so that they run parallel with magnetic north. They make it easier to use magnetic directions with a protractor and map. Declination ruling lines made a lot of sense when maps and compasses were the primary navigation tools, but GPS and declination adjusted compasses have made them much less important.

Given the importance of coordinates (and therefore graticules and/or gridlines) it is not likely that you'll want to further clutter the face of your maps with declination ruling lines. But if you want to put declination rule lines on your map, a straightedge is the only way to apply them. See page 101 for some tips on how to do it.

2.4.3 Dividers and Roamers (UTM)

Dividers and roamers are the primary measurement tools for use with the UTM coordinate system. Working with UTM map coordinates involves measuring horizontal and vertical distances from grid lines. These tools make the job much easier. See page 120 for a detailed description of the UTM coordinate system.

If you're working with a map that has UTM gridlines marked on its face then you can use a roamer. It is the ideal tool to read and apply UTM coordinates. A roamer is a transparent plastic card that has UTM easting and northing rules marked at right angles. You must use a roamer that matches the scale of your map. The roamer in Figure 2-36 covers several different map scales.

To use a roamer, place it on the map so that the point you want to measure is directly beneath the intersection of the two right angle rulers, and the rulers themselves are parallel with the horizontal and vertical gridlines. Read the "easting" value from the closest vertical

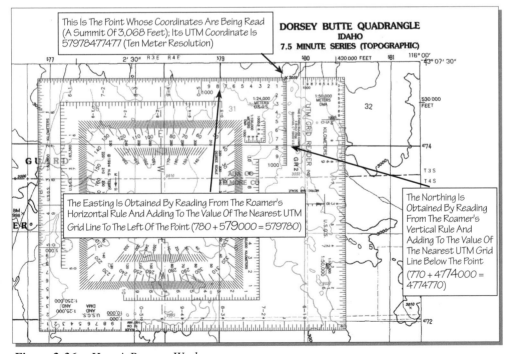

Figure 2-36: *How A Roamer Works*

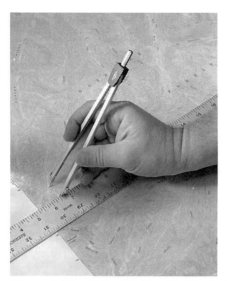

Figure 2-37: *Using Dividers To Obtain UTM Northing Values*

gridline to the left (west) of the point you're reading. Read the "northing" value from the closest horizontal gridline below (south) of the point you're reading. Add these values to the gridline values and you'll have the point's UTM coordinates. It's that simple. Reverse the process to go from coordinates to locations on the map. See Figure 2-36.

It is also possible to read UTM coordinates from a map that has gridlines using just a divider and the printed metric bar scale on the map itself. This works because the UTM grid lines (or tick marks) are always 1,000 meters apart on USGS 7.5-minute and 15-minute topographic maps. A divider is a handy universal tool for reading distance from the printed bar scale on any map.

To obtain the easting value, use the divider to measure the distance from the point of interest to the closest vertical gridline to the left. Then place the divider (be careful not to change its "spread") on the map's metric scale and read the distance. Add that distance to the vertical gridline's value, and you have the easting part of the point's coordinate.

For a northing value, use the divider to measure the distance to the closest horizontal gridline below the point, and read that distance value from the metric distance scale that is printed on the map. Add that distance value to the horizontal gridline's value, and you have the northing part of the point's coordinate.

In the field you can even eyeball the distance between a point of interest and the nearest gridlines below and to the left of the point. While not as precise as using a divider, you can usually get fairly close. You can also fabricate a simple metric distance scale suitable for the map you're using by transferring the 100 meter marks from the map's metric distance scale to the edge of a note card or some other straight-edged piece of paper.

If your map doesn't have UTM gridlines you won't be able to "eyeball" coordinates. You can make a "temporary" grid line, however, by laying your straightedge across the map and connecting the UTM grid marks below or to the left of the point of interest. Then use the divider to obtain the distance from the point of interest to the edge of the straightedge, and read the value from the metric distance scale on the border of the map. This process is shown in Figure 2-37.

2.4.4 Latitude/Longitude Rulers

This tool is used to extract or apply map coordinates expressed in angular — latitude and longitude — units. The ruler must be designed for the specific map series you're working with, i.e. 7.5-minute quadrangles at a 1:24,000 scale. Similar rulers are available for nautical charts, but they won't work on the USGS topographic maps.

The simplest latitude/longitude ruler is designed for the USGS 7.5-minute maps. It has two scales of slightly different lengths that are marked in 1 second increments and span 2.5 minutes, or 150 seconds. The longer of the two scales is used for latitude, and the shorter scale is used for longitude. Two different lengths are used because the distance between lines of latitude remains stable at approximately 69 miles per degree anywhere on earth, but the distance between lines of longitude "shrinks" as you move north or south away from the equator. Most of the continental U.S. lies between latitude 25°N and latitude

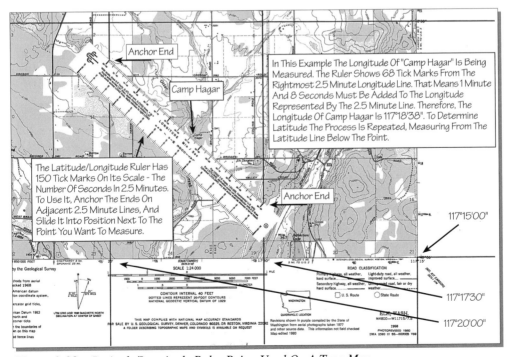

Figure 2-38: Latitude/Longitude Ruler Being Used On A Topo Map

49°N. In this region the length of a degree of longitude varies from 63 miles to 45 miles per degree of longitude.

Another type of latitude/longitude ruler is printed on a clear base and has five scales that are designed for maps from 1:24,000 scale to 1:250,000 scale. It works on more maps than the simpler model, but it is bulkier and more prone to scratching since it is made of clear plastic.

To work with any latitude/longitude ruler you first need to draw graticule lines across the face of your map at 2.5-minute intervals (when using a 7.5-minute map) or 5-minute intervals (when using a 15-minute map). These lines should be perfectly straight and they should extend to the physical edge of the map sheet. Use a good straightedge to draw these lines. They will divide the map itself into thirds in both a horizontal and a vertical direction. You now have nine "sub-quadrangles."

Lay the latitude/longitude ruler across the face of the map so that the ends of the scale lie on adjacent parallel graticule lines. Now slide the ruler to the point you're interested in so that the point is aligned with the ruler's scale. The "skewed" angle of the lat/lon ruler is necessary to fit the fixed length of the ruler's scale into the exact distance between the graticules.

To obtain a longitude reading the ruler is skewed to fit between two vertical graticules. You read the number of minutes and seconds the point is away from the right side of the scale (western hemisphere only) and add them to the value associated with the graticule on the right side of the scale.

To obtain a latitude reading the ruler is skewed to fit between two horizontal graticules. You read the number of minutes and seconds up from the bottom of the scale (northern hemisphere only) and add them to the value associated with the graticule on the bottom end of the scale.

2.4.5 Contour Scales

This map reading device is used for measuring the slope of terrain on topographic maps. It doesn't have anything to do with coordinates and GPS receivers, but it can make map reading and land navigation much easier. Contour scales are inexpensive and they can be useful when planning trips into unfamiliar territory.

The typical contour scale is a clear plastic template that is calibrated to work with both a 1:24,000 scale map (7.5-minute) and a 1:62,500 scale map (15-minute). To use it you place the edge of the contour scale over the contour lines you're interested in measuring. Then you match the spacing of the contour lines on the map with the closest set on the contour scale. Finally, you read the percent grade from the table on the contour scale using the row that corresponds to the map series (7.5-minute or 15-minute) and contour interval on the map you're using.

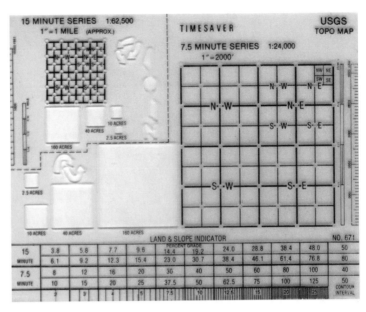

Figure 2-39: A Typical
Contour
Scale

If the contour interval on your map doesn't correspond to the contour intervals on the contour scale, no problem. It will most likely be 1/2 of one of the intervals shown. In this case just halve the percent slope that you read from the scale. If the contour interval on your map is double one of the values on the contour scale's table, then double the slope obtained from that row.

2.4.6 Miscellaneous Map Reading Aids

Several miscellaneous tools can make it easier to work with large-scale topographic maps. A magnifier can come in handy for reading the fine detail. The kind shown in Figure 2-33 is useful when working with a map in advance of a backcountry excursion. You can even find Swiss Army knives with little folding magnifiers that are suitable for taking with you into the field.

A protractor is another handy accessory, with models available in several shapes. Protractors are used to read angles on maps. A circular protractor is the easiest to read, but a square protractor is easier to align with the grid lines of a map. A square protractor also has the benefit of a small built-in straight-edge. Semi-circular protractors seem to offer the advantages of both types, but they really end up with the weaknesses of both. They are awkward to align and difficult to read.

Chapter 3:

Maps

Maps are the single most important source of information for GPS users. Maps can provide you with the coordinates for the places you want to find, and maps can show you where you are when you obtain a GPS position fix. Maps are the "middleman" between your GPS receiver and the world around you.

You can use GPS successfully without maps. In fact, there may be times when you intentionally use only your GPS receiver (along with a compass and spare batteries) for land navigation purposes. In essence, you leave all the details about locations to your GPS receiver and its internal software, simply letting it guide you to the locations that you've previously stored from position fixes.

However, when you integrate maps with GPS you get the best of both. Maps can help you plan a trip into the backcountry. And when you're there, maps can make your travel safer and more efficient.

This chapter provides an understanding of maps that will allow you to realize the full potential of the GPS system. It covers the key information you need to know about maps in general, and large scale topographic maps in particular. After a brief overview, the most important aspects of maps — scale, datum, coordinate systems, contour lines, symbols, dates, and other margin information — are explained in detail.

Following this chapter on maps, the next two chapters cover coordinate systems and direction systems in more detail. Those two topics, while important for most GPS-related uses of maps, are

This Chapter provides a thorough explanation of maps — the "software" needed to realize the full potential of the GPS system.

covered in their own chapters. That's because coordinate systems and direction systems are also relevant by themselves, whether or not you happen to be using a map.

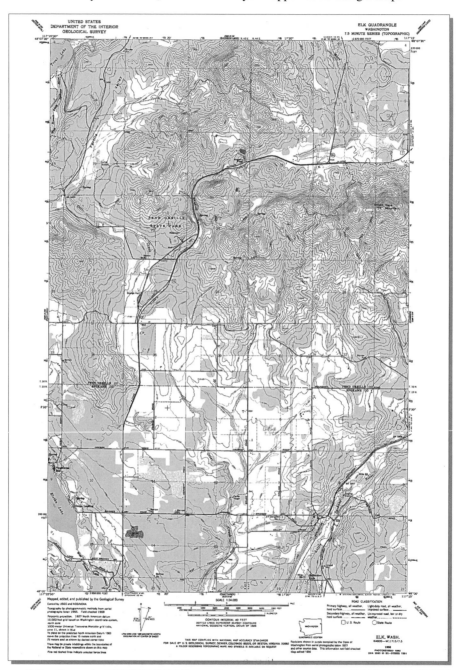

Figure 3-1: *Example Of USGS 7.5-Minute Topographic Map — One Of About 54,000 Maps That Completely Cover The United States*

3.1 Overview

Everyone knows what a map is, yet few of us really understand maps well. We generally think of a map as just a scaled-down representation of some part of the earth. Yet the complexity of a map is easily overlooked, hidden in the apparent (but often elusive) accuracy of its printed rendition of the land.

Perhaps the most fundamental truth about any printed, two-dimensional map of any region on the earth is that it is a distortion of reality. When you stop and consider that a map is an attempt to reduce a spherical surface (the earth) to a plane (the map sheet), it becomes apparent that distortion must and will occur.

Fortunately, the backcountry land navigator is usually concerned with relatively compact regions of land. Large-scale maps that cover these relatively small areas tend to have trivial amounts of distortion. For all practical purposes, the typical maps used for recreational land navigation — United States Geological Survey (USGS) 7.5-minute topographic maps — can be treated as being distortion free.

Nonetheless, it is useful to understand the basic characteristics of maps, including the sources of their distortion. This chapter is designed to make the GPS user familiar with maps in general, and the USGS 7.5-minute quadrangle series topographic maps in particular.

The USGS topographic maps are ideal for most types of outdoor recreation where land navigation is involved. They are available for the entire land area of the United States. It takes almost 54,000 separate USGS 7.5-minute quadrangle series topographic maps to cover every square inch of the continental United States!

So what exactly is a quadrangle series topographic map? Quite simply, the term "quadrangle" refers to a map whose horizontal and vertical borders, called neatlines, coincide exactly with lines of latitude and longitude. By convention, if only one dimension is provided, the ranges of the latitude and the longitude covered by the map are the same (i.e., 7.5-minute). If the map covers differing amounts of latitude and longitude, the latitude and longitude ranges are both given, in that order (i.e., 30-minute by 60-minute).

The term "topographic" refers to a type of map that uses lines and symbols to portray the physical elevation characteristics of the land. Usually the lines represent precise contour intervals, meaning that all the points along a single contour line are the same elevation. However, in some types of maps (but not the USGS topographic maps) the lines are in the form of less precise "hachures," a type of line that suggests elevation by giving the outline and shading of hills, mountains, ridges, etc. Hachures are more akin to sketching.

The USGS 7.5-minute maps are each 7½ minutes of latitude high by 7½ minutes of longitude wide. Eight of these maps side-by-side span one degree of longitude. Eight of these maps stacked vertically span one degree of latitude. Sixty-four of these maps (eight high by eight across) cover a one-degree by one-degree square.

Figure 3-2 shows the relative areas covered by the various USGS quadrangle map series. Four 7.5-minute quadrangles cover the same area as one 15-minute quadrangle, four 15-minute (or sixteen 7.5-minute) quadrangles cover the same area as one 30-minute quadrangle, and so on.

Even though the 7.5-minute quadrangle maps cover equal horizontal and vertical angular distances (7.5 minutes in this case), they are not necessarily square in shape. All USGS 7.5-minute quadrangle maps of the U.S. are rectangular, with greater height than width. That's because the distance covered by a degree (or a minute, or a second) of longitude shrinks as you move away from the equator, but the distance covered by a degree of latitude is approximately the same anywhere on earth.

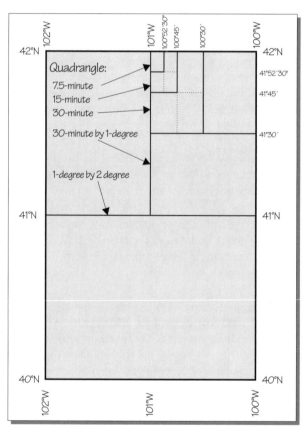

A 7.5-minute quadrangle map will only be square along the equator, where both latitude and longitude cover about 69 miles per degree. Table 3-1 shows the linear distance covered by one degree of latitude and one degree of longitude at various latitudes ranging from the southernmost to the northern-most latitudes found in the continental United States. It also shows the area covered by quadrangle maps at various latitudes.

There are several key items of information that you should know about any map you plan to use with GPS. Those items are the scale, horizontal datum, and the grid system. The map's contour interval and its symbol legend are also important, along with the date(s) of the map and any revisions.

Figure 3-2: *Relative Size Of USGS Topographic Maps*

Other details, such as the projection used to draw the map, are of little practical concern to users of the large scale maps that are most likely to be used in land navigation applications. The final sections in this chapter cover the topics of preparing maps for planning and field use, and where to find maps.

Variations in Distance Per Degree and Quadrangle Area At Various Latitudes					
Latitude	Miles Per Degree of Latitude	Miles Per Degree of Longitude	Area Covered by Quadrangle:		
			7.5-Minute	15-Minute	30-Minute by 1-Degree
48°	69.09	46.37	49.6 mi²	198.3 mi²	1,587 mi²
45°	69.06	48.99	52.4 mi²	209.6 mi²	1,677 mi²
42°	69.02	51.48	55.1 mi²	220.3 mi²	1,763 mi²
39°	68.98	53.83	57.6 mi²	230.4 mi²	1,844 mi²
36°	68.94	56.03	60.0 mi²	239.9 mi²	1,919 mi²
33°	68.91	58.07	62.2 mi²	248.7 mi²	1,990 mi²
30°	68.88	59.96	64.2 mi²	256.8 mi²	2,055 mi²
27°	68.85	61.68	66.1 mi²	264.2 mi²	2,114 mi²
24°	68.82	63.23	67.7 mi²	270.9 mi²	2,167 mi²

Table 3-1: *Variations In Distance Per Degree And Quadrangle Area At Various Latitudes*

3.2 Map Scale

A map's scale is probably the single most important item of information you need to know about any map. It tells you how the actual distances on the map relate to the actual distances on the ground. It is expressed as either a fraction (1/xx,xxx) or a ratio (1:xx,xxx). In these expressions "xx,xxx" simply refers to a number such as 24,000 or 1,000,000. For every 1 unit on the map, there are xx,xxx units on the ground. The technical term used to refer to a map's scale is "representative fraction", or RF. In a moment you'll see why this is an apt description.

An important characteristic of the RF is that it has no dimension. It is not specific to feet, meters, or any other unit of measurement. For that reason it is well suited to serve any measurement system you choose.

To see why RF is dimensionless, consider that a map scale of 1/24,000 (also expressed as 1:24,000) means that one inch on the map represents 24,000 inches on the ground. But it also means that one centimeter on the map represents 24,000 centimeters on the ground.

Since there are 12 inches per foot, a 1:24,000 map can also be said to represent 2,000 feet on the ground with one inch on the map (24,000 inches ÷ 12 inches per foot). Likewise, one centimeter on the map represents 0.24 kilometers on the ground (24,000 centimeters ÷ 100,000 centimeters per kilometer).

Miles (on the ground) per inch (on a 1:24,000 scale map) can also be found by performing a similar conversion. Multiply 5,280 feet per mile times 12 inches per foot to yield 63,360 inches per mile. Since one inch on the map equals 24,000 inches on the ground, divide 24,000 by 63,360 to get the answer of 0.37878787…, or about .38 miles per inch.

As long as you know a map's scale, it doesn't really matter what units of measurement you are interested in using. You just need to do the appropriate arithmetic. It is generally true, however, that certain units of measurement will usually work better with maps of a particular scale.

A map with a scale of 1:1,000,000 (a scale that is typically used to portray an entire state) has one map inch representing 1,000,000 inches on the ground, or about 15.7828 miles

USGS Map Scales — Ground Distances and Quadrangles

Map Scale (RF)	Feet & Miles *On The Ground*		Meters & Kilometers *OTG*		Topographic Quadrangle Coverage:
	Per Inch	Per Centimeter	Per Inch	Per Centimeter	
1:20,000	1,667 ft .3157 mi	656 ft .1243 mi	508 m 0.508 km	200 m 0.200 km	Puerto Rico 7.5-minute
1:24,000	2,000 ft .3789 mi	787 ft .1491 mi	610 m 0.610 km	240 m 0.240 km	All Continental U.S. & Hawaii 7.5-minute
1:25,000	2,083 ft .3946 mi	820 ft .1553 mi	635 m 0.635 km	250 m 0.250 km	Selected Metric Scale Maps
1:50,000	4,167 ft .7891 mi	1,640 ft .3107 mi	1,270 m 1.270 km	500 m 0.500 km	Defense Mapping Agency 15-minute
1:62,500	5,208 ft .9864 mi	2,050 ft .3883 mi	1,588 m 1.588 km	625 m .0625 km	Continental U.S. 15-minute (discontinued)
1:63,360	5,280 ft 1.000 mi	2,079 ft .3937 mi	1,609 m 1.609 km	634 m 0.634 km	Standard Series Alaska 15-minute
1:100,000	8,333 ft 1.578 mi	3,281 ft .6214 mi	2,540 m 2.540 km	1,000 m 1.000 km	Cont. U.S. & Hawaii 30- x 60-minute

Table 3-2: USGS Map Scales — Ground Distances And Quadrangles

per inch (1,000,000 ÷ 63,360 = 15.7828…). This scale is much better suited to metric measurements, where 1 centimeter on the map equals 10 kilometers on the ground (1,000,000 ÷ 100,000 =10). Maps with scales of 1:50,000 and 1:25,000 also tend to work best with metric units.

Maps drawn at the scale 1:63,360 work best with English distance units, since one inch on the map equals exactly one mile on the ground. Maps drawn at the scale of 1:62,500 also work best with English units, since one inch equals 0.99 miles.

The relationship between distance on a map and distance on the ground is usually shown visually on the map in the form of a bar scale. A bar scale provides representations of common real-world linear dimensions drawn at the scale of the map. They are very handy when using a divider to determine distances (see page 63).

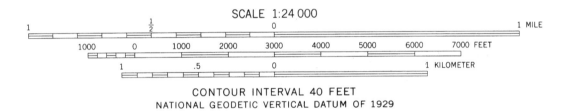

Figure 3-3: Sample Of A Bar Scale From A USGS 7.5-Minute Map (Shown Actual Size)

Maps are sometimes characterized as large scale (where a normal sized map sheet covers a relatively small land area) and small scale (where a normal sized map sheet covers a relatively large land area). To avoid confusion with these terms, think of small and large as it relates to a map's detail. A large scale map has large detail, so it covers a small area. Conversely, a small scale map has small detail, so it covers a large area.

Another way to think of the "size" of a map's scale is with the representative fraction. If the representative fraction is a relatively large number (such as 1/24,000), then it is a large scale map. If the representative fraction is a relatively small number (such as 1/1,000,000), then it is a small scale map.

Maps with scales of 1:25,000 and larger are generally considered large scale. Maps with scales of 1:250,000 and smaller are considered small scale. Maps with scales of 1:50,000 to 1:100,000 are considered medium scale maps.

An obvious tradeoff associated with map scale has to do with keeping map sheet sizes manageable. A given size of map sheet can either **[1]** cover more area with less detail (small scale), or **[2]** cover less area with more detail (large scale). Your intended use of a map determines the scale that is best suited to your particular purpose. If you are flying across the United States, you'd probably want a small scale map. If you are hiking to a hidden backcountry lake, you'd probably want a large scale map.

The USGS 7.5-minute topographic maps are the ideal size for the type of land navigation addressed by this book (on foot, horse, ski, bike, motorcycle, snowmobile, etc). They are readily available and they provide plenty of detail.

For the continental United States and Hawaii, USGS 7.5-minute topographic maps have a scale of 1:24,000. These 7.5-minute maps are ideal for most recreational users. The standard quadrangle series maps for Alaska are published at a scale of 1:63,360 and they cover 15 minutes of latitude by 20 to 36 minutes of longitude. The extra longitude is provided because Alaska is much closer to the north pole than the lower 48 states, and the distance covered by a minute of longitude at Alaska's latitudes would lead to very narrow maps if they were only 15 minutes wide.

USGS 15-minute maps of the continental U.S. have been discontinued, although they may be found in libraries. They cover four times more area than the 7.5-minute maps. They typically have a scale of 1:62,500. They are in the medium scale category, and they are borderline in terms of their usefulness for backcountry navigation. That's because medium scale maps don't show enough terrain detail.

Other USGS map series (30x60-minute, 1x2-degree) are generally too small scale to be useful on the ground, although they can be helpful in trip planning, driving to a trailhead, and similar functions. Older 7.5x15-minute maps have a 1:25,000 scale, but the map sheet is so large that they are unwieldy for field use.

Classification of Map Sizes		
Size Category	Representative Fraction	Preferred Uses
Very Large Scale	Under 1:10,000	Architecture, Engineering, Etc.
Large Scale	1:20,000 to 1:25,000	Backcountry Travel
Medium Scale	1:50,000 to 1:100,000	Trip Planning, Access Planning
Small Scale	1:250,000 and Over	Long Distance Travel

Table 3-3: Map Scale Categories

STANDARD SERIES MAPS

Standard quadrangle maps **cover systematically** subdivided areas of latitude and longitude, and are published at various scales depending on the size of the area-mapped

Standard quadrangle formats **range from 7.5x7.5** minutes covering geographic areas of 49 to 71 square miles to 1x2 degrees covering areas of 4580 to 8669 square miles

Standard quadrangle map scales **range from** 1:24 000 (one inch on the map represents 2000 feet on the ground) to 1:250 000 (one inch on the map represents approximately 4 miles on the ground)

Other quadrangle maps **are published at scales of** 1:20 000 (Puerto Rico) to 1:63 360 (Alaska) and 1:1 000 000 (International Map of the World)

Special area maps **are published at scales of 1:50 000** and 1:100 000 (County, Regional, and National Park Maps), and 1:500 000 (State Base Maps).

MAP SERIES COMPARISON

Illustrated opposite is the relative comparison of the size of the area covered by the various map series. Comparatively, the number of maps required to cover an area of 1 degree latitude by 2 degrees longitude is:

    128 —7.5 minute maps
      64 —7.5x15 minute maps
      32 —15 minute maps
        4 —30x60 minute maps
        1 —1x2 degree map

The amount of detail shown on a map is proportionate to the scale of the map; the larger the map scale, the more detail that is shown. For example, individual houses are shown on 1:24 000-scale 7.5-minute maps, whereas only landmark buildings are shown on 1:100 000-scale 30x60-minute maps.

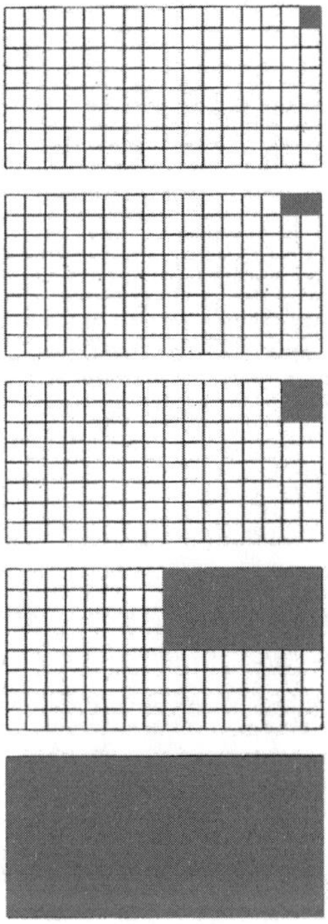

7.5 MINUTE SERIES

Map scale[1]	1:24 000
Map to ground ratio	1 inch represents 2000 feet
Area covered	49–71 square miles
Paper size (approx.)	22"x27"
Contours and elevations[2]	shown in feet

7.5 X 15 MINUTE SERIES

Map scale	1:25 000
Map to ground ratio	1 inch represents 2083 feet
Area covered	100–140 square miles
Paper size (approx.)	24"x40"
Contours and elevations	shown in meters

15 MINUTE SERIES

Map scale[3]	1:62 500
Map to ground ratio	1 inch represents about 1 mile
Area covered	197–282 square miles
Paper size (approx.)	18"x22"
Contours and elevations[2]	shown in feet

30 X 60 MINUTE SERIES

Map scale	1:100 000
Map to ground ratio	1 inch represents 1.6 miles
Area covered	1578–2167 square miles
Paper size (approx.)	29"x44"
Contours and elevations[2]	shown in meters

1 X 2 DEGREE SERIES

Map scale	1:250 000
Map to ground ratio	1 inch represents about 4 miles
Area covered	4580–8669 square miles
Paper size (approx.)	22"x32"
Contours and elevations[2]	shown in feet

[1] 1:25 000 scale on selected maps
[2] Shown in meters on selected maps
[3] 1:50 000 scale on selected maps

Figure 3-4: USGS Standard Series Maps

Unfortunately, scale on a map is not really as simple as it has been portrayed so far. Since a flat map is being used to portray a spherical surface (the earth, or a portion of it), there is inevitably going to be some distortion introduced. Cartographers can control various aspects of map distortion by their choice of map projection methods, but they can't eliminate distortion.

Because of the distortion caused by projecting a round world onto a flat map, scale is not fixed on a map. It varies over the surface of the map. How it varies depends on the type of projection used to construct the map. Fortunately, this scale variation is not a practical issue with the large scale maps typically used by land navigators. The dimensional instability of the paper used for USGS 7.5-minute topographic maps (that is, the paper's expansion and shrinkage as its moisture content varies) exceeds the variation in scale found on different areas of such a map!

3.3 Datums

The datum of a map is its spatial foundation — its "tie-in" to the real world. There are two kinds of datum, horizontal and vertical. The horizontal datum is the one you will use with your GPS receiver. Vertical datums are not of practical concern to backcountry GPS users.

You'll want to make sure that the horizontal datum setting in your receiver matches the horizontal datum of the map (or numeric coordinate data) you are using. The horizontal datum you specify is used by the GPS receiver to "align" its readouts to the spatial reference system used by the makers of the map (or coordinates) you are using.

Many times you may find that coordinates are listed without any indication of the associated datum. This sloppy practice has been acceptable because most U.S. coordinates are based on either NAD27, NAD83, or WGS84. The latter two are almost identical, and the first one has horizontal offsets of no more than 200 meters from the other two. Before the advent of GPS, 200 meters of coordinate error didn't matter to the average hiker or hunter. Now, with GPS, errors related to an incorrect datum will be noticeable.

In simple terms the horizontal datum of a map consists of **[1]** an ellipsoid that represents the surface of the earth at approximately sea level and **[2]** a point of origin on the ellipsoid. An ellipsoid is used instead of a sphere because the earth is not actually round. The rotation of the earth causes a bulge on the plane of the equator. The circumference of the earth at sea level is actually 42 miles greater around the equator compared to the circumference around the poles.

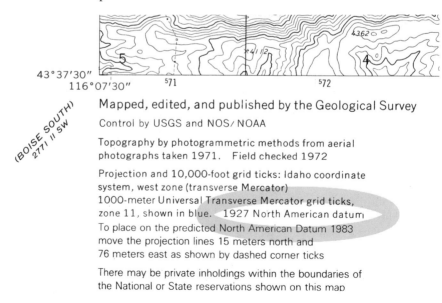

Figure 3-5: *Datum Specification On USGS Topographic Map*

On modern maps the point of origin is defined by the intersection of the equatorial plane (0° latitude) and a polar plane that passes through a "prime meridian" (0° longitude). The prime meridian for maps produced in the U.S. is the meridian that passes through a specific point at the British Royal Observatory in Greenwich, England. Hence the term "Greenwich Meridian." Over the years maps produced in other countries have used many different locations to define the "prime meridian." Other cities that are (or have been) home to their country's prime meridian include Athens, Brussels, Istanbul, Lisbon, Moscow, Paris, Peking, and Tokyo.

Most of the coordinate differences between the various North American datums is related to the different ellipsoids they use. The North American datum of 1927 (NAD27) uses an ellipsoid known as *Clarke 1866*. The newer North American datum of 1983 (NAD83) uses GRS80.

Maps and coordinate data for the continental United States will usually be based on either NAD27 or NAD83. Although USGS topographic maps are tied to NAD27, the newer USGS maps also show the offset for coordinates based on NAD83. Some commercial map products (such as Street Atlas USA) are based on WGS84. Other commercial products (such as electronic maps produced by ETAK for automotive use) are based on NAD27. The bottom line is it's hard to tell what datum is used for a particular map or set of coordinate data without explicit documentation. Sometimes you may be forced to guess between NAD27 and NAD83 or WGS84. If so, just remember that means up to an additional 200 meters of error in the coordinates you use.

Once you leave the continental United States the issue of datum specification becomes much more complicated. Using your GPS receiver with a local map outside the continental U.S. will mean that you need to specify the appropriate datum so that your GPS readings will properly "line up" with the map you are using. If you use the wrong datum it can mean an error of considerable distance — hundreds of meters in some cases!

3.4 Coordinate Systems

The coordinate system(s) found on any map will be either angular (latitude/longitude) or rectangular (UTM, state plane, etc). The angular coordinate system is designed for a three-dimensional object, i.e. a sphere that represents the surface of the earth. The rectangular coordinate system is designed for a two-dimensional object, i.e. a flat page that is used for the sheet of a map. They both provide horizontal and vertical guide lines for locating positions on the map.

As it happens, the USGS topographic maps contain both coordinate systems. That means you are free to choose the system that works best for you. You'll probably find that you switch between latitude/longitude and UTM (Universal Transverse Mercator) depending on the task at hand. Fortunately, GPS receivers make that switch extremely simple.

Since coordinate systems are so fundamental to using GPS receivers (with or without maps) they are covered in depth in the next chapter. The rest of this section gives an overview of the basic coordinate systems used on USGS topographic maps.

Geographic coordinate systems are shown on a map as a grid system that is drawn as either complete lines or tick marks on the border. If tick marks are used, then you have to visualize the lines that connect the tick marks on opposite sides of the map. In the case of rectangular coordinates the lines are called grids. In the case of the angular coordinate system the lines are called graticules. Graticules **are** lines of latitude (horizontal lines) or lines of longitude (vertical lines). Grids usually **are not** lines of latitude or longitude.

You will find latitude/longitude tick marks and UTM grid tick marks on the top, bottom, and sides of most topographic maps. In the case of USGS 7.5-minute maps the horizontal

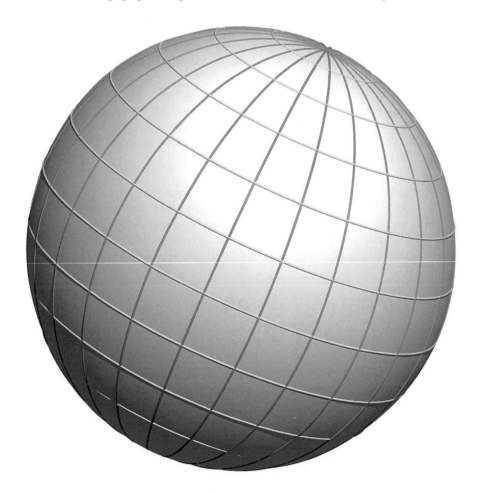

Figure 3-6: Angular "Grid" — It's Definitely Designed For A Sphere

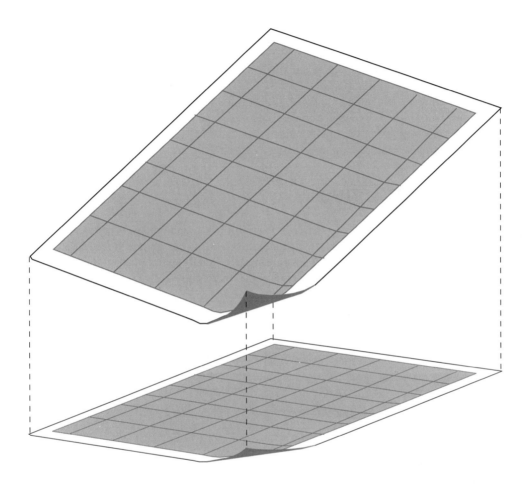

Figure 3-7: *Rectangular Grid — Designed For A Sheet Of Paper*

and vertical borders of the map are lines of latitude and longitude that are 7.5 minutes apart — hence the name 7.5-Minute Quadrangle Series. These are far and away the most important maps available to backcountry land navigators.

Newer editions of USGS 7.5-minute maps that are still based on the North American datum of 1927 have tick marks at the corners that show the offset for translating the latitude/longitude graticules to the newer North American Datum of 1983. The same offset also applies to the UTM grid and tick marks.

There are 2½ minute graticule tick marks (including four interior cross-hair symbols) on the USGS 7.5-minute maps. They can be used to divide the map into nine 2½ minute by 2½ minute rectangles. These graticule tick marks are especially important if you are going to use a latitude/longitude ruler with the map. See page 65 for more information.

UTM grid tick marks can be found along the edges of the USGS topographic maps, and they are usually printed in blue ink. On some of the newer USGS maps the full UTM grid is actually printed on the face of the map. This UTM fineline grid is very handy for GPS users. Increasing GPS usage will eventually lead to more maps with UTM fineline grids.

The numbering system behind the UTM gridlines and tick marks is difficult to explain in just a few words. The next chapter on coordinates covers that topic in detail. Suffice it to say that it is worth taking the time to understand the UTM grid system. Once you do, it makes topographic maps very simple to use.

3.5 Contour Lines

Contour lines bring the earth's landscape to life in topographic maps. The information contained in contour lines can be divided into three general categories: the elevation, the slope, and the shape of the terrain. Contour lines are usually light brown, and every fifth line is bolded to represent an "index" contour line. Index contour lines are added to make topographic maps easier to read.

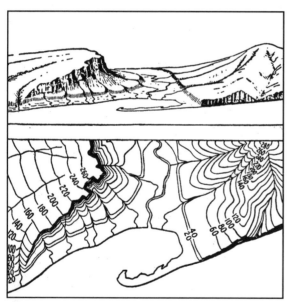

A contour line on a topographic map traces a path of constant elevation. The elevation represented by a contour line is the vertical distance above the map's vertical datum. The term "vertical datum" is usually equivalent to "mean sea level."

The vertical distance between adjacent contour lines (the contour interval) will vary on different maps depending on the overall steepness of the terrain shown on the particular map. The contour interval will not vary on a single map, although some areas on a single map may have supplementary contour lines that fall between the map's regular contour lines.

Figure 3-8: *A Perspective View And Contour Map*

A USGS 7.5-minute topographic map that covers an area that is relatively flat might have a 5 foot contour interval (with every fifth bolded index line representing 25 vertical feet), while a map of the same size and scale that covers an area with steep terrain may use a 40 foot contour interval (with every fifth bolded index line representing 200 vertical feet).

You will usually find the contour interval information for a particular map specified near the bar scale of the map. On USGS topographic maps the contour interval is shown centered in the bottom margin of the map sheet. See Figure 3-24 on page 95.

On maps that have a wide range of steepness within the area covered by the map supplementary contour lines may be used. Supplementary contour lines will appear only in

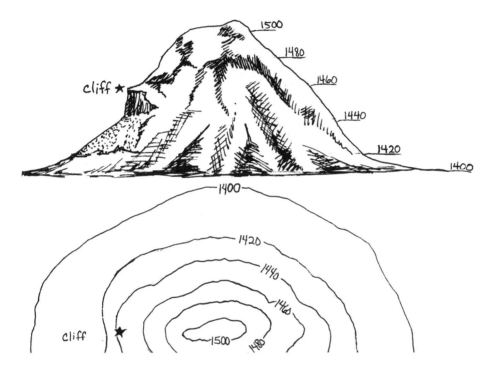

Figure 3-9: *Terrain Features Can Fall Between Contour Intervals*

certain areas of the map. They will be represented by dashed lines that appear between regular contour lines. The legend will indicate the vertical interval of supplementary contour lines. They usually represent one-half of the regular contour interval.

It is very important that you understand what contour intervals do not show. They leave out any features (such as small cliffs) that fall within their interval. Contour intervals are only representative of the general shape and slope of the terrain they cover. They do a good job of representing the average slope and shape of the land, but they are limited by the resolution of the map's vertical interval.

With experience a topographic map user can learn to "read between the lines" and get more out of contour intervals than their literal elevation content. Until that experience is gained, caution is the best policy when interpreting contour lines.

3.5.1 Elevation

Elevation is the simplest and most direct information you can obtain from the contour lines of a topographic map. Elevation is simply a numeric value, and it is the same anywhere along a particular contour line.

Usually every fifth bolded index line will have the elevation (in feet or meters above mean sea level) printed somewhere along its path, with the top of the numbers usually (but not always) on the uphill side of the slope. Each successive regular contour line is 1/5 of the elevation distance between the bolded (and labeled) index contour lines.

If you want to know the elevation of a point that doesn't lie on a contour line, interpolate. The convention is to consider the point to be either **[1]** at the elevation of the contour line (if it is within one-fourth of the distance to the next contour line), or **[2]** at an elevation 1/2 of the vertical distance between contour lines (if the point lies between one-fourth and three-fourths of the way to the next adjacent contour line). This means that the implied vertical resolution of a topographic map is one-half of the contour interval.

Elevations on a topographic map are also indicated for specific points in the form of benchmarks and spot elevations. Benchmarks are usually more accurate and are used by

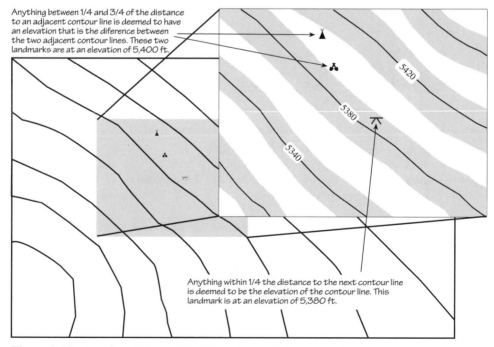

Figure 3-10: Reading Between The Lines: Interpolating Elevation

surveyors as vertical control points. Spot elevations correspond to physical features such as hilltops, road junctions, and other selected point features. See Figure 3-21 on page 92.

3.5.2 Slope

Slope characteristics can also be obtained from contour lines. Slope can be expressed as an angle, a percentage, or a ratio (rise over run). Percentage is probably the easiest form of slope to work with. Angular slope involves trigonometry so it is not too practical. Slope expressed as a ratio is similar to percent, just the inverse. Ratio slope is not used very often.

Slope Measurements — An Assortment Of Units

Percentage	Ratio	Angular
10%	1:10	~5°43'
~17.6%	~22:125	10°
20%	1:5	~11°20'
30%	3:10	~16°42'
~57.7%	~577:1,000	30°
100%	1:1	45°
150%	3:2	~56°19'
~173.2%	~433:250	60°
200%	2:1	~63°24'

Table 3-4: *Comparison Of Angular, Percentage, And Ratio Slope*

To calculate percent slope, just divide the vertical rise by the horizontal distance (using the same units, of course) and multiply the result times 100. A rise of 200 feet over a horizontal distance of 1,000 feet is a 20% slope. A rise of 1,000 feet over the same distance

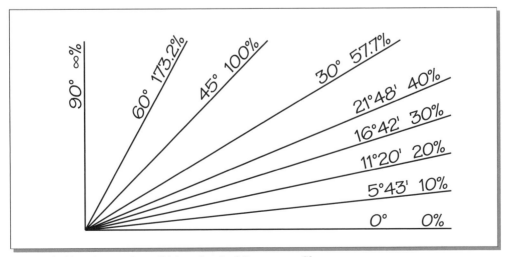

Figure 3-11: *Comparison Of Angular And Percentage Slopes*

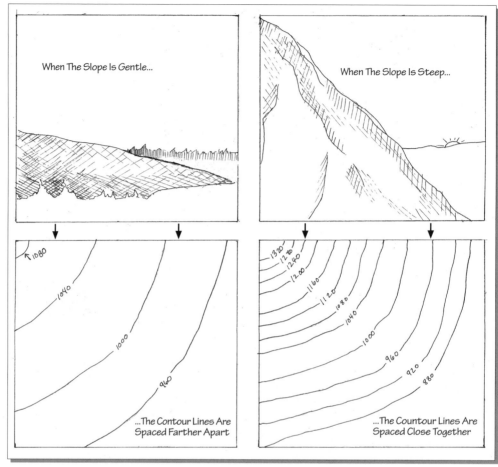

Figure 3-12: *Slope Is Directly Related To Spacing Of Contour Lines*

would be a 100% slope. On a topographic map, widely spaced contour lines indicate gentle slopes and closely spaced contour lines indicate steep slopes. See Figure 3-12.

Another important aspect of a slope is whether it is convex or concave. A pattern involving a change from widely spaced contour lines to closely spaced contour lines (as you move downslope) indicates a convex slope. A pattern involving a change from closely spaced contour lines to widely spaced contour lines (as you move downslope) indicates a concave slope. A single slope can exhibit both characteristics, with the usual pattern being convex near the top and concave near the bottom. See Figure 3-13.

It is fairly easy to calculate slope on a USGS 7.5-minute topographic map. To see how, recall that at a scale of 1:24,000 one inch on the map equals 2,000 feet on the ground. If the elevation difference between two points one inch apart is 300 feet, the slope is $300 \div 2000 = 0.15$, or 15%. Unless this is a sand dune, you can bet that there will be some sections of this 2,000 feet that have more than 15% slope and other sections that have less than 15% slope. If the points are only one-half inch apart, the slope would be 300 ÷ 1000 = .3, or 30%. At two inches it would be 300 ÷ 4000 = .075, or 7.5%.

If you don't like doing arithmetic there are simple plastic templates called contour scales that are available. They allow you to directly read the slope from a topographic map. Each scale on the contour scale is specific to a particular map scale and contour interval. See page 66 in the chapter on hardware for more information.

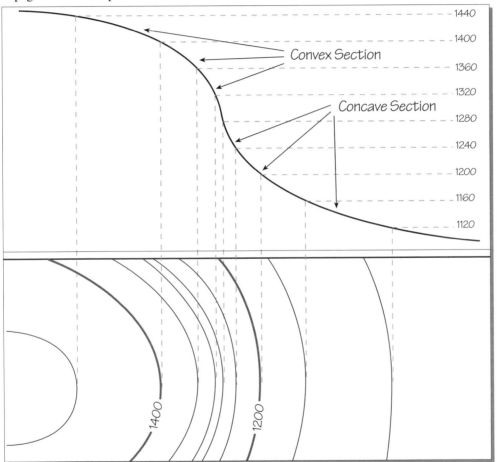

Figure 3-13: Concave And Convex Slopes

3.5.2 Shape

The shape of the land is the most difficult characteristic to read from a set of contour lines. Shape is a different concept than slope, but they are closely related. Shape is observed by noting the curves and angles in the contour lines, both individually and in relationship to each other.

There are several basic land forms that provide the foundation for reading the shape of land from a topographic map. Those forms are hills, valleys, draws, ridges, spurs, saddles, depressions, cuts & fills, and cliffs.

Each of these land forms has a distinct "signature" on a topographic map. You need to learn to recognize these basic shapes of land both on the map and in the real world. As you gain an intuitive recognition of these shapes, you will become fluent in the language of topographic maps.

The following are descriptions and examples of how each of the basic land forms are reflected in the contour lines of a topographic map:

Hill

This is a high point that is characterized by the ground sloping away in all directions. It can be a gentle slope, or the very steep peaks found throughout the Rockies, Cascades, and other "young" mountain ranges of the world. A hill's contour lines will be roughly circular, with successive outer rings being lower in elevation.

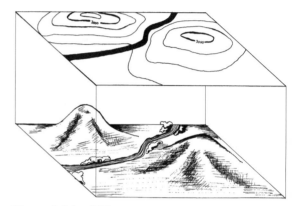

Figure 3-14: Hill

Valley

This feature is usually associated with a stream course that has some relatively level ground bordered by steeper sides. It is characterized by contour lines that run parallel to the stream for some distance before bending across the stream course in a "U" shape. The open end of the "U" is always on the down-slope side of a valley.

Draw

This is a stream course that has essentially no level land within its confines, and is usually, but not necessarily, steeper than a valley. The contours indicating a draw are more "V" shaped, with the point of the "V" pointing up slope along the bottom of the draw.

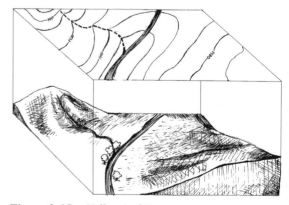

Figure 3-15: Valley And Draw

Ridge

This is a line of high ground that has ground sloping away on opposite sides for some linear distance. The spine of a ridge may have slope, but it is distinctly less than the sides of the ridge. A ridge is characterized by contour lines that run approximately parallel for some distance on opposite sides of the ridge's spine. Contour lines on a ridge may bend back on themselves in either a "U" or a "V" shape indicating a gentle (U) or sharp (V) falloff from the spine of the ridge. The bottom of the "U" or "V" always points downslope on a ridge.

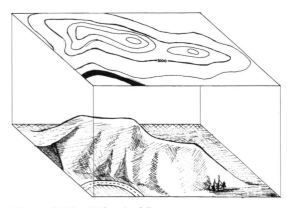

Figure 3-16: *Ridge And Spur*

Spur

This is to a ridge as a draw is to a valley. A spur is a shorter and continuously sloping branch of a ridge. Its contour lines also form a "U" or a "V", but they don't have an appreciable length of parallel run.

Saddle

This is a dip along the spine of a ridge, characterized by ground sloping down and away in two opposite directions, and up in the other two opposite directions. A saddle's contour lines will bend away from each other on the upslope sides, and be enveloped by parallel contour lines on the opposite downslope sides of the ridge.

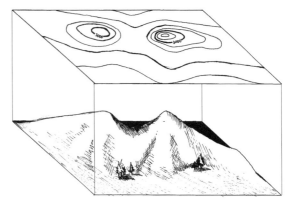

Figure 3-17: *Saddle*

Depression

This is just a dip in the ground that slopes downward on all sides. It is the opposite of a hill. Its contour lines are rings that typically have short hachure lines that point downslope.

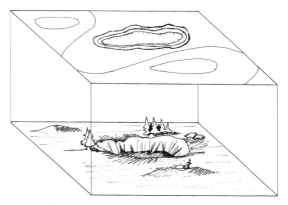

Figure 3-18: *Depression*

Cut & Fill

These are usually man-made features associated with roadways or railroad beds. They are the places where land was either removed or added to make a level bed for the right-of-way. They are characterized by abrupt direction changes in contour lines, and may have hachures indicating the downslope direction.

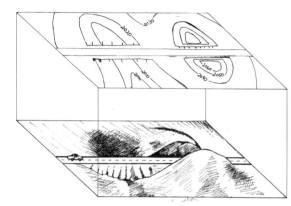

Figure 3-19: *Cut & Fill*

Cliff

This is a section of ground that is so steep that the contour lines converge as one. It is a vertical or near-vertical slope. A cliff contour may have hachure lines pointing downslope.

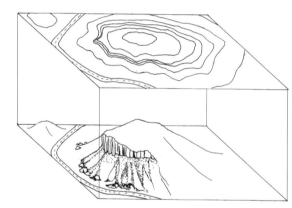

Figure 3-20: *Cliff*

3.6 Map Symbols

Map symbols are the written language of maps. They translate words into a form suitable for the limited space available on a map. Map symbols consist of lines, icons, and shading that are used to represent physical, cultural, and political features on a map.

While many symbols are intuitively obvious, it is a good idea to familiarize yourself with the exact meaning of the symbols that are found on a map you intend to use. Sheet maps typically have limited legends printed on them. In the case of USGS maps the legend on the map is limited to road symbols, but a more comprehensive symbol "dictionary" can be obtained separately from either USGS or the vendors of USGS maps. A comprehensive set of USGS symbol definitions is shown in Figures 3-21 and 3-22.

Most features identified on a map correspond to physical things such as rivers, roads, towns, peaks, etc. However, some features shown on a map have no corresponding physical counterpart in the real world. A county line or a national forest boundary are examples of non-physical features that are shown on maps.

Not all features shown on a map (including USGS topographic maps) are "accurate." United States National Map Accuracy Standards specify that for horizontal accuracy "not more than 10 percent of the points tested shall be in error by more than 1/30 inch, measured on the publication scale," and for vertical accuracy "not more than 10 percent of the elevations tested shall be in error more than one-half the contour interval." Maps that conform to this accuracy standard will have the statement "This map complies with National Map Accuracy Standards" printed on the margin. Translated, this means that a USGS 7.5-minute topographic map (that complies with National Map Accuracy Standards) will show horizontal positions to within 20 meters for at least 9 out of 10 places.

Another source of map inaccuracy is time. A map that was perfectly accurate when it was originally produced will become increasingly inaccurate over time as changes occur to the land, man-made features, and boundaries of various types. Roads or trails shown on an older map may have overgrown, and new trails and roads may have been built since the map was published. That's why you need to pay very close attention to the date(s) associated with any map you rely on for navigation.

CONTROL DATA AND MONUMENTS

Aerial photograph roll and frame number*   3-20

Horizontal control

Third order or better, permanent mark	Neace △ Neace ⬥
With third order or better elevation	BM △ 45.1 Pike ⬥ BM 45.1
Checked spot elevation	△ 19.5
Coincident with section corner	Cactus △ — Cactus ⬥
Unmonumented*	+

Vertical control

Third order or better, with tablet	BM × 16.3
Third order or better, recoverable mark	× 120.0
Bench mark at found section corner	BM + 18.6
Spot elevation	× 5.3

Boundary monument

With tablet	BM □ 21.6 B.M ⊹ 71
Without tablet	□ 171.3
With number and elevation	67 □ 301.1
U.S. mineral or location monument	▲

CONTOURS

Topographic

Intermediate	
Index	
Supplementary	
Depression	
Cut; fill	

Bathymetric

Intermediate	
Index	
Primary	
Index Primary	
Supplementary	

BOUNDARIES

National	— —
State or territorial	— —
County or equivalent	— — —
Civil township or equivalent	— — —
Incorporated city or equivalent	— — — —
Park, reservation, or monument	— · —
Small park	— — — — —

LAND SURVEY SYSTEMS

U.S. Public Land Survey System

Township or range line	———
Location doubtful	— — —
Section line	———
Location doubtful	— — —
Found section corner; found closing corner	— + — ⊥ —
Witness corner; meander corner	WC + MC

Other land surveys

Township or range line	············
Section line	············
Land grant or mining claim; monument	— ·· — □
Fence line	— — — — — —

SURFACE FEATURES

Levee	——— Levee
Sand or mud area, dunes, or shifting sand	Sand
Intricate surface area	Strip mine
Gravel beach or glacial moraine	Gravel
Tailings pond	Tailings Pond

MINES AND CAVES

Quarry or open pit mine	✕
Gravel, sand, clay, or borrow pit	✕
Mine tunnel or cave entrance	⤙
Prospect; mine shaft	X ■
Mine dump	Mine dump
Tailings	Tailings

VEGETATION

Woods	
Scrub	
Orchard	
Vineyard	
Mangrove	Mangrove

GLACIERS AND PERMANENT SNOWFIELDS

| Contours and limits | |
| Form lines | |

MARINE SHORELINE

Topographic maps

| Approximate mean high water | |
| Indefinite or unsurveyed | |

Topographic-bathymetric maps

| Mean high water | |
| Apparent (edge of vegetation) | |

*Provisional Edition maps only

Provisional Edition maps were established to expedite completion of the remaining large scale topographic quadrangles of the conterminous United States. They contain essentially the same level of information as the standard series maps. This series can be easily recongnized by the title "Provisional Edition" in the lower right hand corner.

Figure 3-21: USGS Topographic Map Symbols

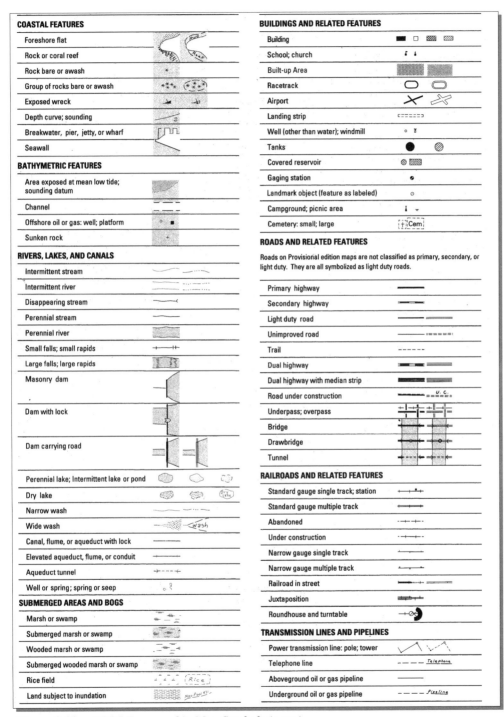

COASTAL FEATURES

Foreshore flat	
Rock or coral reef	
Rock bare or awash	
Group of rocks bare or awash	
Exposed wreck	
Depth curve; sounding	
Breakwater, pier, jetty, or wharf	
Seawall	

BATHYMETRIC FEATURES

Area exposed at mean low tide; sounding datum	
Channel	
Offshore oil or gas: well; platform	
Sunken rock	

RIVERS, LAKES, AND CANALS

Intermittent stream	
Intermittent river	
Disappearing stream	
Perennial stream	
Perennial river	
Small falls; small rapids	
Large falls; large rapids	
Masonry dam	
Dam with lock	
Dam carrying road	
Perennial lake; Intermittent lake or pond	
Dry lake	
Narrow wash	
Wide wash	
Canal, flume, or aqueduct with lock	
Elevated aqueduct, flume, or conduit	
Aqueduct tunnel	
Well or spring; spring or seep	

SUBMERGED AREAS AND BOGS

Marsh or swamp	
Submerged marsh or swamp	
Wooded marsh or swamp	
Submerged wooded marsh or swamp	
Rice field	
Land subject to inundation	

BUILDINGS AND RELATED FEATURES

Building	
School; church	
Built-up Area	
Racetrack	
Airport	
Landing strip	
Well (other than water); windmill	
Tanks	
Covered reservoir	
Gaging station	
Landmark object (feature as labeled)	
Campground; picnic area	
Cemetery: small; large	

ROADS AND RELATED FEATURES

Roads on Provisional edition maps are not classified as primary, secondary, or light duty. They are all symbolized as light duty roads.

Primary highway	
Secondary highway	
Light duty road	
Unimproved road	
Trail	
Dual highway	
Dual highway with median strip	
Road under construction	
Underpass; overpass	
Bridge	
Drawbridge	
Tunnel	

RAILROADS AND RELATED FEATURES

Standard gauge single track; station	
Standard gauge multiple track	
Abandoned	
Under construction	
Narrow gauge single track	
Narrow gauge multiple track	
Railroad in street	
Juxtaposition	
Roundhouse and turntable	

TRANSMISSION LINES AND PIPELINES

Power transmission line: pole; tower	
Telephone line	
Aboveground oil or gas pipeline	
Underground oil or gas pipeline	

Figure 3-22: USGS Topographic Map Symbols (cont.)

3.7 Dates

Know the date of a map you're using. Dates are important because they tell you something about the reliability of the information contained on the map. For example, a map published in 1956 may show trails that no longer exist, and that same map will fail to show new trails that have been put in since 1956. Even roads that are shown (or not shown) on maps are prone to change. Areas of vegetation are also subject to change over time, as are buildings and other man-made structures. Geologic features such as slopes, peaks, valleys, etc. are far less likely to change over time. In general, the older the map the less reliable it is likely to be, especially in its depiction of man-made features.

Finding the date of a map is not always straightforward. That's because there can be several dates associated with a single map. USGS topographic maps can have different dates for the year of the map's publication, the year the aerial photography was done, the year field checks were performed, the year a revised map was published, the year of a provisional release, and the year the map was printed.

A USGS topographic map will have the original publication date shown below the name of the map in the lower right margin of the map sheet (see Figure 3-28). This date tells you when the map was first released to the public in its current printed form. Other pertinent dates will be shown on the lower left margin of the map sheet (see Figure 3-26). They usually indicate such things as the year the map's aerial photographs were taken, the year that field checks were conducted to verify positions and features shown on the map, and the year the map was edited.

Provisional maps are labeled as such and typically have their marginal information printed in brown. These maps have been released under an accelerated time frame and are subject to further scrutiny before final release. The data on a provisional map should not be considered as accurate as a final published map, although it is probably more than adequate for land navigation purposes. Even the name of a provisional map is subject to change before final publication.

The date of any revision subsequent to the initial publication of a map will be indicated beneath the publication date. On revised maps, the revision date and any changes made to the map itself will be shown in a special color, usually purple. Notes pertaining to the revisions, such as their source, field checks, and so on, will usually be shown in the margin in the special color used to identify the revision.

The date a map was actually printed and the location of the printing plant will be shown just below the lower right neatline (see Figure 3-28). The printing date is not relevant when you are trying to judge the quality of the map's content.

3.8 Margin Information

A wealth of information can be found in the margins of most maps. This section gives a thorough, but concise, explanation of the layout of the information found in the margins of large-scale USGS topographic maps. These samples are taken from the 7.5-minute quadrangle series.

Upper Center

The cooperative credit block identifies any federal, state, and/or municipal agencies that contributed funding for the production of the map. Minor contributors are listed in the credit legend located in the lower left margin. This one was produced with the assistance of the Forest Service. On many maps this block is empty.

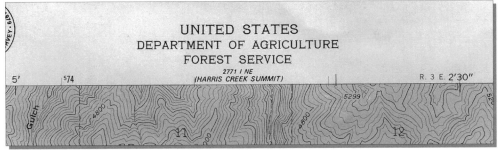

Figure 3-23: Upper Center Margin

Lower Center

The scale block is located in the center of the lower margin and includes the map's scale expressed as a ratio, bar scales in various linear units of distance, a contour interval statement, a vertical datum statement, a shoreline and tide-range statement (if applicable), and a map accuracy statement. Omission of the map accuracy statement indicates that the map may not fully comply with national map accuracy standards.

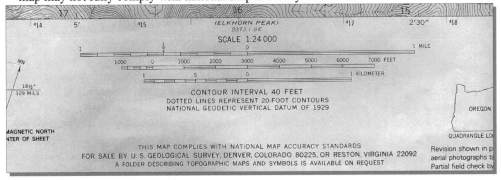

Figure 3-24: Lower Center Margin

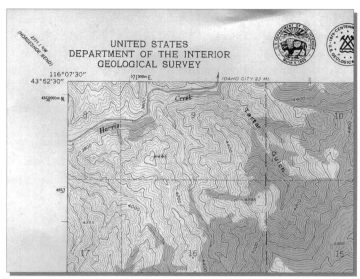

Figure 3-25: *Upper Left Margin*

Upper Left

The USGS heading block identifies the issuing agency. It is always the same in the case of USGS topographic maps.

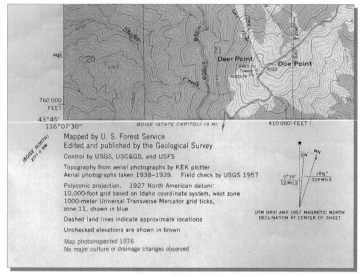

Figure 3-26: *Lower Left Margin*

Lower Left

The credit legend gives information on the name of the mapping agency; the name of the editing and publishing agency; the name of the agency that provided geodetic controls; methods used in producing the map; credits for hydrographic data, projection and horizontal control datum information; the UTM zone; and other explanatory and informational data.

The magnetic declination diagram is located to the right of the credit legend. It shows the grid declination and the magnetic declination relative to true north. The latter, magnetic declination, is specified as of the year of field survey. You should be aware that magnetic declination at a particular location changes over time, so this information loses its accuracy as time passes. Also, the angles shown in the diagram may not be accurate. Only use the numbers.

Upper Right

The name block gives the quadrangle name, the state or states included in the quadrangle, the county or counties included in the quadrangle if they are not shown on the face of the map, the series (minutes or degrees covered) and type (topographic or planimetric) of the map, and (for 7.5 minute quadrangles only) the name and position of the 15-minute quadrangle that covers the same area.

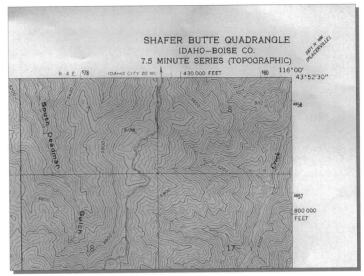

Figure 3-27: Upper Right Margin

Lower Right

The title block of the map includes the name of the map, the primary state it is in, the associated 15-minute map (if this is a 7.5-minute map), the geographic index number, the latest date of field completion (and revisions, if applicable), and the Army Mapping Service reference number.

A quadrangle location diagram is placed to the left of the title block. It shows the approximate location of the quadrangle within a miniature map of the state.

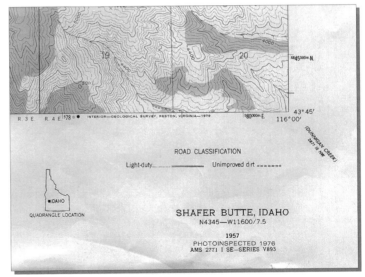

Figure 3-28: Lower Right Margin

The responsible agency, the printing plant, and the date the map was printed are shown in the lower right margin just below the neatline. A road symbols legend explains the various road symbols used on that particular quadrangle map.

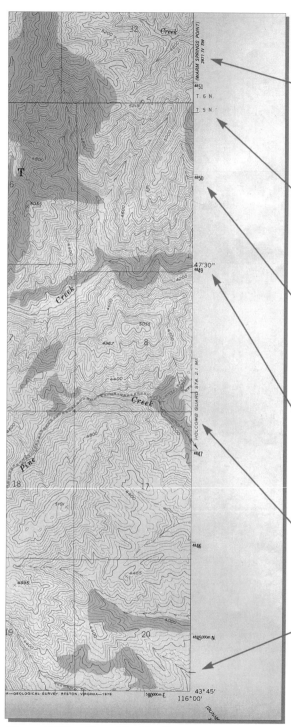

Figure 3-29: *Along The Neatlines*

Along The Neatlines

Adjoining quadrangle names are printed along the neatlines. Same-series quadrangles are identified by name only. Different series quadrangles are identified by their scale. If the adjoining border is covered by multiple map series, only the same-series map name is identified.

Township and range numbers are printed in pairs along the neatlines when applicable. If crowding occurs with other information, they are moved to avoid the conflict and are located at an equidistant spacing from the location of the grid line.

UTM grid tickmarks are printed in blue at 1,000 meter (1 kilometer) intervals on the neatlines of maps that have no UTM grid on the face of the map. UTM tick mark labels are printed in black and may be omitted in crowded sections of the margin.

Latitude and longitude are labeled at each of the four corners. Latitude and longitude tickmarks are also printed in black and labeled along the neatlines at 2.5 minute intervals on 7.5-minute quadrangles and at 5 minute intervals on 15-minute quadrangles.

Road destinations are shown just outside the neatlines for selected roads and highways, with distances given to the next town, major road junction, etc.

State plane tickmarks are printed in black. Numeric coordinate values are shown along the neatlines in the vicinity of the southwest and northeast corners of the quadrangle (see Figures 3-26 and 3-27). In cases where a map lies in more than one state plane zone, the second zone's tickmarks are labeled near the southeast and northwest corners.

3.9 Map Preparation

Preparing a map for use with a GPS receiver consists of adding gridlines, graticules, and/or declination rule lines. Choosing which of these lines to add to a map depends on the type of coordinate system you plan to use, and whether you plan to use your compass in magnetic or declination adjusted mode. Map preparation may also include having the map laminated. You may want to read the section on map reading aids in Chapter 2 (page 59) for more information about the mechanics of how to modify and use maps.

3.9.1 UTM Gridlines

Some USGS topographic maps published after 1978 include printed UTM gridlines. These gridlines are a real benefit to users of GPS receivers. They make it easy to use a roamer on these maps. It is also fairly easy to "eyeball" UTM coordinates on a map with UTM gridlines. Unfortunately, many of the USGS maps available today were published prior to 1978. Also, the USGS abandoned their declared policy of printing fineline UTM grids. Consequently, most USGS maps only have UTM grid tick marks along the neatlines of the map.

If you're working with a map that doesn't have UTM gridlines, but you want the convenience of being able to use a roamer, no problem. You can apply UTM gridlines yourself by connecting the UTM grid tick marks that are on the border of all USGS

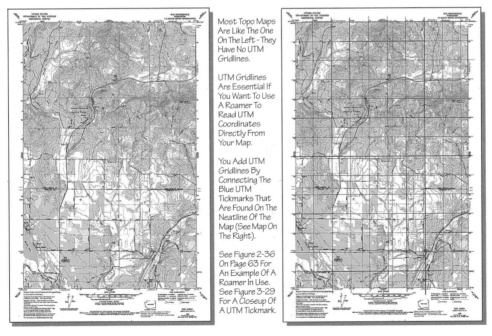

Most Topo Maps Are Like The One On The Left - They Have No UTM Gridlines.

UTM Gridlines Are Essential If You Want To Use A Roamer To Read UTM Coordinates Directly From Your Map.

You Add UTM Gridlines By Connecting The Blue UTM Tickmarks That Are Found On The Neatline Of The Map (See Map On The Right).

See Figure 2-36 On Page 63 For An Example Of A Roamer In Use. See Figure 3-29 For A Closeup Of A UTM Tickmark.

Figure 3-30: *Preparing Your Topo Map For Use With A Roamer*

topographic maps. You'll need a good straightedge ruler, a fine-point pen or pencil, and a steady hand.

Adding your own UTM gridlines will increase the clutter on the face of the map. You can avoid adding UTM gridlines if you're willing to work strictly from the margins. This is OK if you only plan to use the map indoors on a large, flat surface. If you plan to use the map in the field, the added clutter of UTM gridlines is probably a worthwhile tradeoff. They allow you to use a simple plastic roamer to obtain UTM coordinates. See page 63 for information on how to use a roamer.

If you choose to work with UTM coordinates without gridlines on the face of the map, you'll need a way of making precise measurements from the point you're interested in to the closest "imaginary" gridlines below and to the left of the point. A good straightedge ruler and a divider can be used for this purpose. Again, see page 63 for instructions on how to use these tools.

Be aware that the UTM grid will not necessarily line up parallel to the neatlines of a USGS topographic map. Unless your map happens to be on the central meridian of a UTM zone, there will be grid declination. This means that you shouldn't be alarmed if the straightedge ruler is slightly skewed relative to the neatlines of the map. That's just one of the UTM coordinate system's characteristics.

3.9.2 Latitude/Longitude

The other major coordinate system, latitude/longitude, requires that you apply guidelines if you want to use your map with a latitude/longitude ruler. To do this you simply draw additional graticules at 2.5-minute latitude and longitude intervals within the map. You will need to extend these lines as close to the edge of the map sheet as possible. This is so that you can read points near the edge of the map with a properly skewed latitude/longitude ruler. See page 65 for a detailed description of using the "tools" that will assist you in working with latitude/longitude coordinates on a map.

3.9.3 Adding Your Own Grid System To A Map

If you are working with a map that doesn't have either UTM gridlines or latitude/longitude graticules you can add these lines yourself. It is a tedious process that starts with finding a map that covers the same (or similar) area that does have UTM or latitude/longitude grid(s). Your task is to find locations common to both maps and transfer coordinates from the grided map to the non-grided map.

These transferred coordinates become the basis for horizontal and vertical grid lines. It helps to transfer as many common points as possible. Once you've transferred these points you can complete the grid system using interpolation and/or extrapolation. The level of

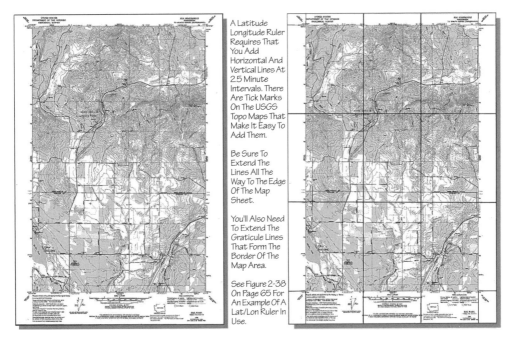

A Latitude Longitude Ruler Requires That You Add Horizontal And Vertical Lines At 2.5 Minute Intervals. There Are Tick Marks On The USGS Topo Maps That Make It Easy To Add Them.

Be Sure To Extend The Lines All The Way To The Edge Of The Map Sheet.

You'll Also Need To Extend The Graticule Lines That Form The Border Of The Map Area.

See Figure 2-38 On Page 65 For An Example Of A Lat/Lon Ruler In Use.

Figure 3-31: *Preparing Your Topo Map For Use With A Latitude/Longitude Ruler*

precision of a manual grid transfer depends on operator diligence. The completion of the 7.5-minute quadrangle series for the entire U.S. should make it unnecessary to add grids to your own map. But if for some reason the need should arise, all it takes is lots of patience and care.

3.9.4 Declination Rule Lines

In the old days map preparation meant adding declination ruling lines. These lines are drawn from the top to the bottom of the map, and their angle is set at exactly the amount of magnetic declination in the area covered by the map.

Magnetic declination ruling lines were important when directions were the primary means of determining your location. They made it much easier to work with a compass that was not (or could not be) adjusted for magnetic declination. Both of these factors are now a thing of the past. GPS receivers are used to obtain position fixes, and declination adjustability is very common in compasses. Nonetheless, if you don't have or use declination adjustment on your compass, and you don't mind the clutter, declination ruling lines can make it much easier to work with magnetic directions on a map.

To apply declination ruling lines you must first obtain the amount of east or west magnetic declination for the map you're using. Be careful with older maps (check the publication date) because declination shifts over time. Also be aware that the declination drawing on the lower left margin of USGS topographic maps is not drawn "to scale." The best way to set the correct declination angle is to use a protractor. Apply the declination angle to one of the vertical neatlines of the map you're preparing. Then make as many (or few) parallel declination lines as you want.

3.10 Map Sources—Paper

Entire books are written on the subject of map sources. Probably the best overall book on this topic is "The Map Catalog: Every Kind Of Map And Chart On Earth And Even Some Above It" by Joel Makower. This book can be very helpful for someone needing to find a map for a specialized purpose or for an overseas location. Fortunately, land navigators in the U.S. have easy access to the large scale topographic maps produced by the U.S. government. These maps — the USGS 7.5-minute series — cover the entire land area of the nation and they are available at a reasonable cost.

These USGS 7.5-minute topographic maps are ideal for backcountry travelers in the United States. They can be purchased from a variety of different outdoor recreation retailers (backpacking/camping, fishing/hunting, etc). USGS topographic maps are also available at blueprint and surveyor supply stores.

Another group of maps that are somewhat limited for actual backcountry use, but can be very useful for trip planning and trailhead access, are the medium scale maps. With representative fractions in the range of 1:50,000 to 1:100,000, these maps are limited in detail, but they cover much larger areas than the 7.5-minute maps. Sources for these maps include the USGS, the BLM (United States Department of Interior, Bureau of Land Management), the U.S. Forest Service (part of the Department of Agriculture), and various state highway departments.

Commercial map makers offer a variety of options, including DeLorme's atlas series that cover entire states, and the Green Trails maps that cover popular outdoor recreation areas. Most of these options are medium scale, so they are not as useful as the USGS 7.5-minute maps. You also need to be careful to make sure that any map you buy for use with GPS has a compatible coordinate system.

You can also find topographic maps at libraries if you just need to scout areas that you may want to travel. Look for a Map Depository Library in your area. Although you can't take library maps with you into the field, you can obtain coordinates from the maps held in libraries. A divider and a straight edge are all the tools you need to extract precise UTM coordinates from any USGS topographic map.

If you are going to use your GPS receiver overseas, the map issues become more complex. The Makower book cited above is a good place to start. The U.S. Defense Mapping Agency also has military maps for selected areas overseas that are available to the public. When using maps overseas be very careful that you set the proper datum and grid system in your receiver, otherwise your GPS receiver's coordinate information may be off by considerable distances relative to the map's coordinates.

3.11 Map Sources—Digital

Computerized maps open up a vast array of possibilities for GPS users. More than anything else, they make it incredibly easy to extract precise and accurate coordinate information from maps. They also make it very easy to see where coordinates you collect with your GPS receiver (position fixes) are located on a map.

Digital map choices range from high precision electronic versions of the individual USGS 7.5-minute topographic maps (when complete, it will take over 800 CD-ROMs to cover the entire U.S.) to seamless electronic "road maps" that cover the entire United States on one CD-ROM. And there's lots in-between.

Don't let the size difference fool you. The designers of the one CD-ROM road map type programs pack an incredible amount of information into the 640 MB that is available on a single CD-ROM disc. They do this by foregoing any raster graphics (image files) that take up large amounts of storage space. Instead, they rely strictly on line maps (vector graphics) that can cover vast areas with surprising detail very efficiently.

As is the case in many newly emerging technologies, changes are occurring rapidly and advances are taking place at a dizzying pace. Many of the options available (or almost available) as of early-1997 are in the early prototype stages. Early purchasers of these programs may feel like the unpaid R&D staff for the vendors. Nonetheless, the benefits they offer can be compelling.

Some of the products described here are in the early stages of a multi-year development process. So keep in mind that when it comes to the bleeding edge of high technology, circumstances change almost faster than ink dries. You will need to do your own research on the status of digital mapping technology if this topic is important to you. What follows is offered in the spirit of giving an overview of where digital mapping (of the kind that is useful to backcountry GPS users) stands as of early-1997.

3.11.1 "Atlas" Type Digital Road Maps

There are a number of different brands of electronic "road maps" available on CD-ROM. The only ones worth considering are those that have the ability to provide a readout of the geographic coordinates based on the location of the cursor. Delorme Mapping Company's STREET ATLAS USA is a good example of such an electronic map. Its coverage of the entire U.S. fits on just one CD-ROM. Its coordinates are remarkably accurate based on the author's own experience. A similar electronic map is offered by Chicago Precision Mapping, and it has received very favorable reviews.

You can easily zoom in and out on the atlas-type electronic maps, going from a full view of the entire U.S. to an area that shows a neighborhood in just a few keystrokes (or mouse clicks). Amazingly, STREET ATLAS USA even contains crude elevation contours. While these atlas-type electronic maps are of limited use for planning backcountry outings, they do have a surprising amount of coverage of Forest Service access roads and the like. They can help you get to the trailhead.

The latest release of STREET ATLAS USA (version 4) has added the ability to communicate directly (in real-time) with a GPS receiver through the computer's serial port. When connected to a GPS receiver, STREET ATLAS USA can show your current position on the map. This feature may be of interest to someone using a laptop computer when traveling in a car, or someone conducting a cross-country mapping exercise, but it has relatively little applicability for the typical backcountry land navigator.

STREET ATLAS USA also has a limited ability to upload and download stored waypoints. This is appealing for anyone who dislikes the scroll method of data entry found on most handheld GPS receivers. Unfortunately, this feature is very primitive in Street Atlas. Dedicated waypoint management software from the GPS receiver's manufacturer usually does a much better job.

3.11.2 Digital Raster Graphics

Another category of electronic maps use digitized USGS topographic maps as their foundation. These electronic maps offer all the detail of the printed version of the map, with the added bonus that you can read precise and accurate coordinates very easily by using the cursor, and you can print sections of the map that relate to your area of interest.

The USGS is planning to have its 7.5-minute topo maps (all 54,000 of them) digitized and available on CD-ROM by the end of 1998. A handful were actually available as of early 1997.

The technical term for these electronic topo maps is "DRGs," or digital raster graphics. DRGs are just high-resolution scanned versions of paper maps that have been geo-referenced. "Geo-referenced" means that the image file (in TIFF format, for all you techno-junkies out there) is accompanied by another file (called a "world" file) that the viewing software uses to convert pixels (the image's coordinates) into real-world UTM coordinates. The viewing software provided on each DRG CD-ROM is a free version of ArcView, a popular GIS program. ArcView can be used to read the geographic coordinates anywhere on the map, measure distances in real world units (feet, meters, miles, kilometers, etc.), and print out sections of the map to your laser or inkjet printer.

Geo-referencing of DRGs is an incredible benefit to GPS users. It allows you to use your cursor to obtain the precise coordinates for any location on the digital map without the use of roamers, dividers, latitude/longitude scales, etc. All you need to do is point your cursor and click on the location whose coordinate you want. It is incredibly simple!

Each CD-ROM produced by the USGS will cover an area of 1° latitude by 1° longitude, and is priced at $32. That's 50 cents per map since there are sixty-four 7.5-minute quadrangles in each 1° x 1° area — an incredible bargain! Besides the 7.5-minute topo maps, each CD includes a copy of the GIS viewing software, and several smaller scale maps of the area covered (two 1:100,000 maps and one 1:250,000 map).

The USGS DRGs are a must for GPS users who also have personal computers. The only problem at this point (early-1997) is that very few of the CDs have actually been released. Hopefully the project will stay on schedule, and complete coverage of the U.S will be available by sometime in 1998.

3.11.3 On The Horizon

The future is bright for digital maps. As more people discover the remarkable benefits of GPS, the marketplace should bring further innovations. The currently available technology (digital road maps and DRGs) are just the beginning of what digital maps have to offer. A small company in California is a good example of what the future holds.

Wildflower Productions has combined DRGs (and other USGS electronic map products) with their own GIS software to produce a product called TOPO! that is targeted specifically at backcountry enthusiasts. Their product is similar to the USGS digital maps, but it takes the concept much further.

TOPO! doesn't cover 1-degree by 1-degree areas, but rather areas of interest. The San Francisco Bay Area, Los Angeles, Sequoia National Park, and Yosemite National Park are each covered on a single CD. TOPO! also eliminates the borders on the scanned 7.5-minute topo maps, allowing the entire area to be covered seamlessly. In contrast, the USGS DRGs are individual maps, complete with borders.

TOPO! adds what are known as digital elevation models (DEMs), thereby allowing users to perform a variety of elevation related functions with this electronic map. While you can obtain elevation from a DRG in exactly the same way as on a paper topographic map (i.e., by reading the nearest countour line), products like TOPO! give elevation as a readout. This works just like the coordinate read-out provided by DRGs and atlas-type maps. One of the advantages offered by including digital elevation models is the ability to automatically calculate the gross and net elevation change along a user-specified route of travel. TOPO! can also produce an elevation profile from a path you trace-out on the map.

Although TOPO! is currently available only for select locations in California and Colorado, Wildflower Productions has plans to extend the coverage to other regions of the country. There is not currently a direct GPS interface built into TOPO!, but that is also a part of the future development plans for this product.

Chapter 4:

Coordinate Systems

Coordinate systems are the most fundamental "link" between maps and the world they represent. They are also the critical link between GPS receivers and the physical world around us. In fact, it is not exaggerating to say that coordinates are the foundation of the GPS system. This chapter describes and explains the primary coordinate systems that are used in GPS receivers and on USGS topographic maps.

Coordinates define precise physical locations in remarkably simple and elegant terms. Six digits of latitude and seven digits of longitude are all it takes to specify a location to within 50 feet of precision — anywhere on earth!

GPS represents such a remarkable advance in navigation technology that it can allow land navigators to function effectively without any use of maps. Try that with a compass! Coordinates are the key to this functionality. Indeed, GPS has made it possible to use waypoint coordinates in their raw numeric form to precisely navigate complex routes with no map and no difficulty.

Nonetheless, maps continue to play a major role in land navigation. Maps supply an important description of the landscape within which coordinates lie. GPS can both enhance your use of maps, and free you from the necessity of using maps. It's up to you.

As mentioned earlier, there are two basic categories of coordinate systems used in cartography and navigation. The most familiar

Coordinates are the foundation of the Global Positioning System...you can use them to navigate complex routes with ease.

107

category of coordinate system relies on angular measurements — usually degrees, minutes, and seconds — to represent actual locations on earth. The other category of coordinate system relies on rectangular measurements — Cartesian coordinates expressed in feet or meters — to represent actual locations on the earth. You will probably find both of these coordinate systems useful when you work with maps and GPS receivers.

4.1 Angular Coordinates

Angular coordinates are the basis for the familiar latitude and longitude lines found on most maps. If you look at a side view of the earth, with the north pole at the top, lines of latitude are circles that are parallel to the equator and to one another. That's why lines of latitude are also called "parallels." Lines of longitude are half-circles that extend from the north pole to the south pole. Lines of longitude are also called "meridians".

Figure 4-1: *Lines Of Latitude And Longitude Wrap Around The Globe That Is The Earth — They Look Like A Grid, But They're Actually Formed By Rays*

Lines of latitude run east-west, but they are used to measure north-south distances. All points on a particular line of latitude are the same angular <u>and</u> linear distance north or south of the equator (or any other specific parallel).

Lines of longitude run north-south, but they are used to measure east-west distances. All points on the same line of longitude are the same angular distance east or west of the "prime meridian" (or any other specific meridian). Since lines of longitude converge at the north and south poles, the linear distance between any two meridians is not constant. The linear distance between any two meridians is greatest at the equator and shrinks to zero at the two poles.

Angular coordinates are designed for the spherical surface of the earth. They specify points based on an angular distance from a reference point. That point is the intersection of the equator and the "prime meridian." In a moment you'll see how this reference point, or "origin," is selected.

There are a variety of different units used for angular measurements. They include degrees, mils, radians, and grads. Each divides the circumference of a circle into a number of equal arc segments. Degrees divide a circle into 360 arc segments, mils divide a circle into 6,400 arc segments, radians divide a circle into 2*pi arc segments, and grads divide a circle into 400 arc segments.

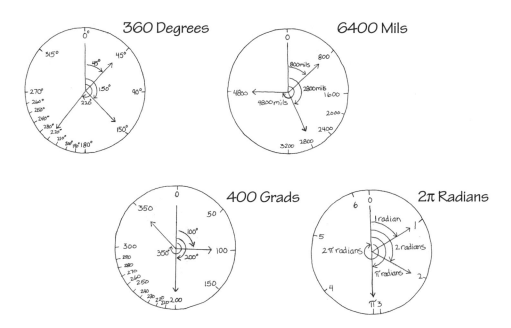

Figure 4-2: *Examples Of Different Angular Units — Different Ways Of Dividing Circles*

Degrees are the only type of angular measurement of concern to civilian land navigators. A degree ($^1/360$ of a circle) can be broken down further into minutes ($^1/60$ of a degree, or $^1/21,600$ of a circle), and minutes can be divided further into seconds ($^1/60$ of a minute, or $^1/1,296,000$ of a circle).

4.1.1 Building Angular Coordinates — From Scratch

To really understand geographic coordinates (latitude and longitude) it helps to start in two dimensions — a circle. Any point on a circle can be can be specified (relative to some other point on the circle) by the angle of the arc between the rays that pass through the two points. Figure 4-3 shows three rays that originate at the center of a circle. The angle between those rays is the angular distance between the points. An important observation is that we don't measure absolute length with an arc, only an angle. The exact same angular distance will have completely different absolute lengths on circles of different diameters.

Now consider a sphere. Any point on a sphere can be specified (relative to some other point on the sphere) by two angles measured on "right circles" (see Figure 4-5). The right circles are formed by the intersection of the sphere and two planes. The planes both pass through the center of the sphere and a common point on its surface, and they are at

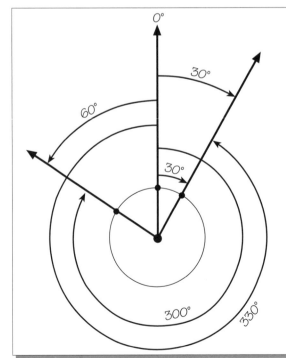

Angles are the amount of arc between two rays. Angles don't measure distance (notice the different length of the two 30° arcs).

Angles can be measured in either a clockwise or a counter clockwise direction. Thus the same two rays can have two different angular values (see the 60° counter clockwise arc and the 300° clockwise arc, or the 30° clockwise arc and the 330° counter clockwise arc).

In geographic coordinates (latitude and longitude) the rays that are being measured start at the center of the earth and pass through points on the surface of the earth.

In compass directions the rays that are being measured start at a location on the surface of the earth and point in a horizontal direction.

***Figure 4-3**: Measuring Angles — The Foundation Of Angular Coordinate Systems*

right angles to each other. Notice that neither right circle needs to pass through the point being measured.

In effect, once the right circles are specified, two numbers (angles) can be used to uniquely identify any point on the sphere. These angles (that we call coordinates) really specify the angle of a ray in 3-dimensional space. That ray originates from the exact center of the sphere and passes through the point we are measuring on the sphere's surface.

Something that should be noted at this point is the term "sphere" is being used loosely when it is applied to the earth. In reality, ellipsoids have been used to represent the earth's surface at sea level for well over a century. Ellipsoids are just flattened spheres. The earth is slightly flattened at the poles and bulges at the equator. That bulge is the result of the earth's axial spin. This discussion refers to the earth as a sphere strictly for the sake of simplicity, and nothing of importance is lost in the process. Now, back to the "spherical" model of the earth.

Angular coordinates alone do not tell you the size — the radius — of the sphere being described. In the case of the earth, the coordinates pertain to a sphere whose radius is the distance from the center of the earth to mean sea level. In other words, the "surface of the sphere" is mean sea level in the case of the earth. A third number, elevation, specifies the height of a point above, on, or below the surface of that sphere.

Elevation is relevant because it is needed to complete the full 3-dimensional specification of a point in space (or on the irregular surface of the earth). For the most part, elevation is not an essential item of information for GPS land navigation — you already know you're on the surface of the earth. In certain situations, however, elevation can be very critical when you're using GPS. See page 41 for a discussion of the role of elevation and 2D operating mode. See page 55 for a discussion of why altimeters are better than GPS receivers for giving your elevation.

One of the basic issues encountered when you work with coordinates on a sphere is how to determine a suitable point to represent the origin — the place on the surface of the sphere where the two right circles intersect. If you think about it, a sphere has no beginning and no end, nor any corners such as you find on a rectangle. Ultimately, the selection of a reference point for the origin is arbitrary. Fortunately, certain physical characteristics of the sphere we're concerned with — the earth — offer a partial answer to our need for a reference point, the "origin."

Since the earth spins around an axis (thereby giving us night and day), we can conveniently use this spin axis as the starting point for aligning the right planes. Start by aligning one plane with this polar axis. It follows that a second right plane must be perpendicular to the spin axis. In fact, to pass through the center of the sphere the second plane must divide the earth at a distance exactly halfway between the poles. Its intersection with the sphere forms the circle we call the equator.

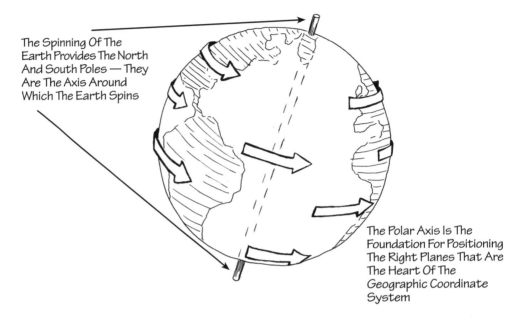

The Spinning Of The Earth Provides The North And South Poles — They Are The Axis Around Which The Earth Spins

The Polar Axis Is The Foundation For Positioning The Right Planes That Are The Heart Of The Geographic Coordinate System

Figure 4-4. *The Earth's Spin Axis Is The Starting Point For The Angular Coordinate System*

At this point the second plane (and along with it, the circle called the equator) is fixed in place, but the first plane is not. All that is specified for the first plane is that it must pass through the polar axis. It can intersect the equator anywhere. An infinite number of possibilities exist for this "polar plane." Indeed, there is more than one such plane used on various maps of the world.

Any point on earth (except the exact north or south pole) can be designated to have the first plane pass through it, and thereby fix the circle that gives us the "prime meridian." Once this is done, the intersection of the equator and the "prime meridian" establish our spherical reference point, the "0° latitude, 0° longitude" coordinate. Note that the "prime meridian" is actually one-half of a circle. Unlike parallels, meridians only "wrap" around one-half of the earth's sphere. You would need to travel along two meridians to fully circumnavigate the globe around the poles.

The meridian designated as "prime" is given an angular value of zero. All other meridians can be specified by the angle their plane forms with the prime meridian. Meridians (lines of longitude) are labeled in terms of their angle either east or west of the prime meridian (0° longitude). This limits meridians to values between 0° and 180°. They must, however, be labeled as east (E) or west (W) to cover the full 360° arc of the equator (or whatever parallel the point is on).

Meridians converge at the poles, so they appear on the surface of the earth similar to the segments of an orange. All points along the same meridian are the same number of degrees east or west of the prime meridian. The angular distance between any two meridians, measured in degrees, is the same regardless of whether the degrees are measured at the equator or at the arctic circle. The linear distance between two meridians is not constant, since meridians are not parallel. On the equator each degree between meridians is about 69 miles long. At the arctic circle (latitude 66½ degrees north) each degree between meridians is 26 miles long. As meridians converge at the poles, this distance shrinks to zero.

Now let's return to the equator. (Whew — it's hot and humid all of a sudden.) We can specify any point on a particular meridian by the angle it forms in relation to the equator. If all such points at this angle on all meridians are connected, we have a line of latitude, or a parallel. Parallels are just circles around the earth that are parallel to the equator.

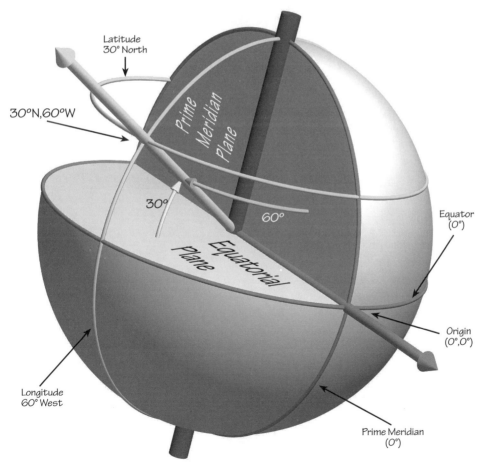

Figure 4-5: *Angular Coordinates On A Sphere — It's Really Just Two (Right) Circles*

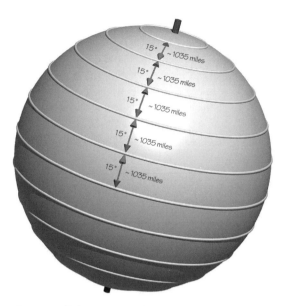

Figure 4-6: *Any Two Parallels — Everywhere The Same Linear Distance Apart*

The angle of a parallel can be from 0° (the equator) to 90° (one or the other of the poles). To avoid using negative numbers we need to indicate a direction. Thus, lines of latitude (parallels) are specified as being north (N) or south (S) of the equator. Since they range from 0° to 90° (plus N or S for hemisphere), they cover a pole to pole arc of 180°.

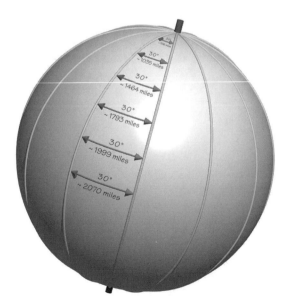

Figure 4-7: *Any Two Meridians — Ever Changing Linear Distance*

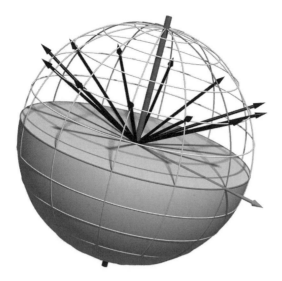

Figure 4-8: *All Possible Rays Through A Parallel Form A Cone*

Parallels are on planes that "slice" the polar axis of the earth at right angles, but the "rays" that make up each parallel actually form a cone. The point of the cone is located at the exact center of the earth, and it radiates out around the polar axis. It passes through the surface of the earth at a right angle to the surface.

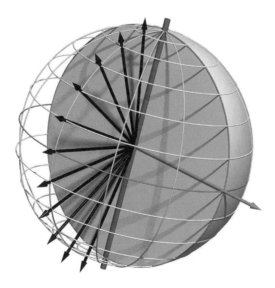

Figure 4-9: *All Possible Rays Through A Meridian Form One-Half Of A Plane*

4.1.2 Latitude and Longitude — Putting It All Together

Now to put this all together. The angular coordinate of any point on earth can be specified by identifying the parallel and the meridian it lies on. A parallel is identified by its degrees north or south of the equator. This is the latitude. A meridian is identified by the number of degrees it lies east or west of the prime meridian. This is the longitude. It is customary to list the latitude first, then the longitude, as in "44°N, 114°W."

When reading latitude on a map the numbers increase going up (north) in the northern hemisphere and increase going down (south) in the southern hemisphere. When reading longitude on a map the numbers increase going left (west) in the western hemisphere and increase going right (east) in the eastern hemisphere.

In the case of the 180° meridian (the international date line) no direction indicator is needed. That's because it is both 180° east of the prime meridian and 180° west of the

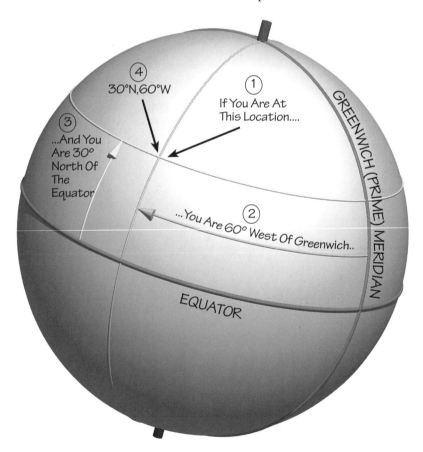

Figure 4-10: *Putting It All Together: Finding Your Spot On The Globe*

prime meridian. In the case of the poles (latitudes 90°N and 90°S) no longitude value is needed since all lines of longitude pass through both poles.

Sometimes latitude and longitude are expressed without a letter for the hemisphere. Some computer programs, for example, can't work with letters. In these cases the numeric values are made negative in the western hemisphere (for longitude) and the southern hemisphere (for latitude). "44°N,114°W" would be written "44,-114" in such a system.

Angular coordinates define a specific position on a sphere of any particular radius. Since the surface of the earth is not a smooth sphere, we need a third value to fully describe a point on (or, for that matter, above or below) the earth. Elevation is that third value.

4.1.3 Elevation

Elevation is a measurement, in feet or meters, that indicates how far out along a ray from the center of the earth our point is located. Rather than specifying elevation relative to the origin of the ray (the center of the earth), cartographers use an "offset" that is defined as either mean sea level or the surface of an ellipsoid that approximates mean sea level.

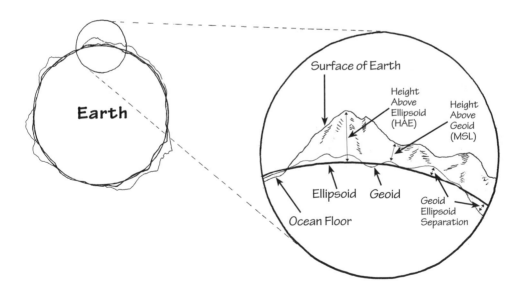

Figure 4-11: *Elevation Can Be Based On The Ellipsoid Or The Geoid — They're Not The Same*

Mean sea level (MSL) is the vertical datum used on USGS topographic maps. MSL is the earth's surface of constant gravity, and it is called the "geoid." The geoid has been described as the surface that would exist if oceans where to replace the earth's continental masses. You can think of the geoid as the gravitational equivalent of an isobar, contour line, isogonic line, etc. The geoid is obtained by local physical observations, and it is irregular over fairly small areas, such as states. See Figure 2-20 for a simulated image of how the geoid appears over the U.S.

The GPS system doesn't use the geoid as its vertical reference. Instead, it uses an ellipsoid to approximate the surface of the earth at sea level. This is a mathematical portrayal of the earth's shape. It is not the same as the surface of the geoid. The vertical difference between the ellipsoid and the geoid is up to 52 meters in the continental U.S. This means GPS elevation does not match the elevation found on most maps. However, many GPS receivers designed for personal navigation use a table to convert from ellipsoidal elevation to geoidal elevation. Doing so gets them to within about 5 meters of the elevation shown on a map.

Getting back to our coordinate system, any point's elevation is just its vertical distance above or below either mean sea level or the surface of the ellipsoid.

4.1.4 Distance Measurement

Before leaving the topic of angular coordinates, we need to examine the units that are used in this system a little more closely. So far we've mostly talked about angles in terms of degrees. Each degree of latitude covers approximately 69 statute miles (or 60 nautical miles) anywhere on earth, and each degree of longitude covers approximately 69 statute miles (also 60 nautical miles) at the equator.

To get more resolution, it is possible to write decimal degrees, such as "44.3564°." One decimal place gives a resolution of 6.9 miles, two decimal places give a resolution of .69 miles, three decimal places give a resolution of 364 feet, four decimal places give a resolution of 36 feet, and so on.

Another way to obtain more resolution is to use minutes (1/60th of a degree) and seconds (1/60th of a minute). A minute gives resolution to 1.15 miles and a second gives resolution to 101 feet. A second carried to one decimal place gives a resolution to 10 feet!

Keep in mind that the foregoing values are close approximations that apply to all degrees of latitude, but for longitude they apply only to distance measurements along the equator. To obtain the approximate distance measurement for a degree of longitude at various latitudes, a little trigonometry is needed. The formula is: distance per degree = 69 x cosine(latitude). The cosine for each degree of latitude is given in Table 4-1. To see how this formula works, the cosine of 43° is 0.7313. The length of a degree of longitude at 43° latitude is 69 x 0.7313 = 50.46 miles. You can substitute the length at the equator of a

Conversion Factors For Angular To Linear Measurements

Latitude	Cosine	Latitude	Cosine	Latitude	Cosine
0°	1.0000				
1°	0.9998	31°	0.8572	61°	0.4848
2°	0.9994	32°	0.8480	62°	0.4695
3°	0.9986	33°	0.8387	63°	0.4540
4°	0.9976	34°	0.8290	64°	0.4384
5°	0.9962	35°	0.8191	65°	0.4226
6°	0.9945	36°	0.8090	66°	0.4067
7°	0.9925	37°	0.7986	67°	0.3907
8°	0.9903	38°	0.7880	68°	0.3746
9°	0.9877	39°	0.7771	69°	0.3584
10°	0.9848	40°	0.7660	70°	0.3420
11°	0.9816	41°	0.7547	71°	0.3256
12°	0.9781	42°	0.7431	72°	0.3090
13°	0.9744	43°	0.7313	73°	0.2924
14°	0.9703	44°	0.7193	74°	0.2756
15°	0.9659	45°	0.7071	75°	0.2588
16°	0.9613	46°	0.6947	76°	0.2419
17°	0.9563	47°	0.6820	77°	0.2249
18°	0.9511	48°	0.6691	78°	0.2079
19°	0.9455	49°	0.6561	79°	0.1908
20°	0.9397	50°	0.6428	80°	0.1736
21°	0.9336	51°	0.6293	81°	0.1564
22°	0.9272	52°	0.6157	82°	0.1392
23°	0.9205	53°	0.6018	83°	0.1219
24°	0.9135	54°	0.5878	84°	0.1045
25°	0.9063	55°	0.5736	85°	0.0872
26°	0.8988	56°	0.5592	86°	0.0698
27°	0.8910	57°	0.5446	87°	0.0523
28°	0.8829	58°	0.5299	88°	0.0349
29°	0.8746	59°	0.5150	89°	0.0174
30°	0.8660	60°	0.5000	90°	0.0000

Table 4-1: *Table Of Cosines (For Converting Between Angular And Linear Measurements)*

minute, second, or whatever angular unit you chose (in place of 69 miles per degree) to obtain the corresponding distance at the latitude of your choice.

4.1.5 Angular Units

When specifying angular coordinates you can choose between decimal degrees, decimal minutes or decimal seconds, but you can't mix them together. The possibilities are decimal degrees (no minutes or seconds); degrees and decimal minutes (no seconds); or degrees, minutes and decimal seconds.

To convert from decimal degrees to degrees and decimal minutes, just take the decimal component of the degree (the part to the right of the decimal place) and multiply it times 60 to get decimal minutes. To convert from decimal minutes to minutes and decimal seconds, multiply the decimal component of the minutes times 60 to get decimal seconds.

Seconds ⮕ Minutes ⮕ Degrees

decimal seconds.....45° 37′ 21.0′′
⇓
decimal minutes.....45° 37 $^{21}/_{60}$′ = 45° 37.35′
⇓
decimal degrees...................................45 $^{37.35}/_{60}$° = 45.6225°

Degrees ⮕ Minutes ⮕ Seconds

decimal degrees.....45.3725°
⇓
decimal minutes.....45° 60 x .3725′ = 45° 22.35′
⇓
decimal seconds......................45° 22′ 60 x .35 = 45° 22′ 21.0′′

Figure 4-12: Converting Between Various Units Of Angular Measurement

To convert from decimal degrees to degrees, minutes, and decimal seconds, just calculate decimal minutes as an intermediate step.

Going the other way, to convert from decimal seconds to decimal minutes, divide the decimal seconds by 60 and add the result to the truncated minute value. To convert from decimal minutes to decimal degrees, divide the decimal minute value by 60 and add the result to the truncated degree value. To convert from decimal seconds to decimal degrees, just calculate decimal minutes as an intermediate step.

If you need to do such conversions very often, it is relatively simple to program a spreadsheet to do the conversions automatically. There are also dedicated computer programs available that will do coordinate conversions for you.

4.2 UTM Rectangular Coordinates

Rectangular coordinates are a response to the weaknesses of the angular coordinate system. The **Universal Transverse Mercator** system is the "grandaddy" of the rectangular coordinate systems. It covers the entire surface of the earth, with the exceptions of the north and south polar regions. The poles are covered by a different coordinate system.

For all their elegance and precision in pinpointing any location on our spherical earth, angular coordinates can be very difficult to work with. Perhaps the most apparent difficulty in working with angular coordinates is the absence of a constant distance relationship. A degree of longitude ranges from about 69 miles long at the equator, to about 49 miles long at the 45th parallel, to about 26 miles long at the arctic circle. A degree of latitude, on the other hand, varies by a negligible amount, and is equal to about 69 miles at any parallel (and at any meridian).

Since land navigation usually involves interacting with just a small part of the world around us, a different coordinate system was devised that makes large scale maps easier to use. By specifying coordinates in a rectangular framework it is possible to directly link the coordinate numbering system to a distance measuring system. That is exactly what the Universal Transverse Mercator (UTM) coordinate system accomplishes. Each UTM coordinate grid is expressed in units of meters, with a particular point on the grid specified as the number of meters east and north of a reference point. There are a total of 60 separate UTM grid zones in the UTM system.

While the UTM grid system is simpler than the angular coordinate system in many ways, it is not independent of the angular system. In fact, the 60 UTM grid zones each span six degrees of longitude and 164 degrees of latitude. Each UTM grid zone extends from latitude 80°S to latitude 84°N, and is centered exactly on a line of longitude.

The regions of the earth below latitude 80°S and above latitude 84°N (the polar regions) are not included in the UTM system. Instead, they are covered by a different grid system

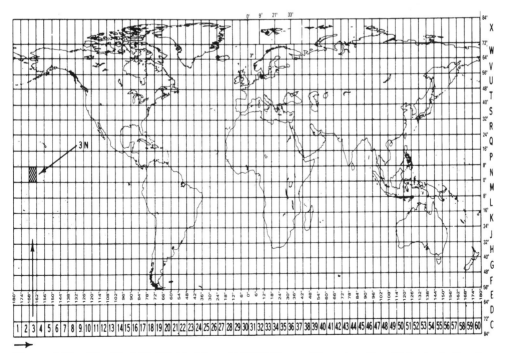

Figure 4-13: *The World Is Divided Into 60 UTM Zones; There Are Also 20 Latitude Bands Labeled C Through X*

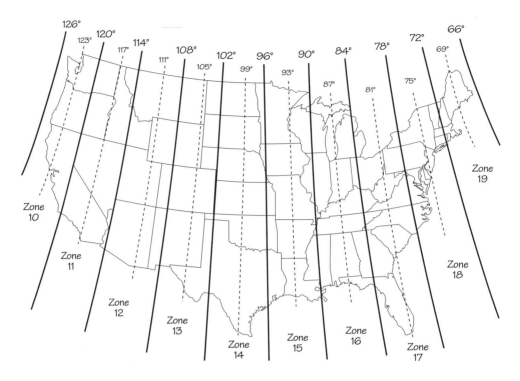

Figure 4-14: *The UTM Zone Coverage Of The United States*

known as UPS — the Universal Polar Stereographic system. The UPS grid system is described briefly in the next section.

The numbering system for UTM zones starts with zone number 1 at longitude 180° (the international date line) and proceeds east. UTM zone 1 extends from longitude 180°W to longitude 174°W. It is actually centered on longitude 177°W. At longitude 0° (the prime, or Greenwich meridian) we reach the eastern edge of UTM zone 30 and the western edge of UTM zone number 31. Continuing east the last UTM zone (zone number 60) begins at longitude 174°E and ends at longitude 180°, or where we started. See Figure 4-13.

In the angular coordinate system longitude values increase in both directions starting at the prime meridian. This means longitude values increase when going west in the Western Hemisphere, and when going east in the Eastern Hemisphere. The UTM grid zone numbers always increase in an easterly direction. Unfortunately, this means that UTM grid zones increase in the opposite direction as longitude in the Western Hemisphere. See Figure 4-14.

Since a rectangular coordinate system is not capable of representing a curved surface without some distortion, the UTM coordinate system has a certain amount of distance related distortion. By using 60 separate zones this distortion is limited to less than 1 part in 2,500 parts, or less than .04 percent.

Each UTM zone is an independent Cartesian grid system that has its own origin. For each zone the origin is located at the intersection of the equator and the zone's central meridian. Thus, the origin of each zone lies on the equator and is exactly 6 degrees of longitude from the origin of adjacent UTM zones.

UTM grids are designed to be "read right then up." This means that the grid numbers always increase from left to right (west to east) and from bottom to top (south to north). Unlike the angular system, this direction of measurement does not depend on which north-south or east-west hemisphere you are working in. Anywhere on earth, the UTM rule is always "read right then up." This also means that UTM coordinates are usually given with the horizontal (easting) value first, then the vertical (northing) value second.

UTM coordinates are often abbreviated when they're used to label maps. Grid and tick-mark labels will often be truncated to a resolution of one kilometer. In order to make them easier to read, UTM grid labels typically have the digits representing thousands of meters and ten-thousands of meters enlarged, like this: "05**64**000mE" or "48**29**000mN." When truncated to one kilometer resolution (for grid or tick mark labels) these numbers become 05**64** for the easting and 48**29** for the northing.

The foregoing UTM coordinates (with resolution to 1,000 meters) can also be written as 05644829. The easting value is always given first, then the northing value. If there are an odd number of digits, that means the leading zero of the easting value has been dropped, as in 5644829. The easting value will always have one less digit than the northing value when an odd number of digits is present. See Figure 4-15.

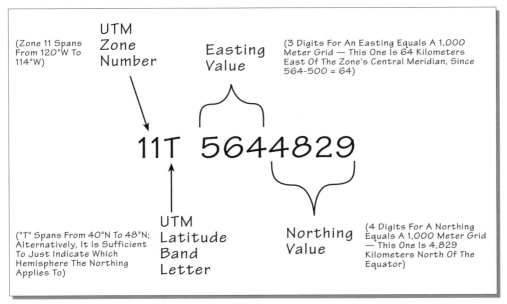

Figure 4-15: UTM Coordinates — Interpreting The Pieces

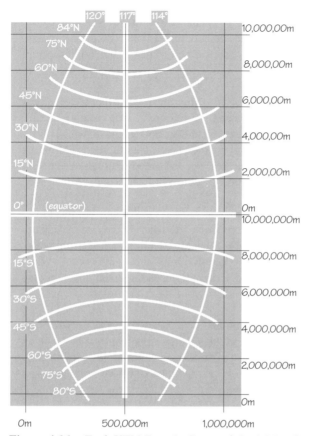

The illustration at left shows how the UTM coordinate system compares to the latitude/longitude coordinate system. This illustration is not drawn to scale, since the vertical dimension covers 20 times the distance covered by the horizontal scale. This does, however, show the essence of how the UTM coordinate system is designed.

The UTM coordinate system is overlaid on top of the geographic (latitude/longitude) coordinate system.

The two systems coincide in each of 60 UTM zones at the equator and at each zone's central meridian (zone 11 is shown, with its central meridian of 117°W).

The boundary of each UTM zone is defined by the meridians that are 3° east and west of the zone's central meridian. In this case those meridians are 120°W and 114°W.

Figure 4-16: *Each UTM Zone Is Centered On A Meridian — The "Central" Meridian*

The reason that the easting value requires one less digit is the "tall narrow" shape of the UTM zones. An easting value will never exceed 999,999 meters. Northing values, on the other hand, start at zero on the equator and reach about 9,300,000 meters at latitude 84° North — the northern-most reach of the UTM zones. This means that meter-level precision requires six digits for the easting and seven digits for the northing.

For a particular UTM zone seven or eight total digits specify a point to within 1,000 meters of precision, nine or ten total digits to within 100 meters of precision, eleven or twelve total digits to within 10 meters of precision, and so on. The zone designator adds two more digits, and a letter of the alphabet is used to designate the southern or northern hemisphere.

A UTM coordinate actually defines a square area, rather than a precise point. The length of the sides of the square are determined by the resolution of the coordinate pair. If the resolution is 1,000 meters, then the sides of the square are 1,000 meters long. If the resolution is 10 meters, then the square has sides that are 10 meters long. Any point that falls within a particular square will have the same coordinate (at that resolution) as any other point that falls within the same square.

The square defined by a UTM coordinate is not centered on the coordinate's values. Instead, the coordinate defines the lower left corner of the square. Since UTM coordinates are always "read right then up," this is equivalent to truncating the insignificant digits.

The coordinate value for the origin of each UTM zone is not 0,0 as you might expect. To avoid the use of negative numbers, the true origin of each zone is assigned a value of 500,000 meters east, 0 meters north for the northern hemisphere, and a value of 500,000 meters east, 10,000,000 meters north for the southern hemisphere. This gives rise to the terms "false origin," "false easting," and "false northing."

The actual point of origin in a particular UTM zone is the same physical location on the equator for both the southern hemisphere and the northern hemisphere. The easting value's false origin of 500,000 meters avoids negative numbers since there is no place that a zone is over 999,999 meters wide. The northern hemisphere's northing origin of zero works fine, but a value of zero would require negative numbers for the grid in the southern hemisphere. That's because of the "read right then up" rule. By setting the value of the northing origin (the equator) to 10,000,000 meters for the southern hemisphere, no negative numbers are needed.

Different false origins for the northern and southern hemispheres mean that UTM coordinate data must specify whether it applies to the northern or southern hemisphere.

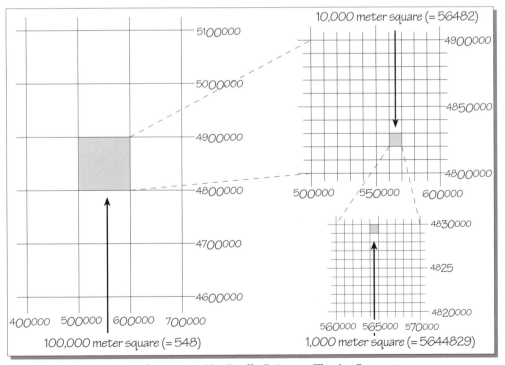

Figure 4-17: *UTM Coordinates Are Not Really Points — They're Squares*

UTM Coordinates:
Resolution Determines The Number Of Digits

UTM Coordinate	Zone	Latitude Band	Easting Meters	Northing Meters	Grid Size (Resolution)
11T 5645764829733	11	T	564,576	4,829,733	1 meter
11T 56457482973	11	T	564,570	4,829,730	10 meter
11T 564548297	11	T	564,500	4,829,700	100 meter
11T 5644829	11	T	564,000	4,829,000	1,000 meter
11T 56482	11	T	560,000	4,820,000	10,000 meter
11T 548	11	T	500,000	4,800,000	100,000 meter

Note: The coordinates shown in this example all describe the first "1 meter" point - the only difference between them is the amount of precision used to describe that point.

Figure 4-18: *UTM Coordinates Specify Both Location And Grid Size*

Actually, the north-south location within a UTM zone is specified by a single alphabetic character that identifies one of 20 successive bands of latitude.

The first 19 bands of latitude (labeled C through W) are each 8 degrees "high." The 20th band (labeled X) is 12 degrees of latitude "high." The labeling starts with "C" at latitude 80°S to 72°S, skips the letters "I" and "O," and ends with "X" representing latitude 72°N to 84°N. The equator is the beginning of band "N," therefore all parts of the northern hemisphere are in bands labeled "N" or higher. Just think of "N" for northern as an easy way to remember this.

The continental U.S. is covered by UTM grid zone 10 (west coast) to UTM grid zone 19 (east coast). This spans sixty degrees of longitude. The latitude bands range from "R" at the tip of Key West, to just inside band "U" at the Washington State/Canadian border. This spans just a little over twenty-four degrees of latitude.

The central meridians of the UTM grid zones in the continental U.S. are 123°W (zone 10), 117°W (zone 11), 111°W (zone 12), 105°W (zone 13), 99°W (zone 14), 93°W (zone 15), 87°W (zone 16), 81°W (zone 17), 75°W (zone 18), and 69°W (zone 19). Anywhere along these meridians the UTM grid easting value is always 500,000 meters.

The grid declination along these 500,000 meter vertical (easting) gridlines is always zero, since they are also lines of longitude. No other vertical UTM gridline in a particular zone is parallel to a line of longitude, therefore all other vertical UTM gridlines have either east or west grid declination relative to true north. The amount of grid declination increases as distance increases away from the zone's central meridian and as distance increases away from the equator.

Among the horizontal (northing) gridlines, only the 0 meter gridline (and its counterpart 10,000,000 meter gridline in the southern hemisphere) correspond exactly to a line of latitude — the equator. As you move north, the horizontal UTM grid lines appear to curve down and away from the lines of latitude as you move away from the zone's central meridian. This is because the lines of latitude are parallel to the equator on a spherical surface, while the UTM horizontal gridlines are parallel to the equator on a rectangular surface.

If you want to see this phenomenon for yourself, just try laying the edge of a sheet of paper flat along the 45th parallel on a globe. Now try it on the equator. The equator can be aligned along the edge of the paper, but the 45th parallel can not! It's the difference between great circles (the equator) and little circles (other lines of latitude), concepts that are explained in the next chapter on page 146. For now you just need to see that the parallels above the equator curve up and away from the edge of the flat sheet of paper. Correspondingly, the UTM grid declination in the Northern Hemisphere is west when the easting value is less than 500,000 meters (i.e., west of the central meridian), and it is east when the easting value is greater than 500,000 meters (i.e., east of the central meridian).

4.3 Other Rectangular Coordinates

There are a number of other rectangular coordinate systems besides UTM. In most situations involving GPS land navigation they do not prove to be particularly useful. The other coordinate systems listed here are included either because they are used in specialized cases for certain GPS users, or because you will encounter them on USGS topographic map products.

4.3.1 Universal Polar Stereographic (UPS)

Universal Polar Stereographic, or UPS, is a metric coordinate system that covers the extreme southern and northern latitudes. It is basically a complement to the UTM system. It relies on a different projection method to cover the extreme polar regions. It is not used anywhere in the United States.

The design of the UPS grid is similar to UTM in that it uses a false origin. The pole (either north or south) is the projection's true origin, but the pole is given a "false" value of 2,000,000 meters North and 2,000,000 meters East. Note that the same false northing value is used at both the North Pole and the South Pole.

In the case of the North Pole, northing values are centered along the 0°/180° meridians (the prime meridian and the international date line) with values increasing as you move north along the prime meridian, then continuing to increase as you move south along the international date line. The easting values increase as you move north along the 90° West meridian, then they continue to increase as you move south along the 90° East meridian.

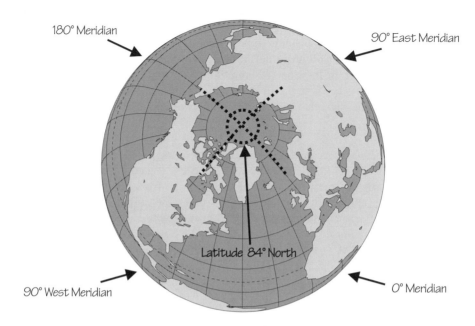

Figure 4-19: *Universal Polar Stereographic (UPS) Grid At The North Pole — It Only Applies Within The Circle Formed By The 84° North Parallel*

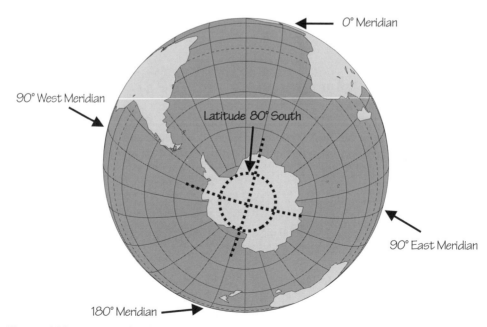

Figure 4-20: *Universal Polar Stereographic (UPS) Grid At The South Pole — It Only Applies Within The Circle Formed By The 80° South Parallel*

Think of it as looking down from directly above the north pole, with the prime meridian at the bottom and the 90°W meridian on the left. See Figure 4-19.

The South Pole grid is laid out in the same way as the North Pole, except the northing value increases as you go south along the 180° longitude line, reaches 2,000,000 meters at the South Pole, then keeps increasing as you move north along the prime meridian. Think of it as looking down from directly above the south pole, with the prime meridian at the top and the 90°W meridian on the left. See Figure 4-20.

4.3.2 Military Grid Reference System (MGRS)

The Military Grid Reference System, or MGRS, was developed by the U.S. Army to simplify the use of rectangular grid coordinate systems. It is a relative of the UTM and UPS grid systems.

The MGRS grid uses the same grid zone identifiers (1 through 60) and band identifiers (C through X) as the UTM system (see Figure 4-13). It then adds two letters to designate 100,000 by 100,000 meter (100 by 100 kilometer) squares. Following those two letters the MGRS system reverts to the standard UTM easting and northing values.

If two digits follow the letters, they specify the lower left corner of a 10,000 by 10,000 meter square. If four digits follow the letters, they specify the lower left corner of a 1,000

ZONES	SET 1 1 7 13 19 25 31 37 43 49 55								SET 2 2 8 14 20 26 32 38 44 50 56								SET 3 3 9 15 21 27 33 39 45 51 57								SET 4 4 10 16 22 28 34 40 46 52 58								SET 5 5 11 17 23 29 35 41 47 53 59								SET 6 6 12 18 24 30 36 42 48 54 60							
2,000,000 m	AV	BV	CV	DV	EV	FV	GV	HV	JE	KE	LE	ME	NE	PE	QE	RE	SV	TV	UV	VV	WV	XV	YV	ZV	AE	BE	CE	DE	EE	FE	GE	HE	JV	KV	LV	MV	NV	PV	QV	RV	SE	TE	UE	VE	WE	XE	YE	ZE
	AU	BU	CU	DU	EU	FU	GU	HU	JD	KD	LD	MD	ND	PD	QD	RD	SU	TU	UU	VU	WU	XU	YU	ZU	AD	BD	CD	DD	ED	FD	GD	HD	JU	KU	LU	MU	NU	PU	QU	RU	SD	TD	UD	VD	WD	XD	YD	ZD
	AT	BT	CT	DT	ET	FT	GT	HT	JC	KC	LC	MC	NC	PC	QC	RC	ST	TT	UT	VT	WT	XT	YT	ZT	AC	BC	CC	DC	EC	FC	GC	HC	JT	KT	LT	MT	NT	PT	QT	RT	SC	TC	UC	VC	WC	XC	YC	ZC
	AS	BS	CS	DS	ES	FS	GS	HS	JB	KB	LB	MB	NB	PB	QB	RB	SS	TS	US	VS	WS	XS	YS	ZS	AB	BB	CB	DB	EB	FB	GB	HB	JS	KS	LS	MS	NS	PS	QS	RS	SB	TB	UB	VB	WB	XB	YB	ZB
1,500,000 m	AR	BR	CR	DR	ER	FR	GR	HR	JA	KA	LA	MA	NA	PA	QA	RA	SR	TR	UR	VR	WR	XR	YR	ZR	AA	BA	CA	DA	EA	FA	GA	HA	JR	KR	LR	MR	NR	PR	QR	RR	SA	TA	UA	VA	WA	XA	YA	ZA
	AQ	BQ	CQ	DQ	EQ	FQ	GQ	HQ	JV	KV	LV	MV	NV	PV	QV	RV	SQ	TQ	UQ	VQ	WQ	XQ	YQ	ZQ	AV	BV	CV	DV	EV	FV	GV	HV	JQ	KQ	LQ	MQ	NQ	PQ	QQ	RQ	SV	TV	UV	VV	WV	XV	YV	ZV
	AP	BP	CP	DP	EP	FP	GP	HP	JU	KU	LU	MU	NU	PU	QU	RU	SP	TP	UP	VP	WP	XP	YP	ZP	AU	BU	CU	DU	EU	FU	GU	HU	JP	KP	LP	MP	NP	PP	QP	RP	SU	TU	UU	VU	WU	XU	YU	ZU
	AN	BN	CN	DN	EN	FN	GN	HN	JT	KT	LT	MT	NT	PT	QT	RT	SN	TN	UN	VN	WN	XN	YN	ZN	AT	BT	CT	DT	ET	FT	GT	HT	JN	KN	LN	MN	NN	PN	QN	RN	ST	TT	UT	VT	WT	XT	YT	ZT
	AM	BM	CM	DM	EM	FM	GM	HM	JS	KS	LS	MS	NS	PS	QS	RS	SM	TM	UM	VM	WM	XM	YM	ZM	AS	BS	CS	DS	ES	FS	GS	HS	JM	KM	LM	MM	NM	PM	QM	RM	SS	TS	US	VS	WS	XS	YS	ZS
	AL	BL	CL	DL	EL	FL	GL	HL	JR	KR	LR	MR	NR	PR	QR	RR	SL	TL	UL	VL	WL	XL	YL	ZL	AR	BR	CR	DR	ER	FR	GR	HR	JL	KL	LL	ML	NL	PL	QL	RL	SR	TR	UR	VR	WR	XR	YR	ZR
1,000,000 m	AK	BK	CK	DK	EK	FK	GK	HK	JQ	KQ	LQ	MQ	NQ	PQ	QQ	RQ	SK	TK	UK	VK	WK	XK	YK	ZK	AQ	BQ	CQ	DQ	EQ	FQ	GQ	HQ	JK	KK	LK	MK	NK	PK	QK	RK	SQ	TQ	UQ	VQ	WQ	XQ	YQ	ZQ
	AJ	BJ	CJ	DJ	EJ	FJ	GJ	HJ	JP	KP	LP	MP	NP	PP	QP	RP	SJ	TJ	UJ	VJ	WJ	XJ	YJ	ZJ	AP	BP	CP	DP	EP	FP	GP	HP	JJ	KJ	LJ	MJ	NJ	PJ	QJ	RJ	SP	TP	UP	VP	WP	XP	YP	ZP
	AH	BH	CH	DH	EH	FH	GH	HH	JN	KN	LN	MN	NN	PN	QN	RN	SH	TH	UH	VH	WH	XH	YH	ZH	AN	BN	CN	DN	EN	FN	GN	HN	JH	KH	LH	MH	NH	PH	QH	RH	SN	TN	UN	VN	WN	XN	YN	ZN
	AG	BG	CG	DG	EG	FG	GG	HG	JM	KM	LM	MM	NM	PM	QM	RM	SG	TG	UG	VG	WG	XG	YG	ZG	AM	BM	CM	DM	EM	FM	GM	HM	JG	KG	LG	MG	NG	PG	QG	RG	SM	TM	UM	VM	WM	XM	YM	ZM
	AF	BF	CF	DF	EF	FF	GF	HF	JL	KL	LL	ML	NL	PL	QL	RL	SF	TF	UF	VF	WF	XF	YF	ZF	AL	BL	CL	DL	EL	FL	GL	HL	JF	KF	LF	MF	NF	PF	QF	RF	SL	TL	UL	VL	WL	XL	YL	ZL
500,000 m	AE	BE	CE	DE	EE	FE	GE	HE	JK	KK	LK	MK	NK	PK	QK	RK	SE	TE	UE	VE	WE	XE	YE	ZE	AK	BK	CK	DK	EK	FK	GK	HK	JE	KE	LE	ME	NE	PE	QE	RE	SK	TK	UK	VK	WK	XK	YK	ZK
	AD	BD	CD	DD	ED	FD	GD	HD	JJ	KJ	LJ	MJ	NJ	PJ	QJ	RJ	SD	TD	UD	VD	WD	XD	YD	ZD	AJ	BJ	CJ	DJ	EJ	FJ	GJ	HJ	JD	KD	LD	MD	ND	PD	QD	RD	SJ	TJ	UJ	VJ	WJ	XJ	YJ	ZJ
	AC	BC	CC	DC	EC	FC	GC	HC	JH	KH	LH	MH	NH	PH	QH	RH	SC	TC	UC	VC	WC	XC	YC	ZC	AH	BH	CH	DH	EH	FH	GH	HH	JC	KC	LC	MC	NC	PC	QC	RC	SH	TH	UH	VH	WH	XH	YH	ZH
	AB	BB	CB	DB	EB	FB	GB	HB	JG	KG	LG	MG	NG	PG	QG	RG	SB	TB	UB	VB	WB	XB	YB	ZB	AG	BG	CG	DG	EG	FG	GG	HG	JB	KB	LB	MB	NB	PB	QB	RB	SG	TG	UG	VG	WG	XG	YG	ZG
0 m	AA	BA	CA	DA	EA	FA	GA	HA	JF	KF	LF	MF	NF	PF	QF	RF	SA	TA	UA	VA	WA	XA	YA	ZA	AF	BF	CF	DF	EF	FF	GF	HF	JA	KA	LA	MA	NA	PA	QA	RA	SF	TF	UF	VF	WF	XF	YF	ZF

Easting labels (repeated per set): 200,000 m 300,000 400,000 500,000 600,000 700,000 800,000 m

Figure 4-21: *Military Grid Reference System 100,000 Meter Square Designations (And A Handy MGRS/UTM Converter)*

by 1,000 meter square. If six digits follow the letters, they specify the lower left corner of a 100 by 100 meter square, and so on. (See Figure 4-23.)

Figure 4-21 provides a comprehensive listing of the MGRS 100,000 meter square identifiers (letter pairs that uniquely identify each 100,000 meter square within a UTM Grid Zone/Latitude Band combination). To convert a UTM coordinate to MGRS (we'll use the coordinate from Figure 4-23), first select the set that corresponds to the coordinate's UTM zone. Then find the easting value along the lower axis (564,576 meters would be truncated to 500,000). This sets the column and establishes the first alphabetic character (N).

Next find the coordinate's northing value on the left axis. Values over 2,000,000 meters must be "recycled," meaning that the second letter sequence repeats every 2,000,000 meters. A northing value of 4,829,733 would be converted to 829,733. This is truncated to 800,000 meters and establishes the second alphabetic character (J).

Remember, if the UTM coordinates are expressed as an odd number of digits it is because the leading zero in the easting value was dropped. In essence, the MGRS grid system replaces either 3 or 4 digits in the UTM system with two alphabetic characters. Although it is meant to be a simplified global coordinate system, MGRS has two different "versions." The 100,000 meter square identifiers shown in Figure 4-21 are for maps that are based on the WGS84 datum. A different sequence of letter pairs (not shown) is used for MGRS coordinates based on the NAD27 datum.

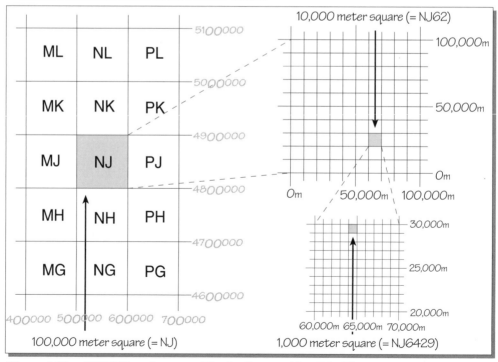

Figure 4-22: *MGRS Zone System — They're Squares (Just Like The UTM System)*

MGRS Coordinates:
Just A Modified Version Of UTM!

UTM Coordinate	MGRS Coordinate	Grid Size (Resolution)
11T 5645764829733	11T NJ6457629733	1 meter
11T 56457482973	11T NJ64572973	10 meter
11T 564548297	11T NJ645297	100 meter
11T 564829	11T NJ6429	1,000 meter
11T 56482	11T NJ62	10,000 meter
11T 548	11T NJ	100,000 meter

Note: The coordinates shown in this example all describe the first "1 meter" point - the only difference between them is the amount of precision used to describe that point. See Figure 3-18 for details of the UTM coordinate used here.

Figure 4-23: MGRS Coordinates – They're Just A Modified Form Of UTM!

The good news about MGRS is that it is not used on USGS 7.5-minute and 15-minute quadrangle series maps, so you probably won't need to worry about it. That's because the entire land area of the United States is covered by USGS 7.5-minute maps, and they use UTM. MGRS is a more valuable feature in a GPS receiver if you intend to use Defense Mapping Agency maps either in the U.S. or overseas.

4.3.3 Township and Range System (USPLSS)

Township and Range grids are printed on all USGS topographic maps that cover areas that have been surveyed by the U.S. Public Land Survey System (USPLSS). This grid system has its origin in the Land Ordnance of 1785.

This system is built on a network of base lines and principal meridians that are lines of latitude and longitude. The intersection of the base line and the principal meridian is known as the "Initial Point." Most states have only one Initial Point, but a few states have several Initial Points. Some states, such as Oregon and Washington, share a single initial point. Figure 4-25 is a U.S. map of base lines and principal meridians.

The USPLSS grid system is built outward from the Initial Point in six mile increments. Township lines intersect the principal meridian every six miles north and south of the Initial Point, and Range lines intersect the base line every six miles east and west of the Initial Point. Each six mile by six mile square is known as a "Township." Townships are divided into 36 one mile by one mile squares known as "Sections."

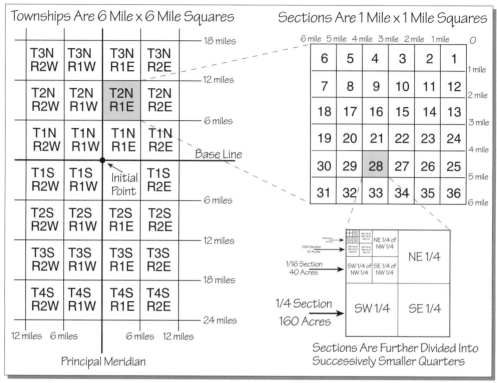

Figure 4-24: *USPLSS — How It Works*

Because of the distortion caused by the earth's curvature every fourth Range and Township line (in other words, every 24 miles) is "corrected" to realign it with a "standard" parallel or a "guide" meridian. This prevents the grid distortion from amplifying (relative to latitude and longitude graticules) as Townships and Ranges extend out from the Initial Point.

The result of this realignment is that townships are not always perfect six mile by six mile squares. That's why the USPLSS grid printed on the face of many USGS topographic maps doesn't always form tidy perpendicular intersections. It is also why the USPLSS grid can't be easily converted to either the latitude/longitude coordinate system or the UTM coordinate system.

The USPLSS grid system is mainly of interest to surveyors and lawyers because it is used for the legal description of public and private land ownership. However, you may be able to use the USPLSS in a pinch to find your location on a topo map. It works by knowing that western lands were given away (to states, land grant universities, railroads, etc.) in one section increments. As a result, long straight fence lines in the backcountry usually indicate a section border. All you need to do is find the section on your topo map. Be careful if you try this, it takes skill to match map features with the world around you.

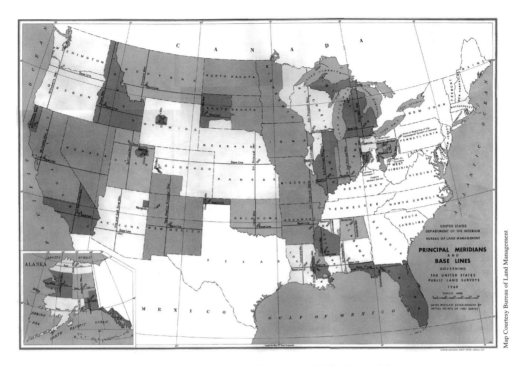

Figure 4-25: USPLSS (Towns And Sections) Coverage Of The United States

4.3.4 State Plane Coordinate System (SPCS)

The State Plane Coordinate System (SPCS) was created in the 1930's. It represented a substantial improvement over the older USPLSS. The continental United States was divided into 125 zones, with each zone representing all or part of a state. In the case of states with multiple zones, the individual zones follow county borders.

State plane coordinates are similar to UTM coordinates in several respects. SPC's have false origins that always yield positive numbers for coordinates, and state plane coordinates are always read in the same "read right then up" manner as UTM. That's right, SPC's represent eastings and northings! The notation used for state plane coordinates is the easting first, then the northing, then the state, and finally the zone. It looks like this: "381170 feet East, 711391 feet North, Idaho, West Zone." In case you're wondering, that's the location of Idaho's State Capitol dome (NAD27).

That example also illustrates one of the key differences between SPC and UTM. State plane coordinates are expressed in feet. In fact, the large scale USGS topographic maps have 10,000 **foot** State Plane Coordinate tick marks on the neatlines.

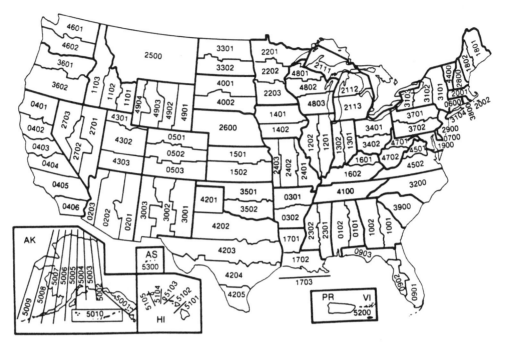

Figure 4-26: *State Plane Coordinate System — Zone Coverage Of The United States*

Another less obvious difference is that State Plane Coordinates are not based on a single standardized projection method. Some states (primarily those that are taller than they are wide) use a Transverse Mercator projection. Most states (all that are wider than they are tall, and some that are taller than they are wide) use the Lambert Conformal projection.

Although State Plane Coordinate tick marks are shown on the neatlines of all large scale USGS topographic maps, they are of no practical use to the backcountry land navigator. Fortunately, they don't clutter up the face of topographic maps, just the borders.

4.4 NAVSTAR's Coordinate System

The NAVSTAR global positioning system uses a special coordinate system that is called "Earth Centered Earth Fixed, xyz" (ECEF). It is a three-dimensional Cartesian coordinate system that relies on the familiar right-angled x, y, and z axis system. The origin (0,0,0) is located at the center of the earth's mass. The z-axis goes through the north pole. The x-axis goes through the intersection of the prime meridian and the equator. The y-axis goes through the intersection of the 90° east meridian and the equator.

This system makes it easy for computers to specify points on the surface of the earth (as well as points in space above the surface of the earth) by their x,y,z coordinates. Relatively simple trigonometry can then be used to obtain distances and directions. Unlike the two-dimensional coordinate system used for mapping the surface of the earth, there is no distortion inherent in the ECEF coordinate system.

Although ECEF coordinates are very convenient in the NAVSTAR system, they are not well suited for direct human use. That's because they don't tie-in to mean sea level the way both angular coordinates and rectangular coordinates do. As such, ECEF coordinates are basically limited to use within a computer environment — such as the NAVSTAR satellites and GPS receivers.

The readouts you obtain from the screen of your GPS receiver are converted (by the receiver) from its internal ECEF format into either latitude/longitude coordinates, UTM coordinates, or whatever other coordinate system you've chosen for your display. Also, regardless of the datum being used for the display, your receiver always stores coordinates in the WGS84 (World Geodetic System 1984) datum. This is the native NAVSTAR datum. Any time you select a different datum, the displayed coordinates are being converted from WGS84.

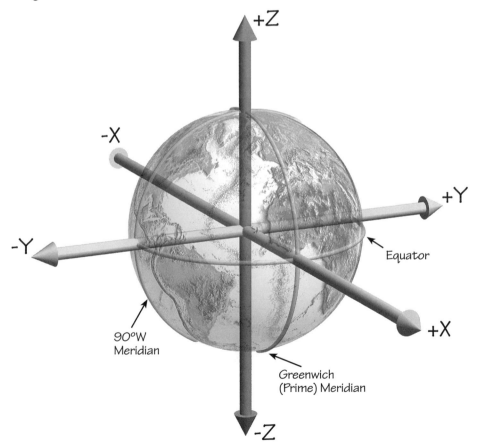

Figure 4-27: *NAVSTAR's Earth Centered, Earth Fixed XYZ Coordinate System*

Chapter 5:

Directions

With the arrival of GPS, the topics covered in this chapter — bearings, azimuths, compass headings, and the like — have all been demoted from the starring role to the supporting cast in land navigation. Gone are the days of tediously using protractors and compass cards to work with bearings and headings on maps. Directions are no longer the primary means of obtaining a "fix" of your location. Position fixes can be completely handled by the GPS system. Coordinates are now the main information you work with on a map. Directions are now a by-product of the satellite navigation system, an output provided by your GPS receiver.

Directions remain important, however, for getting from one location to another. Your GPS receiver is very good at telling you the direction to a location (such as the next waypoint), but it is not very good at telling you which way that direction is on the ground. A compass is still the primary tool for giving directions in the real world. Consequently, you still need to understand the basics of directions as they relate to compasses, maps, and GPS receivers.

To illustrate this, suppose your receiver tells you that it is 225° (exactly southwest) from your position to a certain peak. If you can see the peak, then you know the direction that is 225°. If you can't see the peak, then your receiver has no way of telling you which way to look. It can't point you at 225°. But your compass can.

Although GPS has greatly simplified navigation, there are important reasons to not abandon the "old" navigational skills that rely on compass directions and a map. You need to have non-GPS route

Directions remain important for getting from one location to another... you still need to understand the basics.

finding skills so that you will be able to navigate even when your GPS receiver doesn't. It is very important to have at least a rudimentary understanding of how to use a map and/or compass without GPS. Understanding the basics of directions is an essential foundation for navigating with only your map and/or a compass.

5.1 Which Way Is North?

This may sound like a straightforward or even trivial question, but like many things in navigation it has some underlying complexity. There are three basic "kinds" of north: true north, grid north, and magnetic north. It is important to understand the differences between them. As you'll soon see, using the wrong "kind" of north can have serious consequences when it comes to finding your destination.

5.1.1 True North

True north is the direction from any point on earth to what we commonly refer to as the "north pole." The term "pole" refers to the rotational axis of the earth. All lines of longitude point to the north (and south) poles. On a map, the lines of longitude represent

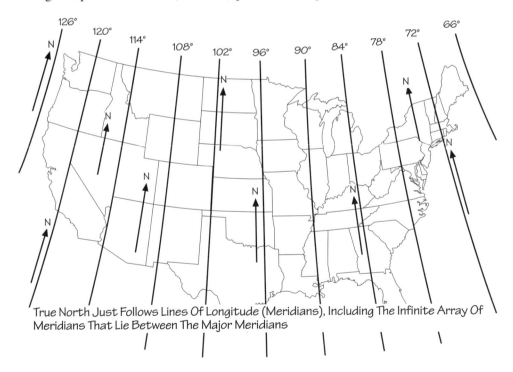

True North Just Follows Lines Of Longitude (Meridians), Including The Infinite Array Of Meridians That Lie Between The Major Meridians

Figure 5-1: *True North Is Found Along Any Meridian*

true north and south, and the lines of latitude represent true east and west. Latitude and longitude are the only "grid" lines on a map that you can count on to follow true north-south and east-west directions. Rectangular grids are all afflicted with direction distortion of some kind.

5.1.2 Grid North

Grid north refers to the declination angle (relative to true north) of a vertical grid line in a rectangular coordinate system. This grid declination (not to be confused with magnetic declination) varies over the area covered by the grid system. When grid declination is specified on a map it usually refers to the amount of declination at the center of the map.

In the case of the Universal Transverse Mercator grid system, the grid declination is zero along the central meridian of each zone (see page 120 for more on UTM). To the east of that central meridian the grid declination is east (i.e., the vertical grid lines point east of true north), and to the west of the central meridian the grid declination is west.

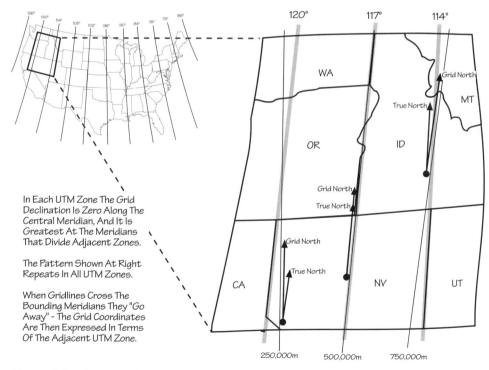

Figure 5-2: An Example Of Grid Declination

This "tilt" of the UTM grid also affects the horizontal gridlines. Except on the equator, the horizontal gridlines appear to bow down as you move outward away from the UTM zone's central meridian. This tilt is more pronounced as your distance increases from both the equator and the central meridian.

You can see UTM grid declination on most USGS topographic maps. Pick a 7.5-minute quadrangle that is at least a degree or two away from a UTM zone central meridian. Lay a straight-edge vertically across the map. Connect UTM tick marks on opposite neatlines (pick marks near the corner of the map). You should notice the "tilt" of the straightedge relative to the nearby neatline. This is the grid declination. Fortunately, grid declination is fairly modest within the continental United States. It rarely reaches as much as two degrees.

The reason behind UTM grid declination is the curvature of the earth. The "easting" part of the UTM grid is in meters, and the number of meters per degree of longitude shrinks as you move north in latitude. That means the gridlines can't possibly line up with more than one meridian. It is identical to the concept that the distance across the outer surface of an orange segment gets narrower as you move closer to its ends (the poles). Grid declination occurs with any rectangular grid system, including the "State Plane Coordinate" system and the "Townships and Sections" system found on USGS topographic maps.

5.1.3 Magnetic North

Quite simply, magnetic north is the direction your compass needle points. This is valid as long as there is no local magnetic interference. See page 53 for information about magnetic interference.

Magnetic north usually differs from true north, and the amount of difference is called magnetic declination. Magnetic declination varies quite a lot depending on your physical location on earth. Lines of constant magnetic declination are called isogonic lines. Think of them as magnetic contour lines. See Figure 5-3 and Figure 5-4.

A line of 0° magnetic declination is a special kind of isogonic line that is called the agonic line. In the U.S. it runs from approximately the northeastern tip of Minnesota to the panhandle of Florida. To the west of this agonic line the magnetic declination is east (that is, a magnetic compass needle points east of true north), and to the east of the agonic line the magnetic declination is west. At the extreme eastern and western tips of Maine and Washington State, respectively, the magnetic declination exceeds 20 degrees. In parts of Alaska magnetic declination exceeds 30 degrees.

Magnetic declination varies not only with location, it also varies at a particular location over time. In some parts of the U.S. the magnetic declination is changing at a rate of 1 degree in 10 years. For this reason, it is important to be aware of the publication date on

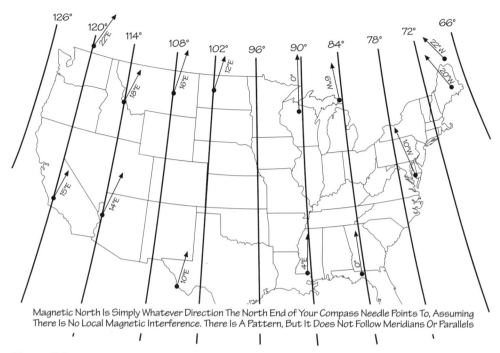

Figure 5-3: *Magnetic Declination Varies Considerably Across The United States*

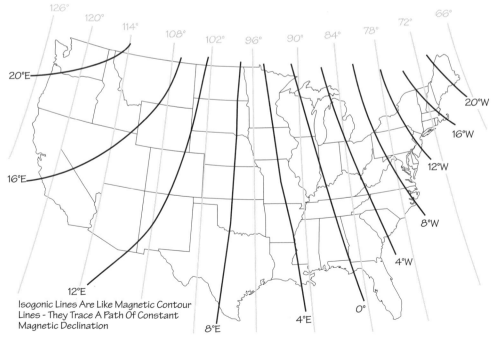

Isogonic Lines Are Like Magnetic Contour
Lines - They Trace A Path Of Constant
Magnetic Declination

Figure 5-4: *Isogonic Lines Show The Pattern Of Magnetic Declination*

any map you use to obtain magnetic declination information. Thirty or forty year old maps are fairly common, and their magnetic declination information can be quite out of date.

If you don't know the current value for magnetic declination at a particular location, you can calculate it yourself. All you need to do is find your position on a topographic map and read the true bearing from your position to an observable landmark on the map. Then take a reading with your compass (being sure that the declination adjustment is set to zero), and compare the result with the true bearing. If the magnetic direction is higher, the difference is west declination and must be subtracted from a magnetic bearing to get the true bearing. If the magnetic direction is lower, the difference is east declination and the difference must be added to a magnetic bearing to get the true bearing.

You can also use your GPS receiver to check your location's magnetic declination. You'll need a stored waypoint that you can see in the distance. Perform a "GoTo" that waypoint and note the **true direction** from your current position to the waypoint. Now use your compass to read the **magnetic direction** to the waypoint. Any difference should be due to magnetic declination. A higher compass reading (to the right on the dial) is west declination. A lower compass reading (to the left on the dial) is east declination.

5.2 Getting Your Bearings

Now that you know about the three different "norths," it's time to get your bearings. This section is about how directions work, including the terminology of directions.

The basic system used for indicating directions divides the arc formed by a full circle into 360 degrees. North is the reference direction, and it is assigned a value of 0°. The numbering system proceeds in a clockwise direction so that 90° is at a right angle pointing east, 180° is opposite 0° and points south, and 270° is at a right angle pointing west. North is both 0° and 360°.

A handy thing to remember is that no matter where you are on earth, a "higher" direction involves turning to your right. Conversely, a lower number for direction involves turning to the left. This is called a "right-handed direction system." As an example, if you're facing south (180°), then 230° is 50° to your right. Likewise, 140° is 40° to your left.

The use of 360 degrees to divide a circle is somewhat arbitrary. A French system (grads) divides a circle into 400 units, and the military uses a system (mils) that divides a circle into 6,400 units. Engineers like a system (radians) that divides a circle into a little over 6 units. No particular system is right or wrong, but they each have their own pluses and minuses.

Our 360 degree directional system originated in ancient Greece, and meshes quite nicely with astronomical observations. With 24 hours in a day, the earth rotates 15 degrees in each hour of the day (and night). Each minute of time the earth rotates one-quarter degree

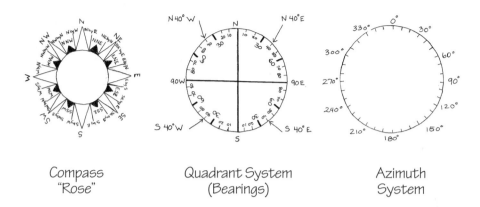

| Compass "Rose" | Quadrant System (Bearings) | Azimuth System |

Figure 5-5: *Degrees Of The Compass — Roses, Quadrants, And Azimuths*

(15 degrees per hour divided by 60 minutes per hour), which is equivalent to 15 angular minutes. Another way to think of this is that it takes four minutes of time for the position of the sun in the sky to shift by one degree. These relationships are useful when calculating local solar noon based on your angular distance from a time zone central meridian. See page 185 for more on that topic.

The two-dimension direction system is similar to the three-dimension angular system used in the latitude/longitude coordinate system, but it is a separate system and should not be confused with position coordinates. The origin of the geographic coordinate system is always the ray from the center of the earth that passes through the intersection of the equator and the prime meridian. The origin of the directional system is the ray from whatever point you specify on the surface of the earth to the North Pole. See Figure 5-6.

5.2.1 Azimuths

The horizontal direction from one point on the earth to another point on the earth is called an azimuth. The measurement unit of an azimuth is degrees. An azimuth is the angle that is formed between two rays that extend from the first point. The first ray extends to the north reference (0°), the second ray extends to the second point. The azimuth is always measured from the north reference ray to the second ray in a clockwise direction. An azimuth can range between 0° (north) and 360° (also north).

On a map you read an azimuth by placing the center of a protractor over the first point. Next, you line up the 0° line on the protractor so that it points north on the map (true, grid, or magnetic, it is your choice). You then read the angle at which the ray to the second point

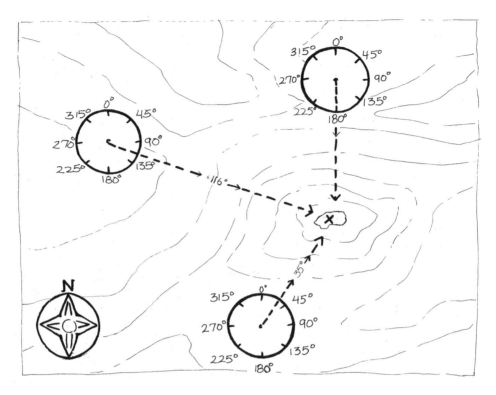

Figure 5-6: *Azimuths Originate At Any Point You Want, But 0° Must Always Line Up With North*

crosses the protractor's scale. See Figure 5-6. That angle is the azimuth from the first to the second point. On the ground you read an azimuth from the scale of a compass that has been oriented with north (see page 49).

With a GPS receiver you can obtain an azimuth by creating a "leg" from the first point to the second point (consult your GPS receiver's manual for the exact procedure). The azimuth is shown on the GPS display as the direction from the first point to the second point. Again, the choice of true, grid, or magnetic direction is up to you. Just be aware of which one you are using.

The direction from the second point to the first point is known as a "back azimuth." Once you have an azimuth, you can quickly and easily calculate a back azimuth by adding or subtracting 180° from the value of the original azimuth. Add if the original azimuth is between 0° and 180°, subtract if the original azimuth is over 180°.

5.2.2 Bearings

So enough of azimuths. What about bearings? The term "bearing" is often used as a synonym for azimuth, although strictly speaking they are not the same. When the term bearing is used to refer to an azimuth it usually causes no problem, because the context makes it clear that an azimuth is what is really meant. Azimuths can range over a full 360 degrees, but bearings are limited to quadrants, a range of 90 degrees. This limited range works by combining alphabetic characters with the numerical component of a bearing.

In essence, bearings are expressed as a variance from either north (an azimuth of 0°) or south (an azimuth of 180°). An azimuth of 30° is equivalent to a bearing of N30°E. This means "north then 30° east." An azimuth of 120° is equivalent to a bearing of S60°E. This means "south then 60° east." An azimuth of 210° is equivalent to a bearing of S30° W. This means "south then 30° west." An azimuth of 330° is equivalent to a bearing of N30°W. Bearings are mostly used by surveyors as a part of the metes and bounds system of describing property boundaries.

An important thing to recognize about bearings is they don't necessarily increase in a clockwise direction. Bearings that are within 90 degrees east of south are measured in a **counter clockwise** direction starting from south. Bearings that are within 90 degrees west

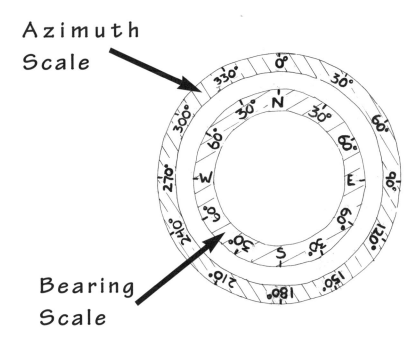

Figure 5-7: *How Bearings Compare To Azimuths*

of north are also measured in a **counter clockwise** direction. Fortunately, GPS receivers don't use bearings in the true sense, they use azimuths.

You should now be able to see why calling an azimuth a bearing is really not a problem. Although technically a "bearing" of 290° doesn't exist, it is clear from the terminology that it is referring to an azimuth.

Degrees used to indicate directions can be further divided into minutes (60 per degree) and seconds (60 per minute). This finer resolution is of no practical use to land navigators, since most handheld compasses can't resolve less than one degree anyway.

Now a final observation about direction terminology in the context of GPS receivers. Most GPS receivers use the term "bearing" to refer to the direction from one location to another. The term "bearing" is not usually used to describe the direction you are moving over the ground. That concept is usually referred to as your heading, your course over ground, or your track. There is a great deal of difference between these concepts. It is important that you understand how your specific GPS receiver refers to these concepts.

5.2.3 Great Circles & Rhumb Lines

Two special geographic concepts that relate to directions and GPS receivers are "great circles" and "rhumb lines." These concepts date back to the origin of navigation, and they help illustrate the intriguing complexity that underlies both making and using maps. Over the years these concepts have also presented long distance navigators with an intriguing tradeoff between simplicity and efficiency. Great circles and rhumb lines are two different paths to get to the same destination.

Great Circles

A great circle can be visualized as a circle formed by the intersection of the surface of the earth and a plane that passes through the exact center of the earth. All meridians (lines of longitude) are great circles. The equator is also a great circle, and it is the only parallel (line of latitude) that is also a great circle. Any plane that intersects the earth that does not pass through the exact center of the earth forms a little circle. All lines of latitude (except the equator) are little circles. Their planes pass through the polar axis at a right angle, but they don't pass through the center of the earth.

Great circles all have the same radius, diameter, and circumference — they are the measurements of the earth itself (at sea level). Little circles all have radii, diameters, and circumferences that are smaller than the earth's, hence the name "little circles."

Great circles are not limited to north-south (a meridian) or east-west (the equator) directions. Any circle around the earth that lies on a plane that passes through the exact

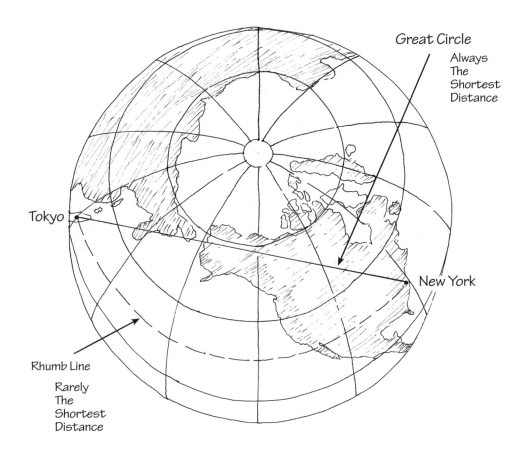

Figure 5-8: *Great Circles And Rhumb Lines — On A Globe*

center of the earth is a great circle. An important characteristic of all oblique great circles (that is, any great circle that is not either the equator or a meridian) is that the compass heading along its path will constantly change.

The significance of great circles is this: the shortest path between any two points on the surface of the earth is along the great circle they lie on. That's right, the shortest path is on a unique great circle.

The downside of great circles is that unless the two points on the surface of the earth both lie on the same meridian or the equator, the compass heading along the great circle path between them will not remain constant. Taken together, these observations about great circles mean that except for points on the same meridian or the equator, the shortest distance between any two points on earth will not be along a path of constant heading.

To illustrate this principle, stretch a piece of string between New York and Tokyo on a globe. When it's drawn tight it lies on the shortest surface path between the two cities. It's a great circle path! Now notice this — even though Tokyo is due west of New York, the path along the taught string first proceeds northwest, then gradually shifts to due west, then about Fairbanks swings southerly at an increasing rate until the heading is southwest as it arrives at Tokyo. Even though Tokyo lies due west of New York, you can't follow a single compass heading to get there in the shortest distance. That only works for travel along a north-south route or east-west travel along the equator.

Now for the punch line — GPS receivers give directions in terms of great circles! Most of the time this is of little consequence for land navigators, since the distances they're concerned with are small. The difference between constant bearing directions (rhumb lines — covered in the next section) and shortest distance directions (great circles) are insignificant over short distances. If you want to use your GPS receiver for long-distance travel, it is important to understand this distinction.

Rhumb Lines

Rhumb lines are the path of constant bearing between two points. As indicated earlier, if the points happen to both be on the same meridian or the equator, then a rhumb line is also a great circle. If the two points happen to be on the same parallel (but not the equator), then the rhumb line is on a little circle.

If the points are not on either the same parallel or meridian, then the rhumb line is neither a little circle or a great circle. It is a loxodromic curve. This is a line that spirals as it moves from point a to point b around the globe. If you follow a rhumb line that is also a loxodromic curve to its end point, you'll end up (after a very long journey) at the north or south pole.

The distinguishing feature of any rhumb line is that it can be followed by staying on a constant compass bearing. This is important to global navigators because it makes rhumb lines relatively easy to follow to a destination. The tradeoff is that the rhumb line path between two points is longer than the great circle path between the same two points (unless, of course, the rhumb line **is** a great circle).

Rhumb lines have long been of interest to navigators because great circle lines have one big weakness — they are hard to follow. Navigators have generally followed a policy of safety over efficiency. Rhumb lines provided much simpler navigation at the expense of a longer route. GPS has forever changed that situation. Modern satellite navigation using the global positioning system provides great circle bearings instantly and accurately, with no calculation required on the part of the user.

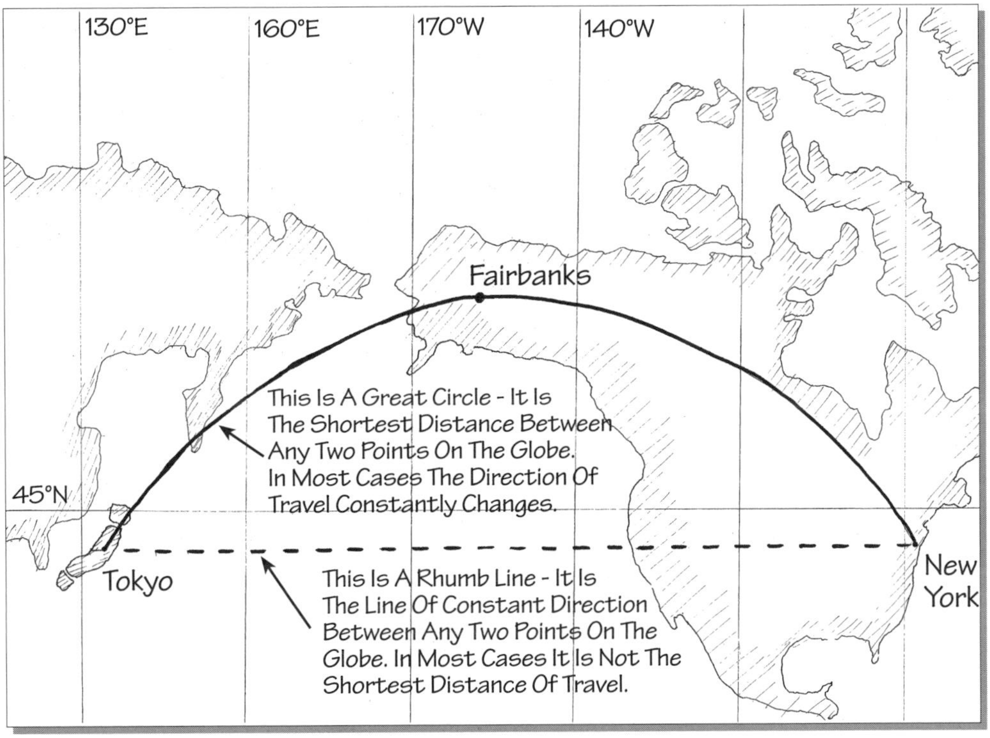
130°E
160°E
170°W
140°W
Fairbanks
This Is A Great Circle - It Is The Shortest Distance Between Any Two Points On The Globe. In Most Cases The Direction Of Travel Constantly Changes.
45°N
Tokyo
This Is A Rhumb Line - It Is The Line Of Constant Direction Between Any Two Points On The Globe. In Most Cases It Is Not The Shortest Distance Of Travel.
New York

Figure 5-9: *Great Circles And Rhumb Lines — On A Mercator Map Projection*

Chapter 6:

GPS Skills

The main objective of this book is to help you successfully use your GPS receiver in the great outdoors. Using a GPS receiver will allow you to travel the backcountry with much more confidence. With GPS you will find it's easy to know exactly where you are, and how to get where you want to go. That means you can go farther, spend less time worrying about navigating, and spend more time enjoying the reason you're outdoors in the first place. What could be sweeter!

Before starting out, a strong word of caution: *what follows is only advice*. The backcountry is a complex and unpredictable environment. *No amount of technology and planning can replace one vital element: your good judgement*. Only you can judge whether you have the necessary know how to safely handle anything nature (or technology) might throw at you.

Once you own a GPS receiver you'll probably find that it has many more uses than you initially imagined. You'll also find that the way you use your GPS receiver varies depending on your activity.

At times you may want to use your GPS receiver by itself with no map, as a backup in case you get lost. Other times you'll want to use your GPS receiver as an occasional navigational aid to supplement your use of a map, in order to confirm your position on the map. There also may be times that you'll want to combine your GPS receiver with careful advance planning, and make the GPS receiver your primary means of finding your way, with or without a map along.

The way you choose to use your GPS receiver is up to you. One thing is certain: once you own a GPS receiver, it makes no sense to ever again go into

Once you own a GPS receiver... you won't want to leave home without it.

the backcountry without having it along. In fact, even if you're just going out for a day of alpine skiing at your favorite ski area, slipping your receiver into your pack or pocket can be a lifesaving precaution. People who get lost seldom know in advance that they are about to lose their way.

The next section of this chapter looks at how to gain the most benefit from using your GPS receiver by itself, without using a map. From there the next two sections look at the advantages offered by combining maps and GPS receivers. First we look at how maps can be used with a GPS receiver in the field, followed by using maps to plan a trip in advance.

Finally, the last section of this chapter covers the rudiments of finding your way without your GPS receiver. As reliable as the global positioning system is, it is always a good idea to have a backup plan. You'll never know in advance when your receiver will become lost, broken, or just plain run out of power. Old mariners have a saying: "never rely on only one navigation system." That's how they became **old** mariners.

Unless otherwise noted, all sections in this chapter assume that you are using a compass to augment your GPS receiver. If you are not familiar with the limitations of using a GPS receiver as a compass, you should probably read the section about limitations of GPS receivers on page 43.

6.1 Using GPS Without A Map

Field Equipment: GPS Receiver
Spare Batteries
Compass
Altimeter (optional)

While maps clearly enhance the use of GPS for land navigation, the reality is that much backcountry recreation is done without maps. Just because GPS came along doesn't mean that outdoor enthusiasts are suddenly going to carry maps everywhere they go. But GPS receivers are so compact, versatile, and beneficial that one should go with you even if maps don't.

It doesn't take much effort to use your GPS receiver by itself. In fact, it only requires that you have the GPS receiver along, understand its basic operation, and follow a few simple procedures as you make your way. You don't need to worry about coordinates or datums to use a GPS receiver by itself, without a map.

Using a GPS receiver without a map is quite simple, and it can also be very valuable. Having a GPS receiver with you as a safety backup can make the difference between wandering aimlessly and getting home. If conditions are severe, in a winter storm for example, a GPS receiver can be the difference between life and death.

Sometimes even when you have a map with you it is only a crude trail guide with no geographic coordinates or grids identified. With GPS, you can add a new level of confidence when you travel without a map or with a crude map. It's as easy as remembering to put your GPS receiver in your pocket or pack and storing a few waypoints.

6.1.1 The Basic Process

Using a GPS receiver without a map involves two basic operations:

[1] Storing position fixes as waypoints in your receiver's memory, and

[2] Obtaining the distance and direction to those locations.

Once you get comfortable with using your GPS receiver (and its novelty wears off) you may find that you do much more of the first operation and relatively little of the second operation. That's because in the final analysis, GPS is a backup system that you'll mostly use when you don't know where you are. Even if you find that all you end up doing is storing waypoints, that's OK. You must store waypoints for a GPS receiver to be of any use by itself. Those stored waypoints are what make your receiver valuable when you find that you need it. See pages 28-31 if you need information about how to store waypoints

The cardinal rule when storing position fixes is *make sure your receiver is not in 2D mode*. Storing a position fix is generally a fairly foolproof way to obtain a waypoint. You don't need to worry about either the datum or coordinate system settings when you store a position fix, but you must be sure that your receiver is operating in 3D mode. This means that you must have a lock on at least four satellites. For backcountry GPS users, 2D mode is nothing but trouble waiting to happen. See page 41 for more information on this important topic.

6.1.2 Traveling On A Trail

Whenever you embark at a trailhead take a few minutes before you head out to obtain a position fix. Store the trailhead position fix as a waypoint, being sure to label it so that later you will know what that point represents. Even if you don't plan to actively navigate with your GPS receiver, *store the trailhead position fix as a waypoint*. That way, if you later become disoriented you will be able to use that stored waypoint to find your way back to your starting point.

During your travel on a trail, whether it is a loop or an out and back journey, occasionally store a waypoint so that you can backtrack if necessary. Pick a junction, saddle, ridge, lake, or any distinctive feature for these intermediate waypoints. It is probably a good idea to log a waypoint at least every 2-3 miles if you're on foot, or at least every hour or so if you're on horseback or in a vehicle of some kind.

It is also a good idea to make a note (either in the GPS receiver or on a notepad) about your direction of travel if the waypoint involves a junction. It's important to use a consistent point of reference when indicating direction of travel. Pick a method that works for you, then stick with it. Remember, it is best to use your compass to obtain these direction of travel readings.

There are several different ways to note your direction of travel at a junction. One way is to use compass points such as N (for a heading of 0°), NW (for a heading of 315°), SSE (for a heading of 157.5°), etc. This gives you 16 possible directions by using only 3 characters.

If you prefer to use numbers, as in bearings, that works too. Bearings have an advantage in that they can be read directly from the dial of your compass. It is a good idea to fill-in leading zeros (005°, 020°, etc.) to avoid errors and/or confusion. See page *xiv* for a discussion of direction terminology.

Another option is to use bearings rounded to the nearest 10 degrees. This gives 36 possible directions with just two digits. Again, leading zeros help avoid confusion and errors. North would be 00, twenty degrees would be 02, east would be 09, south would be 18, etc. Add the degree symbol (°) if it helps keep the bearings in context.

Note your direction of travel at a junction as you move in and out of the junction. If they're the same, noting one direction will suffice. For example, a notation of "N;NW" means that you entered the junction heading north, then you made a left turn on the trail to a heading of northwest. A notation of "NW" means that you proceeded straight through the junction on a heading of northwest.

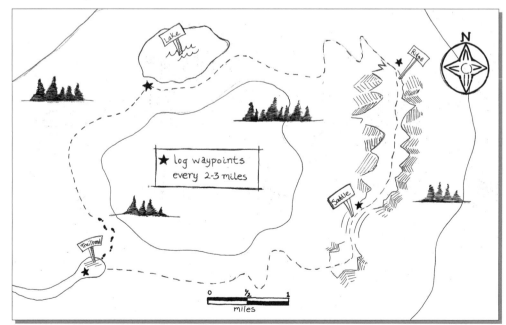

Figure 6-1: *Selecting Locations To Store As Waypoints*

When you want to backtrack, simply reverse the directions on your way back. If you use numeric notation, just add 18 (or 180) if the direction is from 0° to 180°, or subtract 18 (or 180) if the direction is from 180° to 360°. If you use compass points it is just as easy. Just replace N's with S's, S's with N's, E's with W's, and W's with E's. For example, the back-bearing for N is S. The back-bearing for SW is NE. The back-bearing for ESE is WNW. Also reverse the order of two-part junctions where you changed directions. Our earlier example of "N;NW" becomes "SE;S" when backtracking.

As you mark waypoints along a trail be careful to keep track of their sequence. It is easy to lose track of the location a particular coordinate represents. It can also be confusing to try and remember which number you started with if you store waypoints under your receiver's default numbering scheme, and you didn't start this trip at #1. Many receivers will store the time a waypoint was logged along with the coordinates. This feature can be used to "reconstruct" the sequence of waypoints. A good habit is to delete or rename old waypoints (after you've concluded a trip) so that auto-numbered waypoints on a future trip will clearly apply only to that trip.

Once you're ready to reverse your course simply select the last waypoint you saved and tell your receiver to "GoTo" that location. As you pass each waypoint, pick the next one and "GoTo" all over again. Continue this process until you've reached your starting point.

The foregoing procedure involves storing individual waypoints in sequence and manually charting a reverse course. This is a simple, straight forward, and relatively foolproof method. You can do it with any GPS receiver.

A way to keep track of a series of waypoints is through the use of a route. If your receiver has this capability (most do), you can group the trailhead and intermediate waypoints into a route as you progress through your journey. This "on the fly" route defining automatically keeps track of the sequence of your waypoints. You can also wait until you are ready to backtrack, then build the route "home" using the waypoints you stored on the way out.

Another handy feature your receiver may have is the ability to reverse a route. This simply tells the GPS receiver to backtrack, and automatically selects the waypoints in reverse order as you proceed past them.

6.1.3 Practice Makes Perfect

Before using your GPS receiver on a real backcountry excursion you should practice in familiar territory. This section describes a way to practice using your GPS receiver with nothing more than waypoints that are obtained from satellite fixes. Later in this chapter (see page 175) you'll find a description of a GPS game that is similar to orienteering. It exercises many more of the skills you need to develop before relying on GPS in the real world. But first things first: Walk before you run.

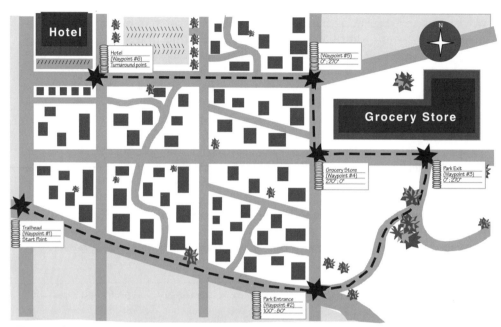

Figure 6-2: *Practice Storing Position Fixes And Navigating In Your Neighborhood*

Your initial practice excursions can be done anywhere, even in your neighborhood — unless you happen to live among skyscrapers where satellite signals are likely to be blocked. Consult your receiver's operating manual for the exact methods used to define waypoints and descriptive memo fields. Start out doing practice excursions using only waypoints. In other words, *don't use your receiver's route function until you've mastered "manual" use of waypoints.*

Go on a long walk, marking waypoints at appropriate intervals. For practice purposes every 10 to 15 minutes is about right. To accurately simulate a real excursion turn the receiver off between waypoints to conserve battery power. Note your direction of travel at each waypoint. Record both the entering and exiting directions for the waypoints where you change directions. Figure 6-2 illustrates this process.

When you're ready to reverse course, use your GPS receiver to guide you from waypoint to waypoint. Even though you know the way, follow the GPS receiver. Remember, use the GPS receiver to tell you the bearing and distance to the next waypoint, but use your compass to actually guide you there. At walking speeds the direction of travel displayed by a GPS receiver is usually not very reliable.

The idea here is to establish your capability to navigate strictly by following your receiver's direction to the waypoints you stored (and your directional notes). Think of it as IFR — instrument flying rules. Until you can successfully find your way "home" by using GPS in familiar territory, you shouldn't count on it in the backcountry.

This practice exercise will serve a number of useful purposes. You'll learn how to store position fixes as waypoints, you'll get familiar with using a compass and noting directions, and you'll learn how to select stored waypoints as "GoTo" destinations. You'll also see first hand the effects of Selective Availability (SA). By doing this practice exercise you'll learn how to cope with the error it introduces. See page 10 for info on how SA works.

The impact of Selective Availability on backcountry GPS users is not crippling, but it is also not trivial. As long as you have a lock on at least four satellites with good geometry (not always an easy feat in the backcountry) you can count on a 95% probability that the position fix displayed on your screen is within 100 meters of the place where you are standing. But there is more...

The effect of Selective Availability is compounded when you store a position fix as a waypoint and then later use GPS to return to that stored waypoint. There is a 95% probability that the stored location is within 100 meters of the actual location you were at when you originally stored the position fix. Later, when you return, there is also a 95% probability that you are within 100 meters of the stored location when your current position fix says you're there. Taken together, that means you have a 99.75% probability of being within 200 meters of the actual location you were at when you stored the position fix the first time.

The practical meaning of all this is you must use a healthy dose of judgement and awareness of your surroundings when using GPS. Think in terms of a 200 meter radius "circle of error" when returning to a waypoint that you stored using a position fix. Your receiver will probably get you much closer than this, but you can't be sure.

By practicing GPS navigation in a familiar setting it becomes a little easier to see what you are dealing with as a result of SA. Figure 6-3 shows a typical street grid that has 16 blocks to the mile. Each block is about 100 meters long. When you stand in the middle of an intersection and record a position fix, the coordinates logged in memory have a 95% probability of being within 100 meters of the intersection you're standing in. That means those coordinates *could* be closer to any one of the surrounding eight intersections.

When you later decide to return to the intersection, the receiver "aims" for the coordinates that you stored, not the true coordinates of the intersection you were standing in. Since Selective Availability is still on, there's another 100 meters of random error introduced at this point. That means your receiver could be pointing to the actual intersection you stood in, or to any of the 20 surrounding intersections.

To illustrate this, Figure 6-3 shows a circle around the original intersection that has a radius of 2 blocks. There are 8 other intersections that lie within the circle, and 12 more that are on or near the edge. That's a total of **20** wrong intersections that may be picked as the correct intersection by the GPS receiver. If you didn't record the names of the intersecting streets (or some other distinctive feature) when you stored the original position fix, you have no way of sorting this puzzle out.

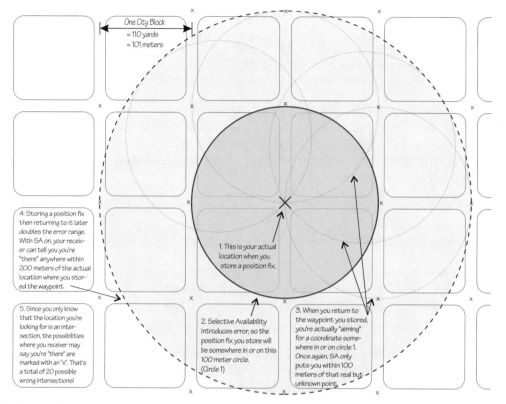

One City Block
= 110 yards
= 101 meters

4. Storing a position fix then returning to it later doubles the error range. With SA on, your receiver can tell you you're "there" anywhere within 200 meters of the actual location where you stored the waypoint.

5. Since you only know that the location you're looking for is an intersection, the possibilities where your receiver may say you're "there" are marked with an "x". That's a total of 20 possible wrong intersections!

1. This is your actual location when you store a position fix.

2. Selective Availability introduces error, so the position fix you store will be somewhere in or on this 100 meter circle. (Circle 1)

3. When you return to the waypoint you stored, you're actually "aiming" for a coordinate somewhere in or on circle 1. Once again, SA only puts you within 100 meters of that real but unknown point.

Figure 6-3: *Selective Availability Does Impact GPS Accuracy*

Fortunately, when you're in the backcountry you don't usually have to deal with anything like a uniform street grid. The challenge isn't picking which one of twenty possible trail junctions you should take, it is finding the trail period. While that can be difficult, at 200 meters GPS can still get you pretty darn close. Just don't count on GPS to pick between two trail junctions that are 100 meters apart.

Once you've mastered following a GPS course in familiar territory you've probably established the basic skills needed to operate your GPS receiver. You should be ready to hone those skills by using your GPS receiver during an actual backcountry journey. But make it an easy one! If you rely on your receiver before you're completely comfortable with its operation you may find yourself applying the lessons of the next section.

6.1.4 If You Do Get Lost

If you suddenly find yourself unsure of your course, it means that the time of reckoning has arrived — you're lost! It is time to put you and your GPS receiver to the real test. The basic thing you need to do in this situation is find your way to a known waypoint. It may

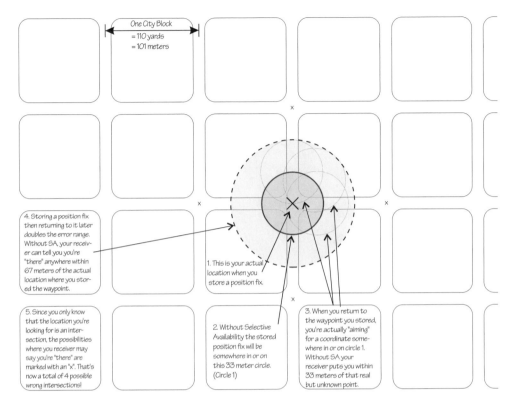

One City Block
= 110 yards
= 101 meters

4. Storing a position fix then returning to it later doubles the error range. Without SA, your receiver can tell you you're "there" anywhere within 67 meters of the actual location where you stored the waypoint.

1. This is your actual location when you store a position fix.

5. Since you only know that the location you're looking for is an intersection, the possibilities where you receiver may say you're "there" are marked with an "x". That's now a total of 4 possible wrong intersections!

2. Without Selective Availability the stored position fix will be somewhere in or on this 33 meter circle. (Circle 1)

3. When you return to the waypoint you stored, you're actually "aiming" for a coordinate somewhere in or on circle 1. Without SA your receiver puts you within 33 meters of that real but unknown point.

Figure 6-4: *The Range Of Error Is Much Smaller Without Selective Availability*

be a simple matter of figuring out which way to proceed on a trail. It may be more complicated if you've lost the trail itself.

Begin by obtaining a position fix at your current location. You may need to find a clearing, wait for a change in satellite positions, or move to higher ground. Next, find the closest waypoints to your current position. Some GPS receivers have the ability to provide a graphic display of waypoints in your vicinity. Some have the ability to show a list of the closest waypoints.

If your GPS receiver doesn't have a closest waypoint capability, cycle through each of the waypoints you marked along your course of travel to find the closest ones. If you've been using sequential numbers in your naming scheme, it should be easy. You may need to execute a "GoTo" command to determine the bearing and distance to each waypoint. Once you've located the nearest waypoints, make a note of their distance and direction from your current position.

Now for the tricky part: Since you're "lost" it is not safe to assume that the waypoint you're trying to locate is actually on the same trail you are currently on, nor is it safe to

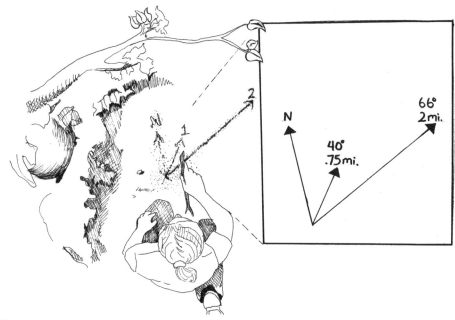

Figure 6-5: *Lost Without A Map? — Draw Your Own*

assume that your best route "home" is through the last waypoint you recorded. While those facts are usually the case, sometimes they're not. It is possible that somewhere along the way you inadvertently took a wrong fork or turn and you are now on a completely different trail. If your course has involved a large loop, backtracking may not be the most economical way to get to your destination — the starting point. You did store a waypoint at your starting point — didn't you?

It is even possible that you've not only lost the correct trail, you may have lost the trail altogether. This can be a problem during winter travel on snow, or in little traveled areas that have game trails that are better than the human trails. In any case, you need to find your way back to one of your stored waypoints.

If your GPS receiver has a graphic display you should be able to see the nearest waypoints on the screen. If it doesn't have a graphic display, obtain the distance and direction to the closest three or four waypoints and the trailhead. To help you visualize the route you're seeking, draw an ad hoc "map" that shows your current location and each nearby waypoint.

If necessary use the ground or snow to draw this map. Be very careful to properly orient the map you draw, especially if it is on the ground. To do this mark a spot for your location, then draw a ray from your location that actually points to either true or magnetic north. Be consistent about using either true or magnetic north when going between the GPS receiver, compass, and your drawn map. If your compass has declination adjustment capability it may be easiest to work with true north. If not, you can set your GPS receiver to show magnetic bearings. Then it will be consistent with the magnetic directions shown by your compass. Whichever method you choose to use, just be consistent.

When you draw your ad hoc map, mark the waypoints using direction and distance information from your GPS receiver. Use rays that originate at your position and point in the appropriate direction (relative to the ray that represents north).

Set the "scale" for the map you're drawing by spacing the relative distance to each of the waypoints. For example, if the closest waypoint is ¾ mile away and the next closest waypoint is 2 miles away, space the mark for the second waypoint a little less than three times (2 divided by .75 equals 2.67) farther out its ray. Place the farthest waypoint on the "map" first so that you will not run out of space when you place subsequent marks.

If necessary to get a good idea of the layout of the trail, add marks for additional waypoints. Use as many marks as you need to get a clear sense of where your route is relative to the landscape around you.

Be especially careful when setting the angle of each ray on your ad hoc map. Try to be as accurate as possible. Align your compass card (the part with the degree scale — you did bring your compass, didn't you?) on the mark representing your current location and use it as a protractor to set the waypoint rays. If you miss an angle by 10 degrees, the closest you'll get to a waypoint that is 2 miles away will be 1,800 feet, or over 1/3 of a mile. A 10 degree error on a waypoint 4 miles away will yield a distance error of 3,700 feet, or over 2/3 of a mile. If your angle is off by 20 degrees for a waypoint 4 miles away, the closest you'll get to the actual location is 7,200 feet, or over 1 1/3 miles. You can see why it is important to strive for accuracy in setting these angles.

Once you've drawn your ad hoc map on paper, the ground, or snow, use it to visualize the location of the route and waypoints you want to reach. Compare the map layout with what you know of the actual terrain around you. Your goal is to find the best path back to your point of origin. This is where a strong dose of judgement comes into play.

If you're still on a trail consider whether it may be a different trail than the one you need to be on. It can be difficult to tell if a trail will lead you to your objective. Remember that there are few straight lines in nature. A trail that seems to go the wrong way may actually be circumnavigating an obstacle such as a ravine or a mountain.

If there's no trail, or the terrain permits, maybe a cross-country course of travel in the direction of your route makes the most sense. Just be careful to consider the impact of known or potential obstacles, and try to take a course that minimizes the difficulty of getting back to your original route. You'll need to weigh the tradeoff between distance on a trail versus overland travel where you may encounter dense brush, streams, steep slopes, avalanches, and other hazards.

Another very important consideration applies any time you make a decision to go off-trail. If you stay lost, for whatever reason, it will probably be easier for searchers to find you on a trail as compared with an off-trail location. Once you leave a trail there are no guarantees you'll be able to find your way back to a trail.

6.1.5 Cross-Country Land Navigation

Intentionally traveling off-trail in the backcountry without a map is inherently risky business. Although a properly utilized GPS receiver can make off-trail travel considerably safer, you should always try to carry a map of the area. If you do choose to navigate off-trail without a map, here's some advice on how to get the most from your GPS receiver.

First, follow the instructions for marking waypoints when traveling on a trail, and treat every waypoint as a junction. That means note your direction of travel at all waypoints you store. Be very aware of distinct features either in your surroundings or on your course, and make a note of them. Store a waypoint for any major change in course direction, whether horizontal or vertical. That means store a waypoint wherever you begin either climbing or descending.

Second, be extra careful when making notes about course changes at waypoints you store — your direction of travel going into and exiting the waypoint. Also make a note about any elevation related course change — where you begin climbing or descending. These steps are especially important if you plan to backtrack, but you should follow them regardless — just in case you do get lost.

Finally, if you aren't on a course to any particular destination (say you're hunting), it still makes good sense to periodically mark a waypoint — just in case you get lost. That way you won't be faced with as much unknown terrain between you and your starting point or destination. If you do become lost, follow the instructions in the previous section for some ideas on what to do.

6.1.6 GPS As A Safety Backup

Your GPS receiver can also be useful when you're in familiar territory, and even when you're not on a backcountry outing. Maybe you're going to a familiar hiking area, or you're spending the day alpine skiing at your favorite ski area. It still makes sense to carry your GPS receiver.

When you go out for the day, store your starting position (say, at the lodge or where you parked your car) so that you will be able to return to that point if something unexpected happens (a white-out, a wrong turn through the trees, etc.) and you end up lost. You'd be surprised how easy it is to become lost in "familiar" territory or doing "safe" activities!

If you regularly ski at one (or several) ski areas, it probably makes sense to keep the coordinates for those locations stored as permanent waypoints. That way you don't need to reacquire a satellite fix each time you embark on a day of skiing. It also is wise to keep a written log of such waypoints close to your GPS receiver in case you lose (or accidentally erase) the stored coordinates. And don't forget to carry a spare set of batteries.

6.2 Navigating With GPS And A Map

Field Equipment: GPS Receiver
Spare Batteries
Compass
Map
Small Protractor (optional)
Roamer (optional)
Latitude/Longitude Scale (optional)
Altimeter (optional)

Navigating with both a map and a GPS receiver greatly enhances the value of each of these tools. This is a good example of synergy in action. The whole (a map and a GPS receiver together) is worth more than the sum of the parts (a map alone or a GPS receiver alone). If you can handle taking a map along, it is definitely the best way to go.

This section assumes that you have not stored waypoints or routes in your GPS receiver in advance of your trip (that's covered in the next section on advance planning). Here you rely primarily on your map to locate some desired destination(s). You'll just use your GPS receiver to keep track of your progress and confirm your location on the map.

6.2.1 The Basic Process

Using a GPS receiver with a map in the field involves two additional skills:

[1] **Translating GPS position coordinates (for either your current position or a stored waypoint) from the receiver to a physical location on the map, and**

[2] **Translating physical locations on the map (your destination, a point along the way, some other point of interest) into coordinates that can be used in the GPS receiver.**

In this section we'll look at the process of obtaining coordinates from the GPS receiver and figuring out where they are on the map. We'll look at going the other way (reading coordinates on a map and entering them into the GPS receiver) in the next section on planning with GPS and maps.

For coordinate values to properly line-up between your GPS receiver and your map, the map's datum must be correctly specified in the receiver's setup parameters. ***Using the correct datum setting is critical whenever you use GPS with a map***. See page 78 for a discussion of datums, and page 44 for a discussion of setup parameters.

Before you head out to the backcountry with a map and your GPS receiver, you should be familiar with the advice contained in the previous section on using a GPS receiver by itself, without a map. You should plan to store waypoints for the trailhead and other key points along your journey. That way you will be able to retrace your route using GPS position fixes if necessary. This section simply adds the step of using GPS position fixes to identify where you are on the map.

You can use your GPS receiver to locate your position on a map in several different ways. The most straightforward method is to directly apply the numeric coordinates using the grid system on your map. This is usually done with a roamer, a divider, or a latitude/longitude ruler. This is illustrated in Figure 6-6. Also, Chapter 2, page 59 provides a detailed explanation of various ways to translate numeric coordinate values to their corresponding physical location on the map. It helps to have a properly prepared map (see Chapter 3, page 99).

You can also locate your position on a map using the distance and direction features available in your GPS receiver. You do this by working from a reference point on the map.

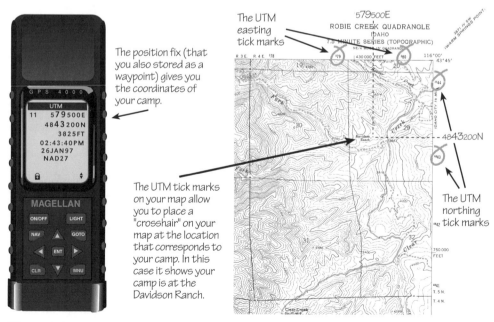

Figure 6-6: Waypoints - In Your Receiver And On Your Map

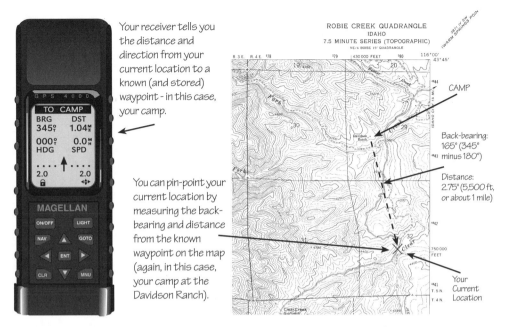

Your receiver tells you the distance and direction from your current location to a known (and stored) waypoint - in this case, your camp.

ROBIE CREEK QUADRANGLE
IDAHO
7.5 MINUTE SERIES (TOPOGRAPHIC)
NE/4 BOISE 15' QUADRANGLE

CAMP

Back-bearing:
165° (345° minus 180°)

Distance:
2.75" (5,500 ft, or about 1 mile)

You can pin-point your current location by measuring the back-bearing and distance from the known waypoint on the map (again, in this case, your camp at the Davidson Ranch).

Your Current Location

Figure 6-7: Finding Your Location On A Map — Without Using Coordinates

In this context a "reference point" means a location you can pinpoint on the map and whose coordinates are (or can be) stored in the receiver as a waypoint.

The reference point can be virtually anything, from the trailhead to a nearby peak whose coordinates you previously stored from a position fix. The 2.5-minute hash marks on the edge or interior of a 7.5-minute topographic map are especially handy, since you can easily find them on the map and their coordinates are **very** accurate. The key is to use a point whose coordinates you know **and** that you can identify on the map.

Locating your position on the map using the reference point requires that you draw a back-bearing line from that point. To obtain the back-bearing just enter the coordinates for the reference point (if they're not already stored as a waypoint) then perform a "GoTo" from your current location. Note the distance and direction, then add or subtract 180° from the direction (depending on whether it is under or over 180°). The result is the back-bearing — the direction from the reference point to you!

Now use a protractor (or use your compass as a protractor) and draw a line from the reference point in the direction of the back-bearing. You are somewhere on that line! There are several ways to pinpoint your location on that line.

One method is to use the distance from the reference point. Convert the actual distance to map distance and measure that distance from the reference point on the line you just drew. That's where you are.

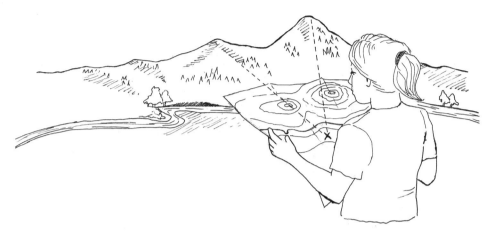

Figure 6-8: *Orient Your Map (Using Your Surroundings)*

If you're traveling on a trail and the line from the reference point is roughly perpendicular to the trail, you don't need to measure the distance from the reference point (although doing so is a good idea). The point where the back-bearing ***intersects*** the trail is your location. Just be aware that if the line from the reference point is roughly parallel to the trail (such as a line from the trailhead) the intersection method won't work.

Another method involves triangulation (just like using a compass). You need a second reference point that you can use for a second back-bearing. When using the triangulation method two important factors impact accuracy. One is the angle formed by the intersection of two lines. The closer it is to 90° the more accurate the location of the intersection. Also, the closer each reference point is to the intersection of the lines, the more accurate the location of the intersection. Again, the 2.5-minute hash marks on USGS 7.5-minute topographic maps are very convenient for this method of locating your position.

Now that you've pinpointed your position on your map, there's another very important skill that you need in order to use that information successfully. You need to orient your map. The advent of GPS does not eliminate this fundamental navigation skill.

Map orienting involves aligning the directions on your map with the actual directions on the ground. The north side of the map (usually the top) should always be aligned with real-world north whenever you are reading the map. That way, when you face north, the north side of the map is away from you. When you face south, the south side of the map is away from you. When you face east, the east side of the map is away from you; and so on.

There are two basic ways to orient your map. One is to visually align it with the world around you. For visual orientation you must be able to see enough distinctive landmarks to

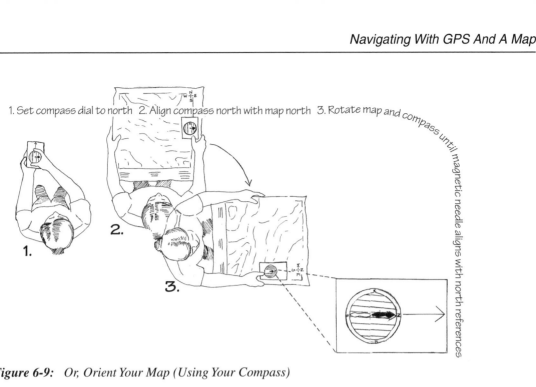

1. Set compass dial to north 2. Align compass north with map north 3. Rotate map and compass until magnetic needle aligns with north references

1.

2.

3.

Figure 6-9: *Or, Orient Your Map (Using Your Compass)*

position your map without first knowing directions. In fact, this method of orienting a map yields direction (although it is crude) as an output. When you've visually oriented your map, the north side of the map faces real-world north and the direction on the map that's away from you is the direction you're actually facing.

The other way to orient your map involves using your compass. If you can't see a sufficient number of distinctive landmarks, or you are unsure about them, you can use the invisible magnetic field of the earth to help you orient the map. Place your compass on the map and hold it so that the compass north reference is aligned with north on the map. Now rotate the map and compass together so that the magnetic needle on the compass points to north on both the map and the compass north reference. A baseplate compass is ideal for this purpose.

Don't forget to allow for magnetic declination. East declination is added to the compass readout, west declination is subtracted from the compass readout. If the declination is 20° east, the map is oriented when the north end of the compass needle points to 20° on the map. If the declination is 15° west, the map is oriented when the compass needle points to 345° on the map (360° minus 15°). If you're visually orienting the map you don't need to worry about magnetic declination.

By properly orienting your map you will ensure that it is "synchronized" with the world around you. This allows you to more easily visualize the relationship between the features on the map and those same features in the physical world it describes.

6.2.2 A Journey To Trout Heaven Lake

Now, let's take a hypothetical hike to a place you've never been to see how your map and GPS receiver complement one another.

Assume that we're on our way to remote Trout Heaven Lake. This lake contains the biggest trout ever known to man (or so we've been told). The lake is four miles from the trailhead. The first two miles are north on forest trail #79, then east (right) for two more miles on forest trail #136.

You've checked the datum setting in your receiver to make sure it is the same as the datum specified on the map. You've also stored our position fix at the trailhead and named it "TRHEAD." Finally, we set out on our hike. We reach a trail junction 30 minutes later, but there's no sign that indicates if this is trail #136. It doesn't seem like we've covered two miles, but a trail does go off to the right. Our map doesn't show any other intersecting trail before trail #136.

At this point a GPS position fix tells us we're at latitude 44°12'35"N by longitude 115°05'26"W. That's nice to know, but neither of us have our latitude/longitude ruler along. We can't place these coordinates on the map with enough precision to be sure if this is the junction or not. We could switch the receiver to display UTM coordinates, but the junction is in the middle of the map and we haven't drawn a UTM grid on it. Obtaining precise measurements with a compass ruler would be tedious at best. However, we can lay your compass ruler on the map and note that from the trailhead to the junction is four inches.

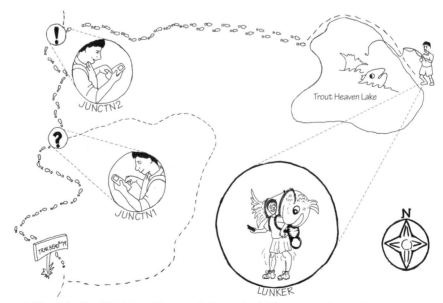

Figure 6-10: *The Trail To Trout Heaven Lake — And Waypoints Along The Way*

Looking at the map scale, we note that one inch on the map equals 2,000 feet on the ground. That makes sense since this is a USGS 7.5-minute topographic map. So, four inches is 8,000 feet, or a little over 1½ miles. The trail meanders a little, so it seems plausible that 2 miles on the trail is equivalent to a little over 1½ miles of straight-line distance.

Now we can tell your GPS receiver to "GoTo" the waypoint you initially logged at the trailhead. We find that it is 1 mile from our present position to the trailhead. Since the map shows it is a little over 1.5 miles from the trailhead to the junction, we'll store our current position as "JNCTN1" then proceed on through the junction without turning.

We find another junction about a half of a mile further on the original trail. You obtain a position fix and find that this location is 1.52 miles from the trailhead. There's no sign indicating the name or number of this intersecting trail, but it seems to be the right distance from the trailhead. After storing this position as "JNCTN2" we turn right and proceed. An hour later you're struggling to land the biggest trout either of us has ever laid eyes on.

Later, before leaving the lake, you obtain a position fix and store it in a waypoint called "LUNKER." We definitely want to find this spot again! After we return home you call the local Forest Service district office and ask about the unmarked trail. You're told that the first junction is a new trail that has been added since the map you're using was published, and it circles back to the trailhead!

6.2.3 Wandering About - Off Trail With GPS

Just because you have a GPS receiver and a map doesn't necessarily mean you have a specific route (or even a trail) to travel. Whether you're hunting for elk or a spectacular photograph, your preferred method of operation may be to explore the terrain as you go, without the benefit or security of a trail.

Using a GPS receiver in this situation is very similar to traveling on a trail, but you need to be more alert and cautious. As always, be sure to store a waypoint at the "trailhead," which is presumably where you left your car or truck. And make sure that the datum setting that you select in your GPS receiver matches the datum for the map you're using.

When you're traveling cross-country it's a good idea to store a waypoint periodically while you are moving, say every 30 to 60 minutes. Some receivers have a feature that logs the date and time a waypoint is stored. This can be very helpful if you later need to put the position fixes in sequence. Adding waypoints to a route or using a sequential numbering scheme can give a similar result.

It may be worthwhile to get in the habit of keeping a notebook handy and recording relevant information about waypoints that you log — things such as your direction of travel as you enter and exit the waypoint, and a few words that describe the surroundings.

Also, as a precaution, look back where you came from as you store waypoints. That way you will have a better chance of recognizing the way back. This kind of attention to detail takes very little effort, yet can be very helpful if your GPS receiver quits working and you need to use a backup navigation system.

It also pays to locate your position on your map when you store a position fix. You may even want to mark and label the waypoints on your map. This can take the place of logging data in a notebook. It is also important that you know how to use both a compass and an altimeter to locate yourself in case you can't get a position fix with your GPS receiver.

As long as you know where you are on your map, you should be fine. It is important to visually "cross-check" the location your GPS receiver is providing with the surroundings indicated on your map. They should be consistent, and if they're not, figure out why. You might be making mistakes when translating the coordinates from your receiver to your map. Or maybe your receiver is lying to you — see 2D Mode on page 41.

When you want to return to your starting point (or your destination, if it's different) tell your receiver to "GoTo" that waypoint. If your plan is to backtrack, you may not want to go directly to the waypoint that is your ultimate destination. Instead, you may want to "GoTo" the waypoints you stored, but in the reverse order.

6.3 Advance Planning & Preparation

Field Equipment:	GPS Receiver
	Spare Batteries
	Compass
	Map (optional)
	Small Protractor (optional)
	Roamer (optional)
	Latitude/Longitude Scale (optional)
	Altimeter (optional)

Using a map to plan your use of GPS in advance takes full advantage of all the tools available to you. Before you even arrive at the trailhead, you have planned your route and stored relevant coordinates in your receiver. Your map is along as a reference tool, but you don't really need it to get where you're going. You have all the necessary route finding information stored in your GPS receiver's memory!

Nonetheless, your map is a valuable guide to your surroundings, and its importance as a backup tool can't be overstated. You should always carry a map in the backcountry (even if you don't plan to use it) because there's a risk of getting lost should your GPS receiver fail.

6.3.1 Preparing To Use GPS On A Trip

Once you know where you want to go, there are several basic steps to prepare for your backcountry journey. These steps involve obtaining and preparing the maps that you will use in the course of the trip.

For the backcountry part of your trip you will probably want to use the USGS 7.5-minute topographic map series. If your map(s) don't already have UTM gridlines, you may want to add them so that it will be possible to use a roamer (see page 63). If you prefer working with latitude and longitude, you may want to extend the neatline graticules to the edge of the map sheet and add horizontal and vertical graticules at the 2.5 minute tick marks (see page 100). Extending and adding graticules makes it possible to use a latitude/longitude ruler.

You also may want to laminate the map either before or after marking on it. If you don't laminate it, use a plastic map holder (a gallon size zip-lock bag works nicely) to protect it in the field. See page 61 for a description of the best way to fold a map so that it will fit in the holder and be easy to use.

If you will be using a map that doesn't have a coordinate system of any kind (but it has a reasonable amount of geographic "fidelity") you may want to add a coordinate system yourself. You can follow the instructions on page 100 to accomplish this painstaking feat.

An important and not always trivial consideration in planning a trip is getting to the trailhead. Don't forget that a GPS receiver can be a very useful tool when navigating in a vehicle through unfamiliar terrain (with a dedicated navigator, of course). If you've never been to the trailhead for your backcountry trip don't hesitate to use your GPS receiver to get you there.

Maps that are useful for showing access roads include 1:100,000 scale topo maps, Forest Service and BLM maps, Delorme Atlases, or any number of other medium scale maps that may be available for the area you're interested in reaching. You can even use 7.5-minute topo maps for the trip to the trailhead, but they usually have too large a scale (and hence cover too small an area) to be convenient for the driving part of a trip.

When you set up checkpoints for the drive to the trailhead think in terms of the entire route after it leaves the regular highway system. Backcountry roads are rarely marked with street signs. Obtain and store the coordinates for any junction that requires a turn.

6.3.2 Picking A Route

Once you have gathered and prepared the maps you need to plan your trip, you can select the route you intend to travel. This part of the planning process has an infinite number of possibilities. Ultimately, your choice of routes depends on the purpose of your trip.

If you have a specific destination in mind there may be an obvious "best" way to get there. On the other hand, if your goal is simply to see an area, you may just want to wander wherever your fancy takes you. You can select your destinations as you plan, picking the places that have the greatest potential for scenic splendor, wildlife viewing, exciting riding, or whatever it is that is drawing you into the backcountry in the first place.

As you plan a backcountry journey you must keep in mind the need for periodic position fixes. The key to successfully planning a GPS assisted land navigation route is in waypoint selection. The obvious waypoints you should include are the start point and the end point of the trip. If it is a loop, then they will be the same. If your trip involves going out and back, then the turnaround point is the end point. In between the start point and the end point lie the intermediate waypoints you will use to guide you and to gauge your progress.

When you select the intermediate waypoints you need to weigh two separate and sometimes conflicting considerations. One is the relevance of the waypoint, the other is the likelihood of being able to get a position fix. Both are very important.

The most obvious and relevant waypoints you can select are junctions and major direction changes. The latter are especially important if you're traveling off-trail. Also store waypoints for saddles, ridges, valleys, streams, and other distinctive features that you must cross. Don't get too carried away with intermediate waypoints, or you'll spend all your time taking position fixes. Think in terms of allowing about 30-90 minutes of travel time between intermediate waypoints.

Try to use distinctive physical features as intermediate waypoints so they can be easily correlated with features shown on the map. That way you can visually verify your location on your map.

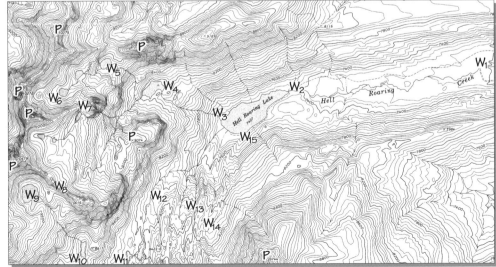

Figure 6-11: *Plan Your Route And Store Appropriate Waypoints — "W" Marks Places Along Your Route, "P" Marks Peaks You Want To Identify*

Keep in mind that a location must be fairly exposed to the sky in order to be "GPS friendly." Avoid selecting the bottom of ravines or cliffside locations if possible. Sometimes an important waypoint (such as a major trail junction) may be in a poor reception location. In this case select a nearby location along your path that offers a good likelihood of obtaining a position fix.

Depending on the duration and complexity of your trip (and the capabilities of your receiver) you may want to divide your travel plans into several different routes. You could link several short routes into one much longer route, or you could have a main route and one or more "side routes" that represent planned or potential side trips.

6.3.3 "Load" Your Receiver

Once you have selected a route (and its associated waypoints), it's time to "load" your GPS receiver. The specific steps you undertake at this point are: [1] name the waypoints on the map, [2] read the coordinates of the waypoints from the map, [3] set the correct datum (from the map) in the GPS receiver, and [4] enter the names and coordinates for the waypoints into the GPS receiver.

When you name the waypoints consider both the flow of the trip and the limitations of your receiver. If your route is a simple loop, a sequential numbering system may be best. A receiver that doesn't have route capability makes this very appealing. If your receiver has route capabilities then more meaningful names may work better for you. If you're using routes, but you have more waypoints than will fit into one route, split the trip into multiple routes. If you do this, "overlap" the waypoints. That is, start the next route with the last waypoint of the preceding route. If the trip has side excursions, consider making them separate routes. That will also help conserve waypoints for the primary route.

If your receiver has route-reversal capabilities you won't need to duplicate waypoints to cover the return portion of an out-and-back trip. If your receiver doesn't have route-reversal capabilities you may want to simplify things by storing your waypoints in a second route (in reverse order) for the return part of the trip. That way you have one route for the trip out, and a second route for the trip back.

Another consideration when planning the waypoints for your trip is recording "off-trail" points of interest. Peaks, cliffs, and lakes are just some of the points of interest that you may want to add to your waypoint list. By having their coordinates stored you will be able to confirm their locations (even from a distance) by using your receiver's "GoTo" function. In fact, you can store coordinates for peaks and other points of interest that are completely off the map you will use on your journey. It can be quite satisfying to use your GPS receiver's "GoTo" function and a compass bearing to identify a peak that may be dozens of miles from your actual location.

When you plan route and waypoint names, you again need to take into consideration the limitations of your receiver. Obvious considerations are the number of characters available for these names, and the number of waypoints that can be placed in a route. You may have the option to add additional information for a waypoint in a memo field, and you can always supplement the information in your receiver with entries in a notebook.

Remember, if your receiver doesn't have routes, or you don't care to use them, an alphabetically or numerically ordered naming scheme makes it easy to switch from one waypoint to the next. That will make your backcountry navigation easier.

6.3.4 In The Field

Probably the first thing you will need to do in the field is get to the trailhead. When you're unfamiliar with the drive to the trailhead, use your GPS receiver to help get you there. If the trailhead is fairly remote, you should have stored waypoints for each of the critical junctions along your drive to the trailhead. "GoTo" each successive waypoint that you stored. It helps to have an external power source (such as the vehicle's 12 volt electrical system) so you can use your receiver continuously as you proceed to the trailhead.

When you're driving to the trailhead you may find there are more crossroads, junctions, and forks than are shown on the map. If you become confused at an unmarked intersection, you'll be able to use your receiver's "GoTo" feature to help you sort it out. Don't panic if you find yourself going in a direction other than the exact direction to your objective. You may even find yourself going away from your destination at some points in your travels. Remember: on land, the path to your destination is rarely a straight line.

Once you arrive at the trailhead, obtain a position fix and compare it with your previously stored trailhead waypoint. They should match to within a few seconds (latitude/longitude coordinate system) or several hundred meters (UTM coordinate system). This amount of "error" is acceptable when allowing for the combined effects of Selective Availability and measurement imprecision when you read the coordinates from the map.

If your position fix at the trailhead doesn't closely match your stored coordinates for the trailhead, find out why before relying on any of the other waypoint coordinates you have stored. Make sure you entered the waypoints correctly (including the correct datum specification). Also make sure your receiver is not operating in 2D mode. Two-dimensional mode can lead to large (as in miles) position errors. See page 41 for more information.

Once you've confirmed the accuracy of your trailhead position (your position fix at the trailhead closely matches the previously stored coordinates for that location) you can proceed on your journey with confidence. Simply "GoTo" each successive waypoint that you previously stored in your receiver's memory. Periodically take a position fix just to ensure that you're on course. The "GoTo" screen (or its equivalent) will tell you the distance and direction to the selected waypoint.

Once you arrive at a waypoint its stored coordinates should match your current position fix within a couple of hundred yards (or a few seconds if you're using latitude/longitude). Don't worry if the locations aren't a perfect match. Handheld civilian GPS receivers aren't perfect, they're just darn good.

If you find that your stored waypoints and actual position fixes don't match up, store those position fixes (labeled in a meaningful way, of course) so you can use them to navigate your way back if necessary. Later, you can use those stored position fixes to diagnose the reason they don't match the original stored waypoints.

Most likely you'll spend a lot of time using your GPS receiver when it is new. Once the novelty wears off you'll probably use it more off and on (so to speak). It is conceivable that once you arrive in the field you may not actually use all the waypoints you've entered. If you feel comfortable that you know where you are, nothing says you must use your GPS receiver. It is a good idea, however, to use it at least occasionally just to verify you're on track and to make sure that your receiver is in good working order.

6.3.5 Fun & Games - Developing GPS Skills

Many new GPS users experience difficulty in becoming familiar with all the various features and functions of GPS receivers. Learning to use this rather sophisticated electronic gear can be intimidating. It is not easy to learn how to use GPS, but once learned, GPS is easy to use. The following "game" is designed to help you learn how to use GPS.

For a group willing to invest the time, this game can be a useful tool for teaching each other many of the skills necessary to use GPS. It not only covers most aspects of backcountry GPS receiver use, it also brings compass skills directly into the picture.

This game will help novice (and not so novice) GPS users gain skills and become quite comfortable with this technology. Think of it as a GPS version of a scavenger hunt. It is similar to the sport of orienteering, but the role of the magnetic compass is secondary — analogous to what GPS has done to compasses in the "real world."

The basic idea is to have a volunteer (preferably someone already familiar with GPS) serve as a game master. The game master selects half a dozen actual locations that the players will find using only their GPS receivers and compasses. At each selected location, the game master attaches a ribbon (or some other marker) to a branch, sign post, shrub or any convenient spot that allows the players to verify that they found the location. The game master prepares a *waypoint/bearing sheet* that lists each location by its geographic coordinates and localized compass bearings (see Figure 6-13). The game begins when the game master gives the players the waypoint/bearing sheet. Once a player has found all of the locations, he or she has completed the game.

The locations selected for this game should offer a good view of the sky (urban canyons are poor choices), and they should have distinctive local features that allow for precise compass bearings. The locations should also be selected so that their precise coordinates can be accurately read from a topo map. It is preferable to obtain coordinates from a map (as opposed to relying on a GPS receiver to obtain a position fix at each selected location). Using map coordinates avoids the error inflicted by Selective Availability. A USGS 7.5-minute topographic map of the game area (or an equivalent map) is a good tool for pinpointing the coordinates of the selected locations. Nonetheless, the game master should take a GPS position fix at each location as a cross-check on the accuracy of the map-based coordinates. The GPS coordinates and the map-based coordinates should be relatively close. If not, it indicates that something is wrong.

Since Selective Availability is a reality of GPS use, players will only be able to reliably get within about 100 meters of each selected location. Because of this, each location needs to be further defined by a compass triangulation that uses two (or three) observable bearing points. The specification for the compass bearings should only makes sense once the player is in the vicinity of the waypoint. This allows for very precise positioning (much "tighter" than with GPS alone), and as an added bonus teaches participants how to use a compass if they haven't already acquired that skill.

The compass bearings should be specified relative to objects that are in the immediate vicinity of the waypoint, not to objects that are far away. In other words, use a flag pole, fire hydrant, playground slide, or some other distinctive local object. Do not use a distant

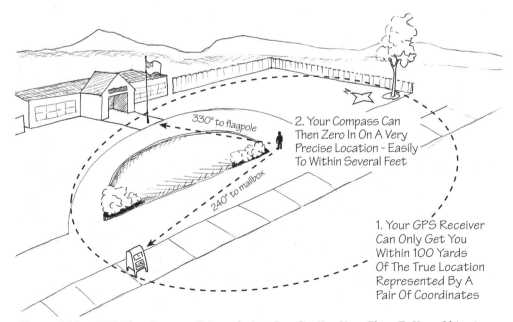

Figure 6-12: GPS Plus Compass Triangulation Can Get You <u>Very</u> Close To Your Objective

peak, distant smoke stack, distant skyscraper, etc. A compass bearing should be able to achieve an accuracy of plus or minus one degree. A two degree arc is 10 feet wide at a distance of 300 feet from a bearing point. A two degree arc is 550 feet wide at a distance of 3 miles from a bearing point.

It also helps to select bearing points that are approximately at right angles to one another. The idea is to use the compass bearings to zero in on the location so that the player can line up with the compass bearings and literally touch the ribbon left at that location. It will not work if the bearings are 180° apart. All this will do is put the player somewhere on a line between the two bearing points.

GPS Orienteering Exercise
Waypoint Worksheet

All Coordinates Based On NAD27 Datum

All Compass Bearings Magnetic

Waypoint #1
43°34'34''N   Compass Bearings: 330° to flagpole
116°09'30''W   240° to U.S. mailbox

Waypoint #2
43°34'32''N   Compass Bearings: 330° to large weathervane
116°09'05''W   240° to "Road Closed" sign

Waypoint #3
43°34'48''N   Compass Bearings: 330° to eagle statue
116°09'22''W   240° to swimming pool slide

Waypoint #4
11 567979 E   Compass Bearings: 330° to pine tree w/broken top
4825292 N   240° to school bus shelter

Figure 6-13: *Here's A Sample Of A Waypoint Worksheet*

An example of using localized triangulation goes something like this: "the waypoint is located at a bearing of 240° to the mail box and 330° to the flag pole." Unless you live in a very small town, this location would be impossible to find without GPS first getting you into the close vicinity. When selecting the bearing points it is important to strike a balance between objects that are so unique they give the location away without GPS navigation — "125° to the Liberty Bell, 200° to the street sign" — and objects that are so commonplace that being within 100 meters doesn't narrow it down enough — "125° to the fire hydrant, 200° to the door."

This game can be scaled to fit any area you want. It can range from a walking exercise (limited to, say, a single square mile) to a driving exercise where the waypoints are spread out over an entire metropolitan area. One consideration is that a larger area involves more maps. A good map library can make that feasible. Also, if the players are going to drive to waypoints it is a good idea to require teams so that one person can drive while the other uses the GPS receiver to navigate. It is even possible to use a familiar hiking, biking, or horseback riding area, but this will probably be more difficult from the game master's standpoint.

The waypoint/bearing sheets provided to players can range from quite basic (one datum, one coordinate system, magnetic compass bearings) to more complex (various datums, various coordinate systems, and a mix of magnetic and true compass bearings). The level of complexity should be scaled to the skill level of the players involved. More complex waypoint/bearing sheets can be used to challenge more advanced GPS users.

This game is very helpful in accomplishing two important goals. One is teaching the GPS user to correctly enter the various setup parameters and coordinates. The other is teaching the GPS user to navigate to a completely unknown point using nothing more than the GPS receiver and a compass. All the fun that is had in the process is strictly a bonus!

6.4 If Your Receiver Breaks Down

This is an important topic for anyone who uses the GPS system to guide them through the backcountry. Although GPS has brought unparalleled ease and simplicity to land navigation (once you learn how to use it), it has a feature that is common to virtually any mechanical or electronic equipment — it can break.

Whether you run out of battery power, drop it over a cliff, run over it with your bike, it's stepped on by your horse, or you simply lose it, one thing is certain: You need a backup navigation plan in case you can't use your GPS receiver.

This section is intended to provide you with a basic understanding of the ways to deal with a GPS system failure. It is not meant to be a comprehensive guide to backcountry safety. You will need to be familiar with much more than the backup navigation information that follows on the next few pages.

Several good books that go into much more detail on the topic of traditional navigation are identified in the Bibliography on page 247. Further reading on this topic is highly recommended for anyone who is serious about backcountry land navigation.

A backup navigation plan for backcountry GPS users is built on two fundamental legs. One is acquiring the skills that can help you find your way without using your GPS receiver. The other is constantly staying aware of your approximate location relative to key reference points when you're in the field, while you are able to use your GPS receiver. Both legs of your backup plan involve steps taken in advance of a GPS receiver failure.

The following sections provide an overview of the ways that you can minimize the problems that you will face if you lose the use of your GPS receiver (and possibly your compass) in the field. It is impossible, however, for this or any other book to provide you with the judgement needed to deal with an equipment failure. Ultimately you must make fundamental decisions such as staying put (if you are lost) versus attempting to proceed using alternative means of navigation.

6.4.1 Awareness and Preparedness

Hopefully, if your GPS receiver quits working, it won't happen at a time when you are also lost. Indeed, if you get in the habit of staying aware of your location at all times, the odds are that you'll be dealing with one or the other of these situations, but not both.

A key element of maintaining awareness is using your GPS receiver to keep track of your distance and direction from either the trailhead, your destination, or both. That way when your receiver quits working (or a squirrel carts it away) you won't be too out of touch with your approximate location. You will know approximately where you are.

Besides keeping track of bearings and distances to key locations, you should also try to make notes (mental or written) about the terrain you are traveling through. In mountainous areas be aware of your travel relative to drainages and ridges. In flat or rolling forests, think about the location of streams (including their direction of flow) relative to your course of travel. If there are any prominent landmarks, such as distinctive peaks, distant cliffs, etc., note their location relative to your course of travel.

When you have a map along, maintain awareness by using it regularly. That way you will have the best possible understanding of your position. If you don't have a map along then it may be worthwhile to make notes about key landmarks — how you approach this is your choice, since it is your memory that you must rely on.

There are also a few items of information that can be useful to have on hand in the event you lose the services of your GPS receiver **and** your compass. The bearings of sunrise and sunset for a particular date and latitude can be obtained from Table 6-1 on page 185. Record the appropriate values for the date and area of travel on a notecard and take it with you. Then you can refer to these values when the need arises. You can also use them to confirm the magnetic declination setting for the area where you are operating.

Another important data item is the precise time of "solar" noon for the date and longitude of the area you are navigating. With an accurately set watch (something you should always have as a GPS owner!) you can determine the moment the sun is in exactly a southerly direction, thereby obtaining an accurate heading. How to use these tools in a pinch is covered in the next section. The point being made here is that you must have this information with you in order to use it. You don't need to carry a book or even the whole table, all you need are the values that pertain to the date and location of your trip. See Figure 6-19 for an example.

It is also a good idea to keep a written copy of the sunrise, sunset, and solar noon data separate from your GPS receiver. That way if the "failure" of your receiver is because it was lost, you may still have the backup data. It also doesn't hurt to keep a spare copy with the receiver itself. And if you want to be thoroughly prepared you may want to keep a hardcopy of important waypoint coordinates. That way you'll be prepared if your receiver's memory is accidentally cleared.

6.4.2 Map & Compass — Back To Basics

If your GPS receiver breaks down (or you lose it) you'll need to know how to:

[1] Locate your position on a map using a compass, landmarks, and/or other traditional orienteering skills, and

[2] Find your destination (and possibly intermediate waypoints) using only your map and your compass.

When your GPS receiver is working, it tells you the directions you need to dial into your compass in order to navigate. Without your GPS receiver, **you** need to figure out the direction to go. Usually that's a two-step process. First you must find your location on your map. Then you must determine the direction you need to travel, and use your compass to follow that direction.

Finding your location on a map can be as simple as identifying a landmark you know is nearby. It is usually more complicated, and involves a process known as triangulation.

Triangulation is usually done by finding at least two distinct points that you can see both on your map and in the real world. Peaks are usually a good choice, but any distinct (and identifiable) point will do. Use your compass to determine the direction to each point, then draw a *back-bearing* line on your map from each of the points.

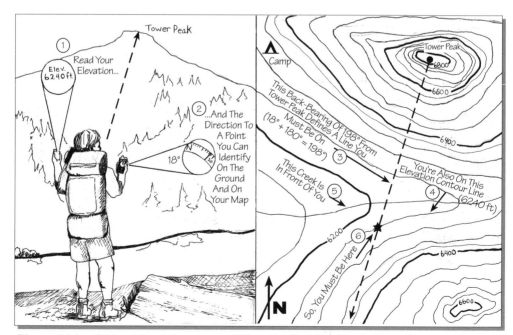

Figure 6-14: *Taking A Back-Bearing And Elevation Reading To Find Your Location On A Map*

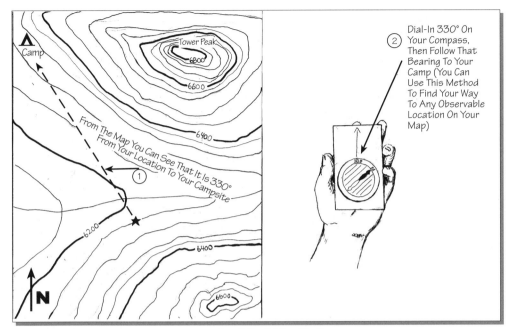

Figure 6-15: *Using A Map To Figure Out Which Way To Go*

The back-bearing is just the direction from you to the distinct point, plus or minus 180 degrees. The use of 180 degrees reverses the direction, and you add or subtract to keep the result in the range of 0 to 360 degrees.

Each back-bearing line has a very important characteristic — you are somewhere on it! By drawing two back-bearing lines, you can find your location at the point where they cross. When you pick points for back-bearings you should try to find points that are as close to 90 degrees apart as possible. That way the back-bearing lines will be approximately perpendicular, and this improves the accuracy of this method.

Triangulation won't work if the points are 180 degrees apart. In that case the two back-bearing lines won't intersect. Instead, they merge into one, and then you can't tell where you are on those lines.

Probably the most difficult aspect of triangulation is finding suitable points that you can identify on both your map and in the real world. You can only draw a back-bearing if you can see a distinct feature and also identify it on your map.

Sometimes you can reduce the required number of back-bearings to one. You can do this by substituting a contour line for one of the back-bearings. You'll need an altimeter that you've kept calibrated. Observe your elevation and look for points where the single back-bearing crosses that elevation contour line. There may be several, so you'll need to pick the right one based on surrounding terrain features and/or distance estimates. See Figure 6-14 for an illustration of how this works.

Once you know your location on your map, you need to determine the direction you want to travel. Draw a straight line from your current position to your objective. Use your compass (or protractor, if you have one) to read the bearing you need to follow. Do this by placing the center of the compass (or protractor) on your current position, and orient north on the degree scale with north on the map. The bearing you need to follow is indicated where the line to your objective intersects the degree scale. See Figure 6-15.

You should also note the distance from your current position to your objective. As you proceed along the compass course toward your objective, try to estimate the amount of distance you cover. This is known as dead reckoning, and simply means that you are using distance traveled to estimate your position. As the opportunities arise use triangulation to reassess your position. Then make any course corrections that might be needed.

6.4.3 Finding Directions Without A Compass

If you lose both your GPS receiver <u>and</u> your compass it is still possible to establish directions on the ground. Perhaps the simplest (and crudest) way to find direction is to note that moss tends to grow on the north side of trees. Unfortunately, moss is not always present. In arid regions timber usually grows on north facing slopes, with grass or sage on the south. Another possibility is to orient your map with your surroundings (see page 166). This works well if you can identify landmarks on both your map and the real world.

The following methods for finding directions are based on astronomical observations — they'll work in a pinch as long as you're in the northern hemisphere.

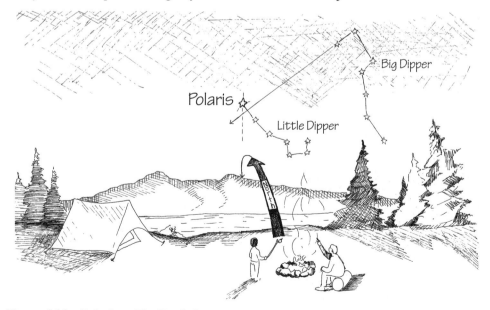

Figure 6-16: *Polaris — The North Star*

Polaris — The North Star

The classic celestial method for finding north involves locating Polaris in the night sky. Actually, it is there even in the daytime, you just can't see it during daylight hours without special instruments. Polaris is a reliable indicator of north year-round, with the only obstacle being cloud cover. Find Polaris and you've found north.

The key to finding the north star is the Little Dipper. Polaris is the star located at the end of the handle, opposite the "cup." It is also handy to know that Polaris' height in the night sky (at a particular latitude) doesn't vary. In fact, the angular height of Polaris (its "elevation") is the same as the latitude from which you're viewing it. If you're near Miami, Florida (at 25°N) then Polaris will always be about 25° above the horizon. If you're near Portland, Oregon or Minneapolis, Minnesota (both are at about 45°N) Polaris will always be about 45° above the horizon.

When you search the sky for the Little Dipper be aware that its attitude is always changing. In effect, the Little Dipper (along with the rest of the stars in the sky) rotates around Polaris on a daily and seasonal cycle. This means the cup of the dipper can be above, below, or beside the end of the handle. Only Polaris remains fixed in its position.

Another factor associated with finding Polaris is the Big Dipper. Make sure that you don't mistake it for the Little Dipper. In fact, the Big Dipper can actually help you locate Polaris.

If you imagine a line extending from the two stars that make up the front edge of the Big Dipper's cup, that line points almost exactly at Polaris. See Figure 6-16.

Waiting for darkness may not be the most desirable way to find north. There are also ways to find north (and thereby any other direction) during the daylight hours by using the sun. The three methods that follow involve either measurements of some kind (distance or time), or values taken from a table. Let's start with the least complicated method — using the shadow cast by the sun at solar noon to find north.

The Shadow Method

The shadow method of finding north involves precisely measuring the shadow cast by a tall stick that you've planted in a level piece of ground. The stick doesn't

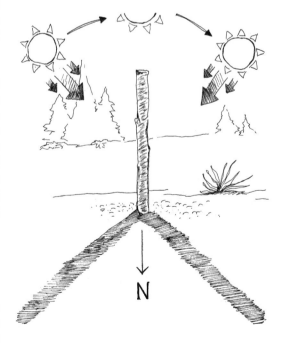

Figure 6-17: *The Shadow Method Of Finding North*

need to be straight, but the top of the stick must be exactly above the point where its base enters the ground. You can use a makeshift plumb-bob to accomplish this. You also need to find the most level ground possible.

Start performing the shadow method of finding north thirty or forty minutes before the sun reaches its highest point in the sky. Draw a ray from the base of the vertical stick to the tip of its shadow. Now watch as the length of the shadow shrinks as the sun continues to rise in the sky. It is a slow process, so you might want to have lunch.

After the sun passes its highest point in the sky the shadow will begin to grow. When the shadow has grown to exactly the same length it was when you drew the first ray, draw a second ray from the base of the vertical stick to the tip of the shadow.

A third ray that is exactly half way between the first two rays points at true north. If your stick is vertical, the ground is level, and your distance measurement is correct, the accuracy of this method can be very good — to within a few degrees.

You don't need to know the exact time to use this method, but you do need a sense of when the sun will reach its highest point in the sky so that you can begin the procedure prior to that time. Solar noon is the moment when the sun is at its highest point in the sky. If you're in doubt about when solar noon will occur, it doesn't hurt this method to start early. Just be aware that however long before solar noon you start, you won't finish until that amount of time has passed after solar noon.

The critical element of this method is being able to precisely measure the length of the shadow cast by the sun. You don't need to know the actual distance, you just need to know when the ever-changing length of the sun's shadow is exactly the same as it was when you first measured it before noon. You can make this precise measurement by marking the length on a makeshift "ruler" or "tape" that you have at hand. A stick, tent pole, belt, or whatever should work just fine. Just be sure that whatever you use doesn't stretch.

The Bearing Of Sunrise/Sunset Method

This method of direction finding relies on a simple table (see Table 6-1) that gives the direction of the sun when it rises and when it sets. You will only be able to use this method if you had the foresight to carry a copy of the table with you, or you wrote down the values for the area and time of year that you are traveling.

To use this table, select the row that corresponds to the time of year that you are traveling. Select the columns that correspond to the latitude of the area you're traveling through. Interpolate if you need to obtain intermediate values.

Write the values for the bearing of sunrise and sunset in a notepad that you can carry with you on your trip. You can use these bearing values to find directions if your compass and

	Bearing of Sunrise at Latitude:						Bearing of Sunset at Latitude:					
	25°N	30°N	35°N	40°N	45°N	50°N	25°N	30°N	35°N	40°N	45°N	50°N
Jan 1	116	117	118	121	124	127	245	243	241	239	236	233
Jan 15	113	115	116	118	121	124	247	245	244	242	240	236
Feb 1	109	110	111	113	114	117	251	250	249	247	246	243
Mar 1	98	99	99	100	101	102	262	261	261	260	259	258
Apr 1	85	85	85	84	84	83	275	275	276	276	276	277
May 1	73	73	71	70	68	66	287	287	289	290	292	294
Jun 1	66	64	63	60	58	54	294	296	297	299	302	306
Jun 15	64	63	61	59	56	52	296	297	299	301	304	308
Jul 1	64	63	61	59	56	52	295	297	298	300	304	308
Jul 15	66	65	63	61	59	55	294	295	297	299	301	304
Aug 1	70	69	68	66	64	61	290	291	292	293	296	298
Sep 1	81	80	80	79	78	77	279	279	280	280	281	283
Oct 1	93	94	94	94	95	95	266	266	266	265	265	265
Nov 1	106	107	108	109	110	113	254	253	252	251	249	247
Dec 1	114	115	117	119	121	125	246	245	243	241	238	235
Dec 15	116	117	119	121	124	128	244	243	241	239	236	232

Table 6-1: The Bearing Of Sunrise And Sunset By Date And Latitude

GPS receiver quit working. You can also use these bearings for verifying the magnetic declination in the area you're traveling.

The Solar Noon Method

This is the most difficult of the three methods described for direction finding. Its advantage is that it works in daylight (like the shadow method) **and** it is quick. The way it works is by observing the direction of a shadow cast by a vertical stick at exactly solar noon. That shadow points to the north.

The trick to this method is determining the exact moment of solar noon at your location. If you're on a time-zone standard meridian, solar noon can be read directly from Table 6-2. If you're not on your time zone's standard meridian you'll need to calculate an adjustment factor to apply to the values found in Table 6-2.

To determine the solar noon adjustment factor for the area you will be operating in, start by noting the longitude of that location. You need to be precise to the nearest minute of longitude. Next, calculate how many degrees and minutes that location is away from its time zone standard meridian. The time zone standard meridians are shown in Figure 6-18.

Solar Noon At Any Time Zone Central Meridian - 1998

Jan 1......12:03:31	Mar 1......12:12:23	May 1......11:57:07	Jul 1......12:03:49	Sep 1......12:00:03	Nov 1......11:43:36
Jan 2......12:04:00	Mar 2......12:12:11	May 2......11:57:00	Jul 2......12:04:00	Sep 2......11:59:44	Nov 2......11:43:35
Jan 3......12:04:27	Mar 3......12:11:59	May 3......11:56:54	Jul 3......12:04:12	Sep 3......11:59:24	Nov 3......11:43:35
Jan 4......12:04:55	Mar 4......12:11:46	May 4......11:56:48	Jul 4......12:04:22	Sep 4......11:59:05	Nov 4......11:43:35
Jan 5......12:05:22	Mar 5......12:11:33	May 5......11:56:42	Jul 5......12:04:33	Sep 5......11:58:45	Nov 5......11:43:36
Jan 6......12:05:48	Mar 6......12:11:19	May 6......11:56:38	Jul 6......12:04:43	Sep 6......11:58:24	Nov 6......11:43:38
Jan 7......12:06:14	Mar 7......12:11:05	May 7......11:56:33	Jul 7......12:04:53	Sep 7......11:58:04	Nov 7......11:43:41
Jan 8......12:06:40	Mar 8......12:10:50	May 8......11:56:30	Jul 8......12:05:02	Sep 8......11:57:43	Nov 8......11:43:44
Jan 9......12:07:05	Mar 9......12:10:35	May 9......11:56:27	Jul 9......12:05:11	Sep 9......11:57:22	Nov 9......11:43:49
Jan 10......12:07:29	Mar 10......12:10:20	May 10......11:56:24	Jul 10......12:05:20	Sep 10......11:57:01	Nov 10......11:43:54
Jan 11......12:07:53	Mar 11......12:10:04	May 11......11:56:22	Jul 11......12:05:28	Sep 11......11:56:40	Nov 11......11:44:01
Jan 12......12:08:17	Mar 12......12:09:48	May 12......11:56:20	Jul 12......12:05:36	Sep 12......11:56:19	Nov 12......11:44:08
Jan 13......12:08:39	Mar 13......12:09:32	May 13......11:56:20	Jul 13......12:05:43	Sep 13......11:55:58	Nov 13......11:44:16
Jan 14......12:09:01	Mar 14......12:09:16	May 14......11:56:19	Jul 14......12:05:50	Sep 14......11:55:37	Nov 14......11:44:24
Jan 15......12:09:23	Mar 15......12:08:59	May 15......11:56:20	Jul 15......12:05:56	Sep 15......11:55:15	Nov 15......11:44:34
Jan 16......12:09:43	Mar 16......12:08:42	May 16......11:56:20	Jul 16......12:06:02	Sep 16......11:54:54	Nov 16......11:44:45
Jan 17......12:10:03	Mar 17......12:08:24	May 17......11:56:22	Jul 17......12:06:07	Sep 17......11:54:33	Nov 17......11:44:56
Jan 18......12:10:23	Mar 18......12:08:07	May 18......11:56:24	Jul 18......12:06:12	Sep 18......11:54:11	Nov 18......11:45:08
Jan 19......12:10:41	Mar 19......12:07:50	May 19......11:56:27	Jul 19......12:06:16	Sep 19......11:53:50	Nov 19......11:45:22
Jan 20......12:10:59	Mar 20......12:07:32	May 20......11:56:30	Jul 20......12:06:20	Sep 20......11:53:29	Nov 20......11:45:35
Jan 21......12:11:17	Mar 21......12:07:14	May 21......11:56:33	Jul 21......12:06:23	Sep 21......11:53:08	Nov 21......11:45:50
Jan 22......12:11:33	Mar 22......12:06:56	May 22......11:56:38	Jul 22......12:06:26	Sep 22......11:52:47	Nov 22......11:46:06
Jan 23......12:11:49	Mar 23......12:06:38	May 23......11:56:43	Jul 23......12:06:28	Sep 23......11:52:26	Nov 23......11:46:22
Jan 24......12:12:04	Mar 24......12:06:20	May 24......11:56:48	Jul 24......12:06:30	Sep 24......11:52:05	Nov 24......11:46:39
Jan 25......12:12:18	Mar 25......12:06:02	May 25......11:56:54	Jul 25......12:06:30	Sep 25......11:51:44	Nov 25......11:46:57
Jan 26......12:12:31	Mar 26......12:05:44	May 26......11:57:00	Jul 26......12:06:31	Sep 26......11:51:23	Nov 26......11:47:15
Jan 27......12:12:44	Mar 27......12:05:26	May 27......11:57:07	Jul 27......12:06:31	Sep 27......11:51:03	Nov 27......11:47:35
Jan 28......12:12:56	Mar 28......12:05:08	May 28......11:57:14	Jul 28......12:06:30	Sep 28......11:50:43	Nov 28......11:47:55
Jan 29......12:13:07	Mar 29......12:04:50	May 29......11:57:22	Jul 29......12:06:28	Sep 29......11:50:23	Nov 29......11:48:15
Jan 30......12:13:17	Mar 30......12:04:32	May 30......11:57:30	Jul 30......12:06:26	Sep 30......11:50:03	Nov 30......11:48:37
Jan 31......12:13:26	Mar 31......12:04:14	May 31......11:57:39	Jul 31......12:06:23		
Feb 1......12:13:35	Apr 1......12:03:56	Jun 1......11:57:48	Aug 1......12:06:20	Oct 1......11:49:43	Dec 1......11:48:58
Feb 2......12:13:42	Apr 2......12:03:38	Jun 2......11:57:57	Aug 2......12:06:16	Oct 2......11:49:24	Dec 2......11:49:21
Feb 3......12:13:49	Apr 3......12:03:21	Jun 3......11:58:07	Aug 3......12:06:11	Oct 3......11:49:05	Dec 3......11:49:44
Feb 4......12:13:55	Apr 4......12:03:03	Jun 4......11:58:17	Aug 4......12:06:06	Oct 4......11:48:46	Dec 4......11:50:08
Feb 5......12:14:00	Apr 5......12:02:46	Jun 5......11:58:27	Aug 5......12:06:00	Oct 5......11:48:28	Dec 5......11:50:32
Feb 6......12:14:05	Apr 6......12:02:29	Jun 6......11:58:38	Aug 6......12:05:54	Oct 6......11:48:10	Dec 6......11:50:57
Feb 7......12:14:08	Apr 7......12:02:12	Jun 7......11:58:49	Aug 7......12:05:47	Oct 7......11:47:53	Dec 7......11:51:23
Feb 8......12:14:11	Apr 8......12:01:55	Jun 8......11:59:00	Aug 8......12:05:39	Oct 8......11:47:35	Dec 8......11:51:49
Feb 9......12:14:13	Apr 9......12:01:38	Jun 9......11:59:11	Aug 9......12:05:31	Oct 9......11:47:19	Dec 9......11:52:15
Feb 10......12:14:14	Apr 10......12:01:22	Jun 10......11:59:23	Aug 10......12:05:22	Oct 10......11:47:03	Dec 10......11:52:42
Feb 11......12:14:14	Apr 11......12:01:06	Jun 11......11:59:35	Aug 11......12:05:13	Oct 11......11:46:47	Dec 11......11:53:10
Feb 12......12:14:14	Apr 12......12:00:50	Jun 12......11:59:47	Aug 12......12:05:03	Oct 12......11:46:32	Dec 12......11:53:37
Feb 13......12:14:13	Apr 13......12:00:35	Jun 13......12:00:00	Aug 13......12:04:52	Oct 13......11:46:17	Dec 13......11:54:06
Feb 14......12:14:11	Apr 14......12:00:19	Jun 14......12:00:12	Aug 14......12:04:41	Oct 14......11:46:03	Dec 14......11:54:34
Feb 15......12:14:08	Apr 15......12:00:05	Jun 15......12:00:25	Aug 15......12:04:30	Oct 15......11:45:49	Dec 15......11:55:03
Feb 16......12:14:05	Apr 16......11:59:50	Jun 16......12:00:38	Aug 16......12:04:18	Oct 16......11:45:36	Dec 16......11:55:32
Feb 17......12:14:01	Apr 17......11:59:36	Jun 17......12:00:51	Aug 17......12:04:05	Oct 17......11:45:24	Dec 17......11:56:01
Feb 18......12:13:56	Apr 18......11:59:23	Jun 18......12:01:04	Aug 18......12:03:52	Oct 18......11:45:12	Dec 18......11:56:31
Feb 19......12:13:51	Apr 19......11:59:09	Jun 19......12:01:17	Aug 19......12:03:38	Oct 19......11:45:00	Dec 19......11:57:00
Feb 20......12:13:44	Apr 20......11:58:57	Jun 20......12:01:30	Aug 20......12:03:24	Oct 20......11:44:50	Dec 20......11:57:30
Feb 21......12:13:38	Apr 21......11:58:44	Jun 21......12:01:43	Aug 21......12:03:10	Oct 21......11:44:40	Dec 21......11:58:00
Feb 22......12:13:30	Apr 22......11:58:32	Jun 22......12:01:56	Aug 22......12:02:55	Oct 22......11:44:31	Dec 22......11:58:30
Feb 23......12:13:23	Apr 23......11:58:21	Jun 23......12:02:09	Aug 23......12:02:40	Oct 23......11:44:22	Dec 23......11:59:00
Feb 24......12:13:14	Apr 24......11:58:10	Jun 24......12:02:22	Aug 24......12:02:24	Oct 24......11:44:14	Dec 24......11:59:30
Feb 25......12:13:05	Apr 25......11:57:59	Jun 25......12:02:35	Aug 25......12:02:08	Oct 25......11:44:07	Dec 25......12:00:00
Feb 26......12:12:55	Apr 26......11:57:49	Jun 26......12:02:48	Aug 26......12:01:51	Oct 26......11:44:00	Dec 26......12:00:31
Feb 27......12:12:45	Apr 27......11:57:40	Jun 27......12:03:01	Aug 27......12:01:34	Oct 27......11:43:54	Dec 27......12:00:59
Feb 28......12:12:34	Apr 28......11:57:31	Jun 28......12:03:13	Aug 28......12:01:17	Oct 28......11:43:49	Dec 28......12:01:28
	Apr 29......11:57:23	Jun 29......12:03:25	Aug 29......12:00:59	Oct 29......11:43:45	Dec 29......12:01:58
	Apr 30......11:57:15	Jun 30......12:03:37	Aug 30......12:00:40	Oct 30......11:43:41	Dec 30......12:02:26
			Aug 31......12:00:22	Oct 31......11:43:38	Dec 31......12:02:55

Table 6-2: *Solar Noon At Any Time-Zone Central Meridian In 1998 (Times For 1999 And Beyond Can Be Obtained From The **Nautical Almanac** — See Page 247)*

Figure 6-18: *Time Zone Standard Meridians, Continental U.S.*

Each degree of longitude away from the time-zone standard meridian is worth four minutes of time and each minute of longitude away is worth four seconds of time. Add the amount of time corresponding to a location west of the standard meridian, or subtract the amount of time corresponding to a location east of the standard meridian. If your excursion is during daylight savings time add an hour to the adjustment factor values you just calculated. Write down these values and keep them handy in case you need to refer to them. If you're going to be out for an extended length of time you may want to note the local time of solar noon for each day of your outing. See Figure 6-19 for an example.

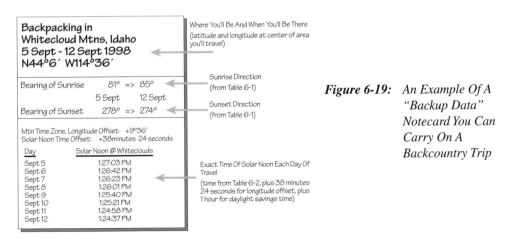

Figure 6-19: *An Example Of A "Backup Data" Notecard You Can Carry On A Backcountry Trip*

Appendix 1: Highest Points

The following table is a listing of the highest named point in each county in each state. The latitude and longitude of that named point are provided to the nearest second, which is a resolution of approximately 100 feet. The highest point in the state is identified with an asterisk (*) at the end of the county name(s). Not all counties are included, since some counties don't have even a single named highest point. The states that have a named point listed for every county in that state have an asterisk (*) following the state name.

Some highest points are identical for more than one county in a state (or across states). This can happen when the highest point is on the boundary of the county and that point is then "shared" by multiple counties. Every effort has been made to verify that the highest point actually lies within the county indicated, but the nature of the underlying data source (the USGS Geographic Names Information System) precludes making any guarantees. In other words, it is possible that some of the peaks listed actually lie just outside the county they are listed under.

The coordinates are from the USGS 7.5-minute quadrangle series topographic maps. The datum for these coordinates is NAD27. The elevation listed for each point should be quite accurate (within National Map Accuracy Standards) since these locations are, in most cases, distinct landmarks. They do not, however, necessarily correspond to elevations shown on the display of your GPS receiver. See page 117 for information on differences between GPS and topo map elevations.

The uses for this information ranges from the GPS equivalent of trivial pursuits (How far and what direction is it from where we are to the highest point in the county?) to actually identifying and/or traveling to these landmarks when you are in their vicinity.

Alabama

County	Highest Point	Elevation	Latitude	Longitude
Autauga	Parker Mountain	566	32°33'49"N	86°50'34"W
Baldwin	Stony Hill	215	30°47'40"N	87°52'34"W
Barbour	Graveyard Hill	690	31°56'21"N	85°25'53"W
Bibb	Sand Mountain	745	33°14'11"N	87°03'19"W
Blount	Sand Mountain	1,740	34°57'01"N	85°32'51"W
Bullock	Wolfpit Hill	660	31°55'21"N	85°46'57"W
Calhoun	Morton Hill	2,063	33°41'35"N	85°44'20"W
Cherokee	Flagpole Mountain	1,968	34°01'49"N	85°25'32"W
Chilton	Perry Mountain	700	32°45'36"N	86°57'23"W
Choctaw	Scott Mountain	555	32°07'36"N	88°21'41"W
Clarke	Orange Hill	490	31°43'10"N	87°44'29"W
Clay	Hernandez Peak	2,344	33°27'30"N	85°48'48"W
Cleburne*	Cheaha Mountain*	2,405*	33°29'08"N	85°48'33"W
Coffee	Coston Hill	460	31°32'55"N	86°07'01"W
Colbert	Summer House Mtn	940	34°43'12"N	87°54'38"W
Coosa	Terrapin Hill	1,261	33°00'48"N	86°15'00"W
Covington	Red Wash Hill	305	31°08'03"N	86°30'23"W
Crenshaw	Carmel, Mount	657	32°01'14"N	86°20'57"W
Cullman	Haynes Mountain	945	34°08'00"N	86°55'28"W
Dallas	Wildcat Hill	477	32°04'46"N	87°03'28"W
DeKalb	Lookout Mountain	2,242	34°59'00"N	85°21'00"W
Elmore	Bald Knob	590	32°32'02"N	86°11'05"W
Escambia	Sandstone Hill	250	31°03'21"N	86°43'54"W
Etowah	Lookout Mountain	2,242	34°59'00"N	85°21'00"W
Fayette	Ford Mountain	800	33°46'47"N	87°44'50"W
Franklin	Suggs Mountain	1,041	34°27'23"N	87°41'02"W
Geneva	Buffalo Hill	216	31°03'13"N	86°07'50"W
Greene	Hays Mount	295	32°45'41"N	87°58'28"W
Henry	Vickers Hill	500	31°38'17"N	85°18'49"W
Jackson	Johnson Top	1,870	34°58'32"N	86°18'46"W
Jefferson	Butler Mountain	1,445	33°43'10"N	86°36'52"W
Lauderdale	Pettipoole Hill	760	34°54'33"N	87°58'35"W
Lawrence	Penitentiary Mountain	1,074	34°26'08"N	87°20'18"W
Limestone	Baker Hill	760	34°49'52"N	87°06'02"W
Lowndes	Barganier Hill	587	31°59'16"N	86°36'51"W
Madison	Johnson Top	1,870	34°58'32"N	86°18'46"W
Marengo	Grant Hill	245	32°21'46"N	87°52'07"W
Marion	Ikes Knob	917	34°15'31"N	87°42'09"W
Marshall	Gunters Mountain	1,380	34°33'58"N	86°10'39"W
Mobile	Big Rock	210	31°06'14"N	88°05'44"W
Monroe	Lookout Hill	443	31°47'09"N	87°20'08"W
Montgomery	Carter Hill	567	31°58'01"N	86°09'24"W
Morgan	Whitesburg Mountain	1,270	34°30'50"N	86°36'29"W
Perry	Bull Mountain	600	32°46'37"N	87°04'56"W
Pike	Becks Mountain	675	31°56'05"N	86°03'45"W
Randolph	Plunkett Mountain	1,232	33°23'01"N	85°34'39"W
Shelby	Signal Mountain	1,570	33°23'49"N	86°34'51"W
St. Clair	Bald Rock Mountain	1,594	33°36'15"N	86°25'18"W
Sumter	Alamuchee Hill	385	32°26'30"N	88°19'02"W
Talladega	Horn Mountain	1,912	33°17'50"N	86°04'30"W
Tallapoosa	Hog Mountain	1,090	33°04'33"N	85°50'59"W
Tuscaloosa	Round Mountain	788	33°21'56"N	87°16'01"W
Walker	Lockhart Hill	820	33°46'14"N	87°29'07"W
Washington	Dwight Hill	320	31°09'24"N	88°15'38"W
Wilcox	Grumpton Hills	450	31°57'08"N	87°16'02"W
Winston	Balls Mountain	990	34°16'08"N	87°29'09"W

Alaska

County	Highest Point	Elevation	Latitude	Longitude
Aleutian Islands	Shishaldin Volcano	9,372	54°45'22"N	163°58'03"W
Anchorage	Bashful Peak	8,005	61°18'29"N	148°52'05"W
Bethel	Mount Oratia	4,658	59°55'47"N	160°00'49"W
Dillingham	South Buttress	15,885	61°42'49"N	154°13'17"W
Fairbanks North Star	West Point	5,865	64°57'15"N	144°40'51"W
Haines	Mount Service	7,847	59°05'23"N	134°26'47"W
Juneau	Boundary Peak 93	8,584	58°43'46"N	133°50'17"W
Kenai Peninsula	Mount Torbert	11,413	61°24'34"N	152°24'42"W
Ketchikan Gateway	Mount Reid	4,592	55°42'24"N	131°14'52"W
Kobuk	Mount Angayukaqsraq	4,760	67°42'30"N	159°24'00"W
Kodiak Island	Mount Glottof	4,405	57°32'58"N	153°06'47"W
Matanuska-Susitna	Mount Hunter	14,573	62°57'03"N	151°05'22"W
Nome	Mount Osborn	4,714	64°59'35"N	165°19'45"W
North Slope	Mount Isto	9,050	69°12'03"N	143°47'41"W
Northwest Arctic	Mount Igikpak	8,510	67°24'18"N	154°58'01"W
Prince of Wales-Outer Ketchikan	Mount Jay John	7,499	56°08'31"N	130°25'29"W
Sitka	Mount Ada	4,528	56°40'50"N	134°41'38"W
Skagway-Yakutat-Angoon	Mount Saint Elias	18,008	60°17'36"N	140°55'46"W
Southeast Fairbanks	Mount Hayes	13,832	63°37'12"N	146°42'58"W
Valdez-Cordova	Mount Bona	16,500	61°23'08"N	141°44'55"W
Wade Hampton	Mount Chiniklik	2,625	61°57'15"N	161°11'49"W
Wrangell-Petersburg	Kates Needle	10,002	57°02'42"N	132°02'39"W
Yukon-Koyukuk*	Mount McKinley*	20,320*	63°04'10"N	151°00'13"W

Arizona*

County	Highest Point	Elevation	Latitude	Longitude
Apache	Baldy Peak	11,403	33°54'22"N	109°33'44"W
Cochise	Chiricahua Peak	9,798	31°50'47"N	109°17'27"W
Coconino	Humphreys Peak*	12,633*	35°20'47"N	111°40'40"W
Gila	Mazatzal Peak	7,903	34°03'45"N	111°27'39"W
Graham	Graham, Mount	10,720	32°42'06"N	109°52'15"W
Greenlee	Blue Peak	9,346	33°33'43"N	109°17'47"W
La Paz	W C P Peak	3,200	33°56'55"N	113°33'40"W
Maricopa	Browns Peak	7,657	33°41'03"N	111°19'29"W
Maricopa	Four Peaks	7,657	33°40'38"N	111°19'35"W
Mohave	Hualapai Peak	8,417	35°04'30"N	113°54'00"W
Navajo	Brookbank Point	7,684	34°19'45"N	110°44'50"W
Pima	Lemmon, Mount	9,157	32°26'35"N	110°47'16"W
Pinal	Apache Peak	6,441	32°33'05"N	110°45'03"W
Santa Cruz	Wrightson, Mount	9,453	31°41'46"N	110°50'52"W
Yavapai	Union, Mount	7,979	34°24'54"N	112°24'13"W
Yuma	Harquahala Mountain	5,681	33°48'40"N	113°20'46"W

Arkansas

County	Highest Point	Elevation	Latitude	Longitude
Baxter	Lee Mountain	1,608	35°52'34"N	92°26'52"W
Benton	Whitney Mountain	1,808	36°24'05"N	93°55'02"W
Boone	Piney Mountain	2,140	36°12'12"N	93°14'32"W
Bradley	Cane Hill	92	33°18'34"N	92°18'15"W
Calhoun	Boones Mound	100	33°22'46"N	92°34'15"W
Carroll	Dodson Mountain	2,160	36°07'46"N	93°21'28"W
Clark	Sugarloaf Knob	740	34°18'20"N	93°26'03"W
Clay	Bunker Hill	295	36°26'29"N	90°30'01"W
Cleburne	Choppy Knob	1,327	35°41'35"N	92°11'27"W
Conway	Woolverton Mountain	1,078	35°25'55"N	92°33'12"W
Crawford	Shepherd Mountain	2,321	35°45'01"N	93°57'34"W
Drew	Gaster Hill	380	33°39'27"N	91°48'43"W
Faulkner	Buffalo Hump	882	35°20'27"N	92°13'19"W
Franklin	Hare Mountain	2,440	35°45'33"N	93°45'25"W
Fulton	Wallace Knob	1,136	36°22'36"N	91°51'47"W
Garland	Ouachita Pinnacle	1,961	34°43'48"N	93°13'35"W
Hempstead	Rocky Mound Hill	480	33°40'26"N	93°30'30"W
Hot Spring	Needles Eye Mountain	1,270	34°21'46"N	93°12'00"W
Howard	Big Tom Mountain	1,677	34°20'56"N	93°57'23"W
Independence	Round Mountain	1,150	35°44'02"N	91°49'15"W
Izard	Brandenburg Mountain	1,700	35°59'05"N	92°02'45"W
Jackson	Throckmorton Hill	660	35°27'14"N	91°33'59"W
Jefferson	Jennings Hill	433	34°21'28"N	92°11'51"W
Johnson	Garlands Knob	2,360	35°43'49"N	93°28'46"W
Lafayette	Boyd Hill	390	33°27'50"N	93°40'34"W
Lawrence	Cave Hill	700	36°11'15"N	91°18'25"W
Lee	Morrells Hill	360	34°38'50"N	90°38'31"W
Lincoln	Twin Mounds	175	33°48'26"N	91°37'52"W
Little River	Lime Rock Hill	450	33°42'02"N	94°24'24"W
Logan*	Signal Hill*	2,753*	35°10'02"N	93°38'41"W
Lonoke	Haymes Hill	440	35°02'19"N	92°03'55"W

County	Highest Point	Elevation	Latitude	Longitude
Madison	Isaac Knob	2,447	35°48'01"N	93°40'08"W
Marion	Clark Hill	1,341	36°19'48"N	92°51'32"W
Miller	Krause Hill	463	33°24'40"N	93°49'48"W
Mississippi	Chickasawba Mound	275	35°55'54"N	89°55'50"W
Montgomery	Mast Mountain	2,195	34°38'57"N	93°55'10"W
Newton	Turner Ward Knob	2,463	35°51'48"N	93°27'13"W
Ouachita	Rocky Hill	290	33°45'44"N	92°54'39"W
Perry	Deckard Mountain	1,812	34°47'11"N	93°07'52"W
Pike	Hogpen Mountain	1,710	34°20'51"N	93°49'07"W
Poinsett	Miller Mound	215	35°30'48"N	90°27'09"W
Polk	Rich Mountain	2,662	34°41'33"N	94°26'29"W
Pope	Walker Mountain	2,128	35°40'17"N	92°51'45"W
Prairie	Sand Hill	205	35°00'20"N	91°26'16"W
Pulaski	Shinall Mountain	1,060	34°47'57"N	92°29'48"W
Randolph	Bellah Hills	749	36°28'18"N	91°06'50"W
Saline	Angling Pinnacle	1,768	34°46'28"N	92°57'53"W
Scott	Hickory Knob	2,201	34°57'59"N	94°14'14"W
Searcy	Horn Mountain	2,203	35°54'51"N	92°56'06"W
Sebastian	Poteau Mountain	2,669	34°57'44"N	94°22'09"W
Sevier	Steele Hill	460	33°54'18"N	94°05'05"W
Sharp	Peter Martin Hill	793	35°58'27"N	91°40'07"W
Stone	Strand Knob	1,840	35°52'19"N	92°21'50"W
Union	Pigeon Hills	160	33°16'25"N	92°21'34"W
Van Buren	Hatley Mountain	2,000	35°33'38"N	92°46'09"W
Washington	Denny Mountain	2,366	35°49'43"N	93°59'11"W
White	Schoolhouse Hill	862	35°19'35"N	92°04'11"W
Woodruff	Blockade Hill	225	35°20'41"N	91°15'37"W
Yell	Petit Jean Mountain	2,439	35°01'22"N	93°41'59"W

California*

County	Highest Point	Elevation	Latitude	Longitude
Alameda	Cedar Mountain	3,675	37°33'36"N	121°36'20"W
Alpine	Sonora Peak	11,459	38°21'14"N	119°38'03"W
Amador	Thunder Mountain	9,415	38°40'30"N	120°05'20"W
Butte	Humboldt Peak	7,087	40°09'03"N	121°25'45"W
Calaveras	Flagpole Point	7,933	38°27'34"N	120°06'35"W
Colusa	Snow Mountain East	7,056	39°23'01"N	122°45'03"W
Contra Costa	Diablo, Mount	3,849	37°52'54"N	121°54'46"W
Del Norte	Baldy Peak	6,775	41°40'25"N	123°43'09"W
El Dorado	Freel Peak	10,881	38°51'28"N	119°53'58"W
Fresno	North Palisade	14,242	37°05'38"N	118°31'19"W
Glenn	Black Butte	7,448	39°43'36"N	122°52'16"W
Humboldt	Salmon Mountain	6,956	41°11'00"N	123°24'36"W
Imperial	Blue Angels Peak	4,548	32°37'19"N	116°05'26"W
Inyo	Williamson, Mount	14,370	36°39'22"N	118°18'37"W
Kern	Johnson, Mount	12,868	37°07'44"N	118°35'06"W
Kings	Zwang Peak	3,078	35°56'48"N	120°14'48"W
Lake	Harbin Mountain	12,585	38°47'31"N	122°38'43"W
Lassen	Hat Mountain	8,737	41°08'57"N	120°07'32"W
Los Angeles	San Antonio, Mount	10,064	34°17'20"N	117°38'45"W
Madera	Ritter, Mount	13,140	37°41'22"N	119°11'53"W
Marin	East Peak	2,571	37°55'45"N	122°34'34"W
Mariposa	Clark, Mount	11,522	37°41'47"N	119°25'39"W
Mendocino	Anthony Peak	6,954	39°50'47"N	122°57'48"W
Merced	Laveaga Peak	3,801	36°53'26"N	121°10'37"W
Modoc	Eagle Peak	9,892	41°17'01"N	120°11'59"W
Mono	White Mountain Peak	14,246	37°38'04"N	118°15'17"W
Monterey	Junipero Serra Peak	5,862	36°08'44"N	121°25'06"W
Napa	Berryessa Peak	3,057	38°39'50"N	122°11'20"W
Nevada	Lola, Mount	9,143	39°25'59"N	120°21'48"W
Orange	Santiago Peak	5,687	33°42'38"N	117°32'00"W
Placer	Granite Chief	9,006	39°11'54"N	120°17'09"W
Plumas	Ingalls, Mount	8,360	39°59'38"N	120°37'35"W
Riverside	San Jacinto Peak	10,804	33°48'52"N	116°40'42"W
Sacramento	American Ranch Hill	2,486	39°10'06"N	121°06'47"W
San Benito	Willow Creek Peak	12,437	36°35'09"N	121°13'16"W
San Bernardino	San Gorgonio Mountain	11,490	34°06'02"N	116°49'40"W
San Diego	Cuyamaca Peak	6,512	32°56'48"N	116°36'20"W
San Francisco	Davidson, Mount	925	37°44'18"N	122°27'00"W
San Joaquin	Boardman, Mount	3,600	37°28'53"N	121°28'13"W
San Luis Obispo	Caliente Mountain	5,106	35°02'11"N	119°45'33"W
San Mateo	Borel Hill	2,572	37°19'13"N	122°11'53"W
Santa Barbara	San Rafael Mountain	6,593	34°42'39"N	119°48'51"W
Santa Clara	Copernicus Peak	4,360	37°20'49"N	121°37'44"W
Santa Cruz	Bielawski, Mount	3,231	37°13'24"N	122°05'30"W
Shasta	Lassen Peak	10,457	40°29'16"N	121°30'14"W
Sierra	Babbitt Peak	8,760	39°36'09"N	120°06'23"W
Siskiyou	Shasta, Mount	14,162	41°24'34"N	122°11'38"W
Solano	Vaca, Mount	2,819	38°24'01"N	122°06'18"W
Sonoma	Saint Helena, Mount	4,343	38°40'10"N	122°37'56"W
Stanislaus	Maclure, Mount	12,880	37°44'37"N	119°16'47"W
Sutter	South Butte	2,117	39°12'21"N	121°49'09"W
Tehama	Brokeoff Mountain	9,235	40°26'43"N	121°33'32"W
Trinity	Thompson Peak	8,994	41°00'05"N	123°02'50"W
Tulare*	Mount Whitney*	14,491*	36°34'45"N	118°17'30"W
Tuolumne	Lyell, Mount	13,114	37°44'22"N	119°16'14"W
Ventura	Pinos, Mount	8,831	34°48'42"N	119°08'47"W
Yolo	Berryessa Peak	3,057	38°39'50"N	122°11'20"W
Yuba	Barton Hill	3,850	39°33'07"N	121°07'50"W

Colorado

County	Highest Point	Elevation	Latitude	Longitude
Alamosa	Blanca Peak	14,345	37°34'38"N	105°29'07"W
Archuleta	Summit Peak	13,300	37°21'03"N	106°41'46"W
Baca	Little Black Mesa	4,730	37°00'53"N	102°55'47"W
Bent	Mothers Hill	4,519	37°40'51"N	103°18'20"W
Boulder	Longs Peak	14,255	40°15'17"N	105°36'55"W
Chaffee	Harvard, Mount	14,420	38°55'28"N	106°19'12"W
Cheyenne	Eureka Hill	4,700	38°58'40"N	102°51'48"W
Clear Creek	Grays Peak	14,270	39°38'02"N	105°49'01"W
Conejos	Conejos Peak	13,172	37°17'19"N	106°34'13"W
Costilla	Blanca Peak	14,345	37°34'38"N	105°29'07"W
Crowley	Antelope Mesa	4,850	38°22'43"N	103°54'29"W
Custer	Crestone Needle	14,197	37°57'53"N	105°34'34"W
Delta	Lamborn, Mount	11,396	38°48'11"N	107°31'20"W
Denver	Inspiration Point	5,415	39°47'13"N	105°03'31"W
Dolores	Wilson, Mount	14,246	37°50'21"N	107°59'27"W
Douglas	Thunder Butte	9,836	39°10'18"N	105°11'49"W
Eagle	Mount of the Holy Cross	14,005	39°28'05"N	106°28'45"W
El Paso	Pikes Peak	14,110	38°50'26"N	105°02'38"W
Elbert	Eagle Rock	6,234	39°13'24"N	104°15'44"W
Fremont	Bushnell Peak	13,105	38°20'29"N	105°53'20"W
Garfield	Flat Top Mountain	12,354	40°00'03"N	107°04'58"W
Gilpin	James Peak	13,294	39°51'08"N	105°41'22"W
Grand	Pettingell Peak	13,553	39°43'45"N	105°54'15"W
Gunnison	Castle Peak	14,265	39°00'35"N	106°51'39"W
Hinsdale	Uncompahgre Peak	14,309	38°04'18"N	107°27'41"W
Huerfano	Blanca Peak	14,345	37°34'38"N	105°29'07"W
Jackson	Clark Peak	12,951	40°36'24"N	105°55'46"W
Jefferson	Kenosha Mountains	12,429	39°22'05"N	105°36'17"W
La Plata	Eolus, Mount	14,083	37°37'22"N	107°37'15"W
Las Animas	West Spanish Peak	13,626	37°22'32"N	104°59'35"W
Lake*	Mount Elbert*	14,433*	39°07'04"N	106°26'41"W
Larimer	Hagues Peak	13,560	40°29'05"N	105°38'45"W
Logan	Eagle Point Hill	4,608	40°30'12"N	103°05'39"W
Mesa	Leon Peak	11,236	37°04'46"N	107°50'36"W
Mineral	Baldy Cinco	13,383	37°57'20"N	107°06'09"W
Moffat	Black Mountain	10,815	40°47'29"N	107°23'13"W
Montezuma	Hesperus Mountain	13,232	37°26'42"N	108°05'18"W
Montrose	Flat Top	10,144	38°11'00"N	107°56'19"W
Morgan	Judson Hills	4,921	40°26'59"N	103°56'59"W
Otero	Merker Hills	4,990	37°39'57"N	103°55'34"W
Ouray	Sneffels, Mount	14,150	38°00'12"N	107°47'30"W
Park	Lincoln, Mount	14,286	39°21'05"N	106°06'39"W
Phillips	Fiddler Peak	4,028	40°28'28"N	102°22'36"W
Pitkin	Castle Peak	14,265	39°00'35"N	106°51'39"W
Prowers	Two Buttes	4,711	37°39'34"N	102°32'30"W
Pueblo	Greenhorn Mountain	12,347	37°52'53"N	105°00'46"W
Rio Blanco	Trappers Peak	12,002	39°56'29"N	107°15'01"W
Rio Grande	Bennett Peak	13,203	37°29'00"N	106°26'00"W
Routt	Zirkel, Mount	12,180	40°49'53"N	106°39'45"W
Saguache	Crestone Peak	14,294	37°58'00"N	105°35'05"W
San Juan	Vermilion Peak	13,894	37°47'57"N	107°49'40"W
San Miguel	Wilson Peak	14,017	37°51'37"N	107°59'03"W
Sedgwick	Marks Butte	4,072	40°48'56"N	102°30'24"W
Summit	Grays Peak	14,270	39°38'02"N	105°49'01"W
Teller	Sentinel Point	12,527	38°50'26"N	105°06'15"W
Washington	Flat Top	5,402	39°34'36"N	103°35'48"W
Weld	Simpson Mesa	6,212	40°58'42"N	104°45'32"W
Yuma	Mount Yuma	4,161	40°00'34"N	102°35'37"W

Connecticut*

County	Highest Point	Elevation	Latitude	Longitude
Fairfield	College Hill	1,551	42°01'01"N	73°13'33"W
Hartford	Morrison Hill	1,202	42°01'23"N	72°56'57"W
Litchfield*	Mount Frissell*	2,380*	42°03'04"N	73°28'57"W
Middlesex	Meshomasic Mountain	897	41°37'49"N	72°32'33"W
New Haven	Lindsley Hill	1,046	41°37'22"N	72°57'57"W
New London	Sweet Hill	644	41°40'14"N	72°13'49"W
Tolland	Burley Hill	1,315	42°01'01"N	72°12'33"W
Windham	Snow Hill	1,202	41°57'15"N	72°12'38"W

Delaware*

County	Highest Point	Elevation	Latitude	Longitude
Kent	Kitts Hummock	10	39°06'10"N	75°24'10"W
New Castle*	Iron Hill*	320*	39°38'19"N	75°45'08"W
Sussex	Wilson Hill	53	38°42'40"N	75°28'43"W

District of Columbia*

County	Highest Point	Elevation	Latitude	Longitude
District of Columbia*	Mount Saint Alban*	382*	38°55'50"N	77°04'15"W

Florida

County	Highest Point	Elevation	Latitude	Longitude
Alachua	Underwood Hill	163	29°49'37"N	82°33'38"W
Baker	Ellicotts Mound	121	30°34'07"N	82°12'53"W
Brevard	Mulberry Mound	27	27°52'34"N	80°47'08"W
Broward	Melaleuca Head	9	26°00'41"N	80°44'53"W
Charlotte	Cash Mound	22	26°48'21"N	82°10'47"W
Collier	Sand Hill	22	26°03'45"N	81°45'23"W
Dade	Panther Mound	15	25°34'22"N	80°45'33"W
Duval	Indian Mound	80	30°21'57"N	81°25'28"W
Escambia	Sunny Hill	205	30°44'01"N	87°23'23"W
Franklin	Sugar Hill	7	29°43'28"N	84°44'21"W
Hamilton	Jim Mike Hill	117	30°20'51"N	82°49'02"W
Hendry	Tonys Mound	22	26°33'15"N	80°56'26"W
Hernando	Chinsegut Hill	274	28°37'08"N	82°21'53"W
Hillsborough	Big Cockroach Mound	36	27°41'04"N	82°31'19"W
Holmes	Hudson Hill	298	30°51'22"N	85°56'18"W
Jackson	Sixteenth Hill	204	30°44'30"N	85°46'13"W
Jefferson	Texas Hill	231	30°33'23"N	83°52'18"W
Lake	Sugarloaf Mountain	312	28°38'57"N	81°44'00"W
Lee	Faulkner Mound	16	26°37'43"N	82°13'38"W
Levy	Spring Hill	131	29°25'30"N	82°35'33"W
Liberty	Red Hill	51	30°13'19"N	85°03'58"W
Manatee	Portavant Indian Mound	17	27°31'51"N	82°37'34"W
Martin	Pisgah Hill	57	27°13'03"N	80°13'04"W
Monroe	Basin Hills	12	25°14'16"N	80°19'31"W
Nassau	McClure Hill	56	30°40'54"N	81°27'00"W
Orange	Mulberry Mound	24	28°21'47"N	80°52'29"W
Osceola	Bunker Hill	186	28°19'19"N	81°35'57"W
Palm Beach	Big Mound	22	26°52'28"N	80°28'40"W
Pasco	LeHeup Hill	242	28°18'48"N	82°12'04"W
Pinellas	Sunset Hills	21	28°09'24"N	82°46'57"W
Polk	Iron Mountain	295	27°56'11"N	81°34'39"W
Santa Rosa	Mound, The	10	30°44'19"N	87°17'04"W
Sarasota	Caloosa Indian Mound	19	27°17'46"N	82°15'49"W
Seminole	Moccasin Mound	16	28°37'49"N	81°00'50"W
St. Johns	Squirrel Hill	32	29°49'06"N	81°26'25"W
Suwannee	Rocky Hill	155	30°09'53"N	82°53'19"W
Volusia	Bumcombe Hill	43	29°10'38"N	81°09'46"W
Walton	Danley Hill	302	30°58'24"N	86°11'44"W
Washington*	High Hill*	323*	30°43'52"N	85°29'07"W

Georgia

County	Highest Point	Elevation	Latitude	Longitude
Banks	Kelley Mountain	1,220	34°28'22"N	83°26'34"W
Bartow	Hanging Mountain	1,917	34°17'52"N	84°41'21"W
Bibb	Lamar Mounds	300	32°48'44"N	83°35'33"W
Brooks	Kennedy Hill	230	30°55'15"N	83°36'10"W
Burke	High Head	240	33°05'09"N	81°45'49"W
Camden	London Hill	25	30°51'14"N	81°36'23"W
Carroll	Blackjack Mountain	1,545	33°26'12"N	85°15'57"W
Catoosa	White Oak Mountain	1,495	34°54'40"N	85°06'00"W

County	Highest Point	Elevation	Latitude	Longitude
Chattahoochee	Bush Hill	699	32°21'46"N	84°42'11"W
Charlton	Ellicotts Mound	121	30°34'07"N	82°12'53"W
Chattooga	Lookout Mountain	2,242	34°59'00"N	85°21'00"W
Cherokee	Pine Log Mountain	2,331	34°19'15"N	84°38'29"W
Clay	Johnny Moore Hill	481	31°44'01"N	85°00'10"W
Clinch	Bird Sand Hill	138	30°51'53"N	82°36'16"W
Cobb	Kennesaw Mountain	1,808	33°58'34"N	84°34'47"W
Coffee	Rose Hill	310	31°39'42"N	82°56'24"W
Columbia	Carmel, Mount	500	33°36'20"N	82°24'46"W
Coweta	Dunbar Mountain	860	33°14'44"N	84°54'24"W
Dade	Lookout Mountain	2,242	34°59'00"N	85°21'00"W
Dawson	Black Mountain	3,600	34°36'48"N	84°12'17"W
DeKalb	Stone Mountain	1,683	33°48'22"N	84°08'45"W
Dooly	Sugar Hill	371	32°17'21"N	83°39'21"W
Dougherty	Fossil Sand Dunes	250	31°34'08"N	84°07'56"W
Douglas	Andy Mountain	1,340	33°43'51"N	84°51'14"W
Early	River Hill	300	31°27'00"N	85°03'22"W
Fannin	Cowpen Mountain	4,149	34°53'23"N	84°34'27"W
Floyd	Johns Mountain	1,723	34°31'17"N	85°08'39"W
Forsyth	Sawnee Mountain	2,060	34°14'12"N	84°09'38"W
Gilmer	Big Bald Mountain	4,081	34°45'04"N	84°19'15"W
Glynn	Liz Hill	22	31°19'41"N	81°32'37"W
Gordon	Baugh Mountain	1,188	34°32'38"N	85°01'16"W
Grady	Curry Hill	330	30°55'51"N	84°21'23"W
Greene	Cemetery Hill	640	33°34'53"N	83°10'53"W
Gwinnett	Lanier Mountain	1,200	33°50'58"N	84°02'11"W
Habersham	Tray Mountain	4,430	34°48'04"N	83°41'02"W
Hall	Buckhorn Mountain	1,479	34°24'20"N	83°51'15"W
Hancock	Granite Hill	520	33°17'32"N	82°56'08"W
Haralson	Reeds Mountain	1,560	33°42'06"N	85°07'57"W
Harris	Dowdell Knob	1,395	32°50'26"N	84°44'45"W
Heard	Stone Mill Mountain	992	33°18'14"N	85°07'47"W
Houston	Sugar Hill	371	32°17'21"N	83°39'21"W
Jackson	Price Mountain	1,210	34°10'28"N	83°45'46"W
Jenkins	Paramore Hill	280	32°45'49"N	81°54'40"W
Lamar	Hog Mountain	1,020	33°04'10"N	84°08'39"W
Lincoln	Graves Mountain	890	33°44'29"N	82°31'28"W
Lumpkin	Blood Mountain	4,458	34°44'23"N	83°56'13"W
McIntosh	Pilcher Hill	65	31°28'37"N	81°35'43"W
Meriwether	Betts Mountain	1,280	32°55'05"N	84°34'24"W
Monroe	Providence Hill	640	32°59'30"N	83°53'20"W
Murray	Bald Mountain	4,005	34°51'53"N	84°37'42"W
Muscogee	Watson Hill	380	32°25'13"N	84°52'25"W
Newton	Cornish Mountain	975	33°40'24"N	83°48'50"W
Oglethorpe	Big Mountain	760	33°48'16"N	83°01'55"W
Paulding	Vinson Mountain	1,320	33°55'52"N	85°02'44"W
Pickens	Oglethorpe, Mount	3,288	34°29'10"N	84°19'49"W
Pike	Indian Grave Mountain	1,264	32°59'37"N	84°21'03"W
Polk	Shorty Mountain	1,600	34°01'46"N	85°24'00"W
Rabun	Rabun Bald	4,696	34°57'56"N	83°18'00"W
Richmond	Rhodes Mound	115	33°15'41"N	81°51'57"W
Rockdale	Panola Mountain	940	33°38'07"N	84°10'13"W
Spalding	Barrow Hill	990	33°14'24"N	84°13'09"W
Stephens	Currahee Mountain	1,740	34°31'45"N	83°22'33"W
Talbot	Rockhouse Mountain	1,064	32°52'33"N	84°30'15"W
Taliaferro	Gunn Hill	600	33°32'59"N	82°56'22"W
Towns*	Brasstown Bald*	4,784*	34°52'20"N	83°48'36"W
Troup	Hogg Mountain	860	32°57'12"N	85°04'25"W
Union*	Brasstown Bald*	4,784*	34°52'20"N	83°48'36"W
Upson	Dorster Mountain	1,280	32°58'14"N	84°25'41"W
Walker	Round Top	2,340	34°50'15"N	85°24'18"W
Walton	Alcovy Mountain	1,070	33°43'57"N	83°44'41"W
Warren	Stony Hill	560	33°21'39"N	82°42'25"W
White	Tray Mountain	4,430	34°48'04"N	83°41'02"W
Walker	Johns Mountain	1,723	34°31'17"N	85°08'39"W
Whitfield	Dug Mountain	1,820	34°43'59"N	85°01'08"W
Wilcox	High Rock	390	32°00'52"N	83°32'42"W
Wilkes	War Hill	528	33°41'31"N	82°52'59"W
Wilkinson	Hillhouse Hill	410	32°55'42"N	83°09'02"W

Hawaii*

County	Highest Point	Elevation	Latitude	Longitude
Hawaii*	Mauna Kea*	13,796*	19°49'25"N	155°28'15"W
Honolulu	Puu Kaua	3,127	21°26'41"N	158°06'06"W
Kauai	Kawaikini	5,208	22°03'34"N	159°30'00"W
Maui	Red Hill	10,023	20°42'45"N	156°15'19"W

Idaho*

County	Highest Point	Elevation	Latitude	Longitude
Ada	Shaw Mountain	5,904	43°36'19"N	116°03'37"W
Adams	Monument Peak	8,957	45°13'37"N	116°33'25"W
Bannock	Bonneville Peak	9,271	42°45'47"N	112°08'23"W
Bear Lake	Meade Peak	9,957	42°29'49"N	111°14'53"W
Benewah	Reeds Baldy	6,153	47°22'32"N	116°22'31"W
Bingham	Birch Creek Mountain	7,486	43°16'31"N	111°51'40"W
Blaine	Hyndman Peak	12,009	43°44'57"N	114°07'48"W
Boise	Cramer, Mount	10,716	44°00'40"N	114°58'54"W
Bonner	Scotchman Peak	7,009	48°11'20"N	116°04'51"W
Bonneville	Baird, Mount	10,025	43°21'47"N	111°05'39"W
Boundary	Parker Peak	7,670	48°52'26"N	116°35'12"W
Butte	Diamond Peak	12,197	44°08'32"N	113°04'59"W
Camas	Baker Peak	10,174	43°40'12"N	114°40'44"W
Caribou	Meade Peak	9,957	42°29'49"N	111°14'53"W
Canyon	Pickles Butte	3,083	43°29'20"N	116°42'41"W
Cassia	Cache Peak	10,339	42°11'08"N	113°39'37"W
Clearwater	Rhodes Peak	7,930	46°40'30"N	114°46'58"W
Custer*	Borah Peak*	12,662*	44°08'14"N	113°46'46"W
Elmore	Snowyside Peak	10,651	43°56'18"N	114°58'14"W
Franklin	Wilderness Peak	9,460	42°02'26"N	111°38'46"W
Fremont	Targhee Peak	10,300	44°43'21"N	111°23'15"W
Gem	Wilson Peak	7,865	44°27'27"N	116°09'30"W
Gooding	Wrangle Hill	5,668	43°10'59"N	114°50'12"W
Idaho	He Devil	9,393	45°19'26"N	116°32'54"W
Jefferson	Sand Mountain	5,360	43°58'04"N	111°58'41"W
Jerome	Hazelton Butte	4,401	42°33'32"N	114°05'38"W
Kootenai	Latour Peak	6,408	47°26'02"N	116°21'39"W
Latah	Bald Mountain	5,334	47°01'54"N	116°34'15"W
Lemhi	Bell Mountain	11,612	44°14'12"N	113°11'40"W
Lewis	Mason Butte	4,639	46°11'47"N	116°33'39"W
Lincoln	Twin Oaks	5,894	43°08'37"N	114°33'39"W
Madison	Red Butte	8,108	43°39'38"N	111°20'22"W
Minidoka	Bear Den Butte	5,104	43°10'43"N	113°30'23"W
Nez Perce	Craig Mountain	5,290	46°04'34"N	116°51'02"W
Oneida	Elkhorn Peak	9,095	42°20'12"N	112°19'38"W
Owyhee	Cinnabar Mountain	8,403	42°58'27"N	116°39'23"W
Payette	Hog Cove Butte	3,782	44°07'03"N	116°33'16"W
Power	Deep Creek Peak	8,748	42°28'16"N	112°39'19"W
Shoshone	Illinois Peak	7,690	47°01'35"N	115°04'16"W
Teton	Piney Peak	9,020	43°37'48"N	111°21'28"W
Twin Falls	China Mountain	7,550	42°03'21"N	114°51'25"W
Valley	Big Baldy	9,705	44°46'58"N	115°13'05"W
Washington	Cuddy Mountain	7,715	44°47'04"N	116°47'26"W

Illinois

County	Highest Point	Elevation	Latitude	Longitude
Calhoun	Sugar Loaf	682	39°08'23"N	90°38'07"W
Franklin	Grammer Hill	549	38°02'16"N	89°00'42"W
Fulton	Tampico Mounds	572	40°24'55"N	90°01'17"W
Gallatin	High Knob	929	37°36'01"N	88°19'41"W
Hardin	Hicks Dome	677	37°31'53"N	88°22'06"W
Henderson	Gittings Mound	759	40°38'12"N	91°03'01"W
Jackson	Grassy Knob	811	37°36'50"N	89°25'46"W
Jersey	Tucker Knob	892	38°58'55"N	90°30'28"W
Jo Daviess*	Charles Mound*	1,235*	42°30'15"N	90°14'24"W
Kane	Johnsons Mound	898	41°51'51"N	88°25'45"W
Kankakee	Langham, Mount	733	41°03'39"N	87°46'21"W
Lake	Gander Mountain	957	42°29'37"N	88°11'33"W
Madison	Browns Mound	593	38°42'14"N	89°54'18"W
Marion	Lowe Mound	598	38°47'27"N	88°58'11"W
Monroe	Potato Hill	730	38°16'43"N	90°17'51"W
Montgomery	Bald Knob	767	39°10'31"N	89°15'54"W
Pope	Williams Hill	1,064	37°34'56"N	88°28'32"W
Saline	Cave Hill	923	37°40'56"N	88°25'04"W
St. Clair	Turkey Hill	611	38°28'11"N	89°54'02"W
Union	Government Rock	831	37°34'33"N	89°26'08"W

Indiana

County	Highest Point	Elevation	Latitude	Longitude
Bartholomew	Taylor Hill	1,018	39°10'43"N	86°02'14"W
Benton	Nebo, Mount	830	40°41'30"N	87°14'30"W
Brown	Weed Patch Hill	1,058	39°10'01"N	86°13'03"W
Cass	Morgan Hill	710	40°43'35"N	86°20'41"W
Clark	Round Knob	1,001	38°31'11"N	85°51'35"W
Clay	Cromwell Hill	660	39°25'28"N	86°59'16"W
Crawford	Pilot Knob	930	38°18'22"N	86°21'11"W
Daviess	Knob Hill	660	38°34'47"N	86°58'38"W
Dearborn	Harrison Hill	990	39°14'40"N	84°51'19"W
Dubois	Goss Hill	730	38°30'37"N	86°45'30"W
Elkhart	Buzzard Hill	940	41°27'55"N	85°49'07"W
Floyd	Hickman Hill	1,006	38°14'28"N	85°55'52"W
Franklin	English Hill	1,019	39°21'47"N	84°55'10"W
Gibson	Wilson Hill	626	38°16'26"N	87°21'27"W
Greene	Tunnel Hill	789	38°55'39"N	86°44'42"W
Harrison	Hayes Hill	940	38°04'13"N	86°11'49"W
Jackson	Pinnacle	966	38°52'36"N	85°59'34"W
Jay	Twin Hills	1,000	40°30'38"N	85°07'07"W
Johnson	Kelly Hill	870	39°36'57"N	86°05'04"W
Knox	Barefoot Nation Hills	596	38°46'25"N	87°21'55"W
Kosciusko	Dunham Hill	960	41°16'22"N	85°42'41"W
Lagrange	Knob, The	1,040	41°39'08"N	85°21'15"W
Lawrence	Gobblers Knob	910	38°42'01"N	86°35'17"W
Marion	Mann Hill	829	39°39'12"N	86°14'28"W
Martin	Sampson Hill	810	38°38'20"N	86°47'19"W
Monroe	Bearwallow Hill	1,033	39°15'03"N	86°12'59"W
Montgomery	Truax Hill	820	39°59'48"N	87°03'14"W
Morgan	Nebo, Mount	1,000	39°24'23"N	86°20'30"W
Noble*	Sand Hill*	1,060*	41°30'51"N	85°13'30"W
Ohio	Henschen Hill	820	38°59'51"N	84°51'52"W
Orange	Airie, Mount	906	38°34'25"N	86°38'11"W
Owen	Hale Hill	886	39°22'52"N	86°49'42"W
Parke	Vinegar Hill	670	39°26'51"N	87°01'45"W
Perry	Plock Knob	820	37°57'46"N	86°35'30"W
Pike	Turkey Hill	566	38°21'42"N	87°17'23"W
Porter	Holden, Mount	763	41°39'51"N	87°03'05"W
Posey	Aldrich Mound	372	38°02'45"N	88°02'04"W
Pulaski	Bunker Hill	750	41°06'08"N	86°34'09"W
Putnam	Moser Hill	934	39°32'58"N	86°46'03"W
Ripley	Hassmer Hill	960	39°05'08"N	85°14'54"W
Shelby	McFarren Hill	856	39°27'14"N	85°51'59"W
Spencer	Fisher Knobs	643	37°59'44"N	87°05'24"W
St. Joseph	Vargo Hill	920	41°33'43"N	86°20'38"W
Starke	Pigeon Roost Hill	745	41°10'28"N	86°36'58"W
Sullivan	Ladd Hill	630	39°08'19"N	87°31'08"W
Switzerland	Potato Bug Hill	910	38°44'28"N	85°06'46"W
Tippecanoe	Mound, The	740	40°23'26"N	86°44'34"W
Vigo	Sanford Hill	680	39°20'35"N	87°21'44"W
Warren	Copeland Hill	670	40°20'34"N	87°19'17"W
Warrick	Dyson Knob	650	38°12'52"N	87°17'03"W
Washington	Rock Knob	1,010	38°35'48"N	85°48'08"W

Iowa

County	Highest Point	Elevation	Latitude	Longitude
Clayton*	Sugar Loaf*	1,065*	42°38'36"N	90°57'36"W
Dubuque*	Sugar Loaf*	1,065*	42°38'36"N	90°57'36"W

Kansas

County	Highest Point	Elevation	Latitude	Longitude
Barber	Gypsum Hills	1,801	37°22'00"N	98°37'45"W
Bourbon	Guthrie Mountain	1,010	37°59'30"N	94°53'24"W
Butler	Oil Hill	1,380	37°50'10"N	96°53'07"W
Chase	Texaco Hill	1,637	38°05'23"N	96°22'46"W
Cherokee	Blue Mound	970	37°00'15"N	94°49'26"W
Clark	Nebo, Mount	2,441	37°16'53"N	99°45'42"W
Clay	Table Mounds	1,500	39°18'44"N	97°16'37"W
Cloud	Twin Mounds	1,521	39°30'32"N	97°30'40"W
Coffey	Jackrabbit Hill	1,100	38°14'03"N	95°43'44"W
Cowley	Hogback Hill	1,160	37°11'15"N	96°34'08"W
Crawford	Breezy Hill	1,016	37°32'10"N	94°39'00"W
Doniphan	Lookout Mountain	1,195	39°53'30"N	95°10'03"W
Douglas	Coon Point	1,110	39°00'15"N	95°25'32"W
Elk	Osage Cuestas	1,411	37°25'30"N	96°27'30"W
Ellis	King Hill	2,077	39°08'10"N	99°08'37"W
Ellsworth	Buzzard Roost	1,651	38°44'58"N	97°57'53"W
Ford	Boot Hill	2,510	37°45'14"N	100°01'15"W
Franklin	Fowler Hill	1,040	38°42'10"N	95°11'00"W
Geary	Franks Hill	1,320	39°01'27"N	96°46'03"W
Graham	Twin Mound	2,136	39°17'48"N	99°13'08"W
Greenwood	Temple Knob	1,650	37°41'58"N	96°29'39"W

Jefferson	Nolan Hill	1,036	39°06'32"N	95°18'07"W
Johnson	Observation Bluff	910	38°54'28"N	95°02'53"W
Kiowa	Iron Mountain	2,040	37°26'07"N	99°10'47"W
Labette	Bender Mounds	1,020	37°20'25"N	96°28'36"W
Leavenworth	Pilot Knob	1,100	39°17'50"N	94°56'10"W
Linn	Graveyard Mound	940	38°15'53"N	94°45'51"W
Logan	Twin Butte	3,340	38°47'08"N	101°23'03"W
Marshall	Twin Mounds	1,390	39°36'56"N	96°30'28"W
McPherson	Twin Mounds	1,540	38°31'02"N	97°29'45"W
Meade	Twin Hills	2,708	37°06'38"N	100°35'46"W
Mitchell	Williams Butte	1,808	39°15'22"N	98°27'14"W
Montgomery	Timber Hill	1,046	37°13'47"N	95°06'00"W
Nemaha	Albany Hill	1,272	39°56'13"N	95°47'52"W
Neosho	Long Mound	1,030	37°34'17"N	95°30'43"W
Norton	Horseshoe Hill	2,400	39°48'20"N	99°53'20"W
Osage	Elkhorn Knob	2,000	38°41'57"N	95°51'32"W
Pawnee	Jenkins Hill	2,095	38°10'36"N	99°09'42"W
Phillips	Blue Mound	2,030	39°50'25"N	99°08'39"W
Pottawatomie	Ephraim, Mount	1,260	39°23'19"N	96°24'02"W
Pratt	Pilot Knob	2,060	37°40'41"N	98°52'20"W
Riley	Sumner Hill	2,000	39°06'27"N	96°44'07"W
Rooks	King Hill	2,077	39°08'10"N	99°08'37"W
Saline	Soldier Cap Mound	1,578	38°42'58"N	97°47'42"W
Scott	Pawnee Mound	2,988	38°16'53"N	100°49'17"W
Shawnee	Burnett Mound	1,140	39°00'35"N	95°44'10"W
Sherman*	Mount Sunflower*	4,039*	39°01'19"N	102°02'12"W
Stafford	Pilot Knob	1,880	37°53'18"N	98°36'29"W
Trego	Round House Rock	2,360	38°44'02"N	99°39'07"W
Wabaunsee	Gun Barrel Hill	1,600	38°49'05"N	96°12'20"W
Wallace	Rock Hill	3,890	38°47'24"N	101°58'21"W
Wilson	Three Mounds	1,050	37°33'20"N	95°32'04"W
Woodson	Silver City Dome	1,125	37°45'06"N	95°47'30"W

Kentucky

County	Highest Point	Elevation	Latitude	Longitude
Bath	Tater Knob	1,388	38°03'18"N	83°32'33"W
Bell	Brush Mountain	3,153	36°39'34"N	83°34'00"W
Boyle	Parksville Knob	1,364	37°35'32"N	84°53'24"W
Breathitt	Drill Knob	1,450	37°28'18"N	83°07'23"W
Bullitt	Martins Hill	847	38°00'26"N	85°47'21"W
Butler	Buffalo Hill	640	37°20'11"N	86°35'41"W
Caldwell	Bald Knob	766	37°04'21"N	87°47'19"W
Carter	Hunts Knob	1,089	38°17'32"N	82°53'01"W
Casey	Green River Knob	1,789	37°09'12"N	84°50'42"W
Clay	Asher Knob	2,000	37°00'07"N	83°32'56"W
Clinton	Haw Knob	1,370	36°46'51"N	85°01'45"W
Crittenden	Cave Hill	901	37°18'48"N	88°14'08"W
Edmonson	Brooks Knob	852	37°11'30"N	86°12'09"W
Elliott	Locust Knob	1,316	38°08'17"N	83°01'59"W
Estill	Chrisman Mountain	1,499	37°37'23"N	84°06'13"W
Franklin	The Backbone	867	38°14'11"N	84°49'45"W
Gallatin	Johnson Hill	854	38°46'01"N	84°53'48"W
Grayson	Dug Hill	882	37°21'48"N	86°08'17"W
Green	Pilot Knob	1,031	37°08'34"N	85°39'38"W
Hardin	Blueball Hill	1,017	37°44'15"N	86°02'34"W
Harlan*	Black Mountain*	4,139*	36°54'51"N	82°53'38"W
Hart	Maxey Knob	1,082	37°16'01"N	85°42'10"W
Hopkins	Yarbro Hill	542	37°25'04"N	87°36'56"W
Jefferson	Dodge Hill	832	38°04'57"N	85°50'10"W
Jessamine	Wagon Bed Knob	1,382	37°55'03"N	83°51'22"W
Johnson	Stuffley Knob	1,508	37°46'59"N	82°55'13"W
Knott	Yellow Mountain	1,641	37°25'58"N	82°56'56"W
Knox	Kirby Mountain	699	36°59'17"N	83°56'54"W
Laurel	Cutoff Knob	1,654	37°09'03"N	83°59'32"W
Leslie	Chestnut Knob	2,605	36°54'30"N	83°24'14"W
Letcher	Halls Butt	3,115	37°01'56"N	82°48'51"W
Lincoln	Dry Knob	1,277	37°25'23"N	84°48'11"W
Livingston	Randle Hill	613	37°13'27"N	88°25'25"W
Logan	Buzzard Knob	853	36°49'12"N	86°48'32"W
Madison	Pinnacle Knob	1,597	37°32'04"N	84°14'19"W
Marion	Cooley Knob	1,127	37°31'53"N	85°02'56"W
Martin	Spring Knob	1,565	37°41'42"N	82°31'35"W
McCreary	Ryans Creek Mountain	2,165	36°39'18"N	84°18'21"W
McLean	Bates Knob	571	37°29'09"N	87°12'33"W
Meade	Hogback Hill	928	37°54'47"N	86°16'53"W
Menifee	Cedar Knob	1,367	37°57'39"N	83°46'12"W
Metcalfe	Pilot Knob	1,031	37°08'34"N	85°39'38"W

Monroe	White Hill	1,127	36°39'56"N	85°36'04"W
Montgomery	Westbrook Mountain	1,394	37°55'34"N	83°53'25"W
Morgan	Granddaddy Knob	1,272	37°58'22"N	83°09'06"W
Muhlenberg	Tooley Hill	703	37°07'01"N	87°07'49"W
Nelson	Watson Knob	984	37°41'37"N	85°31'51"W
Ohio	Seminary Hill	578	37°17'54"N	86°51'26"W
Pendleton	Pleasant Hill	877	38°46'22"N	84°18'27"W
Perry	Lost Mountain	1,847	37°19'03"N	83°11'00"W
Pike	Skeet Rock Knob	3,000	37°15'36"N	82°23'02"W
Powell	Rotten Point	1,425	37°54'34"N	83°55'31"W
Pulaski	Cash Knob	1,439	37°14'49"N	84°26'30"W
Rockcastle	Owens Knob	1,615	37°29'31"N	84°17'48"W
Rowan	Limestone Knob	1,435	38°08'16"N	83°28'36"W
Shelby	Jeptha Knob	1,188	38°10'38"N	85°04'11"W
Simpson	Pilot Knob	928	36°49'20"N	86°40'29"W
Todd	Pilot Rock	966	36°55'16"N	87°17'10"W
Trigg	Buie Knob	813	36°57'04"N	87°40'22"W
Trimble	Bunker Hill	686	38°36'21"N	85°15'34"W
Warren	Little Knob	772	37°03'21"N	86°13'39"W
Wayne	Bridgeman Mountain	1,724	36°42'48"N	84°56'05"W
Webster	Gobblers Knob	427	37°25'59"N	87°55'14"W
Whitley	Bear Wallow Mountain	2,188	36°39'27"N	83°59'26"W

Louisiana

County	Highest Point	Elevation	Latitude	Longitude
Avoyelles	Les Grandes Cotes	75	31°03'00"N	92°10'00"W
Beauregard	High Hill	58	30°23'13"N	93°42'41"W
Bienville*	Driskill Mountain*	535*	32°25'28"N	92°53'50"W
Bossier	Delaney Mount	461	32°55'46"N	93°44'49"W
Caddo	Pine Hills	395	32°35'18"N	93°51'49"W
Caldwell	Bayou Dan Hills	254	31°56'04"N	91°59'44"W
Cameron	Latania Hill	7	29°55'15"N	92°50'30"W
Catahoula	Chalk Hills	282	31°51'11"N	91°59'35"W
De Soto	Sand Hill	250	31°51'58"N	93°48'58"W
Grant	Johns Hills	305	31°41'29"N	92°29'06"W
Jackson	Buckenham Hill	272	32°28'44"N	92°33'47"W
La Salle	Bald Hill	291	31°45'21"N	92°05'06"W
Livingston	Rose Mound	13	30°22'57"N	90°33'57"W
Natchitoches	Negro Foot Hill	395	31°24'15"N	92°58'22"W
Ouachita	Pargoud Indian Mound	105	32°32'47"N	92°07'28"W
Rapides	Dough Hills	245	31°20'11"N	92°48'35"W
Red River	Couchanda Hill	220	32°00'14"N	93°24'07"W
Sabine	Eagle Hill	463	31°23'59"N	93°17'01"W
St. Bernard	Magnolia Mound	11	29°53'18"N	89°32'03"W
Washington	Bogue Chitto Mountain	350	30°58'31"N	90°09'40"W
Webster	Duncan Hill	425	32°53'40"N	93°15'27"W
Winn	Jordan Hill	160	31°51'38"N	92°31'41"W

Maine*

County	Highest Point	Elevation	Latitude	Longitude
Androscoggin	Shackley Hill	1,122	44°25'02"N	70°15'33"W
Aroostook	Peaked Mountain	2,270	46°34'13"N	68°48'52"W
Cumberland	Douglas Mountain	1,416	43°52'18"N	70°41'49"W
Franklin	Crocker Mountain	4,168	45°02'49"N	70°22'57"W
Hancock	Lead Mountain	1,475	44°51'53"N	68°06'35"W
Kennebec	Round Top	1,130	44°32'50"N	69°56'27"W
Knox	Megunticook, Mount	1,385	44°14'28"N	69°04'03"W
Lincoln	Haskell Hill	496	44°13'28"N	69°27'49"W
Oxford	Old Speck Mountain	4,180	44°34'15"N	70°57'18"W
Penobscot	East Turner Mountain	2,441	45°56'47"N	68°49'16"W
Piscataquis*	Mount Katahdin*	5,267*	45°54'16"N	68°55'22"W
Sagadahoc	Fuller Mountain	277	43°48'51"N	69°50'16"W
Somerset	West Peak	4,150	45°08'51"N	70°17'20"W
Waldo	Frye Mountain	1,139	44°28'34"N	69°13'03"W
Washington	Pleasant Mountain	1,374	44°53'24"N	68°01'07"W
York	Hosac Mountain	1,320	43°45'04"N	70°46'52"W

Maryland

County	Highest Point	Elevation	Latitude	Longitude
Allegany	Dans Rock	2,895	39°34'53"N	78°53'51"W
Anne Arundel	Eagle Hill	157	39°05'21"N	76°29'08"W
Baltimore	Spook Hill	780	39°38'06"N	76°43'12"W
Caroline	Opossum Hill	60	38°47'09"N	75°48'24"W
Cecil	Egg Hill	400	39°39'34"N	75°53'57"W
Charles	Rose Hill	160	38°31'13"N	77°01'43"W
Dorchester	Sand Hill	13	38°27'44"N	75°59'41"W

Frederick	Salamander Rock	1,842	39°34'32"N	77°29'18"W
Garrett*	Backbone Mountain*	3,360*	39°13'44"N	79°29'39"W
Harford	Kilgores Rocks	540	39°41'28"N	76°25'38"W
Howard	Annapolis Rock	618	39°16'47"N	77°07'55"W
Kent	Daves Hill	69	39°20'00"N	75°54'57"W
Montgomery	Hunting Hill	510	39°05'05"N	77°11'54"W
Somerset	Backbone Hill	40	38°15'38"N	75°37'25"W
St. Mary's	Blue Gull Hill	90	38°07'48"N	76°22'19"W
Washington	Quirauk Mountain	2,140	39°41'47"N	77°30'47"W
Wicomico	Ryles Hill	27	38°19'25"N	75°52'47"W

Massachusetts*

County	Highest Point	Elevation	Latitude	Longitude
Barnstable	Pine Hill	306	41°42'31"N	70°33'58"W
Berkshire*	Mount Greylock*	3,487*	42°38'15"N	73°10'00"W
Bristol	Copicut Hill	384	41°43'17"N	71°03'38"W
Dukes	Peaked Hill	311	41°21'23"N	70°44'22"W
Essex	Holt Hill	420	42°38'28"N	71°06'24"W
Franklin	Crum Hill	2,841	42°42'39"N	73°01'13"W
Hampden	Round Top Hill	1,794	42°15'20"N	72°59'12"W
Hampshire	West Mountain	2,125	42°31'55"N	72°57'33"W
Middlesex	Jones Hill	1,302	42°41'45"N	71°50'37"W
Nantucket	Sauls Hills	108	41°16'45"N	70°00'30"W
Norfolk	Great Blue Hill	635	42°12'43"N	71°06'58"W
Plymouth	Pine Hills	395	41°56'00"N	70°35'24"W
Suffolk	Bellevue Hill	335	42°16'35"N	71°08'40"W
Worcester	Wachusett Mountain	2,006	42°29'20"N	71°53'15"W

Michigan

County	Highest Point	Elevation	Latitude	Longitude
Allegan	Baldy	835	42°44'37"N	86°12'12"W
Baraga*	Mount Arvon*	1,979*	46°45'20"N	88°09'21"W
Barry	Hogback, The	934	42°28'39"N	85°23'46"W
Cass	Misery, Mount	1,040	41°57'13"N	85°46'34"W
Charlevoix	Richardson Hill	1,079	45°10'45"N	85°05'42"W
Chippewa	Velvet Hill	689	46°25'55"N	84°17'12"W
Crawford	Cote Dame Marie	1,524	44°35'58"N	84°47'44"W
Dickinson	Pine Mountain	1,523	45°49'59"N	88°04'55"W
Emmet	Emmet Heights	1,316	45°28'51"N	84°57'17"W
Gogebic	Wolf Mountain	1,826	46°26'30"N	89°46'15"W
Grand Traverse	McCrea Hill	933	44°42'05"N	85°39'24"W
Houghton	Tolonen Hill	1,506	47°02'10"N	88°41'44"W
Jackson	Prospect Hill	1,227	42°01'56"N	84°15'30"W
Kalkaska	Cleary Hill	1,476	44°35'56"N	84°53'00"W
Keweenaw	Gratiot Mountain	1,490	47°23'04"N	88°06'18"W
Leelanau	Sleeping Bear, The	1,044	44°52'20"N	86°04'03"W
Mackinac	Brulee Point	583	45°58'12"N	84°27'49"W
Marquette	Summit Mountain	1,873	46°27'00"N	87°37'48"W
Menominee	Buck Hill	771	45°25'49"N	87°50'02"W
Missaukee	Allen Hill	1,378	44°29'02"N	85°01'42"W
Montcalm	Maple Hill	896	43°22'04"N	85°28'46"W
Montmorency	Comstock Hills	1,449	44°51'23"N	84°19'04"W
Oakland	Waterford Hill	1,151	42°42'40"N	83°24'40"W
Ontonagon	Government Peak	1,850	46°47'00"N	89°43'51"W
Oscoda	Tom, Mount	1,462	44°44'45"N	84°08'03"W
Otsego	Redner Hill	1,424	44°52'19"N	84°35'33"W
Roscommon	Emery Hill	1,366	44°15'36"N	84°41'11"W
Van Buren	Thunder Mountain	821	42°15'21"N	86°20'54"W
Washtenaw	Peach Mountain	1,035	42°24'10"N	83°55'29"W
Wexford	Briar Hill	1,706	44°21'58"N	85°40'46"W

Minnesota

County	Highest Point	Elevation	Latitude	Longitude
Aitkin	Quadna Mountain	1,589	46°57'47"N	93°35'12"W
Becker	Toad Mountain	1,755	46°52'10"N	95°30'42"W
Cass	Maple Hill	1,546	46°38'55"N	94°29'14"W
Clearwater	Jack Pine Hill	1,951	47°15'23"N	95°30'10"W
Cook*	Eagle Mountain*	2,301*	47°53'51"N	90°33'36"W
Dakota	Buck Hill	1,195	44°43'23"N	93°17'13"W
Douglas	Tower Hill	1,582	45°51'10"N	95°37'06"W
Itasca	Big Thunder Peak	1,752	47°07'21"N	93°40'37"W
Kandiyohi	Tom, Mount	1,375	45°19'34"N	95°01'57"W
Lake	Stony Tower Hill	2,080	47°36'15"N	91°26'07"W
Norman	Frenchmans Bluff	1,354	47°11'57"N	96°10'56"W
Sherburne	Blue Hill	1,090	45°29'55"N	93°42'47"W
St. Louis	Lookout Mountain	1,851	47°34'24"N	92°32'08"W

Mississippi

County	Highest Point	Elevation	Latitude	Longitude
Adams	Emerald Mound	415	31°38'09"N	91°14'49"W
Alcorn	Crum Mountain	724	34°51'36"N	88°43'59"W
Attala	Arnold Mountain	555	33°15'31"N	89°33'24"W
Benton	Hamer Hill	712	34°51'28"N	89°14'21"W
Calhoun	Johnny Main Mountain	525	34°01'37"N	89°15'03"W
Carroll	Millers Hill	370	33°25'05"N	90°04'54"W
Chickasaw	Witch Dance Hill	549	33°57'34"N	88°55'02"W
Choctaw	Noxubee Hills	660	33°20'45"N	89°09'20"W
Claiborne	Petit Gulf Hills	265	31°53'44"N	91°11'11"W
Clarke	Bill Mountain	525	32°11'33"N	88°27'17"W
Clay	Reid Hill	420	33°42'12"N	88°52'14"W
George	Whiskey Creek Hills	207	30°55'38"N	88°49'14"W
Greene	Silver Hill	250	31°13'02"N	88°35'49"W
Grenada	Little Mountain	486	33°47'53"N	89°43'54"W
Harrison	Camp Hill	150	30°31'35"N	88°59'50"W
Hinds	Bailey Hill	365	32°16'23"N	90°11'55"W
Jackson	Carrol Hill	152	30°38'35"N	88°42'31"W
Jasper	Moss Hill	585	32°08'17"N	89°03'38"W
Jefferson	Blue Hill	475	31°45'45"N	90°53'37"W
Jones	Buffalo Hill	404	31°38'08"N	89°13'15"W
Kemper	White House Mountain	620	32°55'35"N	88°38'50"W
Lafayette	Thacker Mountain	623	34°19'41"N	89°34'46"W
Lamar	Hub HIll	435	31°06'35"N	89°38'41"W
Lauderdale	Tunnel Hill	555	32°20'46"N	88°49'11"W
Lawrence	Hope Hill	440	31°22'06"N	90°14'07"W
Marion	Red Hill	391	31°06'17"N	89°42'01"W
Monroe	Colberts Hill	320	33°58'20"N	88°33'43"W
Neshoba	Circle Hill	690	32°40'24"N	89°00'07"W
Newton	Nance Hill	603	32°15'24"N	89°13'37"W
Noxubee	Gholson Mountain	580	32°57'31"N	88°41'06"W
Panola	Terrapin Mountain	610	34°18'06"N	89°43'42"W
Perry	Deadman Hill	293	31°03'30"N	88°53'48"W
Pontotoc	Dozier Hill	509	34°18'23"N	88°53'38"W
Prentiss	Lebanon Mountain	790	34°34'17"N	88°43'44"W
Rankin	Indian Mound Hill	565	32°09'39"N	89°48'37"W
Scott	Sherman Hill	618	32°16'34"N	89°23'08"W
Sunflower	Prentiss Mound	130	33°17'49"N	90°37'36"W
Tippah	Wicker Mountain	745	34°47'15"N	88°56'44"W
Tishomingo*	Woodall Mountain*	806*	34°47'16"N	88°14'30"W
Union	Rockpile Hill	700	34°35'17"N	88°45'53"W
Warren	Fort Hill	350	32°22'12"N	90°52'09"W
Washington	Hardwood Hill	125	33°23'37"N	91°08'52"W
Webster	Sand Mountain	670	33°36'00"N	89°19'08"W
Wilkinson	Greenwood Hill	430	31°14'37"N	91°08'14"W
Winston	Smallwood Hills	716	32°58'00"N	89°15'54"W
Yalobusha	Spyglass Hill	388	34°08'16"N	89°47'16"W

Missouri

County	Highest Point	Elevation	Latitude	Longitude
Atchison	Brickyard Hill	1,140	40°28'29"N	95°34'33"W
Barry	Eggleston Mountain	1,574	36°32'09"N	94°00'21"W
Barton	Blue Mound	963	37°38'09"N	94°35'46"W
Bates	Long Mound	985	38°20'06"N	94°16'22"W
Bollinger	Turkey Hill	750	37°20'02"N	89°58'25"W
Buchanan	King Hill	1,068	39°43'09"N	94°51'32"W
Butler	Gobbler Knob	363	36°38'54"N	90°34'50"W
Caldwell	Needmore Hill	938	39°37'16"N	94°05'15"W
Camden	Deers Leap Hill	900	37°58'33"N	92°46'11"W
Cape Girardeau	Cave Hill	450	37°23'00"N	89°49'20"W
Carroll	Stokes Mound	895	39°35'18"N	93°28'52"W
Carter	Stegall Mountain	1,348	37°04'42"N	91°11'59"W
Cass	Christiansen Mound	988	38°31'33"N	94°28'14"W
Cedar	The Mound	1,095	37°39'34"N	93°40'20"W
Christian	Tater Hill	1,290	36°53'38"N	92°59'06"W
Clay	Arsenal Hill	914	39°11'56"N	94°24'23"W
Crawford	Crooked Hill	1,349	37°42'51"N	91°16'26"W
Dade	Sand Mountain	1,056	37°28'07"N	93°45'54"W
Dallas	Blue Mounds	1,275	37°33'34"N	93°09'34"W
Dent	Ball Hill	1,260	37°34'30"N	91°23'10"W
Douglas	Keyger Mountain	1,660	36°59'32"N	92°51'02"W
Franklin	Lone Hill	816	38°13'47"N	91°04'13"W

Greene	Fair Grove Mound	1,445	37°22'04"N	93°09'21"W
Henry	The Mound	889	38°14'30"N	93°58'20"W
Howell*	Queens Mountain	1,472	37°00'59"N	91°53'38"W
Iron*	Taum Sauk Mountain*	1,772*	37°34'13"N	90°43'40"W
Jackson	Bowler Hill	1,086	38°53'16"N	94°23'39"W
Jefferson	Vinegar Hill	1,065	38°01'04"N	90°32'11"W
Johnson	Knobs	917	38°46'36"N	93°33'07"W
Lafayette	Wagon Knob	1,005	38°56'41"N	93°57'37"W
Lawrence	Spanish Fort	1,212	37°03'23"N	93°49'58"W
Lincoln	Old Monroe Mounds	445	38°55'58"N	90°44'46"W
Madison	Black Mountain	1,506	37°28'09"N	90°29'40"W
Maries	Indian House Mounds	1,060	38°09'50"N	91°46'46"W
Marion	Harrison Hill	730	39°43'18"N	91°22'42"W
McDonald	High Point	1,287	36°35'16"N	94°14'01"W
Miller	House Mounds	653	38°10'19"N	92°18'26"W
Montgomery	Boland Knob	898	38°44'21"N	91°30'22"W
New Madrid	Indian Mound	317	36°34'19"N	89°35'18"W
Oregon	Mosby Hill	961	36°46'56"N	91°16'57"W
Osage	Grapevine Hill	765	38°29'20"N	91°58'30"W
Ozark	Bear Cave Mountain	1,465	36°40'43"N	92°25'35"W
Perry	High Knoll	677	37°45'50"N	90°00'26"W
Phelps	Blue Knob	1,288	37°47'41"N	91°32'12"W
Pike	Buffalo Knob	1,001	39°16'57"N	91°03'25"W
Polk	Blue Mound	1,328	37°35'14"N	93°11'09"W
Ralls	Lookout Mountain	807	39°38'14"N	91°15'20"W
Reynolds	Proffit Mountain	1,720	37°34'08"N	90°46'52"W
Ripley	Wolf Mountain	923	36°38'00"N	91°05'37"W
Scott	Scott County Hills	500	37°04'34"N	89°36'20"W
Shannon	Thorny Mountain	1,359	37°05'40"N	91°10'43"W
St. Clair	Kibbie Hill	887	38°03'05"N	93°50'29"W
St. Francois	Brown Mountain	1,650	37°40'57"N	90°35'56"W
Ste. Genevieve	Beehive Knob	987	37°48'21"N	90°14'48"W
Stoddard	Horsehead Knoll	340	37°01'34"N	90°08'49"W
Stone	Bread Tray Mountain	1,354	36°34'50"N	93°28'45"W
Taney	Baird Mountain	1,349	36°34'59"N	93°17'32"W
Vernon	Vetters Hill	973	37°49'21"N	94°36'51"W
Washington	Pruitt Mountain	1,582	37°44'20"N	90°50'06"W
Wayne	Mudlick Mountain	1,310	37°15'43"N	90°31'27"W
Webster	North View Hill	1,460	37°18'08"N	93°00'22"W
Wright	Lead Hill	1,744	37°06'04"N	92°38'14"W

Montana*

County	Highest Point	Elevation	Latitude	Longitude
Beaverhead	Tweedy Mountain	11,154	45°28'50"N	112°57'52"W
Big Horn	Lookout, Point	7,245	45°06'53"N	107°53'06"W
Blaine	Barber Butte	6,035	48°16'38"N	109°25'26"W
Broadwater	Baldy, Mount	9,472	46°26'25"N	111°14'48"W
Carbon	Castle Mountain	12,612	45°05'56"N	109°37'47"W
Carter	West Butte	4,450	45°05'27"N	105°01'15"W
Cascade	Long Mountain	8,621	46°56'37"N	110°41'29"W
Chouteau	Highwood Baldy	7,670	47°26'33"N	110°37'49"W
Custer	Hayes Point	3,764	45°49'03"N	106°01'32"W
Daniels	Gregerson Hill	2,972	48°51'11"N	105°53'25"W
Dawson	Antelope, Mount	3,464	47°16'06"N	105°23'53"W
Deer Lodge	West Goat Peak	10,793	45°57'46"N	113°23'39"W
Fallon	Seven-up Butte	3,487	46°10'54"N	104°32'08"W
Fergus	Greathouse Peak	8,681	46°46'07"N	109°21'18"W
Flathead	Stimson, Mount	10,142	48°30'52"N	113°36'34"W
Gallatin	Wilson Peak	10,700	45°19'37"N	111°19'29"W
Garfield	Smoky Butte	4,054	47°19'55"N	107°04'56"W
Glacier	Cleveland, Mount	10,466	48°55'32"N	113°50'50"W
Golden Valley	Tepee Point	8,409	46°44'56"N	109°22'14"W
Granite	Warren Peak	10,463	45°59'12"N	113°27'34"W
Hill	Baldy Mountain	6,916	48°08'55"N	109°39'00"W
Jefferson	Crow Peak	9,414	46°17'38"N	111°54'12"W
Judith Basin	Big Baldy Mountain	9,175	46°58'07"N	110°36'20"W
Lake	McDonald Peak	9,820	47°22'58"N	113°55'06"W
Lewis & Clark	Red Mountain	9,411	47°07'00"N	112°44'16"W
Liberty	Brown, Mount	6,958	48°52'26"N	111°08'18"W
Lincoln	Snowshoe Peak	8,738	48°13'23"N	115°41'18"W
Madison	Koch Peak	11,286	45°02'13"N	111°27'33"W
McCone	Lower Summit	2,910	47°13'30"N	105°31'21"W
Meagher	Baldy, Mount	9,472	46°26'25"N	111°14'48"W
Mineral	Illinois Peak	7,690	47°01'36"N	115°04'13"W
Missoula	Holland Peak	9,356	47°32'06"N	113°34'53"W
Musselshell	Johnston Mountain	4,677	46°15'28"N	108°22'01"W
Park*	Granite Peak*	12,799*	45°09'48"N	109°48'26"W
Petroleum	Rattlesnake Butte	3,488	46°52'22"N	108°10'37"W
Phillips	Old Scraggy Peak	5,708	47°56'19"N	108°31'38"W
Pondera	Morningstar Mountain	8,376	48°11'25"N	113°01'47"W
Powder River	Home Creek Butte	4,407	45°36'08"N	105°56'11"W
Powell	Powell, Mount	10,168	46°21'01"N	112°58'44"W
Prairie	Big Sheep Mountain	3,625	47°02'30"N	105°43'19"W
Ravalli	Trapper Peak	10,157	45°53'24"N	114°17'48"W
Richland	Flag Butte	2,745	47°48'33"N	104°46'05"W
Roosevelt	Castle Rock	2,757	48°29'21"N	105°36'31"W
Rosebud	Cook Creek Butte	4,505	45°26'02"N	106°43'40"W
Sanders	Snowshoe Peak	8,738	48°13'23"N	115°41'18"W
Sheridan	Kisler Butte	2,650	48°43'08"N	104°44'07"W
Silver Bow	Red Mountain	10,070	45°45'54"N	112°28'52"W
Stillwater	Hague, Mount	12,328	45°15'40"N	109°50'11"W
Sweet Grass	Douglas, Mount	11,298	45°18'24"N	110°08'20"W
Teton	Rocky Mountain	9,392	47°48'45"N	112°47'58"W
Toole	West Butte	6,983	48°55'54"N	111°31'58"W
Treasure	Whiskey Butte	3,652	46°02'20"N	107°13'32"W
Valley	Coal Mine Hill	3,302	48°52'55"N	106°30'43"W
Wheatland	Bluff Mountain	8,233	46°40'54"N	110°15'13"W
Wibaux	Red Top Butte	3,068	46°51'09"N	104°09'37"W
Yellowstone	Stratford Hill	4,971	45°31'07"N	108°35'52"W
Yellowstone National Park	Electric Peak	10,992	45°00'19"N	110°50'12"W

Nebraska

County	Highest Point	Elevation	Latitude	Longitude
Arthur	Bourquim Hill	4,074	41°38'50"N	101°59'04"W
Boone	Pilot Knob	1,998	41°36'00"N	98°13'50"W
Boyd	Harvey Buttes	1,903	42°54'07"N	98°51'00"W
Cherry	Indian Hill	4,184	42°07'18"N	101°58'48"W
Custer	Stop Table	2,900	41°12'51"N	100°03'33"W
Dawes	Coffee Mill Butte	4,180	42°40'27"N	103°04'37"W
Furnas	Rattlesnake Hill	4,319	42°04'27"N	103°45'26"W
Garden	Barn Butte	3,615	41°20'28"N	102°18'15"W
Grant	Wild Horse Hill	4,204	41°55'11"N	101°56'02"W
Greeley	Happy Jack Peak	2,057	41°26'33"N	98°42'31"W
Hall	Topeka Peak	2,099	40°42'09"N	98°35'20"W
Harlan	Sappa Peak	2,244	40°04'39"N	99°32'01"W
Keya Paha	McClain Hill	2,385	42°46'01"N	99°42'09"W
Morrill	Chimney Rock	4,226	41°42'14"N	103°20'52"W
Saunders	Indian Peak	1,471	41°25'53"N	96°46'57"W
Sheridan	Wolf Hill	4,280	42°15'04"N	102°09'40"W
Sioux*	Pine Butte*	4,501*	42°49'27"N	103°35'35"W
Thomas	Signal Hill	3,020	41°48'25"N	100°24'25"W
Thurston	Blackbird Hill	1,403	42°04'48"N	96°17'54"W

Nevada*

County	Highest Point	Elevation	Latitude	Longitude
Churchill	Augusta, Mount	9,966	39°32'23"N	117°55'03"W
Clark*	Fletcher Peak*	13,205*	36°17'13"N	115°37'15"W
Douglas	East Peak	9,591	38°56'33"N	119°54'25"W
Elko	Ruby Dome	11,387	40°37'19"N	115°28'27"W
Esmeralda	Boundary Peak	13,140	37°50'46"N	118°21'00"W
Eureka	Diamond Peak	10,614	39°35'07"N	115°49'04"W
Humboldt	Granite Peak	9,732	41°40'07"N	117°35'21"W
Lander	North Toiyabe Peak	10,793	39°21'36"N	117°04'25"W
Lincoln	Shingle Peak	9,823	38°30'30"N	114°55'37"W
Lyon	East Sister	10,402	38°31'24"N	119°17'19"W
Mineral	Grant, Mount	11,239	38°34'13"N	118°47'26"W
Nye	South Summit	11,941	38°45'08"N	116°55'33"W
Pershing	Star Peak	9,834	40°31'21"N	118°10'12"W
Storey	Davidson, Mount	7,864	39°18'30"N	119°39'44"W
Washoe	Rose, Mount	10,776	39°20'38"N	119°54'58"W
White Pine	Wheeler Peak	13,063	38°59'10"N	114°18'45"W

New Hampshire*

County	Highest Point	Elevation	Latitude	Longitude
Belknap	Whiteface Mountain	1,664	43°29'16"N	71°23'17"W
Carroll	Sandwich Dome	3,925	43°54'02"N	71°29'55"W
Cheshire	Monadnock Mountain	3,165	42°51'40"N	72°06'35"W
Coos*	Mount Washington*	6,288*	44°16'14"N	71°18'17"W
Grafton	Lafayette, Mount	5,249	44°09'25"N	71°38'27"W
Hillsborough	N Pack Monadnock Mtn	2,278	42°53'10"N	71°51'58"W
Merrimack	Kearsarge, Mount	2,937	43°23'00"N	71°51'27"W
Rockingham	Saddleback Mountain	1,184	43°10'49"N	71°12'05"W

Strafford	Blue Job Mountain	1,356	43°19'53"N	71°06'56"W
Sullivan	Grantham Mountain	2,661	43°30'02"N	72°12'10"W

New Jersey

County	Highest Point	Elevation	Latitude	Longitude
Bergen	Bald Mountain	1,164	41°07'15"N	74°12'02"W
Burlington	Apple Pie Hill	205	39°48'26"N	74°35'23"W
Camden	Pine Hill	199	39°47'53"N	74°59'37"W
Cape May	Potato Island	11	39°05'02"N	74°52'43"W
Cumberland	Pine Mount	153	39°25'05"N	75°20'11"W
Essex	Stony Hill	650	40°48'43"N	74°14'38"W
Hudson	Laurel Hill	201	40°45'36"N	74°05'06"W
Hunterdon	Fox Hill	1,035	40°43'58"N	74°48'20"W
Mercer	Strawberry Hill	475	40°19'22"N	74°53'45"W
Monmouth	Crawford Hill	390	40°23'25"N	74°11'04"W
Morris	Bowling Green Mountain	1,385	41°00'28"N	74°33'01"W
Ocean	Forked River Mountain	184	39°50'52"N	74°17'21"W
Passaic	Bearfort Mountain	1,480	41°08'22"N	74°23'32"W
Salem	Coffin Hill	122	39°29'23"N	75°21'31"W
Somerset	Mine Mountain	770	40°43'18"N	74°36'20"W
Sussex*	Sunrise Mountain*	1,653*	41°13'05"N	74°43'15"W
Warren	Kittatinny Mountain	1,549	41°19'15"N	74°39'43"W

New Mexico*

County	Highest Point	Elevation	Latitude	Longitude
Bernalillo	South Sandia Peak	9,782	35°07'13"N	106°25'47"W
Catron	Whitewater Baldy	10,895	33°19'25"N	108°38'28"W
Chaves	One Tree Peak	7,089	32°43'09"N	105°19'45"W
Cibola	Taylor, Mount	11,301	35°14'19"N	107°36'28"W
Colfax	Little Costilla Peak	12,584	36°50'00"N	105°13'18"W
Curry	Boney Hill	4,468	34°56'57"N	103°13'32"W
DeBaca	Alta, Loma	5,583	34°28'50"N	104°51'59"W
Dona Ana	Organ Needle	8,990	32°20'42"N	106°33'39"W
Eddy	Deer Hill	7,056	32°04'50"N	104°48'21"W
Grant	McKnight Mountain	10,165	33°03'07"N	107°50'59"W
Guadalupe	Cerro de Pedro Miguel	6,862	35°10'28"N	105°11'42"W
Harding	Sugarloaf Mountain	6,455	36°12'12"N	104°01'47"W
Hidalgo	Animas Peak	8,531	31°34'48"N	108°46'44"W
Lea	Soldier Hill	4,421	33°19'14"N	103°42'35"W
Lincoln	Capitan Peak	10,083	33°35'28"N	105°15'53"W
Los Alamos	Guaje Mountain	7,636	35°55'17"N	106°16'47"W
Luna	Cookes Peak	8,408	32°32'13"N	107°43'50"W
McKinley	Redondo, Cerro	8,976	35°18'20"N	107°29'12"W
Mora	Truchas Peak	13,102	35°57'45"N	105°38'39"W
Otero	Blanca Peak, Sierra	11,973	33°22'27"N	105°48'32"W
Quay	Palomas Mesa	5,325	35°03'43"N	104°02'36"W
Rio Arriba	Truchas Peak	13,102	35°57'45"N	105°38'39"W
Roosevelt	Mesita de la Madera	7,714	35°16'57"N	107°14'55"W
San Juan	Beautiful Mountain	9,388	36°29'20"N	108°59'19"W
San Miguel	Redonda peak	12,357	35°51'42"N	105°44'40"W
Sandoval	Redondo Peak	11,254	35°52'19"N	106°33'36"W
Santa Fe	Santa Fe Baldy	12,622	35°49'56"N	105°45'28"W
Sierra	McKnight Mountain	10,165	33°03'07"N	107°50'59"W
Socorro	South Baldy	10,783	33°59'27"N	107°11'13"W
Taos*	Wheeler Peak*	13,161*	36°33'24"N	105°24'59"W
Torrance	Manzano Peak	10,098	34°35'27"N	106°26'46"W
Union	Grande, Sierra	8,720	36°42'20"N	103°52'34"W
Valencia	Lucero, Mesa	6,850	34°48'51"N	107°08'40"W

New York

County	Highest Point	Elevation	Latitude	Longitude
Albany	Bennett Hill	1,135	42°33'54"N	73°57'48"W
Allegany	Alma Hill	2,548	42°02'58"N	78°00'45"W
Broome	Tarbell Hill	1,903	42°04'01"N	75°27'18"W
Cattaraugus	Flatiron Rock	2,387	42°01'37"N	78°26'40"W
Cayuga	Jewett Hill	1,447	42°41'58"N	76°26'37"W
Chautauqua	Pickup Hill	2,068	42°16'33"N	79°07'37"W
Chemung	Martin Hill	1,902	42°13'57"N	76°55'50"W
Chenango	Cary Hill	1,957	42°41'30"N	75°47'06"W
Clinton	Averill Peak	3,803	44°41'34"N	73°52'53"W
Columbia	Harvey Mountain	2,065	42°18'46"N	73°25'32"W
Cortland	Virgil Mountain	2,132	42°29'35"N	76°08'24"W
Delaware	Pisgah, Mount	3,345	42°13'16"N	74°44'10"W
Dutchess	Brace Mountain	2,311	42°02'39"N	73°29'35"W
Erie	East Hill	1,671	42°39'16"N	78°42'27"W
Essex*	Mount Marcy*	5,344*	44°06'45"N	73°55'26"W

County	Highest Point	Elevation	Latitude	Longitude
Franklin	Donaldson Mountain	4,108	44°09'14"N	74°12'41"W
Fulton	Pinnacle	2,496	43°13'05"N	74°23'22"W
Genesee	Burks Hill	1,412	42°52'36"N	78°05'17"W
Greene	Hunter Mountain	4,040	42°10'40"N	74°13'51"W
Hamilton	Snowy Mountain	3,899	43°42'01"N	74°23'11"W
Herkimer	Canachagala Mountain	2,606	43°35'17"N	74°53'57"W
Jefferson	Underwood Hill	1,142	43°54'30"N	75°49'45"W
Lewis	Beech Hill	1,152	43°50'45"N	75°21'16"W
Livingston	Scott Hill	1,942	42°29'53"N	77°48'17"W
Madison	Cranson Hill	1,495	43°00'50"N	75°46'03"W
Monroe	Baker Hill	928	43°02'05"N	77°25'25"W
Montgomery	Bean Hill	1,216	42°51'54"N	74°13'51"W
Oneida	Penn Mountain	1,813	43°22'46"N	75°15'37"W
Onondaga	Fellows Hill	2,019	42°48'40"N	76°01'18"W
Ontario	Bald Hill	1,845	42°42'52"N	77°34'52"W
Orange	Spy Rock	1,463	41°23'27"N	74°01'18"W
Orleans	Pine Hill	712	43°10'57"N	78°16'09"W
Oswego	Stone Hill	731	43°25'09"N	75°56'12"W
Otsego	Whalen Hill	1,780	42°41'27"N	75°03'58"W
Putnam	Bull Hill	1,420	41°26'18"N	73°57'22"W
Rensselaer	Berlin Mountain	2,798	42°41'31"N	73°17'12"W
Rockland	Rockhouse Mountain	1,283	41°14'20"N	74°05'29"W
Saratoga	Tenant Mountain	2,777	43°22'06"N	74°06'31"W
Schenectady	Glenville Hill	1,102	42°54'56"N	74°02'30"W
Schoharie	Jefferson, Mount	2,738	42°27'30"N	74°37'12"W
Schuyler	Huey Hill	1,892	42°24'14"N	77°00'16"W
St. Lawrence	Matumbla, Mount	2,688	44°16'57"N	74°33'57"W
Steuben	Call Hill	2,401	42°12'42"N	77°39'38"W
Suffolk	Bald Hill	295	40°52'48"N	72°42'38"W
Sullivan	Denman Mountain	3,053	41°54'10"N	74°32'24"W
Tioga	Prospect Hill	1,705	42°06'49"N	76°27'30"W
Tompkins	Connecticut Hill	2,099	42°23'11"N	76°40'10"W
Ulster	Slide Mountain	4,180	41°59'55"N	74°23'12"W
Warren	Puffer Mountain	3,472	43°39'42"N	74°11'59"W
Washington	Erebus Mountain	2,527	43°34'33"N	73°33'07"W
Wayne	Brantling Hill	681	43°08'51"N	73°04'09"W
Westchester	Titicus Mountain	952	41°19'16"N	73°33'46"W
Wyoming	Cobble Hill	1,693	42°46'19"N	78°17'15"W
Yates	South Hill	1,893	42°41'54"N	77°19'31"W

North Carolina

County	Highest Point	Elevation	Latitude	Longitude
Alamance	Cane Creek Mountains	975	35°56'48"N	79°26'10"W
Alexander	Walnut Knob	2,554	36°00'18"N	81°18'43"W
Alleghany	Peach Bottom Mountain	4,175	36°27'57"N	81°13'17"W
Anson	Gordon Mountain	636	34°54'35"N	80°12'13"W
Ashe	Bluff Mountain	5,100	36°23'27"N	81°34'18"W
Avery	Hump Mountain	5,587	36°08'24"N	82°00'42"W
Bertie	Fox Bark	47	36°11'19"N	77°17'22"W
Bladen	Susies Hill	100	34°43'55"N	78°31'25"W
Brunswick	Sand Hill	55	34°05'53"N	78°31'34"W
Buncombe	Potato Knob	6,420	35°43'47"N	82°17'30"W
Burke	Long Arm Mountain	4,240	35°57'35"N	81°53'54"W
Caldwell	Green Mountain	4,900	36°06'38"N	81°47'00"W
Carteret	High Hill	6	34°40'37"N	76°37'06"W
Caswell	Stony Creek Mountain	914	36°14'40"N	79°24'53"W
Catawba	Baker Mountain	1,700	35°39'27"N	81°24'23"W
Chatham	Terrells Mountain	755	35°51'59"N	79°10'03"W
Cherokee	Weatherman Bald	4,980	35°09'38"N	83°44'41"W
Clay	Signal Bald	5,260	35°08'43"N	83°43'34"W
Cleveland	Benn Knob	2,300	35°33'55"N	81°39'38"W
Columbus	Lynn Hill	140	34°20'34"N	78°45'27"W
Cumberland	Coolyconch Mountain	464	35°08'38"N	79°04'22"W
Currituck	Luark Hill	69	36°25'50"N	75°50'30"W
Dare	Kill Devil Hill	68	36°00'51"N	75°40'06"W
Davidson	Three Hat Mountain	1,180	35°45'10"N	80°08'04"W
Davie	Calahaln Mountain	830	35°55'29"N	80°40'11"W
Forsyth	Baux Mountain	1,008	36°13'35"N	80°12'10"W
Gaston	Crowders Mountain	1,385	35°13'58"N	81°16'37"W
Graham	Huckleberry Knob	5,570	35°19'19"N	83°59'37"W
Guilford	Pisgah Hill	945	36°07'12"N	79°50'28"W
Harnett	Holmes Hill	503	35°18'52"N	79°02'34"W
Haywood	Guyot, Mount	6,621	35°42'18"N	83°15'27"W
Henderson	Stony Bald	4,563	35°26'16"N	82°43'32"W
Hoke	Johnson Mountain	550	35°08'29"N	79°14'30"W
Hyde	Styron Hills	23	35°10'52"N	75°46'52"W
Iredell	Shumaker Mountain	1,820	36°00'09"N	80°59'29"W

Jackson	Richland Balsam	6,410	35°22'02"N	82°59'26"W
Lincoln	Buffalo Knob	1,400	35°33'15"N	81°30'44"W
Macon	Wayah Bald	5,342	35°10'49"N	83°33'38"W
Madison	Gravel Knob	4,860	36°03'40"N	82°37'39"W
McDowell	Pinnacle	5,665	35°42'15"N	82°16'33"W
Mecklenburg	Capps Hill	750	35°17'40"N	80°52'10"W
Mitchell	Roan Mountain	6,285	36°06'16"N	82°07'20"W
Montgomery	Dark Mountain	953	35°28'21"N	79°57'07"W
Moore	Pine Mountain	600	35°30'37"N	79°29'33"W
Northampton	Wilkins Hill	330	36°30'57"N	77°47'22"W
Orange	Pickards Mountain	840	35°57'49"N	79°09'36"W
Pender	Sand Ball Hill	27	34°25'15"N	78°01'29"W
Person	Bethel Hill	3,040	36°30'44"N	78°54'35"W
Pitt	Hill, The	70	35°35'58"N	77°21'53"W
Polk	Tryon Peak	3,235	35°15'58"N	82°14'37"W
Randolph	Shepherd Mountain	1,170	35°45'18"N	79°57'09"W
Richmond	Ingram Mountain	530	35°01'16"N	79°56'38"W
Robeson	Wolf Hill	120	34°31'47"N	78°51'28"W
Rockingham	Cedder Mountain	995	36°25'39"N	79°56'27"W
Rowan	Youngs Mountain	1,970	35°44'15"N	80°38'50"W
Rutherford	Sugarloaf Mountain	3,965	35°24'23"N	82°16'08"W
Stanly	Morrow Mountain	906	35°21'08"N	80°05'35"W
Stokes	Moores Knob	2,579	36°23'53"N	80°16'59"W
Surry	Saddle Mountain	3,100	36°30'03"N	80°55'38"W
Swain	Clingmans Dome	6,643	35°33'46"N	83°29'55"W
Transylvania	Silvermine Bald	5,965	35°18'32"N	82°53'00"W
Union	Red Hill	721	35°03'59"N	80°38'55"W
Wake	Adam Mountain	478	35°57'06"N	78°39'01"W
Watauga	Snake Mountain	5,518	36°19'52"N	81°42'28"W
Wilkes	Thomkins Knob	4,080	36°14'26"N	81°28'39"W
Yadkin	Star Peak	1,562	36°12'32"N	80°47'38"W
Yancey*	Mount Mitchell*	6,684*	35°45'53"N	82°15'55"W

North Dakota

County	Highest Point	Elevation	Latitude	Longitude
Adams	Wolf Butte	3,049	46°09'14"N	102°46'25"W
Barnes	Pilot Knob	1,484	47°03'23"N	97°51'16"W
Benson	Crow Hill	2,523	47°57'15"N	99°03'08"W
Billings	Bullion Butte	3,358	46°41'15"N	103°36'10"W
Bottineau	Boundary Butte	2,541	48°59'58"N	100°25'45"W
Bowman	Camel Butte	3,406	46°00'10"N	103°43'10"W
Burke	Little Butte	2,482	48°38'34"N	102°18'14"W
Burleigh	Haystack Butte	2,205	47°10'24"N	100°20'08"W
Cavalier	Kjemhus Hill	1,483	48°59'01"N	98°06'27"W
Dickey	Cannon Hill	1,452	45°57'52"N	98°22'31"W
Divide	Smoky Butte	2,218	48°40'26"N	103°33'44"W
Dunn	North Killdeer Mountain	3,176	47°30'32"N	102°52'36"W
Eddy	Devils Thumb	1,764	47°40'31"N	98°38'09"W
Emmons	Volk Butte	3,005	46°07'26"N	100°18'46"W
Golden Valley	Sentinel Butte	3,430	46°52'16"N	103°50'06"W
Grant	Pretty Rock Butte	2,799	46°08'28"N	101°48'30"W
Griggs	Butte Michaud	1,605	47°35'45"N	98°08'29"W
Hettinger	Black Butte	3,112	46°31'12"N	102°33'42"W
Kidder	Wagon Wheel Hill	2,195	47°19'03"N	99°41'22"W
Logan	Cactus Point	3,025	46°32'21"N	99°13'05"W
McHenry	Little Butte	1,742	47°54'59"N	100°46'08"W
McKenzie	Saddle Butte	2,823	47°51'33"N	102°53'31"W
McLean	Dogden Butte	2,291	47°48'49"N	100°45'39"W
Mercer	Medicine Butte	2,356	47°07'32"N	101°55'38"W
Morton	Hailstone Butte	2,483	46°54'47"N	101°40'29"W
Mountrail	Big Butte	2,465	48°26'42"N	102°46'45"W
Nelson	Blue Mountain	1,668	47°55'06"N	98°29'38"W
Oliver	Red Butte	2,301	47°11'15"N	101°34'30"W
Ramsey	Devils Lake Mountain	1,637	47°56'23"N	98°33'34"W
Ransom	Standing Rock Hill	1,490	46°37'25"N	97°54'28"W
Richland	Devils Nest	1,146	46°02'47"N	96°52'13"W
Sheridan	Klinks Slope	2,030	47°27'36"N	100°33'29"W
Sioux	Round Top	2,587	46°01'08"N	101°56'42"W
Slope*	White Butte*	3,506*	46°23'12"N	103°18'07"W
Stark	Flagstaff Butte	2,950	46°39'50"N	103°02'20"W
Stutsman	Morian, Mount	2,012	47°18'18"N	99°13'03"W
Ward	Twin Buttes	2,205	48°07'09"N	101°28'22"W
Wells	Hawks Nest	2,121	47°20'32"N	99°17'15"W
Williams	Bull Butte	2,588	48°20'13"N	104°01'54"W

Ohio

County	Highest Point	Elevation	Latitude	Longitude
Adams	Peach Mountain	1,260	38°53'43"N	83°21'43"W
Ashland	Bald Knob	1,220	40°39'16"N	82°14'21"W
Ashtabula	Owens Mound	1,191	41°37'05"N	80°36'30"W
Athens	Nebo, Mount	1,020	39°24'29"N	82°05'15"W
Auglaize	Lookout, Mount	1,118	40°35'52"N	84°01'41"W
Belmont	Galloway Knob	1,397	40°00'42"N	80°58'16"W
Brown	Cedar Hill	889	38°42'43"N	83°48'50"W
Butler	Heitsmanns Hill	900	39°24'20"N	84°37'18"W
Champaign	Beatty Knob	1,240	39°50'51"N	81°24'57"W
Clark	Knobs, The	1,258	39°58'14"N	83°39'53"W
Clermont	Galley Hill	875	39°09'01"N	84°11'55"W
Columbiana	Round Knob	1,446	40°40'19"N	80°40'21"W
Coshocton	Hardscrabble Hill	1,150	40°16'25"N	81°49'50"W
Cuyahoga	Orange Hill	1,180	41°29'26"N	81°26'06"W
Darke	Hills Of Judea	1,085	40°00'10"N	84°40'46"W
Fairfield	Jacobs Ladder	1,205	39°39'06"N	82°38'30"W
Fayette	Dumpling Hill	1,130	39°41'33"N	83°36'32"W
Franklin	Spangler Hill	817	39°51'17"N	83°00'02"W
Gallia	Prospect Hill	900	38°54'05"N	82°14'43"W
Geauga	Sugarloaf	1,396	41°24'00"N	81°06'15"W
Greene	Reeds Hill	975	39°48'34"N	83°59'23"W
Guernsey	Twin Sister Knobs	1,150	40°06'48"N	81°41'04"W
Hamilton	Goat Hill	820	39°07'00"N	84°30'09"W
Harrison	Wills Mountain	1,220	40°17'58"N	81°15'13"W
Highland	McCoppin Hill	1,322	39°09'51"N	83°23'50"W
Hocking	Schultz Hill	1,100	39°30'23"N	82°24'58"W
Holmes	Sand Run Hill	1,160	40°30'59"N	81°53'52"W
Jackson	Big Rock	890	39°05'58"N	82°46'32"W
Jefferson	Norton Hill	1,340	40°24'05"N	80°43'53"W
Knox	Rich Hill	1,362	40°19'29"N	82°43'28"W
Lake	The Knob	1,244	41°38'34"N	81°15'52"W
Lawrence	Stewart Knob	1,049	38°41'43"N	82°33'46"W
Licking	Beavers Hill	1,260	40°04'55"N	82°41'41"W
Logan*	Campbell Hill*	1,549*	40°22'11"N	83°43'14"W
Lucas	Sand Hill	632	41°43'36"N	83°34'14"W
Medina	Acme Hill	1,210	41°01'35"N	81°47'57"W
Meigs	Cedar Hill	860	38°53'27"N	81°54'11"W
Monroe	Boston Hill	1,266	39°39'32"N	80°52'39"W
Montgomery	Miamisburg Mound	981	39°37'38"N	84°16'52"W
Morgan	Green Knobs	1,115	39°44'29"N	81°56'24"W
Morrow	Hulse Hill	1,400	40°23'19"N	82°42'32"W
Muskingum	High Hill	1,285	39°50'03"N	81°46'02"W
Noble	Coffee Knob	1,181	39°43'27"N	81°32'48"W
Ottawa	Sugar Rock	615	41°33'56"N	82°51'21"W
Pickaway	Burning Indian Mound	735	39°34'31"N	82°55'29"W
Pike	Shepherds Mountain	1,310	39°08'25"N	83°19'37"W
Portage	Derthick Hill	1,340	41°18'32"N	81°09'36"W
Preble	Devils Backbone	965	39°37'39"N	84°40'02"W
Richland	Ralston Knob	1,410	40°46'46"N	82°38'12"W
Ross	Horseback Knob	1,342	39°14'16"N	83°05'27"W
Scioto	Mustard Hill	1,176	38°58'04"N	83°15'46"W
Shelby	Jefferson, Mount	968	40°14'35"N	84°20'04"W
Stark	Sponsellers Hill	1,260	40°44'57"N	81°19'01"W
Summit	Coal Hill	1,200	41°05'52"N	81°28'23"W
Trumbull	Trautman Hill	1,280	41°22'26"N	80°31'19"W
Tuscarawas	Elephant Knob	1,260	40°18'46"N	81°30'32"W
Vinton	Peck Hill	1,040	39°17'44"N	82°20'18"W
Warren	Little Mount	940	39°34'29"N	84°16'40"W
Washington	English Hill	1,300	39°33'24"N	81°08'16"W
Wayne	Munson Knob	1,260	40°40'23"N	81°55'47"W
Wood	Indian Hill	640	41°33'10"N	83°39'04"W

Oklahoma

County	Highest Point	Elevation	Latitude	Longitude
Adair	Workman Mountain	1,710	35°43'59"N	94°30'37"W
Atoka	Pine Mountain	1,273	34°37'55"N	95°55'04"W
Bryan	Buffalo Hill	729	34°07'46"N	96°07'57"W
Canadian	Red Hill	1,512	35°27'53"N	98°09'35"W
Cherokee	Blaylock Mountain	1,448	35°39'45"N	94°50'18"W
Choctaw	Bull Mountain	841	34°07'55"N	95°14'19"W
Cimarron*	Black Mesa*	4,973*	36°59'50"N	103°08'00"W
Coal	Flagpole Mountain	908	34°26'58"N	96°17'12"W
Comanche	Scott, Mount	2,464	34°44'40"N	98°31'54"W
Craig	Timber Hill	954	36°47'33"N	95°07'23"W

County	Highest Point	Elevation	Latitude	Longitude
Ellis	Flat Top	2,360	36°18'57"N	99°52'53"W
Grady	Gyp Hill	1,445	34°46'44"N	98°03'43"W
Grant	Red Hill	1,195	36°47'32"N	97°52'35"W
Greer	Walsh Mountain	2,303	34°58'35"N	99°24'37"W
Haskell	Sans Bois Mountain	1,680	35°04'55"N	94°58'28"W
Hughes	Lamar Mountain	1,110	35°04'46"N	96°08'25"W
Jackson	Cable Mountain	1,454	34°41'40"N	99°06'05"W
Jefferson	Monument Hill	1,083	34°14'24"N	97°54'55"W
Johnston	Lookout Mountain	1,097	34°23'43"N	96°40'32"W
Kiowa	King Mountain	2,411	34°52'15"N	99°17'36"W
Latimer	Winding Stair Mountain	2,451	34°42'33"N	94°40'38"W
Le Flore	Sugarloaf Mountain	2,564	35°01'34"N	94°28'06"W
Love	Peak Hill	971	33°55'18"N	97°05'16"W
McCurtain	Goblers Knob	1,507	34°14'57"N	94°33'04"W
Murray	Robbers Roost	1,072	34°29'42"N	96°58'57"W
Muskogee	Holt Mountain	988	35°22'44"N	95°09'50"W
Nowata	Steamboat Mound	1,222	36°49'37"N	95°31'02"W
Okmulgee	Twin Hills	912	35°44'35"N	95°50'45"W
Osage	Holmes Peak	1,030	36°12'26"N	96°02'56"W
Ottawa	Potato Hill	878	36°52'41"N	94°58'12"W
Payne	Twin Mounds	1,039	36°06'57"N	96°46'40"W
Pittsburg	Jackfork Mountain	1,563	34°39'52"N	95°30'02"W
Pushmataha	Middle Mountain	1,619	34°40'06"N	95°29'33"W
Roger Mills	Antelope Hills	2,604	35°54'15"N	99°53'03"W
Rogers	Indian Hills	870	36°10'23"N	95°45'50"W
Sequoyah	Quarry Mountain	1,382	35°36'25"N	94°50'26"W
Stephens	Petticoat Hill	1,268	34°29'52"N	97°52'36"W
Wagoner	Blue Mound	696	35°58'11"N	95°25'32"W
Washington	Blue Mound	1,008	36°49'01"N	95°49'22"W

Oregon*

County	Highest Point	Elevation	Latitude	Longitude
Baker	Red Mountain	9,555	45°03'52"N	117°14'43"W
Benton	Marys Peak	4,097	44°30'16"N	123°33'00"W
Clackamas*	Hood, Mount*	11,239*	45°22'25"N	121°41'33"W
Clatsop	Saddle Mountain	3,257	45°58'09"N	123°41'03"W
Columbia	Long Mountain	2,265	45°47'18"N	123°06'25"W
Coos	Bolivar, Mount	4,319	42°47'31"N	123°50'09"W
Crook	Round Mountain	6,753	44°23'32"N	120°20'47"W
Curry	Brandy Peak	5,316	42°35'50"N	123°52'41"W
Deschutes	South Sister	10,358	44°06'13"N	121°46'05"W
Douglas	Thielsen, Mount	9,182	43°09'11"N	122°03'57"W
Gilliam	Black Butte	3,435	45°10'40"N	120°01'10"W
Grant	Strawberry Mountain	9,038	44°18'45"N	118°42'56"W
Harney	Pueblo Mountain	8,725	42°06'00"N	118°38'55"W
Hood River	Hood, Mount*	11,239*	45°22'25"N	121°41'33"W
Jackson	McLoughlin, Mount	9,495	42°26'42"N	122°18'51"W
Jefferson	Jefferson, Mount	10,497	44°40'28"N	121°47'52"W
Josephine	Grayback Mountain	7,055	42°06'36"N	123°18'42"W
Klamath	Scott, Mount	8,938	42°55'23"N	122°01'00"W
Lake	Crane Mountain	8,456	42°03'46"N	120°14'23"W
Lane	South Sister	10,358	44°06'13"N	121°46'05"W
Lincoln	Yachats Mountain	4,140	44°20'47"N	124°00'44"W
Linn	Jefferson, Mount	10,497	44°40'28"N	121°47'52"W
Malheur	Sand Hills	8,928	43°27'20"N	117°26'03"W
Marion	Olallie Butte	7,215	44°49'15"N	121°45'45"W
Morrow	Black Mountain	5,932	45°12'48"N	119°17'38"W
Multnomah	Cemetery Hill	5,140	45°31'09"N	122°17'44"W
Polk	Laurel Mountain	3,589	44°55'25"N	123°34'20"W
Sherman	Wolf Mountain	2,632	45°11'27"N	120°31'14"W
Tillamook	Pinochle Peak	8,152	45°42'22"N	123°36'32"W
Umatilla	Tower Mountain	6,850	45°03'16"N	118°34'03"W
Union	Eagle Cap	9,595	45°09'49"N	117°18'02"W
Wallowa	Sacajawea Peak	9,839	45°14'42"N	117°17'29"W
Wasco	Wilson, Mount	5,599	45°04'01"N	121°39'25"W
Washington	South Saddle Mountain	3,464	45°32'54"N	123°22'25"W
Wheeler	Sugarloaf Mountain	8,881	44°50'03"N	120°10'25"W
Yamhill	Trask Mountain	3,424	45°22'18"N	123°27'19"W

Pennsylvania*

County	Highest Point	Elevation	Latitude	Longitude
Adams	Strasbaugh Hill	1,980	39°58'04"N	77°25'03"W
Allegheny	Rich Hill	1,273	40°34'55"N	79°50'27"W
Armstrong	Peach Hill	1,525	40°55'58"N	79°32'57"W
Beaver	Big Knob	1,383	40°43'12"N	80°11'59"W
Bedford	Blue Knob	3,120	40°17'18"N	78°33'43"W
Berks	Hemlock Heights	1,519	40°37'43"N	75°58'31"W
Blair	Schaefer Head	2,950	40°19'20"N	78°33'35"W
Bradford	Robwood Mountain	2,354	41°39'09"N	76°24'39"W
Bucks	Maycock Mountain	960	40°29'19"N	75°13'11"W
Butler	Eakin Knob	1,575	41°10'12"N	79°48'20"W
Cambria	Round Top	2,795	40°15'39"N	78°38'58"W
Cameron	Whittimore Hill	2,250	41°28'52"N	78°15'35"W
Carbon	Lake Mountain	2,180	41°02'38"N	75°36'20"W
Centre	Hall Mountain	2,400	40°59'50"N	77°16'42"W
Chester	Thomas Hill	977	40°10'37"N	75°47'50"W
Clarion	Zagst Hill	1,740	41°17'17"N	79°14'58"W
Clearfield	Boone Mountain	2,369	41°14'49"N	78°38'49"W
Clinton	Riansares Mountain	2,325	41°03'07"N	77°22'48"W
Columbia	Red Rock Mountain	2,449	41°18'37"N	76°19'32"W
Crawford	Pleasant Hill	1,662	41°49'05"N	79°54'46"W
Cumberland	Big Flat Tower	2,060	40°00'06"N	77°24'27"W
Dauphin	Big Lick Mountain	1,785	40°35'57"N	76°34'55"W
Delaware	Hunting Hill	412	39°57'36"N	75°27'18"W
Elk	Boone Mountain	2,369	41°14'49"N	78°38'49"W
Erie	Dowd Hill	1,730	41°56'43"N	79°36'37"W
Fayette	Devies Mountain	2,740	39°44'03"N	79°44'01"W
Forest	Bald Hill	1,787	41°36'02"N	79°02'19"W
Franklin	Big Mountain	2,458	39°57'01"N	77°56'13"W
Fulton	Big Mountain	2,458	39°57'01"N	77°56'13"W
Greene	Minnie Knob	1,595	39°44'25"N	80°08'44"W
Huntingdon	Butler Knob	2,320	40°17'36"N	77°58'00"W
Indiana	Penn View Mountain	2,160	40°26'09"N	79°10'39"W
Jefferson	Songer Hill	1,880	41°16'07"N	79°09'10"W
Juniata	Little Mountain	1,062	40°23'40"N	77°32'54"W
Lackawanna	Pinnacle Rock	2,600	41°25'40"N	75°45'08"W
Lancaster	Welsh Mountain	1,047	40°07'04"N	75°55'41"W
Lawrence	Fletcher Hill	1,332	40°55'34"N	80°19'37"W
Lebanon	Eagle Peak	1,280	40°20'18"N	76°11'09"W
Lehigh	Bears Rocks	1,604	40°44'03"N	75°45'36"W
Luzerne	Grand View	2,449	41°18'30"N	76°18'36"W
Lycoming	Laurel Mountain	2,330	41°28'25"N	77°06'11"W
McKean	Prospect Hill	2,340	41°48'47"N	78°22'53"W
Mercer	Wheeler Hill	1,373	41°23'36"N	80°19'27"W
Mifflin	Broad Mountain	2,340	40°44'01"N	77°40'06"W
Montgomery	Mill Hill	700	40°25'55"N	75°30'29"W
Monroe	Pimple Hill	2,212	41°01'44"N	75°30'31"W
Montour	Bald Top	1,051	40°58'37"N	76°38'32"W
Northampton	Gaffney Hill	1,016	40°37'33"N	75°15'20"W
Northumberland	Mahanoy Mountain	1,748	40°45'24"N	76°33'57"W
Perry	Big Round Top	2,210	40°15'31"N	77°38'43"W
Philadelphia	Georges Hill	215	39°59'01"N	75°13'28"W
Pike	High Knob	2,200	41°17'58"N	75°07'28"W
Potter	Bailey Hill	2,583	41°52'47"N	77°42'52"W
Schuylkill	Bears Head	2,094	40°51'00"N	76°04'48"W
Snyder	Hightop	2,100	40°48'14"N	77°15'55"W
Somerset*	Mount Davis*	3,213*	39°47'10"N	79°10'34"W
Sullivan	Huckleberry Mountain	2,503	41°17'21"N	76°29'53"W
Susquehanna	North Knob	2,693	41°42'55"N	75°33'39"W
Tioga	Fork Hill	3,002	41°58'01"N	77°28'04"W
Union	Jones Mountain	2,169	40°58'28"N	77°08'21"W
Venango	Pine Hill	1,688	41°21'21"N	79°32'11"W
Warren	Warren Rocks	3,000	41°53'33"N	79°03'09"W
Washington	Wheeler, Mount	1,516	40°07'52"N	80°14'31"W
Wayne	Ararat, Mount	2,656	41°47'29"N	75°27'21"W
Westmoreland	Birch Rock Hill	2,934	40°02'50"N	79°19'03"W
Wyoming	Bartlett Mountain	2,365	41°30'23"N	76°11'36"W
York	Stone Head	1,371	40°05'06"N	77°05'38"W

Rhode Island*

County	Highest Point	Elevation	Latitude	Longitude
Bristol	Townsend Hill	259	41°40'27"N	71°11'03"W
Kent	Badger Mountain	734	41°58'53"N	71°46'19"W
Newport	Dye Hill	453	41°33'13"N	71°46'27"W
Providence*	Jerimoth Hill*	812*	41°50'58"N	71°46'45"W
Washington	Pine Hill	553	41°34'09"N	71°37'52"W

South Carolina

County	Highest Point	Elevation	Latitude	Longitude
Abbeville	Parsons Mountain	832	34°05'00"N	82°21'48"W
Allendale	Gravel Hill	230	32°57'59"N	81°22'45"W
Anderson	Little Mountain	898	34°26'28"N	82°41'55"W

Bamberg	Quartemans Hill	220	33°16'17"N	81°05'52"W
Barnwell	Barnwell Hill	230	33°14'40"N	81°21'50"W
Beaufort	Indian Hill	30	32°24'03"N	80°34'10"W
Berkeley	Nelson Hill	95	33°20'38"N	80°08'43"W
Calhoun	Haigs Hill	317	33°48'19"N	80°56'05"W
Charleston	Windsor Hills	45	32°56'30"N	80°05'21"W
Cherokee	Thicketty Mountain	1,255	35°06'46"N	81°46'07"W
Chesterfield	Jumping Hills	590	34°41'45"N	80°19'56"W
Dorchester	Rosom Hill	50	32°56'49"N	80°17'28"W
Edgefield	Boles Mountain	647	33°56'36"N	82°02'20"W
Florence	Stockade, The	101	34°10'22"N	79°44'47"W
Georgetown	Sandy Island	62	33°53'23"N	79°07'05"W
Greenville	Coldbranch Mountain	3,357	35°05'49"N	82°40'30"W
Horry	Big Sand Hills	56	34°11'50"N	79°08'46"W
Jasper	Turkey Hill	40	32°28'44"N	81°09'49"W
Kershaw	Buck Hill	470	34°20'59"N	80°44'34"W
Lancaster	Fourty Acre Rock	500	34°40'07"N	80°31'38"W
Laurens	Big Knob	945	34°34'13"N	82°06'57"W
Lexington	Sand Mountain	410	33°51'29"N	81°03'08"W
Marion	Heaven Hill	35	34°01'43"N	79°29'20"W
Marlboro	Beattie Hill	85	34°38'07"N	79°47'15"W
McCormick	Laurel Hill	450	34°01'32"N	82°19'56"W
Newberry	Little Mountain	810	34°11'12"N	81°24'50"W
Oconee	Fork Mountain	3,294	34°59'33"N	83°04'50"W
Pickens*	Sassafras Mountain*	3,554*	35°03'53"N	82°46'39"W
Richland	Brice Hill	400	34°05'06"N	81°04'40"W
Spartanburg	Bird Mountain	1,480	35°10'59"N	82°12'55"W
Union	Beddington, Mount	795	34°43'29"N	81°48'18"W
York	Henry Knob	1,120	35°07'51"N	81°16'28"W

South Dakota

County	Highest Point	Elevation	Latitude	Longitude
Aurora	Archer Hill	1,690	43°48'59"N	98°40'32"W
Bennett	Brushy Butte	3,320	43°21'03"N	101°26'12"W
Brown	Crows Nest	1,465	45°47'21"N	98°39'34"W
Brule	Twin Butte	2,042	43°30'55"N	99°15'26"W
Butte	Castle Rock Butte	3,768	45°00'37"N	103°27'13"W
Charles Mix	Took Tay Hill	1,945	43°18'05"N	98°51'59"W
Clay	Spirit Mound	1,246	42°52'28"N	96°57'32"W
Codington	Punished Womans Mound	2,080	45°04'15"N	96°55'58"W
Corson	Thunder Hawk Butte	2,715	45°55'17"N	101°57'42"W
Custer	Butcher Hill	7,051	43°42'59"N	103°18'38"W
Deuel	Buffalo Hill	2,013	44°48'59"N	96°50'35"W
Dewey	Brewer Butte	2,281	45°26'11"N	101°13'40"W
Fall River	Parker Peak	4,840	43°23'56"N	103°41'28"W
Faulk	Waters Hill	2,035	44°53'58"N	99°15'43"W
Grant	Big Tom Hill	1,175	45°10'45"N	96°29'11"W
Gregory	Burnt Rock, The	2,045	43°05'08"N	99°01'01"W
Haakon	Grindstone Butte	2,682	44°11'49"N	101°47'52"W
Hand	Ree Hills	2,050	44°29'00"N	99°10'50"W
Hanson	Medicine Butte	1,390	43°43'50"N	97°56'10"W
Harding	Harding Peak	4,019	45°22'13"N	103°53'10"W
Hughes	Medicine Knoll	2,037	44°28'26"N	100°02'02"W
Hyde	Peno Hill	2,150	44°19'53"N	99°25'23"W
Jackson	Cedar Butte	2,756	43°37'08"N	101°17'47"W
Jones	White Clay Butte	2,516	43°56'17"N	100°40'42"W
Lake	Macey Hill	1,700	44°03'25"N	96°55'18"W
Lawrence	Crooks Tower	7,137	44°09'21"N	103°55'04"W
Lincoln	Canton Mounds	1,450	43°19'40"N	96°32'51"W
Lyman	Medicine Butte	2,262	43°58'00"N	99°36'03"W
Marshall	Pleasant Peak	2,080	45°49'12"N	97°27'16"W
Meade	Flagstaff Mountain	5,421	44°16'01"N	103°32'19"W
Mellette	Cross Butte	2,641	43°33'36"N	101°10'32"W
Moody	Egan Mounds	1,580	43°58'30"N	96°37'00"W
Pennington*	Harney Peak*	7,242*	43°51'58"N	103°31'52"W
Perkins	White Hill	3,133	45°33'10"N	102°54'20"W
Potter	Sugar Loaf Rock	1,858	44°57'57"N	100°22'30"W
Sanborn	Big Mound	1,310	44°03'19"N	98°05'14"W
Shannon	Porcupine Butte	3,695	43°10'48"N	102°19'23"W
Spink	Bald Mountain	1,480	44°50'52"N	98°39'16"W
Stanley	Standing Butte	2,219	44°34'39"N	100°47'03"W
Sully	Artichoke Butte	2,011	44°51'09"N	100°21'00"W
Todd	Eagle Mans Butte	3,178	43°19'25"N	101°12'54"W
Tripp	Dorian Buttes	2,595	43°10'24"N	100°10'01"W
Ziebach	Thunder Butte	2,755	45°19'12"N	101°52'49"W

Tennessee

County	Highest Point	Elevation	Latitude	Longitude
Anderson	Cross Mountain	3,534	36°11'53"N	84°13'51"W
Bedford	Ransom Hill	1,253	35°37'13"N	86°25'39"W
Benton	Round Top	690	35°51'08"N	88°12'23"W
Bledsoe	Worthington Knob	2,554	35°41'19"N	85°03'01"W
Blount	Thunderhead Mountain	5,527	35°34'07"N	83°42'23"W
Bradley	White Oak Mountain	1,495	34°54'40"N	85°06'00"W
Campbell	Flag Pole, The	3,534	36°11'53"N	84°13'51"W
Campbell	Cross Mountain	3,534	36°11'53"N	84°13'51"W
Cannon	Short Mountain	2,092	35°51'59"N	85°58'33"W
Carroll	Sand Hill	710	35°50'33"N	88°14'39"W
Carter	Roan High Knob	6,285	36°06'16"N	82°07'20"W
Cheatham	Whisky Hill	650	36°21'10"N	87°01'46"W
Chester	Sand Mountain	740	35°27'12"N	88°27'48"W
Claiborne	Bryson Mountain	3,200	36°34'09"N	83°50'07"W
Clay	Pilot Knob	1,410	36°35'18"N	85°28'19"W
Cocke	Old Black	6,370	35°42'53"N	83°15'19"W
Coffee	Big Butte	2,015	35°25'59"N	85°55'09"W
Crockett	Horns Bluff	302	35°51'31"N	89°06'31"W
Cumberland	Hinch Mountain	3,048	35°46'52"N	84°58'43"W
Davidson	Holt Knob	1,066	36°01'50"N	86°43'40"W
DeKalb	Round Hill	830	35°56'35"N	85°54'34"W
Decatur	Coalings, The	725	35°31'04"N	88°03'11"W
Dickson	Center Avenue Hill	810	36°04'20"N	87°23'32"W
Fayette	Gordon Hill	677	35°02'19"N	89°13'15"W
Fentress	Lost Mountain	1,810	36°13'33"N	85°05'36"W
Fentress	Reynolds Mountain	1,810	36°29'39"N	85°01'56"W
Franklin	Flat Top	1,890	35°05'26"N	86°08'25"W
Gibson	Caraway Hills	485	35°55'39"N	88°48'01"W
Giles	Hickman Hill	1,110	35°24'32"N	87°05'02"W
Grainger	Donehew Head	2,210	36°12'33"N	83°41'54"W
Greene	Gravel Knob	4,860	36°03'40"N	82°37'39"W
Grundy	Ross Mountain	2,350	35°21'04"N	85°35'28"W
Hamblen	Stony Mountain	1,720	36°20'18"N	83°10'09"W
Hamilton	Lookout Mountain	2,146	35°00'18"N	85°20'39"W
Hancock	Jabez Knob	2,550	36°33'05"N	83°14'03"W
Hardeman	Porters Mountain	634	35°04'57"N	88°58'24"W
Hardin	Sand Hill	755	35°05'13"N	88°05'29"W
Hawkins	Stone Mountain	3,610	36°22'44"N	82°47'23"W
Haywood	Richmond Hill	430	35°26'57"N	89°16'50"W
Henderson	Little Pine Knob	630	35°35'57"N	88°21'32"W
Henry	Owens Hill	550	36°25'59"N	88°09'43"W
Hickman	Buzzard Roost	870	35°52'26"N	87°24'04"W
Houston	Cooley Hill	650	36°16'31"N	87°49'32"W
Humphreys	Slaughter Hill	800	36°05'23"N	87°39'50"W
Jackson	Seven Knobs	1,020	36°17'07"N	85°35'27"W
Jefferson	English Mountain	3,629	35°54'04"N	83°17'53"W
Johnson	Bald, The	4,657	36°21'13"N	81°48'32"W
Knox	House Mountain	2,085	36°06'42"N	83°46'00"W
Lawrence	Oak Hill	1,015	35°15'48"N	87°13'48"W
Lewis	Cothran Hill	900	35°31'40"N	87°20'45"W
Lincoln	Copperas Hill	1,285	35°16'10"N	86°40'47"W
Loudon	Alexander Knob	1,313	35°42'37"N	84°10'46"W
Macon	Hard Scratch Hill	965	36°28'45"N	86°05'04"W
Madison	Norton Hill	610	35°31'43"N	88°46'47"W
Marion	Red Hill	1,950	35°07'23"N	85°49'49"W
Marshall	Welch Hill	1,250	35°23'37"N	86°44'38"W
Maury	Flanigan Hill	1,170	35°27'31"N	87°07'41"W
McMinn	Starr Mountain	2,290	35°16'10"N	84°30'54"W
McNairy	Peter, Mount	690	35°17'16"N	88°32'03"W
Mcminn	Prospect Knob	1,230	35°21'41"N	84°25'13"W
Meigs	Ten Mile Knob	1,250	35°41'04"N	84°38'57"W
Monroe	Haw Knob	5,472	35°18'34"N	84°01'36"W
Moore	Sam Burt Hill	1,075	35°18'09"N	86°16'11"W
Morgan	Big Fodderstack	3,345	36°06'27"N	84°24'56"W
Obion	Fishgap Hill	509	36°29'03"N	89°17'13"W
Overton	Hampton Mountain	2,025	36°10'49"N	85°14'32"W
Perry	Horseshoe Hill	910	35°29'47"N	87°43'11"W
Pickett	Golman Mountain	1,786	36°35'17"N	85°01'23"W
Polk	Big Frog Mountain	4,220	34°59'58"N	84°31'46"W
Putnam	Verble Knobs	1,995	36°07'21"N	85°12'54"W
Rhea	Lone Mountain	1,750	35°28'37"N	85°03'37"W
Roane	Roosevelt, Mount	2,036	35°51'58"N	84°42'49"W
Robertson	Jones Hill	805	36°32'01"N	86°39'01"W
Rutherford	Gowen Knob	1,425	35°45'01"N	86°14'52"W

Scott	Walnut Knob	3,240	36°10'18"N	84°26'44"W
Sequatchie	Bunker Hill	2,294	35°21'29"N	85°30'26"W
Sevier*	Clingmans Dome*	6,643*	35°33'46"N	83°29'55"W
Smith	Walnut Knob	1,250	36°08'36"N	86°03'39"W
Stewart	Pulley Hill	995	36°25'29"N	87°50'46"W
Sullivan	Rich Knob	4,247	36°30'30"N	81°59'03"W
Sumner	Wolf Hill	1,070	36°27'58"N	86°14'17"W
Tipton	Millstone Mountain	425	35°37'44"N	89°41'29"W
Trousdale	Millstone Knob	1,060	36°25'57"N	86°09'20"W
Unicoi	Big Bald	5,516	35°59'23"N	82°29'24"W
Unicoi	Big Stamp	5,516	35°59'34"N	82°29'25"W
Union	Weavers sKnob	1,680	36°20'34"N	83°54'59"W
Van Buren	Smartt Mountain	2,142	35°34'39"N	85°26'03"W
Warren	Harrison Ferry Mountain	1,946	35°36'46"N	85°37'59"W
Washington	Pinnacle Mountain	3,540	36°13'02"N	82°22'13"W
Wayne	Tie Camp Hill	1,030	35°16'32"N	87°40'56"W
Weakley	Red Hill	508	36°18'28"N	88°42'58"W
White	Chestnut Mountain	2,004	35°53'14"N	85°18'06"W
Williamson	Signal Knob	1,285	35°54'02"N	86°37'06"W
Wilson	Defiance, Mount	1,327	36°04'27"N	86°09'43"W

Texas

County	Highest Point	Elevation	Latitude	Longitude
Anderson	Kickapoo Mountain	568	32°01'58"N	95°28'50"W
Angelina	Moss Hill	406	31°10'39"N	94°24'14"W
Bandera	Taylor Mountain	2,185	29°43'33"N	99°31'37"W
Bastrop	Flag Hill	729	29°54'37"N	97°24'58"W
Bell	Sevenmile Mountain	1,245	31°04'27"N	97°52'15"W
Bexar	Smith, Mount	1,892	29°41'16"N	98°45'46"W
Blanco	Monument Hill	1,801	30°13'40"N	98°26'40"W
Borden	Mushaway Peak	2,862	32°43'26"N	101°24'02"W
Bosque	Jackson Hill	1,221	31°50'50"N	97°51'39"W
Bowie	Glass Hill	437	33°26'10"N	94°25'08"W
Brazoria	Damon Mound	146	29°17'28"N	95°44'45"W
Brewster	Emory Peak	7,825	29°14'44"N	103°18'12"W
Briscoe	Old Flat Top	3,085	34°24'09"N	101°05'56"W
Brooks	Quiteria Hill	75	26°53'01"N	98°00'54"W
Brown	Star Mountain	1,894	31°54'29"N	98°49'11"W
Burnet	Potato Hill	1,585	30°48'31"N	98°16'33"W
Caldwell	Round Mountain	705	29°45'06"N	97°30'19"W
Callahan	Eagle Mountain	2,204	32°16'24"N	99°33'25"W
Cameron	Rincon de las Viejas	36	26°00'13"N	97°21'28"W
Camp	Couch Mountain	538	32°55'35"N	94°47'47"W
Carson	Antelope Peak	3,373	35°35'28"N	101°34'08"W
Cass	Hickory Hill	478	33°13'20"N	94°12'39"W
Cherokee	Pryor Mountain	695	31°43'15"N	95°11'18"W
Coke	Goat Mountain	2,608	31°58'52"N	100°46'49"W
Coleman	Chandlers Peak	2,173	32°01'14"N	99°42'34"W
Colorado	Rocky Hill	450	29°51'09"N	96°38'28"W
Comal	Big Head Mountain	1,473	29°58'52"N	98°19'17"W
Comanche	Long Mountain	1,847	31°54'40"N	98°42'00"W
Cooke	Olive, Mount	837	33°28'05"N	97°04'36"W
Coryell	Fletchers Point	1,365	31°28'29"N	98°05'57"W
Crane	Hilltop	2,795	31°19'05"N	102°20'05"W
Crockett	Southwest Mesa	3,058	31°04'13"N	102°05'50"W
Crosby	Courthouse Mountain	2,986	33°26'05"N	101°24'20"W
Culberson*	Guadalupe Peak*	8,749*	31°53'28"N	104°51'36"W
Deaf Smith	Chalk Hill	4,018	34°49'56"N	102°38'18"W
Denton	Pilot Knob	838	33°09'05"N	97°11'56"W
Dickens	Soldier Mound	2,488	33°32'15"N	100°51'22"W
Donley	Ararat, Mount	3,151	35°06'59"N	100°56'55"W
Duval	San Cajo	712	27°58'15"N	98°29'23"W
Eastland	Coyote Peak	1,882	32°07'41"N	99°01'52"W
Edwards	Kelley Mound	2,242	29°40'24"N	100°07'55"W
El Paso	North Franklin Mountain	7,192	31°54'10"N	106°29'36"W
Erath	Lone Mountain	1,407	32°09'51"N	98°00'16"W
Fannin	Snow Hill	683	33°29'20"N	96°10'32"W
Fayette	Obar Hill	590	29°40'07"N	97°07'05"W
Fisher	Round Mountain	2,235	32°32'36"N	100°33'40"W
Foard	Dixie Mound	1,642	33°57'48"N	99°48'22"W
Fort Bend	Nash Dome	58	29°18'17"N	95°39'12"W
Freestone	Burleson Hill	608	31°36'01"N	96°06'09"W
Frio	Pilot Knob	763	28°56'18"N	99°16'59"W
Gillespie	Hermans Point	2,244	30°26'08"N	99°15'30"W
Gonzales	Russell Hill	504	29°38'11"N	97°09'23"W
Guadalupe	Capote Knob	726	29°29'39"N	97°47'26"W
Hamilton	Deadman Mountain	1,590	31°32'59"N	98°21'27"W

Hansford	Lightning Point	3,018	36°28'23"N	101°07'51"W
Hardeman	Big Mound	1,744	34°11'47"N	99°37'41"W
Harris	Wolf Hill	171	29°53'47"N	95°49'25"W
Hartley	Syndicate Hills	4,230	35°58'24"N	102°48'38"W
Hays	Jack Mountain	1,501	30°05'54"N	98°10'06"W
Henderson	Tater Hill Mountain	763	32°09'05"N	95°38'26"W
Hood	Comanche Peak	1,230	32°22'38"N	97°48'11"W
Houston	Houston Mound	552	31°34'30"N	95°24'33"W
Howard	Signal Peak	2,730	32°12'04"N	101°18'42"W
Hudspeth	Eagle Peak	7,484	30°55'16"N	105°05'05"W
Hutchinson	Signal Hill	3,239	35°50'39"N	101°23'37"W
Irion	Ketchum Mountain	2,725	31°19'28"N	101°02'46"W
Jack	Indian Hills	1,297	33°19'30"N	98°17'32"W
Jasper	Hi Truett Hill	475	31°00'18"N	94°00'27"W
Jeff Davis	Baldy Peak	8,378	30°38'07"N	104°10'22"W
Johnson	Caddo Peak	1,065	32°28'53"N	97°24'28"W
Karnes	Tordillo Hill	525	28°51'49"N	98°08'44"W
Kaufman	Sand Hill	383	32°31'53"N	96°28'17"W
Kendall	Big Hill	2,011	30°06'14"N	98°48'19"W
Kenedy	Alto de la Cruz	79	27°09'21"N	97°43'57"W
Kent	McKenzie Mountains	2,830	32°58'42"N	100°58'24"W
Kerr	Red Hill	2,231	30°05'10"N	99°32'03"W
Kimble	Allison Mountain	2,242	30°27'12"N	99°56'29"W
King	Haystack Mountain	2,019	33°26'58"N	100°26'31"W
Kinney	Boiling Mountain	1,981	29°31'19"N	100°06'45"W
Knox	Cedar Mountain	1,646	33°35'42"N	99°53'00"W
Lampasas	Messanger Mountain	1,647	31°09'31"N	98°22'50"W
Lavaca	Frederick Mound	503	29°35'24"N	97°09'32"W
Liberty	Davis Hill	261	30°18'57"N	94°50'26"W
Limestone	Horn Hill	665	31°32'49"N	96°39'07"W
Llano	Round Mountain	3,827	31°56'39"N	105°08'59"W
Marion	Locks Mountain	379	32°47'48"N	94°36'27"W
Martin	Range Hill	2,820	32°14'49"N	102°00'51"W
Mason	Double Knobs	1,981	30°48'01"N	99°21'07"W
Maverick	Deadmans Hill	912	28°46'07"N	100°23'09"W
McCulloch	Rattlesnake Point	1,988	31°15'58"N	99°32'04"W
McMullen	Pinta, Loma	642	28°04'10"N	98°30'43"W
Medina	Flag Mountain	1,995	29°37'20"N	99°14'29"W
Menard	Target Hill	2,261	30°48'52"N	100°05'56"W
Milam	Hart Mountain	648	30°41'28"N	96°53'15"W
Mills	Long Pompey Mountain	1,762	31°37'51"N	98°38'16"W
Mitchell	Hayrick Mountain	2,616	32°06'51"N	101°14'17"W
Montague	Blue Mound	1,318	33°40'31"N	97°37'52"W
Morris	Buzzard Roost Mountain	537	32°53'14"N	94°41'52"W
Motley	Antelope Hill	2,715	34°05'21"N	100°56'39"W
Nacogdoches	Denny Mountain	655	31°47'42"N	94°50'37"W
Newton	Twin Hills	510	31°07'04"N	93°49'46"W
Nolan	Bench Mountain	2,603	32°17'57"N	100°33'56"W
Ochiltree	Horseshoe Hill	3,007	36°28'57"N	101°02'45"W
Oldham	Torrey Peak	3,677	35°29'03"N	102°28'49"W
Palo Pinto	Crawford Mountain	1,470	32°46'51"N	98°22'18"W
Panola	Porter Hill	481	31°58'44"N	94°19'39"W
Parker	Indian Knob	1,275	32°57'04"N	97°45'19"W
Pecos	Clark Butte	4,797	30°23'26"N	102°54'09"W
Potter	Goat Mountain	3,793	35°14'21"N	102°02'54"W
Presidio	Chinati Peak	7,728	29°57'11"N	104°28'38"W
Randall	Cooley Butte	3,412	34°59'40"N	101°41'18"W
Reagan	Moore Hill	2,616	31°24'15"N	101°27'14"W
Real	Housetop Mountain	2,351	29°44'09"N	99°59'06"W
Red River	Stockbridge Knoll	287	33°24'49"N	94°53'14"W
Reeves	Spring Hills	4,514	31°05'46"N	104°05'18"W
Roberts	Tandy Mesa	2,843	36°01'09"N	100°39'22"W
Runnels	Moro Mountain	2,301	32°03'25"N	99°52'18"W
Rusk	Quinn Mountain	624	31°58'08"N	94°57'50"W
Sabine	Forse Mountain	590	31°31'12"N	93°58'48"W
San Augustine	Height Hill	502	31°33'37"N	94°00'03"W
San Jacinto	Camp Hill	263	30°51'18"N	95°15'17"W
San Saba	Shin Oak Mountain	1,930	30°59'27"N	98°52'17"W
Schleicher	Big Hill	2,429	31°05'05"N	100°32'43"W
Scurry	Flat Top Mountain	2,822	32°57'58"N	101°03'53"W
Shackelford	Indian Knoll	1,474	32°33'36"N	99°05'12"W
Shelby	Hollow Rock Mountain	585	31°47'46"N	94°22'53"W
Smith	Goodman Mountain	631	32°24'39"N	94°59'16"W
Stephens	Brown Pen Mountain	1,528	32°35'16"N	98°51'50"W
Sterling	McWhorter Mountain	2,513	32°01'51"N	100°53'45"W
Stonewall	Poke Mountain	1,905	32°58'22"N	100°16'59"W
Sutton	Twin Buttes	2,371	30°29'00"N	100°12'55"W

Tarrant	Blue Mound	864	32°56'40"N	97°21'06"W
Taylor	Buzzard Mountain	2,410	32°21'39"N	99°57'33"W
Terrell	Vista, Loma	2,100	29°52'13"N	102°05'04"W
Throckmorton	Hoover Mountain	1,583	33°03'17"N	99°23'07"W
Tom Green	Big Hill	2,429	31°05'05"N	100°32'43"W
Travis	Negrohead	1,330	30°33'22"N	98°03'22"W
Tyler	Blackland Hill	266	30°58'18"N	94°28'10"W
Upshur	Underwood Mountain	685	32°42'42"N	94°58'52"W
Upton	King Mountain	3,141	31°17'04"N	102°16'25"W
Uvalde	Sycamore Mountain	1,957	29°28'10"N	99°56'26"W
Val Verde	Blue Hills	2,155	30°03'20"N	101°20'11"W
Victoria	Indian Mound	53	28°42'48"N	97°00'46"W
Walker	Smith Hill	393	30°43'46"N	95°33'46"W
Ward	Hays Hill	2,799	31°29'55"N	103°19'55"W
Washington	Shepherd Mountain	423	30°16'25"N	96°34'54"W
Webb	Dos Hermanos Peaks	801	28°05'35"N	99°49'29"W
Wharton	Peach Break	88	29°22'21"N	95°58'04"W
Wheeler	Lime Hill	2,869	35°34'44"N	100°29'03"W
Wichita	Sunshine Hill	1,207	34°03'41"N	98°47'47"W
Williamson	Pilot Knob	1,208	30°45'41"N	97°53'55"W
Wilson	Rocky Point	781	29°17'27"N	98°13'14"W
Wise	Ball Knob Hill	1,180	33°22'42"N	97°38'26"W
Wood	Stivers Hill	630	32°54'46"N	95°13'45"W
Yoakum	North Windmill	3,792	33°16'50"N	103°03'00"W
Young	Flag Mountain	1,389	33°02'06"N	98°29'09"W
Zapata	Mogotes Hill	562	27°06'37"N	99°12'57"W
Zavala	Batesville Hill	956	29°01'48"N	99°43'00"W

Utah*

County	Highest Point	Elevation	Latitude	Longitude
Beaver	Delano Peak	12,173	38°22'09"N	112°22'14"W
Box Elder	Willard Peak	9,764	41°22'59"N	111°58'24"W
Cache	Naomi Peak	9,979	41°54'41"N	111°40'28"W
Carbon	Monument Peak	10,443	39°36'50"N	111°10'32"W
Daggett	Untermann, Mount	12,074	40°46'16"N	109°52'40"W
Davis	Thurston Peak	9,706	41°04'55"N	111°51'03"W
Duchesne*	Kings Peak*	13,528*	40°46'43"N	110°22'28"W
Emery	East Mountain	10,743	39°28'32"N	111°12'58"W
Garfield	Ellen, Mount	11,522	38°06'31"N	110°48'47"W
Grand	Waas, Mount	12,391	38°32'21"N	109°13'37"W
Iron	Brian Head	11,307	37°40'52"N	112°49'50"W
Juab	Ibapah Peak	12,087	39°49'42"N	113°55'08"W
Kane	Navajo Peak	9,965	37°30'45"N	112°48'30"W
Millard	Mine Camp Peak	10,222	38°52'27"N	112°15'10"W
Morgan	Thurston Peak	9,706	41°04'55"N	111°51'03"W
Piute	Delano Peak	12,173	38°22'09"N	112°22'14"W
Rich	Swan Peak	9,082	41°58'50"N	111°27'53"W
Salt Lake	Twin Peaks	11,330	40°35'38"N	111°43'13"W
San Juan	Peale, Mount	12,721	38°26'18"N	109°13'43"W
Sanpete	South Tent Mountain	11,285	39°23'32"N	111°21'24"W
Sevier	Marvine, Mount	11,610	38°40'06"N	111°38'25"W
Summit	Gilbert Peak	13,442	40°49'24"N	110°20'23"W
Tooele	Twin Peaks	11,489	40°33'07"N	111°39'21"W
Uintah	Marsh Peak	12,240	40°42'40"N	109°49'40"W
Utah	Nebo, Mount	11,928	39°48'39"N	111°45'52"W
Wasatch	Clayton Peak	10,721	40°35'26"N	111°33'32"W
Washington	Signal Peak	10,365	37°19'11"N	113°29'27"W
Wayne	Bluebell Knoll	11,328	38°09'35"N	111°29'57"W
Weber	Ben Lomond	9,712	41°21'48"N	111°57'35"W

Vermont*

County	Highest Point	Elevation	Latitude	Longitude
Addison	Abraham, Mount	4,006	44°07'12"N	72°56'10"W
Bennington	Equinox Mountain	3,852	43°10'13"N	73°06'42"W
Caledonia	Signal Mountain	3,348	44°12'20"N	72°19'31"W
Chittenden	Mayo, Mount	3,143	44°27'43"N	72°50'19"W
Essex	Gore Mountain	3,330	44°55'11"N	71°47'40"W
Franklin	Peaked Mountain	1,931	44°47'13"N	72°44'59"W
Grand Isle	Head, The	246	44°49'52"N	73°20'44"W
Lamoille*	Mount Mansfield*	4,393*	44°32'37"N	72°48'53"W
Orange	Butterfield Mountain	3,166	44°11'00"N	72°20'30"W
Orleans	Jay Peak	3,861	44°55'28"N	72°31'34"W
Rutland	Killington Peak	4,235	43°36'16"N	72°49'14"W
Washington	Ellen, Mount	4,083	44°09'36"N	72°55'47"W
Windham	Snow, Mount	3,556	42°57'32"N	72°55'27"W
Windsor	Gillespie Peak	3,366	43°52'17"N	72°58'40"W

Virginia

County	Highest Point	Elevation	Latitude	Longitude
Accomack	Cherrytree Hill	5	37°59'13"N	75°18'00"W
Albemarle	Big Flat Mountain	3,389	38°14'50"N	78°40'13"W
Alleghany	Big Knob	4,072	37°50'55"N	79°55'38"W
Amherst	Bald Knob	4,040	37°44'24"N	79°13'26"W
Appomattox	Kyles Mountain	1,161	37°28'44"N	78°44'08"W
Arlington	Minor Hill	460	38°54'12"N	77°09'28"W
Augusta	Elliott Knob	4,463	38°09'59"N	79°18'53"W
Augusta	Great North Mountain	4,463	38°09'59"N	79°18'52"W
Bath	Bald Knob	4,240	37°55'27"N	79°51'08"W
Bedford	Apple Orchard Mountain	4,225	37°31'01"N	79°30'38"W
Bland	Gose Knob	4,084	37°08'07"N	81°18'42"W
Botetourt	Apple Orchard Mountain	4,225	37°31'01"N	79°30'38"W
Brunswick	Fort Hill	230	36°42'55"N	77°52'09"W
Buchanan	Big A Mountain	3,706	37°03'09"N	82°02'09"W
Buckingham	Spears Mountain	1,604	37°33'42"N	78°45'47"W
Campbell	Long Mountain	1,428	37°18'03"N	79°04'17"W
Carroll	Pike Knob	5,187	36°42'47"N	80°46'08"W
Charlotte	Lyle Mountain	780	37°12'07"N	78°41'31"W
Chesterfield	Blanco Mount	90	37°21'42"N	77°18'39"W
Clarke	Buzzard Hill	1,301	39°04'53"N	77°54'05"W
Craig	Arnolds Knob	3,932	37°29'31"N	80°20'39"W
Culpeper	Scott Mountain	890	38°32'28"N	78°04'53"W
Dickenson	Skeg Knob	2,720	37°16'19"N	82°20'54"W
Dinwiddie	Gunns Hill	350	37°01'14"N	77°44'04"W
Fairfax	Gantt Hill	520	38°55'29"N	77°13'57"W
Fauquier	Rattlesnake Mountain	2,140	38°51'52"N	78°02'36"W
Floyd	Buffalo Mountain	3,971	36°47'45"N	80°28'38"W
Fluvanna	Little Mountain Hill	530	37°48'51"N	78°17'09"W
Franklin	Cahas Mountain	3,571	37°07'02"N	80°00'57"W
Frederick	Paddy Mountain	3,013	39°00'24"N	78°33'49"W
Giles	Bald Knob	4,361	37°21'00"N	80°32'15"W
Gloucester	Church Hill	100	37°27'54"N	76°36'06"W
Goochland	Sabot Hill	235	37°37'24"N	77°45'33"W
Grayson*	Mount Rogers*	5,729*	36°39'35"N	81°32'41"W
Greene	Hightop	3,587	38°20'11"N	78°33'05"W
Henry	Drag Mountain	1,909	36°33'55"N	79°47'31"W
Highland	Bald Knob	4,480	38°24'26"N	79°42'45"W
James City	Folly, Mount	100	37°26'06"N	76°44'16"W
King & Queen	Dickeys Hill	153	37°45'03"N	76°58'48"W
Lee	Potato Hill	3,680	36°53'11"N	82°53'10"W
Loudoun	Purcell Knob	1,200	39°15'29"N	77°45'00"W
Madison	Hawksbill	4,050	38°33'19"N	78°23'43"W
Mecklenburg	Ivy Hill	402	36°35'17"N	78°26'03"W
Montgomery	Bruisers Knob	3,448	37°21'11"N	80°20'38"W
Nelson	Priest, The	4,063	37°49'11"N	79°03'46"W
Northampton	Isaacs, The	5	37°05'11"N	75°57'30"W
Orange	Cowherd Mountain	1,197	38°09'35"N	78°14'13"W
Page	Hawksbill	4,050	38°33'19"N	78°23'43"W
Patrick	Rocky Knob	3,572	36°49'10"N	80°20'33"W
Pittsylvania	Greer Knob	1,636	36°59'34"N	79°35'41"W
Prince Edward	Baker Mountain	720	37°12'14"N	78°38'58"W
Prince William	High Point Mountain	1,311	38°51'22"N	74°42'52"W
Pulaski	Dead Pine Mountain	3,440	36°55'45"N	80°42'52"W
Rappahannock	Marys Rock	3,514	38°38'59"N	78°19'03"W
Richmond	Bald Eagle Hill	160	38°02'26"N	76°53'34"W
Roanoke	Poor Mountain	3,920	37°11'51"N	80°09'09"W
Rockbridge	Elk Pond Mountain	4,034	37°48'44"N	79°09'54"W
Rockingham	Slate Springs Mountain	4,360	38°30'35"N	79°11'03"W
Russell	Beartown Mountain	4,689	36°56'10"N	81°53'12"W
Scott	Bowling Knob	3,557	36°46'33"N	82°47'28"W
Shenandoah	Mill Mountain	3,293	38°58'42"N	78°37'54"W
Smyth*	Mount Rogers*	5,729*	36°39'35"N	81°32'41"W
Spotsylvania	Hamiltons Thicket	410	38°17'33"N	77°42'39"W
Tazewell	Hutchinson Rock	4,480	37°06'08"N	81°24'03"W
Warren	Hogback Mountain	3,474	38°45'43"N	78°16'27"W
Washington	Beech Mountain	4,966	36°38'10"N	81°37'33"W
Westmoreland	Prospect Hill	150	38°04'25"N	76°43'23"W
Wise	Little Mountain	4,260	36°52'50"N	82°37'59"W
Wythe	Buzzard Rock	3,940	36°45'47"N	81°15'43"W

Washington*

County	Highest Point	Elevation	Latitude	Longitude
Adams	Coyote Butte	1,729	46°52'48"N	118°08'07"W
Asotin	Saddle Butte	5,900	46°04'14"N	117°27'39"W

Benton	Lookout	3,629	46°26'52"N	119°50'20"W
Chelan	Bonanza Peak	9,511	48°14'17"N	120°51'54"W
Clallam	Greywolf Mountain	7,218	47°52'57"N	123°12'20"W
Clark	Pyramid Rock	3,503	45°43'52"N	122°15'15"W
Columbia	Oregon Butte	6,387	46°06'38"N	117°40'41"W
Cowlitz	Goat Mountain	4,965	46°09'50"N	122°17'55"W
Douglas	Moses Stool	3,619	47°29'04"N	120°00'27"W
Ferry	Copper Butte	7,135	48°42'09"N	118°27'51"W
Franklin	Jackass Mountain	911	46°25'44"N	119°04'31"W
Garfield	Diamond Peak	6,379	46°06'56"N	117°32'18"W
Grant	Mounment Hill	2,882	47°19'14"N	119°47'58"W
Grays Harbor	Hoquiam, Mount	4,909	47°31'15"N	123°35'32"W
Island	Goose Rock	484	48°24'07"N	122°38'19"W
Jefferson	West Peak	7,965	47°48'05"N	123°42'35"W
King	Daniel, Mount	7,899	47°33'54"N	121°10'43"W
Kitsap	Goat Mountain	6,579	47°29'07"N	121°04'19"W
Kittitas	Daniel, Mount	7,899	47°33'54"N	121°10'43"W
Klickitat	Indian Rock	5,823	45°59'21"N	120°49'18"W
Lewis	Old Snowy Mountain	7,530	46°30'44"N	121°27'10"W
Lincoln	Lilienthal Mountain	3,568	47°54'37"N	118°13'56"W
Mason	Stone, Mount	6,612	47°36'24"N	123°15'55"W
Okanogan	North Gardner Mountain	8,956	48°30'56"N	120°30'02"W
Pacific	Walville Peak	2,419	46°35'23"N	123°24'53"W
Pend Oreille	Gypsy Peak	7,309	48°56'45"N	117°09'04"W
Pierce*	Mount Rainier*	14,410*	46°51'10"N	121°45'31"W
San Juan	Constitution, Mount	2,454	48°40'28"N	122°50'42"W
Skagit	Buckner Mountain	9,112	48°29'43"N	120°59'48"W
Skamania	Saint Helens, Mount	9,677	46°11'52"N	122°11'28"W
Snohomish	Glacier Peak	10,541	48°06'41"N	121°06'46"W
Spokane	Spokane Mount	5,878	47°55'17"N	117°06'47"W
Stevens	Abercrombie Mountain	7,308	48°55'42"N	117°27'29"W
Thurston	Clam Mountain	2,725	46°45'51"N	122°31'59"W
Wahkiakum	Elk Mountain	1,505	46°19'56"N	123°32'42"W
Walla Walla	Lewis Peak	4,888	46°03'42"N	117°59'50"W
Whatcom	Baker, Mount	10,785	48°46'39"N	121°48'43"W
Whitman	Kamiak Butte	3,641	46°51'45"N	117°09'57"W
Yakima	Adams, Mount	12,276	46°12'10"N	121°29'22"W

West Virginia

County	Highest Point	Elevation	Latitude	Longitude
Barbour	Thorn Knob	2,881	39°04'07"N	79°51'39"W
Berkeley	Third Hill Mountain	2,172	39°26'19"N	78°11'41"W
Boone	Pilot Knob	3,360	37°47'32"N	81°30'56"W
Braxton	Ware Mountain	2,000	38°37'47"N	80°32'17"W
Brooke	Mechling Hill	1,240	40°21'02"N	80°32'24"W
Cabell	Porter Knob	1,138	38°21'38"N	82°09'30"W
Calhoun	Mule Knob	1,584	38°41'59"N	81°03'47"W
Clay	Bird Knob	1,864	38°18'50"N	81°14'01"W
Fayette	Myles Knob	3,460	37°58'29"N	80°48'27"W
Gilmer	Powell Knob	1,450	38°54'06"N	80°48'45"W
Grant	Pigeonroost	3,525	39°11'14"N	79°13'27"W
Greenbrier	Grassy Knob	4,360	38°03'54"N	80°29'50"W
Hampshire	Pinnacle	2,844	39°08'35"N	78°26'06"W
Hancock	Stewart Hill	1,365	40°35'51"N	80°31'34"W
Hardy	Mill Mountain	3,293	38°58'42"N	78°37'54"W
Harrison	Odell Knob	1,560	39°26'22"N	80°20'03"W
Jackson	Garnes Knob	1,225	38°40'16"N	81°40'52"W
Jefferson	Raven Rocks	1,454	39°08'24"N	77°50'06"W
Kanawha	Kayford Mountain	2,898	37°58'11"N	81°22'56"W
Lewis	Moss Knob	1,829	38°49'39"N	80°25'09"W
Lincoln	Mann Knob	1,434	38°01'27"N	82°12'06"W
Logan	Spring Mountain	2,683	37°49'15"N	81°38'51"W
Marion	Bake Oven Knob	1,665	39°36'53"N	80°19'49"W
Marshall	Culley Hill	1,590	39°48'16"N	80°33'05"W
McDowell	Johns Knob	2,975	37°23'13"N	81°21'58"W
Mercer	Huff Knob	3,570	37°35'22"N	81°06'53"W
Mineral	Black Rock	3,180	39°20'35"N	79°06'39"W
Mercer	Buckhorn Knob	4,069	37°17'33"N	80°58'50"W
Mingo	Horsepen Mountain	2,524	37°38'26"N	81°59'37"W
Monongalia	Cheat View	2,216	39°37'14"N	79°49'12"W
Monroe	Arnolds Knob	3,932	37°29'31"N	80°20'41"W
Morgan	Cacapon Mountain	2,615	39°26'37"N	78°20'50"W
Nicholas	Hanging Rock	3,840	38°16'03"N	80°26'12"W
Pendleton*	Spruce Mountain*	4,861*	38°41'59"N	79°31'59"W
Pocahontas	Bald Knob	4,860	38°26'52"N	79°55'53"W
Preston	Brushy Knobs	3,256	39°22'22"N	79°32'49"W
Putnam	Rocky Knob	1,169	38°20'51"N	81°55'29"W

Raleigh	Ivy Knob	3,620	37°47'15"N	81°29'28"W
Randolph	Porte Crayon, Mount	4,770	38°55'44"N	79°27'23"W
Ritchie	King Knob	1,340	39°10'12"N	80°58'48"W
Roane	Weedy Knob	1,470	38°36'04"N	81°07'48"W
Summers	Keeney Knob	3,927	37°46'24"N	80°42'20"W
Taylor	Copeland Knob	1,760	39°18'24"N	80°08'35"W
Tucker	Weiss Knob	4,460	38°59'37"N	79°25'48"W
Tyler	Owlshead	1,444	39°26'20"N	80°57'26"W
Upshur	Big Run Knob	2,401	38°47'40"N	80°15'31"W
Wayne	Kelly Knob	1,513	37°57'34"N	82°19'08"W
Webster	Back Fork Mountain	4,040	38°35'51"N	80°11'29"W
Wetzel	Honsocker Knob	1,652	39°42'04"N	80°24'23"W
Wirt	Ruble Knob	1,325	39°00'44"N	81°17'58"W
Wood	Buzzard Rocks	1,280	39°15'42"N	81°16'21"W
Wyoming	Ivy Knob	3,620	37°47'15"N	

Wisconsin

County	Highest Point	Elevation	Latitude	Longitude
Ashland	Whittlesey, Mount	1,872	46°18'03"N	90°37'02"W
Bayfield	Telemark, Mount	1,650	46°11'06"N	91°15'01"W
Clark	Bruce Mound	1,355	44°26'38"N	90°47'32"W
Dane	Sugarloaf Hill	1,141	43°17'33"N	89°41'31"W
Door	Brussels Hill	851	44°45'06"N	87°35'27"W
Douglas	Sugar Camp Hill	1,256	46°37'15"N	91°36'41"W
Dunn	Otteson Bluff	1,258	44°58'03"N	91°54'32"W
Eau Claire	Moldenhauer Hill	1,104	44°43'38"N	91°13'32"W
Fond Du Lac	Mary Hill	1,092	43°47'12"N	88°21'58"W
Forest	Sugarbush Hill	1,939	45°33'29"N	88°48'47"W
Jackson	Knapp Mound	1,347	44°13'25"N	90°30'14"W
Juneau	Daylight Hill	1,314	43°43'31"N	90°12'07"W
Kewaunee	Cherneyville Hill	1,020	44°25'33"N	87°43'50"W
La Crosse	Wanless Hill	1,368	44°00'21"N	90°58'12"W
Langlade	Baldy Hill	1,831	45°26'14"N	89°24'47"W
Marathon	Rib Mountain	1,924	44°55'15"N	89°41'40"W
Marinette	McCaslin Mountain	1,632	45°23'43"N	88°23'36"W
Monroe	Pikes Peak	1,345	43°59'10"N	90°36'35"W
Oneida	Jack Pine Lookout Tower	1,585	45°40'48"N	89°47'53"W
Pepin	Weisinger Hill	1,160	44°39'55"N	92°06'34"W
Pierce	Hammond Hill	1,124	44°45'26"N	92°10'18"W
Price*	Timms Hill*	1,951*	45°27'04"N	90°11'42"W
Richland	Eysnogel Hill	1,148	43°31'02"N	90°27'08"W
Sauk	Sauk Hill	1,461	43°24'07"N	89°45'33"W
Sawyer	Meteor Hill	1,801	45°41'17"N	91°23'48"W
Trempealeau	Bradys Bluff	1,170	44°01'13"N	91°28'59"W
Waushara	Morris, Mount	1,137	44°07'05"N	89°11'04"W
Wood	North Bluff	1,182	44°19'19"N	90°10'55"W

Wyoming*

County	Highest Point	Elevation	Latitude	Longitude
Albany	Medicine Bow Peak	12,013	41°21'38"N	106°19'03"W
Big Horn	Cloud Peak	13,167	44°22'56"N	107°10'24"W
Campbell	North Butte	6,049	43°47'31"N	105°57'25"W
Carbon	Elk Mountain	11,156	41°38'00"N	106°31'33"W
Converse	Warbonnet Peak	9,414	42°26'05"N	105°47'37"W
Crook	Inyan Kara Mountain	6,368	44°12'48"N	104°20'58"W
Fremont*	Gannett Peak*	13,804*	43°11'04"N	109°39'12"W
Goshen	Big Rawhide Butte	6,052	42°35'12"N	104°29'32"W
Hot Springs	Dome Mountain	12,450	43°45'29"N	109°12'30"W
Johnson	Cloud Peak	13,167	44°22'56"N	107°10'24"W
Laramie	Saddleback Mountain	7,944	41°04'34"N	105°12'16"W
Lincoln	Wyoming Peak	11,378	42°36'16"N	110°37'25"W
Natrona	Garfield Peak	8,244	42°46'57"N	107°15'51"W
Niobrara	Horse Heaven	7,414	42°42'53"N	107°00'46"W
Park	Francs Peak	13,153	43°57'41"N	109°20'20"W
Platte	Squaw Rock	7,014	41°55'30"N	105°13'48"W
Sheridan	Dome Peak	10,828	44°35'44"N	107°22'56"W
Sublette	Mount Woodrow Wilson	13,502	43°10'01"N	109°39'03"W
Sweetwater	Battle Mountain	9,108	41°01'53"N	107°16'53"W
Teton	Grand Teton	13,770	43°44'28"N	110°48'06"W
Uinta	Cottonwood Mountain	9,323	41°01'41"N	110°20'43"W
Washakie	Monument Hill	8,094	43°58'27"N	107°07'43"W
Weston	Pisgah, Mount	6,401	43°59'41"N	104°08'34"W

Appendix 2: State Capitols

The following coordinates of all state capitols (and the U.S. Capitol) are taken from USGS 7.5-minute quadrangles. These are the locations of the buildings themselves. The datum is NAD27, except for Hawaii, which uses the Old Hawaiian Datum.

STATE	CITY	COUNTY	UTM ZONE	EASTING	NORTHING
Alabama	Montgomery	Montgomery	16	565 800	3 582 310
Alaska	Juneau	Juneau	8	534 490	6 462 570
Arizona	Phoenix	Maricopa	12	398 090	3 701 310
Arkansas	Little Rock	Pulaski	15	565 090	3 844 970
California	Sacramento	Sacramento	10	631 350	4 270 670
Colorado	Denver	Denver	13	501 345	4 398 605
Connecticut	Hartford	Hartford	18	692 630	4 625 960
Delaware	Dover	Kent	18	455 080	4 334 150
District of Columbia	Washington	District of Columbia	18	325 730	4 306 250
Florida	Tallahassee	Leon	16	761 090	3 370 270
Georgia	Atlanta	Fulton	16	741 930	3 737 200
Hawaii	Honolulu	Honolulu	4	618 240	2 356 800
Idaho	Boise	Ada	11	564 665	4 829 525
Illinois	Springfield	Sangamon	16	272 700	4 408 540
Indiana	Indianapolis	Marion	16	571 715	4 402 200
Iowa	Des Moines	Polk	15	449 695	4 604 355
Kansas	Topeka	Shawnee	15	268 260	4 325 325
Kentucky	Frankfort	Franklin	16	686 080	4 228 450
Louisiana	Baton Rouge	East Baton Rouge	15	674 060	3 370 625
Maine	Augusta	Kennebec	19	437 610	4 906 065
Maryland	Annapolis	Anne Arundel	18	370 830	4 315 270
Massachusetts	Boston	Suffolk	19	330 000	4 691 410
Michigan	Lansing	Ingham	16	700 120	4 733 920
Minnesota	St Paul	Ramsey	15	491 465	4 977 780
Mississippi	Jackson	Hinds	15	765 350	3 577 400
Missouri	Jefferson City	Cole	15	572 060	4 270 200
Montana	Helena	Lewis and Clark	12	422 040	5 159 425
Nebraska	Lincoln	Lancaster	14	694 060	4 519 780
Nevada	Carson City	none	11	261 110	4 338 410
New Hampshire	Concord	Merrimack	19	293 760	4 786 695
New Jersey	Trenton	Mercer	18	519 695	4 451 795
New Mexico	Santa Fe	Santa Fe	13	414 860	3 949 075
New York	Albany	Albany	18	601 820	4 722 765
North Carolina	Raleigh	Wake	17	713 375	3 961 950
North Dakota	Bismarck	Burleigh	14	364 020	5 186 585
Ohio	Columbus	Franklin	17	329 260	4 425 160
Oklahoma	Oklahoma City	Oklahoma	14	635 780	3 928 460
Oregon	Salem	Marion	10	497 700	4 975 920
Pennsylvania	Harrisburg	Dauphin	18	339 800	4 458 590
Rhode Island	Providence	Providence	19	299 420	4 633 600
South Carolina	Columbia	Richland	17	496 930	3 761 970
South Dakota	Pierre	Hughes	14	392 760	4 913 310
Tennessee	Nashville	Davidson	16	519 400	4 002 150
Texas	Austin	Travis	14	621 195	3 349 690
Utah	Salt Lake City	Salt Lake	12	425 110	4 514 220
Vermont	Montpelier	Washington	18	693 110	4 903 650
Virginia	Richmond	Richmond (city)	18	284 950	4 157 215
Washington	Olympia	Thurston	10	507 330	5 208 940
West Virginia	Charleston	Kanawha	17	446 490	4 243 140
Wisconsin	Madison	Dane	16	305 910	4 771 650
Wyoming	Cheyenne	Laramie	13	515 135	4 554 130

Appendix 3: Highway Junctions

The following pages contain coordinates for the junction of every U.S. Interstate with either another U.S. Interstate or a U.S. Highway. In most cases you don't even need a map to use this information. Just look up a pair of routes and you instantly have highly accurate coordinate values. The listing gives latitude first, then longitude. The datum is NAD27.

The coordinates are provided in degrees and decimal minutes. See page 120 if you need information on how to convert to decimal degrees or decimal seconds. You can use these coordinates in your travels to define waypoints that correspond to highway junctions you wish to find. Then, using the "GoTo" feature of your GPS receiver, you'll always know where those junctions are relative to your position.

U.S. Interstates

The junctions are grouped by Interstate route number in ascending order. For each junction of two Interstates, first find the group heading using the lower numbered Interstate, then find the line with the higher numbered Interstate. For example, the junction of I84 and I90 would be found in the group headed by I84, and the junction of I84 and I5 would be found in the group headed by I5. It doesn't matter which of the Interstates you're traveling on, always look for the lower numbered Interstate first to find the junction.

U.S. Interstates/U.S. Highways

In the case of U.S. Interstate and U.S. Highway junctions, always look for the Interstate first. There are no groups for U.S. Highways, so their junctions will always be listed under an Interstate group.

The junctions are sorted within groups in ascending order first by U.S. Interstate route number, then by U.S. Highway route number. Remember that no group will contain Interstate route numbers lower than the group heading. Those junctions are listed under the group for the lower numbered Interstate.

Often you will find there is more than one occurrence of a particular pair of route numbers. This is especially true of U.S. Interstate/U.S. Highway junctions. To help you find the specific junction you are interested in, the *groups are further sorted by state and county name*.

Often this will result in just one pair of routes, and you have your coordinates. If there are still multiple pairs, *the listing is further sorted on a north-south basis*. You will need to determine which of the two or more possible pairs is the one you want based on their location on a map. The more northerly pairs are listed first in the table.

If the junction pairs lie in an east-west orientation, you can find the one you're interested in by comparing the longitude values. Although they're not sorted by longitude, the higher value for longitude corresponds to a more westerly location.

I4

I75	Hillsborough, FL	28° 0.110'	82°19.642'
I95	Volusia, FL	29° 9.301'	81° 4.556'
I275	Hillsborough, FL	27°57.869'	82°27.068'
US17	Orange, FL	28°33.168'	81°22.941'
US17	Orange, FL	28°30.621'	81°23.839'
US17	Seminole, FL	28°49.950'	81°19.321'
US27	Polk, FL	28°13.930'	81°38.924'
US41	Hillsborough, FL	27°58.067'	82°24.117'
US92	Hillsborough, FL	27°59.737'	82°21.895'
US92	Hillsborough, FL	27°59.711'	82°21.115'
US98	Polk, FL	28° 5.093'	81°58.228'
US192	Osceola, FL	28°19.958'	81°32.711'
US301	Hillsborough, FL	27°59.744'	82°21.468'

I5

I8	San Diego, CA	32°45.569'	117°12.174'
I10	Los Angeles, CA	34° 3.308'	118°12.786'
I10	Los Angeles, CA	34° 2.033'	118°13.200'
I80	Sacramento, CA	38°37.510'	121°30.978'
I84	Multnomah, OR	45°31.516'	122°39.846'
I90	King, WA	47°35.606'	122°19.176'
I105	Lane, OR	44° 3.794'	123° 2.880'
I205	San Joaquin, CA	37°46.020'	121°19.866'
I205	Washington, OR	45°22.140'	122°45.420'
I205	Clark, WA	45°43.431'	122°39.192'
I210	Los Angeles, CA	34°18.989'	118°29.346'
I305	Sacramento, CA	38°34.109'	121°30.588'
I405	Los Angeles, CA	34°17.476'	118°28.008'
I405	Orange, CA	33°38.702'	117°44.088'
I405	Multnomah, OR	45°32.650'	122°40.440'
I405	Multnomah, OR	45°30.306'	122°40.362'
I405	Multnomah, OR	45°30.113'	122°40.362'
I405	King, WA	47°27.726'	122°15.756'
I405	Snohomish, WA	47°49.858'	122°15.708'
I505	Yolo, CA	38°51.285'	121°56.748'
I580	San Joaquin, CA	37°35.873'	121°20.496'
I605	Los Angeles, CA	33°56.477'	118° 5.742'
I705	Pierce, WA	47°14.020'	122°25.842'
I710	Los Angeles, CA	34° 0.968'	118°10.284'
I805	San Diego, CA	32°54.209'	117°13.368'
I805	San Diego, CA	32°32.985'	117° 2.400'
US2	Snohomish, WA	47°58.826'	122°11.220'
US12	Lewis, WA	46°32.845'	122°52.470'
US12	Thurston, WA	46°48.092'	123° 0.360'
US20	Linn, OR	44°37.822'	123° 3.666'
US97	Siskiyou, CA	41°25.178'	122°23.052'
US101	Los Angeles, CA	34° 2.033'	118°13.200'
US101	Thurston, WA	47° 1.290'	122°54.288'
US199	Josephine, OR	42°27.901'	123°19.290'

I8

I10	Pinal, AZ	32°48.980'	111°40.830'
I15	San Diego, CA	32°46.715'	117° 6.678'
I805	San Diego, CA	32°46.295'	117° 7.848'
US95	Yuma, AZ	32°41.913'	114°36.426'

I10

I12	E. Baton Rouge,LA	30°25.064'	91° 7.121'
I12	St. Tammany, LA	30°18.373'	89°44.502'
I15	San Bernardino, CA	34° 4.039'	117°32.640'
I17	Maricopa, AZ	33°27.707'	112° 6.450'
I17	Maricopa, AZ	33°25.639'	112° 2.208'
I19	Pima, AZ	32°11.531'	110°58.512'
I20	Reeves, TX	31° 5.365'	104° 2.946'
I25	Dona Ana, NM	32°15.352'	106°43.692'
I35	Bexar, TX	29°25.829'	98°30.031'

I35	Bexar, TX	29°23.758'	98°30.653'
I37	Bexar, TX	29°23.691'	98°28.673'
I45	Harris, TX	29°46.517'	95°22.116'
I45	Harris, TX	29°46.180'	95°21.920'
I49	Lafayette, LA	30°15.553'	92° 0.930'
I55	St. John the Baptist, LA	30° 5.135'	90°25.910'
I65	Mobile, AL	30°37.679'	88° 6.977'
I75	Columbia, FL	30°15.986'	82°45.275'
I95	Duval, FL	30°19.265'	81°40.939'
I110	Los Angeles, CA	34° 2.298'	118°16.380'
I110	Escambia, FL	30°30.256'	87°13.792'
I110	East Baton Rouge, LA	30°26.231'	91°10.661'
I110	Harrison, MS	30°27.168'	88°53.760'
I110	El Paso, TX	31°46.634'	106°26.520'
I210	Los Angeles, CA	34° 3.907'	117°48.336'
I210	Calcasieu, LA	30°14.751'	93° 9.725'
I210	Calcasieu, LA	30°13.639'	93°18.154'
I215	San Bernardino, CA	34° 3.858'	117°17.730'
I295	Duval, FL	30°18.902'	81°46.241'
I310	St. Charles, LA	30° 0.418'	90°17.675'
I405	Los Angeles, CA	34° 1.867'	118°25.998'
I410	Bexar, TX	29°29.962'	98°32.938'
I410	Bexar, TX	29°26.132'	98°23.389'
I510	Orleans, LA	30° 3.560'	89°56.355'
I605	Los Angeles, CA	34° 3.911'	117°59.952'
I610	Orleans, LA	29°59.690'	90° 6.937'
I610	Orleans, LA	29°59.485'	90° 2.965'
I610	Harris, TX	29°46.836'	95°27.241'
I710	Los Angeles, CA	34° 3.670'	118° 9.858'
US11	Orleans, LA	30° 9.019'	89°51.508'
US19	Jefferson, FL	30°28.522'	83°53.384'
US27	Leon, FL	30°28.945'	84°18.515'
US29	Escambia, FL	30°30.256'	87°15.999'
US31	Baldwin, AL	30°40.639'	87°59.077'
US41	Columbia, FL	30°14.692'	82°40.477'
US49	Harrison, MS	30°25.956'	89° 5.640'
US51	St. John the Baptist, LA	30° 5.301'	90°26.485'
US59	Harris, TX	29°46.161'	95°20.467'
US60	La Paz, AZ	33°39.675'	114° 0.666'
US60	Maricopa, AZ	33°27.694'	112° 5.658'
US60	Maricopa, AZ	33°23.317'	111°58.020'
US61	Ascension, LA	30° 9.214'	90°48.388'
US61	Orleans, LA	29°58.169'	90° 6.576'
US62	El Paso, TX	31°46.649'	106°25.290'
US67	Pecos, TX	30°54.019'	103° 3.234'
US67	Pecos, TX	30°52.646'	102°38.652'
US69	Jefferson, TX	30° 5.768'	94° 8.160'
US69	Jefferson, TX	30° 2.961'	94° 8.705'
US70	Dona Ana, NM	32°16.912'	106°53.034'
US70	Hidalgo, NM	32°20.302'	108°40.470'
US77	Fayette, TX	29°41.582'	96°54.137'
US83	Kimble, TX	30°26.294'	99°42.764'
US85	El Paso, TX	31°48.586'	106°32.586'
US87	Bexar, TX	29°24.158'	98°26.626'
US87	Kendall, TX	29°58.802'	98°54.233'
US87	Kendall, TX	29°49.246'	98°45.336'
US87	Kendall, TX	29°46.024'	98°43.154'
US90	Baldwin, AL	30°39.320'	87°54.712'
US90	Mobile, AL	30°41.491'	88° 1.793'
US90	Mobile, AL	30°34.850'	88°10.217'
US90	Baker, FL	30°14.315'	82°18.223'
US90	Escambia, FL	30°30.409'	87° 9.755'
US90	Gadsden, FL	30°29.377'	84°25.558'
US90	Leon, FL	30°29.107'	84° 9.536'
US90	Suwannee, FL	30°20.568'	83° 5.427'
US90	Calcasieu, LA	30°14.176'	93°11.438'
US90	Calcasieu, LA	30°14.169'	93°16.760'
US90	Calcasieu, LA	30° 9.262'	93°38.281'

US90	Orleans, LA	30° 0.617'	90° 0.783'
US90	Orleans, LA	29°57.383'	90° 4.793'
US90	Orleans, LA	29°57.095'	90° 5.044'
US90	Austin, TX	29°46.463'	96° 7.829'
US90	Austin, TX	29°45.819'	96°11.395'
US90	Culberson, TX	31° 2.401'	104°49.812'
US90	Fayette, TX	29°41.641'	96°50.922'
US90	Gonzales, TX	29°41.320'	97°15.155'
US90	Gonzales, TX	29°39.160'	97°32.722'
US90	Guadalupe, TX	29°35.930'	97°55.505'
US90	Guadalupe, TX	29°33.050'	98° 2.527'
US90	Jefferson, TX	30° 4.080'	94° 8.063'
US95	Riverside, CA	33°36.426'	114°34.194'
US129	Suwannee, FL	30°19.809'	82°57.766'
US165	Jefferson Davis, LA	30°14.906'	92°58.989'
US171	Calcasieu, LA	30°14.754'	93°10.822'
US180	Luna, NM	32°16.220'	107°45.474'
US183	Caldwell, TX	29°39.141'	97°35.546'
US190	St. Tammany, LA	30°17.077'	89°44.974'
US190	Pecos, TX	30°52.107'	102° 5.634'
US191	Cochise, AZ	32°10.579'	109°56.922'
US221	Madison, FL	30°26.021'	83°37.621'
US231	Jackson, FL	30°45.194'	85°22.910'
US277	Sutton, TX	30°34.703'	100°38.850'
US285	Pecos, TX	30°54.043'	102°54.522'
US290	Crockett, TX	30°43.685'	101°33.378'
US290	Kimble, TX	30°17.474'	99°31.616'
US290	Pecos, TX	30°53.644'	102°55.344'
US290	Pecos, TX	30°53.544'	102°50.712'
US290	Pecos, TX	30°44.163'	101°50.178'
US290	Reeves, TX	31° 2.845'	103°58.428'
US290	Reeves, TX	31° 0.017'	103°41.928'
US301	Duval, FL	30°17.324'	81°58.978'
US319	Leon, FL	30°30.073'	84°14.887'
US331	Walton, FL	30°41.531'	86° 7.357'
US377	Kimble, TX	30°30.459'	99°46.460'
US441	Columbia, FL	30°14.483'	82°38.306'
US666	Cochise, AZ	32°21.478'	109°41.256'

I12

I55	Tangipahoa, LA	30°28.717'	90°29.330'
I59	St. Tammany, LA	30°18.373'	89°44.502'
US11	St. Tammany, LA	30°18.590'	89°46.223'
US61	East Baton Rouge, LA	30°25.391'	91° 4.499'
US190	St. Tammany, LA	30°25.733'	90° 5.075'
US190	St. Tammany, LA	30°25.726'	90° 5.061'
US190	Tangipahoa, LA	30°28.717'	90°28.954'

I15

I40	San Bernardino, CA	34°53.156'	117° 0.504'
I70	Millard, UT	38°34.627'	112°36.150'
I80	Salt Lake, UT	40°45.822'	111°54.840'
I80	Salt Lake, UT	40°43.076'	111°54.174'
I84	Box Elder, UT	41°42.643'	112°12.318'
I84	Weber, UT	41°11.254'	112° 0.462'
I86	Bannock, ID	42°54.772'	112°26.352'
I90	Silver Bow, MT	46° 0.476'	112°38.232'
I90	Silver Bow, MT	45°58.811'	112°28.728'
I115	Silver Bow, MT	46° 0.304'	112°34.236'
I215	San Bernardino, CA	34°13.532'	117°24.558'
I215	Davis, UT	40°50.132'	111°54.912'
I215	Salt Lake, UT	40°38.088'	111°54.264'
I515	Clark, NV	36°10.461'	115° 9.222'
US2	Toole, MT	48°30.930'	111°52.530'
US6	Utah, UT	39°58.537'	111°46.302'
US12	Lewis and Clark, MT	46°35.468'	111°59.844'
US20	Bonneville, ID	43°30.263'	112° 3.300'

US20	Bonneville, ID	43°29.808'	112° 3.192'
US26	Bingham, ID	43°11.941'	112°21.774'
US26	Bonneville, ID	43°26.346'	112° 7.236'
US30	Bannock, ID	42°39.656'	112°12.630'
US50	Millard, UT	39°15.826'	112° 6.186'
US50	Millard, UT	39° 8.630'	112°14.112'
US89	Cascade, MT	47°33.764'	111°32.010'
US89	Davis, UT	40°59.167'	111°53.940'
US89	Salt Lake, UT	40°49.019'	111°55.116'
US89	Salt Lake, UT	40°31.610'	111°53.424'
US89	Utah, UT	40°22.603'	111°49.098'
US91	Bannock, ID	42°30.127'	112°10.122'
US91	Bingham, ID	43° 8.989'	112°23.268'
US91	Box Elder, UT	41°29.156'	112° 3.138'
US93	Clark, NV	36°22.858'	114°53.514'
US189	Utah, UT	40°12.466'	111°39.486'
US287	Lewis and Clark, MT	47° 1.098'	112° 2.868'
US395	San Bernardino, CA	34°24.020'	117°24.024'

I16

I75	Bibb, GA	32°51.327'	83°38.252'
I95	Chatham, GA	32° 4.438'	81°14.772'
I516	Chatham, GA	32° 4.264'	81° 8.102'
US1	Emanuel, GA	32°23.989'	82°18.494'
US23	Bibb, GA	32°47.998'	83°34.186'
US25	Bulloch, GA	32°18.439'	81°52.441'
US80	Bibb, GA	32°50.369'	83°37.200'
US129	Bibb, GA	32°50.850'	83°37.636'
US221	Treutlen, GA	32°26.048'	82°30.059'
US280	Bryan, GA	32°10.863'	81°27.623'
US319	Laurens, GA	32°29.258'	82°56.115'

I17

I40	Coconino, AZ	35°10.316'	111°39.702'
US60	Maricopa, AZ	33°28.635'	112° 6.738'

I20

I30	Parker, TX	32°43.232'	97°34.013'
I35E	Dallas, TX	32°38.529'	96°49.381'
I35W	Tarrant, TX	32°40.025'	97°19.217'
I45	Dallas, TX	32°39.696'	96°43.587'
I49	Caddo, LA	32°29.780'	93°45.614'
I55	Hinds, MS	32°16.482'	90°12.432'
I55	Rankin, MS	32°16.536'	90°10.440'
I59	Jefferson, AL	33°32.845'	86°44.936'
I59	Lauderdale, MS	32°20.568'	88°46.236'
I65	Jefferson, AL	33°31.291'	86°49.600'
I75	Fulton, GA	33°44.734'	84°23.368'
I77	Richland, SC	34° 4.072'	80°55.347'
I95	Florence, SC	34°11.574'	79°50.647'
I220	Bossier, LA	32°32.388'	93°37.689'
I220	Caddo, LA	32°27.402'	93°50.625'
I220	Hinds, MS	32°17.316'	90°14.976'
I285	De Kalb, GA	33°42.859'	84°14.491'
I285	Fulton, GA	33°45.875'	84°29.564'
I359	Tuscaloosa, AL	33°10.201'	87°33.164'
I459	Jefferson, AL	33°32.683'	86°38.525'
I459	Jefferson, AL	33°20.568'	87° 1.654'
I520	Richmond, GA	33°29.597'	82° 5.053'
I635	Dallas, TX	32°41.975'	96°37.594'
I820	Tarrant, TX	32°41.366'	97°28.023'
I820	Tarrant, TX	32°40.097'	97°14.422'
US1	Aiken, SC	33°39.992'	81°40.426'
US1	Lexington, SC	33°58.699'	81°11.701'
US1	Richland, SC	34° 4.415'	80°56.873'
US11	Greene, AL	32°59.180'	87°47.351'
US11	Jefferson, AL	33°32.774'	86°44.678'

I20 (cont)

US11	Jefferson, AL	33°21.947'	87° 0.087'
US11	Tuscaloosa, AL	33°15.031'	87° 7.881'
US11	Tuscaloosa, AL	33°10.436'	87°28.447'
US11	Tuscaloosa, AL	33°10.432'	87°24.441'
US11	Lauderdale, MS	32°25.542'	88°27.114'
US11	Lauderdale, MS	32°22.008'	88°40.350'
US11	Lauderdale, MS	32°20.964'	88°44.088'
US15	Lee, SC	34°11.670'	80°16.813'
US19	Fulton, GA	33°44.472'	84°24.499'
US25	Aiken, SC	33°33.896'	81°56.236'
US27	Carroll, GA	33°41.104'	85° 9.075'
US31	Jefferson, AL	33°31.699'	86°48.241'
US45	Lauderdale, MS	32°22.986'	88°38.208'
US45	Lauderdale, MS	32°21.192'	88°41.454'
US49	Rankin, MS	32°16.368'	90° 9.498'
US59	Harrison, TX	32°29.466'	94°21.513'
US61	Warren, MS	32°20.826'	90°49.770'
US61	Warren, MS	32°18.804'	90°53.196'
US65	Madison, LA	32°23.501'	91°11.960'
US67	Dallas, TX	32°39.242'	96°52.639'
US69	Smith, TX	32°28.100'	95°23.248'
US71	Bossier, LA	32°30.788'	93°42.914'
US76	Florence, SC	34°11.159'	79°48.688'
US78	Jefferson, AL	33°32.689'	86°35.530'
US78	Jefferson, AL	33°31.833'	86°42.575'
US78	Jefferson, AL	33°31.248'	86°50.951'
US78	St. Clair, AL	33°36.022'	86°19.243'
US78	St. Clair, AL	33°35.916'	86°12.781'
US78	St. Clair, AL	33°34.678'	86°28.564'
US78	McDuffie, GA	33°30.679'	82°30.143'
US79	Bossier, LA	32°33.964'	93°29.553'
US79	Caddo, LA	32°26.637'	93°56.983'
US79	Webster, LA	32°34.955'	93°23.484'
US80	Bienville, LA	32°33.771'	93° 9.525'
US80	Caddo, LA	32°27.103'	94° 0.680'
US80	Madison, LA	32°19.241'	90°57.671'
US80	Ouachita, LA	32°31.133'	92°19.768'
US80	Hinds, MS	32°20.061'	90°20.273'
US80	Lauderdale, MS	32°20.640'	88°47.790'
US80	Newton, MS	32°20.160'	89°17.334'
US80	Rankin, MS	32°16.724'	90° 0.065'
US80	Rankin, MS	32°16.596'	89°56.946'
US80	Eastland, TX	32°28.509'	98°37.429'
US80	Eastland, TX	32°26.317'	98°41.877'
US80	Eastland, TX	32°24.044'	98°47.350'
US80	Eastland, TX	32°22.498'	99° 0.281'
US80	Harrison, TX	32°29.597'	94° 9.697'
US80	Martin, TX	32° 8.404'	101°45.768'
US80	Martin, TX	32° 6.976'	101°49.728'
US80	Parker, TX	32°45.284'	97°41.872'
US80	Parker, TX	32°43.586'	97°52.801'
US80	Reeves, TX	31°24.372'	103°33.306'
US80	Ward, TX	31°36.468'	102°50.526'
US80	Ward, TX	31°28.367'	103°20.046'
US82	Tuscaloosa, AL	33°10.279'	87°31.483'
US83	Taylor, TX	32°29.024'	99°46.111'
US83	Taylor, TX	32°28.916'	99°46.192'
US84	Nolan, TX	32°26.768'	100°30.342'
US84	Taylor, TX	32°27.547'	99°50.890'
US87	Howard, TX	32°15.817'	101°29.406'
US129	Morgan, GA	33°33.313'	83°28.480'
US165	Ouachita, LA	32°29.956'	92° 4.929'
US167	Lincoln, LA	32°32.389'	92°38.264'
US171	Caddo, LA	32°28.729'	93°46.793'
US175	Dallas, TX	32°41.479'	96°37.936'
US176	Richland, SC	34° 2.355'	81° 5.630'
US178	Lexington, SC	33°48.985'	81°27.136'
US183	Eastland, TX	32°22.466'	98°58.209'
US221	Columbia, GA	33°29.862'	82°18.937'
US231	St. Clair, AL	33°36.377'	86°16.919'
US259	Gregg, TX	32°26.995'	94°42.535'
US259	Gregg, TX	32°26.089'	94°49.643'
US271	Smith, TX	32°26.454'	95° 8.009'
US278	Newton, GA	33°36.424'	83°52.523'
US278	Warren, GA	33°29.935'	82°48.278'
US281	Palo Pinto, TX	32°36.472'	98° 6.675'
US283	Callahan, TX	32°24.105'	99°23.132'
US285	Reeves, TX	31°24.063'	103°28.950'
US287	Tarrant, TX	32°40.208'	97°12.601'
US321	Richland, SC	34° 3.955'	81° 1.361'
US377	Tarrant, TX	32°41.045'	97°27.563'
US378	Lexington, SC	34° 0.650'	81° 8.917'
US385	Ector, TX	31°49.682'	102°21.300'
US401	Darlington, SC	34°12.344'	80° 1.615'
US411	St. Clair, AL	33°33.956'	86°31.267'
US431	Calhoun, AL	33°37.049'	85°43.378'
US521	Kershaw, SC	34°13.010'	80°35.570'
US601	Kershaw, SC	34°11.328'	80°41.282'

I24

I57	Williamson, IL	37°36.572'	88°59.702'
I59	Dade, GA	34°58.339'	85°26.987'
I65	Davidson, TN	36°13.445'	86°46.445'
I75	Hamilton, TN	35° 0.352'	85°12.584'
I124	Hamilton, TN	35° 1.926'	85°19.133'
I440	Davidson, TN	36° 7.557'	86°43.684'
US27	Hamilton, TN	35° 1.091'	85°17.606'
US41	Coffee, TN	35°32.135'	86° 9.800'
US41	Coffee, TN	35°27.450'	86° 3.120'
US41	Davidson, TN	36° 8.218'	86°43.623'
US41	Hamilton, TN	35° 1.118'	85°22.996'
US41	Hamilton, TN	35° 0.854'	85°16.352'
US45	Johnson, IL	37°26.791'	88°53.233'
US45	Massac, IL	37° 9.675'	88°40.961'
US45	McCracken, KY	37° 3.055'	88°39.059'
US60	McCracken, KY	37° 4.693'	88°40.847'
US62	Lyon, KY	37° 4.420'	88° 7.301'
US62	McCracken, KY	37° 3.428'	88°39.289'
US62	Marshall, KY	37° 0.163'	88°19.463'
US64	Marion, TN	35° 2.398'	85°41.426'
US68	McCracken, KY	36°59.679'	88°30.361'
US68	Trigg, KY	36°52.913'	87°44.096'
US79	Montgomery, TN	36°35.993'	87°16.978'
US231	Rutherford, TN	35°48.753'	86°23.787'
US431	Davidson, TN	36°19.448'	86°52.084'

I25

I40	Bernalillo, NM	35° 6.355'	106°37.710'
I70	Denver, CO	39°46.801'	104°59.340'
I76	Adams, CO	39°49.023'	104°58.968'
I80	Laramie, WY	41° 6.839'	104°51.018'
I90	Johnson, WY	44°22.293'	106°41.310'
I225	Denver, CO	39°38.082'	104°54.456'
US6	Denver, CO	39°43.541'	105° 0.756'
US16	Johnson, WY	44°21.257'	106°41.178'
US18	Converse, WY	42°39.415'	105°12.210'
US20	Converse, WY	42°49.407'	105°47.544'
US20	Converse, WY	42°45.595'	105°24.888'
US20	Converse, WY	42°43.889'	105°20.352'
US20	Natrona, WY	42°52.033'	106°20.640'
US20	Natrona, WY	42°51.296'	106°17.382'
US24	El Paso, CO	38°49.680'	104°50.046'
US26	Platte, WY	42°13.852'	105° 1.350'

US30	Laramie, WY	41° 7.117'	104°51.030'
US34	Larimer, CO	40°24.436'	104°59.562'
US36	Adams, CO	39°49.658'	104°58.974'
US40	Denver, CO	39°44.438'	105° 0.804'
US50	Pueblo, CO	38°18.467'	104°36.786'
US50	Pueblo, CO	38°17.281'	104°36.348'
US56	Colfax, NM	36°21.677'	104°36.276'
US60	Socorro, NM	34°25.104'	106°50.292'
US60	Socorro, NM	34° 4.583'	106°53.550'
US64	Colfax, NM	36°53.096'	104°25.818'
US64	Colfax, NM	36°51.628'	104°26.388'
US64	Colfax, NM	36°48.899'	104°26.532'
US70	Dona Ana, NM	32°20.864'	106°46.140'
US84	San Miguel, NM	35°31.229'	105°14.934'
US84	Santa Fe, NM	35°38.062'	105°57.360'
US85	Denver, CO	39°42.439'	104°59.778'
US85	Douglas, CO	39°23.930'	104°51.642'
US85	El Paso, CO	38°48.887'	104°49.302'
US85	El Paso, CO	38°40.381'	104°42.492'
US85	Huerfano, CO	37°39.625'	104°47.742'
US85	Huerfano, CO	37°37.070'	104°45.558'
US85	Colfax, NM	36°54.347'	104°26.298'
US85	Sierra, NM	33° 9.714'	107°15.150'
US85	Sierra, NM	33° 6.795'	107°17.892'
US85	Socorro, NM	34° 2.465'	106°53.316'
US85	Laramie, WY	41°13.990'	104°50.220'
US85	Laramie, WY	41°10.049'	104°50.376'
US160	Las Animas, CO	37°10.178'	104°30.636'
US285	Denver, CO	39°39.175'	104°55.080'
US285	Santa Fe, NM	35°38.188'	105°55.800'
US285	Santa Fe, NM	35°33.266'	105°52.692'
US380	Socorro, NM	33°55.022'	106°52.644'

I26

I40	Buncombe, NC	35°33.262'	82°36.701'
I77	Lexington, SC	33°55.816'	81° 4.400'
I77	Lexington, SC	33°55.590'	81° 4.260'
I95	Orangeburg, SC	33°19.099'	80°32.878'
I126	Richland, SC	34° 1.613'	81° 6.037'
I240	Buncombe, NC	35°33.262'	82°36.701'
I385	Laurens, SC	34°30.787'	81°52.231'
I526	Charleston, SC	32°53.072'	80° 1.227'
US1	Lexington, SC	33°58.847'	81° 6.422'
US15	Dorchester, SC	33°17.199'	80°30.802'
US17	Charleston, SC	32°47.828'	79°56.590'
US21	Lexington, SC	33°55.982'	81° 4.639'
US21	Lexington, SC	33°52.827'	81° 2.212'
US21	Lexington, SC	33°45.868'	80°57.857'
US25	Henderson, NC	35°23.949'	82°30.458'
US29	Spartanburg, SC	34°56.165'	81°59.777'
US64	Henderson, NC	35°20.467'	82°26.404'
US78	Charleston, SC	32°58.727'	80° 4.658'
US176	Richland, SC	34° 8.738'	81°14.290'
US176	Richland, SC	34° 5.928'	81°10.481'
US176	Spartanburg, SC	35° 1.609'	82° 2.124'
US221	Spartanburg, SC	34°50.273'	81°58.257'
US301	Orangeburg, SC	33°27.454'	80°43.773'
US378	Lexington, SC	34° 0.228'	81° 6.617'
US601	Orangeburg, SC	33°33.511'	80°49.431'

I27

I40	Potter, TX	35°11.555'	101°50.202'
US60	Randall, TX	35° 1.775'	101°55.140'
US62	Lubbock, TX	33°34.674'	101°50.454'
US70	Hale, TX	34°11.248'	101°44.946'
US82	Lubbock, TX	33°35.536'	101°50.370'
US84	Lubbock, TX	33°32.266'	101°50.616'

US87	Lubbock, TX	33°31.164'	101°50.616'
US87	Swisher, TX	34°43.280'	101°50.838'
US87	Swisher, TX	34°34.766'	101°47.730'
US87	Swisher, TX	34°20.407'	101°44.592'
US287	Potter, TX	35°11.930'	101°50.136'

I29

I35	Clay, MO	39°10.124'	94°33.522'
I35	Jackson, MO	39° 6.264'	94°34.322'
I80	Pottawattamie, IA	41°13.945'	95°53.482'
I80	Pottawattamie, IA	41°13.729'	95°50.327'
I90	Minnehaha, SD	43°36.763'	96°46.201'
I94	Cass, ND	46°50.856'	96°50.436'
I129	Woodbury, IA	42°26.783'	96°22.486'
I229	Andrew, MO	39°53.300'	94°51.580'
I229	Buchanan, MO	39°42.520'	94°47.293'
I229	Lincoln, SD	43°29.263'	96°47.660'
I435	Platte, MO	39°20.701'	94°44.783'
I435	Platte, MO	39°19.173'	94°41.644'
I480	Pottawattamie, IA	41°15.709'	95°54.443'
I635	Platte, MO	39°11.546'	94°36.923'
I680	Pottawattamie, IA	41°29.614'	95°54.038'
I680	Pottawattamie, IA	41°21.259'	95°53.999'
US2	Grand Forks, ND	47°55.986'	97° 5.580'
US12	Roberts, SD	45°18.914'	97° 3.094'
US14	Brookings, SD	44°18.698'	96°45.472'
US18	Lincoln, SD	43°18.088'	96°47.758'
US18	Lincoln, SD	43°15.472'	96°47.768'
US20	Woodbury, IA	42°26.783'	96°22.486'
US30	Harrison, IA	41°33.005'	95°55.023'
US34	Mills, IA	41° 2.720'	95°49.150'
US34	Mills, IA	41° 0.101'	95°48.369'
US36	Buchanan, MO	39°44.991'	94°47.352'
US59	Andrew, MO	39°58.057'	94°58.318'
US59	Andrew, MO	39°51.483'	94°48.631'
US59	Holt, MO	40°12.465'	95°22.470'
US59	Holt, MO	40°11.632'	95°21.654'
US59	Holt, MO	40° 2.708'	95° 8.287'
US59	Holt, MO	39°58.471'	95° 0.901'
US75	Woodbury, IA	42°26.074'	96°22.491'
US81	Grand Forks, ND	48° 4.656'	97°10.110'
US81	Pembina, ND	48°48.210'	97°13.908'
US81	Codington, SD	44°56.030'	97° 3.315'
US136	Atchison, MO	40°24.425'	95°33.307'
US159	Holt, MO	40° 4.483'	95°11.550'
US169	Buchanan, MO	39°48.907'	94°48.190'
US169	Clay, MO	39°10.982'	94°35.576'
US212	Codington, SD	44°53.394'	97° 3.369'
US275	Pottawattamie, IA	41°13.234'	95°49.923'

I30

I35E	Dallas, TX	32°46.279'	96°48.619'
I35E	Dallas, TX	32°46.121'	96°48.239'
I35W	Tarrant, TX	32°44.821'	97°19.150'
I40	Pulaski, AR	34°46.724'	92°15.573'
I45	Dallas, TX	32°46.729'	96°46.910'
I430	Pulaski, AR	34°39.706'	92°24.144'
I440	Pulaski, AR	34°42.700'	92°16.216'
I630	Pulaski, AR	34°44.047'	92°15.688'
I635	Dallas, TX	32°49.370'	96°37.763'
I820	Tarrant, TX	32°45.580'	97°12.818'
I820	Tarrant, TX	32°44.279'	97°28.861'
US59	Bowie, TX	33°27.124'	94° 5.893'
US67	Miller, AR	33°32.965'	93°52.486'
US67	Pulaski, AR	34°45.359'	92°15.733'
US67	Pulaski, AR	34°40.729'	92°21.259'
US67	Saline, AR	34°32.691'	92°37.866'

I30 (cont)

US67	Hopkins, TX	33° 9.365'	95°25.559'
US67	Titus, TX	33° 9.823'	95° 1.121'
US69	Hunt, TX	33° 6.954'	96° 5.951'
US70	Saline, AR	34°32.042'	92°40.620'
US80	Dallas, TX	32°47.927'	96°40.710'
US80	Tarrant, TX	32°43.231'	97°31.414'
US82	Bowie, TX	33°28.251'	94°27.387'
US259	Morris, TX	33°17.659'	94°44.215'
US270	Hot Spring, AR	34°23.795'	92°49.643'
US271	Titus, TX	33°10.172'	94°59.985'
US287	Tarrant, TX	32°44.860'	97°18.565'
US377	Tarrant, TX	32°44.008'	97°24.209'

I35

I35E	Anoka, MN	45°13.107'	93° 1.723'
I35E	Dakota, MN	44°44.419'	93°16.949'
I35E	Denton, TX	33°12.725'	97° 9.982'
I35E	Hill, TX	32° 3.412'	97° 5.612'
I37	Bexar, TX	29°26.323'	98°28.656'
I40	Oklahoma, OK	35°27.859'	97°28.130'
I40	Oklahoma, OK	35°27.718'	97°29.551'
I44	Oklahoma, OK	35°35.928'	97°25.593'
I44	Oklahoma, OK	35°32.469'	97°27.589'
I70	Jackson, MO	39° 6.410'	94°35.658'
I70	Jackson, MO	39° 6.264'	94°34.322'
I80	Polk, IA	41°39.123'	93°34.523'
I80	Polk, IA	41°35.531'	93°46.626'
I90	Freeborn, MN	43°41.031'	93°19.255'
I135	Sedgwick, KS	37°36.102'	97°19.361'
I235	Polk, IA	41°39.123'	93°34.523'
I235	Polk, IA	41°35.531'	93°46.626'
I235	Oklahoma, OK	35°27.718'	97°29.551'
I240	Oklahoma, OK	35°23.500'	97°29.672'
I335	Lyon, KS	38°24.925'	96°14.218'
I410	Bexar, TX	29°31.444'	98°23.612'
I410	Bexar, TX	29°30.598'	98°23.852'
I410	Bexar, TX	29°28.757'	98°24.225'
I410	Bexar, TX	29°27.323'	98°24.798'
I410	Bexar, TX	29°18.982'	98°36.481'
I435	Johnson, KS	38°56.324'	94°44.824'
I435	Clay, MO	39°12.370'	94°29.543'
I535	St. Louis, MN	46°45.905'	92° 7.367'
I635	Johnson, KS	39° 2.399'	94°40.375'
I670	Jackson, MO	39° 5.766'	94°35.481'
US2	St. Louis, MN	46°44.572'	92° 9.262'
US2	St. Louis, MN	46°43.893'	92°12.110'
US6	Polk, IA	41°36.889'	93°46.600'
US8	Washington, MN	45°17.341'	93° 0.146'
US14	Steele, MN	44° 5.710'	93°14.671'
US14	Steele, MN	44° 3.541'	93°15.034'
US18	Cerro Gordo, IA	43° 8.771'	93°21.335'
US20	Hamilton, IA	42°26.927'	93°34.145'
US30	Story, IA	42° 0.385'	93°34.255'
US34	Clarke, IA	41° 1.593'	93°47.641'
US36	De Kalb, MO	39°45.230'	94°13.186'
US50	Lyon, KS	38°24.814'	96°13.940'
US50	Lyon, KS	38°24.662'	96° 8.115'
US53	St. Louis, MN	46°45.886'	92° 7.384'
US54	Sedgwick, KS	37°40.754'	97°11.411'
US56	Johnson, KS	39° 0.895'	94°41.583'
US56	Johnson, KS	38°48.697'	94°53.007'
US57	Frio, TX	29° 1.595'	99° 2.996'
US59	Franklin, KS	38°34.553'	95°16.044'
US59	Webb, TX	27°31.835'	99°30.157'
US60	Kay, OK	36°41.716'	97°20.728'
US61	Chisago, MN	45°20.188'	93° 0.249'

US62	Oklahoma, OK	35°29.575'	97°27.868'
US64	Noble, OK	36°17.373'	97°19.648'
US64	Noble, OK	36°16.455'	97°19.633'
US65	Freeborn, MN	43°40.160'	93°19.394'
US65	Freeborn, MN	43°36.717'	93°20.508'
US69	Decatur, IA	40°37.424'	93°53.401'
US69	Polk, IA	41°38.999'	93°36.016'
US69	Johnson, KS	38°58.559'	94°42.834'
US69	Wyandotte, KS	39° 2.870'	94°38.771'
US69	Clay, MO	39°16.709'	94°25.275'
US69	Clinton, MO	39°40.064'	94°14.134'
US69	Daviess, MO	39°56.704'	94° 7.008'
US69	Daviess, MO	39°51.251'	94°10.574'
US69	Daviess, MO	39°51.214'	94°10.592'
US70	Carter, OK	34°10.361'	97°10.071'
US70	Carter, OK	34° 8.351'	97° 9.331'
US75	Coffey, KS	38°25.773'	95°43.696'
US77	Butler, KS	37°52.385'	96°51.035'
US77	Cleveland, OK	35°16.858'	97°28.985'
US77	Logan, OK	35°48.726'	97°24.961'
US77	Love, OK	33°44.285'	97° 8.731'
US77	Murray, OK	34°27.012'	97° 8.060'
US77	Murray, OK	34°23.961'	97° 8.467'
US77	Oklahoma, OK	35°39.178'	97°25.436'
US77	Hill, TX	32° 2.674'	97° 5.671'
US77	Hill, TX	31°57.866'	97° 7.103'
US77	McLennan, TX	31°32.144'	97° 7.754'
US79	Williamson, TX	30°31.013'	97°41.267'
US81	Medina, TX	29° 7.030'	98°55.194'
US81	Medina, TX	29° 6.793'	98°55.486'
US81	Webb, TX	27°30.509'	99°30.167'
US82	Cooke, TX	33°38.429'	97° 9.325'
US83	Webb, TX	27°45.238'	99°26.327'
US83	Webb, TX	27°30.405'	99°30.161'
US83	Webb, TX	27°30.362'	99°30.158'
US84	McLennan, TX	31°35.062'	97° 6.571'
US90	Bexar, TX	29°23.758'	98°30.653'
US136	Harrison, MO	40°15.918'	94° 0.743'
US160	Sumner, KS	37°16.603'	97°20.383'
US166	Sumner, KS	37° 3.437'	97°20.288'
US169	Johnson, KS	38°53.022'	94°47.486'
US169	Johnson, KS	38°51.306'	94°48.953'
US169	Wyandotte, KS	39° 4.236'	94°37.094'
US169	Jackson, MO	39° 6.417'	94°35.297'
US177	Kay, OK	36°56.459'	97°20.764'
US183	Travis, TX	30°20.342'	97°41.986'
US190	Bell, TX	31° 5.419'	97°23.204'
US190	Bell, TX	31° 2.862'	97°27.890'
US290	Travis, TX	30°19.310'	97°42.392'
US290	Travis, TX	30°12.934'	97°45.092'
US377	Denton, TX	33°13.802'	97°10.423'
US412	Noble, OK	36°24.009'	97°19.600'

I35E

I35W	Anoka, MN	45°13.107'	93° 1.723'
I35W	Dakota, MN	44°44.419'	93°16.949'
I35W	Denton, TX	33°12.725'	97° 9.982'
I35W	Hill, TX	32° 3.412'	97° 5.612'
I94	Ramsey, MN	44°57.294'	93° 5.470'
I94	Ramsey, MN	44°56.859'	93° 6.202'
I494	Dakota, MN	44°51.770'	93° 8.687'
I635	Dallas, TX	32°54.463'	96°53.850'
I694	Ramsey, MN	45° 2.256'	93° 3.714'
I694	Ramsey, MN	45° 1.949'	93° 5.348'
US67	Dallas, TX	32°42.542'	96°49.768'
US77	Ellis, TX	32°29.860'	96°49.339'
US77	Ellis, TX	32°21.746'	96°51.331'
US287	Ellis, TX	32°25.621'	96°51.774'

US287	Ellis, TX	32°25.598'	96°51.735'

I35W

I94	Hennepin, MN	44°57.964'	93°15.134'
I94	Hennepin, MN	44°57.877'	93°16.139'
I494	Hennepin, MN	44°51.700'	93°17.888'
I694	Ramsey, MN	45° 4.020'	93°11.135'
I820	Tarrant, TX	32°50.361'	97°18.749'
US10	Ramsey, MN	45° 5.293'	93°11.252'
US67	Johnson, TX	32°24.955'	97°13.609'
US81	Johnson, TX	32°17.136'	97°10.618'
US81	Tarrant, TX	32°53.205'	97°19.022'
US287	Tarrant, TX	32°45.354'	97°19.145'
US377	Tarrant, TX	32°45.929'	97°19.076'
US377	Tarrant, TX	32°45.859'	97°19.073'

I37

I410	Bexar, TX	29°19.753'	98°24.926'
US59	Live Oak, TX	28°20.236'	98° 1.598'
US77	Nueces, TX	27°51.805'	97°37.353'
US77	San Patricio, TX	27°54.239'	97°37.882'
US281	Atascosa, TX	28°54.455'	98°25.958'
US281	Live Oak, TX	28°31.658'	98°11.212'

I39

I55	McLean, IL	40°32.333'	89° 0.173'
I80	La Salle, IL	41°22.070'	89° 3.552'
I88	Ogle, IL	41°54.301'	89° 1.208'
I90	Winnebago, IL	42°14.920'	88°57.612'
US20	Winnebago, IL	42°13.217'	89° 0.694'
US24	Woodford, IL	40°44.186'	89° 2.637'
US30	Lee, IL	41°45.637'	89° 0.531'
US34	La Salle, IL	41°33.245'	89° 3.640'
US51	La Salle, IL	41°16.853'	89° 5.200'
US51	Marathon, WI	44°53.830'	89°38.401'
US51	Marathon, WI	44°49.752'	89°39.473'
US52	La Salle, IL	41°28.198'	89° 3.007'

I40

I40 B	Canadian, OK	35°31.772'	98° 2.578'
I40 B	Canadian, OK	35°30.075'	97°56.195'
I44	Oklahoma, OK	35°27.599'	97°34.479'
I55	Crittenden, AR	35°10.255'	90°11.548'
I55	Crittenden, AR	35° 9.337'	90° 9.072'
I65	Davidson, TN	36° 9.257'	86°45.725'
I65	Davidson, TN	36° 8.916'	86°46.543'
I75	Knox, TN	35°57.323'	83°58.445'
I75	Loudon, TN	35°52.132'	84°15.386'
I77	Iredell, NC	35°48.586'	80°51.687'
I81	Jefferson, TN	36° 4.004'	83°23.386'
I85	Guilford, NC	36° 1.937'	79°48.293'
I85	Orange, NC	36° 4.528'	79°15.580'
I85	Orange, NC	36° 3.539'	79° 7.538'
I95	Johnston, NC	35°23.488'	78°30.919'
I240	Buncombe, NC	35°33.865'	82°29.974'
I240	Oklahoma, OK	35°24.242'	97°17.432'
I240	Shelby, TN	35° 9.071'	89°53.123'
I240	Shelby, TN	35° 8.956'	90° 1.320'
I265	Davidson, TN	36°10.449'	86°48.054'
I430	Pulaski, AR	34°49.262'	92°20.351'
I440	Pulaski, AR	34°46.887'	92° 9.633'
I440	Wake, NC	35°45.999'	78°44.159'
I440	Wake, NC	35°45.223'	78°35.770'
I440	Davidson, TN	36° 9.594'	86°49.293'
I540	Crawford, AR	35°27.307'	94°19.277'
I640	Knox, TN	36° 0.727'	83°51.792'
US11E	Knox, TN	36° 0.630'	83°50.522'

US11W	Knox, TN	36° 0.442'	83°52.433'
US15	Durham, NC	35°57.011'	79° 0.014'
US19	Buncombe, NC	35°33.559'	82°38.393'
US21	Iredell, NC	35°48.438'	80°52.588'
US25	Buncombe, NC	35°33.506'	82°32.318'
US25W	Cocke, TN	35°58.172'	83°15.461'
US25W	Jefferson, TN	36° 1.363'	83°28.564'
US27	Roane, TN	35°54.577'	84°35.215'
US29	Guilford, NC	36° 2.629'	79°46.436'
US34	Quay, NM	35° 9.335'	103°42.096'
US41	Davidson, TN	36° 9.059'	86°46.172'
US49	Monroe, AR	34°54.535'	91°11.807'
US51	Shelby, TN	35° 9.090'	90° 2.425'
US54	Guadalupe, NM	34°56.863'	104°38.466'
US54	Guadalupe, NM	34°56.680'	104°40.314'
US54	Quay, NM	35° 9.100'	103°46.530'
US59	Sequoyah, OK	35°26.867'	94°48.355'
US62	Okfuskee, OK	35°25.334'	96°17.963'
US62	Okmulgee, OK	35°25.909'	95°58.257'
US64	Faulkner, AR	35° 5.494'	92°25.349'
US64	Johnson, AR	35°27.910'	93°31.264'
US64	Johnson, AR	35°24.911'	93°23.035'
US64	Burke, NC	35°43.160'	81°41.668'
US64	Davie, NC	35°54.590'	80°37.039'
US64	Iredell, NC	35°52.171'	80°42.620'
US64	Iredell, NC	35°47.625'	80°56.191'
US64	Sequoyah, OK	35°27.025'	94°45.472'
US64	Sequoyah, OK	35°24.302'	94°31.546'
US64	Shelby, TN	35°12.251'	89°46.361'
US64	Shelby, TN	35° 9.193'	89°53.304'
US65	Faulkner, AR	35° 6.723'	92°26.122'
US66	Quay, NM	35°10.209'	103°40.488'
US67	Pulaski, AR	34°46.661'	92°14.126'
US69	McIntosh, OK	35°27.508'	95°32.611'
US70	Buncombe, NC	35°37.162'	82°18.427'
US70	McDowell, NC	35°37.403'	82°11.920'
US70	Wake, NC	35°41.681'	78°34.413'
US70	Davidson, TN	36° 9.338'	86°47.366'
US70	Davidson, TN	36° 7.837'	86°53.929'
US70	Haywood, TN	35°35.098'	89° 5.611'
US70	Madison, TN	35°40.846'	88°44.579'
US70	Wilson, TN	36°11.289'	86°16.151'
US70N	Putnam, TN	36° 8.422'	85°16.685'
US70N	Putnam, TN	36° 8.314'	85°16.015'
US70N	Putnam, TN	36° 8.176'	85°27.016'
US70S	Davidson, TN	36° 4.878'	86°57.392'
US71	Crawford, AR	35°29.337'	94°13.586'
US74	Buncombe, NC	35°33.865'	82°29.974'
US75	Okfuskee, OK	35°25.898'	96° 7.358'
US83	Wheeler, TX	35°13.859'	100°14.916'
US84	Guadalupe, NM	34°58.586'	104°59.442'
US93	Mohave, AZ	35°11.459'	114° 3.972'
US93	Mohave, AZ	35° 9.556'	113°41.724'
US95	San Bernardino, CA	34°52.628'	114°45.258'
US95	San Bernardino, CA	34°49.513'	114°35.838'
US117	Duplin, NC	34°58.142'	78° 4.944'
US117	Pender, NC	34°41.189'	77°56.836'
US127	Cumberland, TN	36° 0.001'	85° 2.725'
US177	Pottawatomie, OK	35°23.018'	97° 0.019'
US180	Coconino, AZ	35°12.520'	111°31.014'
US183	Custer, OK	35°30.040'	98°57.862'
US191	Apache, AZ	35°12.952'	109°19.944'
US191	Apache, AZ	35°11.426'	109°26.112'
US221	McDowell, NC	35°38.607'	81°59.161'
US231	Wilson, TN	36°10.928'	86°17.936'
US266	McIntosh, OK	35°27.836'	95°21.255'
US266	Muskogee, OK	35°28.599'	95°18.362'
US270	Canadian, OK	35°31.747'	98° 6.826'

I40 (cont)

US276	Haywood, NC	35°36.136'	83° 0.399'
US281	Caddo, OK	35°31.742'	98°21.010'
US283	Beckham, OK	35°15.772'	99°38.591'
US285	Torrance, NM	35° 0.491'	105°39.828'
US287	Potter, TX	35°11.560'	101°41.784'
US321	Cocke, TN	35°56.884'	83°12.232'
US321	Cocke, TN	35°52.744'	83°11.212'
US321	Loudon, TN	35°52.439'	84°19.457'
US377	Seminole, OK	35°23.001'	96°40.276'
US385	Oldham, TX	35°14.570'	102°25.680'
US412	Madison, TN	35°39.394'	88°52.486'
US421	Forsyth, NC	36° 4.352'	80°19.534'
US601	Davie, NC	35°55.374'	80°35.427'
US641	Decatur, TN	35°50.459'	88° 5.145'
US666	McKinley, NM	35°31.706'	108°45.552'
US701	Sampson, NC	35°13.523'	78°20.903'

I40 B

US81	Canadian, OK	35°32.211'	97°57.261'

I43

I90	Rock, WI	42°31.654'	88°58.503'
I94	Milwaukee, WI	43° 2.127'	87°55.435'
I894	Milwaukee, WI	42°57.742'	88° 2.234'
US10	Manitowoc, WI	44° 9.206'	87°43.891'
US10	Manitowoc, WI	44° 6.565'	87°43.847'
US12	Walworth, WI	42°40.487'	88°31.304'
US14	Walworth, WI	42°36.572'	88°43.495'
US14	Walworth, WI	42°36.554'	88°43.474'
US18	Milwaukee, WI	43° 2.662'	87°55.540'
US18	Milwaukee, WI	43° 2.587'	87°55.510'
US45	Milwaukee, WI	42°57.345'	88° 2.888'
US141	Brown, WI	44°33.649'	88° 3.265'
US141	Brown, WI	44°27.860'	87°57.383'
US141	Brown, WI	44°26.075'	87°55.058'
US151	Manitowoc, WI	44° 4.407'	87°42.748'

I44

I55	St. Louis city, MO	38°36.620'	90°12.521'
I235	Oklahoma, OK	35°31.772'	97°30.821'
I240	Oklahoma, OK	35°23.773'	97°34.454'
I244	Tulsa, OK	36° 9.744'	95°49.429'
I244	Tulsa, OK	36° 5.378'	96° 2.312'
I270	St. Louis, MO	38°32.910'	90°25.630'
US50	Franklin, MO	38°26.180'	90°54.778'
US59	Ottawa, OK	36°43.505'	94°55.624'
US60	Craig, OK	36°37.791'	95° 8.177'
US61	St. Louis, MO	38°33.569'	90°24.400'
US62	Comanche, OK	34°43.761'	98°23.740'
US62	Comanche, OK	34°37.441'	98°23.202'
US62	Grady, OK	35° 3.089'	97°54.511'
US62	McClain, OK	35°16.936'	97°35.996'
US62	Oklahoma, OK	35°29.596'	97°34.720'
US63	Phelps, MO	37°57.659'	91°45.917'
US64	Tulsa, OK	36° 6.830'	95°53.738'
US65	Greene, MO	37°15.009'	93°13.471'
US69	Craig, OK	36°33.444'	95°13.205'
US70	Cotton, OK	34°10.418'	98°30.092'
US71	Newton, MO	37° 2.777'	94°28.694'
US75	Tulsa, OK	36° 5.332'	96° 0.386'
US77	Oklahoma, OK	35°31.772'	97°30.821'
US160	Greene, MO	37°14.720'	93°20.939'
US166	Newton, MO	36°59.888'	94°36.728'
US169	Tulsa, OK	36° 8.348'	95°51.592'
US277	Comanche, OK	34°46.934'	98°18.226'
US277	Comanche, OK	34°30.434'	98°24.730'

US277	Cotton, OK	34°21.722'	98°24.551'
US277	Wichita, TX	33°54.607'	98°30.143'
US281	Wichita, TX	33°54.466'	98°29.944'
US281	Wichita, TX	33°54.408'	98°30.038'
US287	Wichita, TX	33°56.740'	98°31.375'
US377	Lincoln, OK	35°45.458'	96°39.741'

I45

I610	Harris, TX	29°48.825'	95°22.517'
I610	Harris, TX	29°41.822'	95°17.323'
US59	Harris, TX	29°44.647'	95°21.747'
US75	Dallas, TX	32°47.752'	96°47.537'
US75	Dallas, TX	32°46.046'	96°46.592'
US79	Leon, TX	31°27.053'	96° 4.558'
US84	Freestone, TX	31°42.890'	96°10.565'
US175	Dallas, TX	32°44.755'	96°46.097'
US190	Madison, TX	30°57.889'	95°53.032'
US190	Walker, TX	30°43.088'	95°34.170'
US287	Navarro, TX	32° 9.154'	96°28.040'
US287	Navarro, TX	32° 4.447'	96°26.692'

I49

US71	Rapides, LA	31°19.430'	92°27.736'
US71	Rapides, LA	31°14.516'	92°25.793'
US84	De Soto, LA	32° 3.741'	93°34.050'
US167	Lafayette, LA	30°15.553'	92° 0.930'
US167	Rapides, LA	31°18.176'	92°26.833'
US167	Rapides, LA	31°18.160'	92°26.826'
US167	Rapides, LA	31° 0.967'	92°22.533'
US167	St. Landry, LA	30°35.047'	92° 2.924'
US190	St. Landry, LA	30°31.884'	92° 3.911'

I55

I57	Scott, MO	36°52.409'	89°31.981'
I64	St. Clair, IL	38°37.885'	90° 8.579'
I64	St. Louis city, MO	38°37.222'	90°11.348'
I70	Madison, IL	38°45.140'	89°54.412'
I72	Sangamon, IL	39°48.097'	89°35.721'
I72	Sangamon, IL	39°44.601'	89°38.161'
I74	McLean, IL	40°32.203'	89° 1.461'
I74	McLean, IL	40°26.807'	89° 1.304'
I80	Will, IL	41°29.176'	88°11.842'
I90	Cook, IL	41°50.821'	87°38.588'
I155	Logan, IL	40°10.699'	89°24.961'
I155	Pemiscot, MO	36°12.956'	89°44.881'
I220	Madison, MS	32°24.666'	90° 8.832'
I240	Shelby, TN	35° 4.328'	90° 1.565'
I255	Madison, IL	38°40.374'	90° 1.918'
I270	Madison, IL	38°45.140'	89°54.412'
I270	St. Louis, MO	38°30.227'	90°20.361'
I294	Cook, IL	41°45.647'	87°53.517'
I355	Will, IL	41°42.202'	88° 1.975'
US6	Will, IL	41°27.364'	88°11.741'
US24	McLean, IL	40°44.458'	88°44.242'
US30	Will, IL	41°35.015'	88°10.115'
US40	Madison, IL	38°42.962'	89°55.241'
US41	Cook, IL	41°50.911'	87°36.770'
US50	St. Louis, MO	38°30.696'	90°20.148'
US51	St. John the Baptist, LA	30° 5.555'	90°26.263'
US51	Tangipahoa, LA	30°28.176'	90°28.945'
US51	Hinds, MS	32° 6.054'	90°18.114'
US51	Shelby, TN	35° 3.794'	90° 1.410'
US52	Will, IL	41°31.286'	88°11.328'
US61	Crittenden, AR	35°23.520'	90°16.406'
US61	Mississippi, AR	35°53.216'	89°55.100'
US61	Cape Girardeau, MO	37°25.577'	89°38.306'
US61	Cape Girardeau, MO	37°20.983'	89°36.124'

US61	Jefferson, MO	38°20.899'	90°23.721'
US61	Jefferson, MO	38°11.516'	90°23.731'
US61	Jefferson, MO	38° 9.472'	90°21.454'
US61	New Madrid, MO	36°38.155'	89°32.708'
US61	New Madrid, MO	36°34.339'	89°34.638'
US61	Scott, MO	37°12.830'	89°32.605'
US61	Shelby, TN	35° 7.480'	90° 4.018'
US61	Shelby, TN	35° 4.728'	90° 3.423'
US62	Scott, MO	36°53.555'	89°32.001'
US64	Crittenden, AR	35°12.726'	90°12.385'
US67	Jefferson, MO	38°11.832'	90°23.995'
US70	Crittenden, AR	35° 8.844'	90° 7.714'
US80	Rankin, MS	32°16.824'	90°10.356'
US82	Montgomery, MS	33°29.196'	89°45.864'
US84	Lincoln, MS	31°32.508'	90°28.770'
US98	Pike, MS	31°17.306'	90°28.706'
US98	Pike, MS	31°13.248'	90°28.962'
US136	McLean, IL	40°18.695'	89° 9.704'
US150	McLean, IL	40°29.093'	89° 1.706'
US190	Tangipahoa, LA	30°30.249'	90°30.212'
US412	Pemiscot, MO	36°13.860'	89°43.892'

I57

I64	Jefferson, IL	38°20.174'	88°57.383'
I64	Jefferson, IL	38°15.895'	88°55.864'
I70	Effingham, IL	39° 8.982'	88°30.498'
I70	Effingham, IL	39° 5.653'	88°34.868'
I72	Champaign, IL	40° 7.187'	88°18.311'
I74	Champaign, IL	40° 8.761'	88°17.019'
I80	Cook, IL	41°33.968'	87°44.609'
I94	Cook, IL	41°42.919'	87°37.481'
I294	Cook, IL	41°37.108'	87°41.227'
US6	Cook, IL	41°36.107'	87°42.530'
US24	Iroquois, IL	40°45.088'	88° 0.366'
US30	Cook, IL	41°30.378'	87°44.540'
US36	Douglas, IL	39°47.494'	88°15.864'
US45	Champaign, IL	39°54.335'	88°16.780'
US45	Coles, IL	39°25.586'	88°22.669'
US45	Cumberland, IL	39°19.832'	88°25.994'
US45	Effingham, IL	39° 8.689'	88°32.025'
US45	Kankakee, IL	41° 4.596'	87°52.151'
US50	Marion, IL	38°37.442'	88°58.319'
US60	Mississippi, MO	36°55.250'	89°19.097'
US60	Scott, MO	36°52.409'	89°31.981'
US136	Champaign, IL	40°18.494'	88°11.045'
US150	Champaign, IL	40° 8.577'	88°17.255'

I59

I459	Jefferson, AL	33°35.873'	86°39.223'
I759	Etowah, AL	34° 0.514'	86° 4.622'
US11	De Kalb, AL	34°28.649'	85°42.711'
US11	Jefferson, AL	33°33.998'	86°43.506'
US11	St. Tammany, LA	30°21.187'	89°44.429'
US11	Forrest, MS	31°15.618'	89°20.244'
US11	Jones, MS	31°43.284'	89° 6.240'
US11	Jones, MS	31°39.852'	89° 9.552'
US11	Jones, MS	31°38.010'	89°10.854'
US11	Pearl River, MS	30°28.182'	89°41.268'
US49	Forrest, MS	31°21.395'	89°20.796'
US84	Jones, MS	31°41.850'	89° 7.026'
US84	Jones, MS	31°40.783'	89° 9.310'
US98	Forrest, MS	31°14.652'	89°19.578'
US98	Lamar, MS	31°19.482'	89°21.144'
US231	St. Clair, AL	33°51.760'	86°17.234'
US278	Etowah, AL	34° 1.141'	86° 4.483'

I64

I65	Jefferson, KY	38°15.474'	85°44.498'
I70	St. Louis city, MO	38°37.222'	90°11.348'
I71	Jefferson, KY	38°15.698'	85°43.572'
I75	Fayette, KY	38° 6.969'	84°31.573'
I75	Fayette, KY	38° 3.274'	84°25.838'
I77	Kanawha, WV	38°21.607'	81°38.011'
I77	Kanawha, WV	38°18.995'	81°33.723'
I77	Kanawha, WV	38°18.548'	81°33.824'
I77	Raleigh, WV	37°43.783'	81°11.689'
I81	Augusta, VA	38° 7.258'	79° 2.876'
I81	Rockbridge, VA	37°47.648'	79°23.879'
I95	Richmond, VA	37°35.036'	77°28.225'
I95	Richmond, VA	37°32.959'	77°26.100'
I164	Gibson, IN	38°10.114'	87°28.191'
I170	St. Louis, MO	38°37.783'	90°20.604'
I195	Richmond, VA	37°35.198'	77°28.509'
I255	St. Clair, IL	38°37.132'	90° 4.143'
I264	Jefferson, KY	38°16.541'	85°48.568'
I264	Jefferson, KY	38°14.265'	85°37.389'
I264	Chesapeake, VA	36°47.270'	76°23.934'
I264	Norfolk, VA	36°50.709'	76°11.802'
I265	Floyd, IN	38°18.196'	85°51.003'
I265	Jefferson, KY	38°13.369'	85°30.343'
I270	St. Louis, MO	38°38.317'	90°26.935'
I295	Henrico, VA	37°39.322'	77°36.337'
I295	Henrico, VA	37°31.215'	77°16.243'
I464	Chesapeake, VA	36°45.758'	76°16.102'
I564	Norfolk, VA	36°55.002'	76°16.043'
I664	Chesapeake, VA	36°47.108'	76°24.922'
I664	Hampton, VA	37° 1.916'	76°22.696'
US1	Richmond, VA	37°33.157'	77°26.652'
US11	Augusta, VA	38° 1.490'	79° 8.478'
US11	Rockbridge, VA	37°50.473'	79°22.055'
US11	Rockbridge, VA	37°48.052'	79°24.894'
US13	Chesapeake, VA	36°46.863'	76°25.804'
US13	Chesapeake, VA	36°46.295'	76°21.873'
US13	Norfolk, VA	36°52.492'	76°11.860'
US15	Louisa, VA	37°58.612'	78°12.836'
US17	Chesapeake, VA	36°45.503'	76°20.704'
US17	Newport News, VA	37° 5.350'	76°27.566'
US19	Raleigh, WV	37°45.358'	81° 9.276'
US23	Boyd, KY	38°22.788'	82°36.418'
US27	Fayette, KY	38° 4.555'	84°27.353'
US29	Albemarle, VA	38° 1.236'	78°32.216'
US31	Jefferson, KY	38°15.519'	85°45.170'
US31W	Jefferson, KY	38°16.148'	85°46.930'
US33	Henrico, VA	37°35.834'	77°29.503'
US35	Putnam, WV	38°26.873'	81°50.939'
US35	Putnam, WV	38°26.750'	81°50.663'
US40	St. Louis, MO	38°38.317'	90°26.935'
US41	Gibson, IN	38°10.081'	87°33.021'
US42	Jefferson, KY	38°15.355'	85°43.279'
US45	Wayne, IL	38°15.967'	88°20.860'
US51	Washington, IL	38°23.368'	89°10.210'
US52	Cabell, WV	38°24.086'	82°28.827'
US52	Cabell, WV	38°23.998'	82°28.541'
US52	Wayne, WV	38°23.440'	82°34.420'
US60	Bath, KY	38° 8.377'	83°43.343'
US60	Boyd, KY	38°21.922'	82°46.271'
US60	Carter, KY	38°19.580'	83° 7.081'
US60	Clark, KY	38° 2.095'	84° 4.665'
US60	Clark, KY	38° 1.021'	84° 9.401'
US60	Franklin, KY	38°10.424'	84°48.679'
US60	Jefferson, KY	38°15.478'	85°43.378'
US60	Montgomery, KY	38° 5.308'	83°53.934'
US60	Alleghany, VA	37°49.615'	79°47.602'

I64 (cont)

US60	Alleghany, VA	37°48.569'	79°51.011'
US60	Alleghany, VA	37°48.519'	80° 3.695'
US60	Alleghany, VA	37°46.337'	79°57.792'
US60	Rockbridge, VA	37°51.140'	79°28.759'
US60	Hampton, VA	37° 1.411'	76°19.796'
US60	Norfolk, VA	36°57.958'	76°17.521'
US60	Cabell, WV	38°24.796'	82°20.906'
US60	Greenbrier, WV	37°54.206'	80°38.008'
US60	Greenbrier, WV	37°47.501'	80°16.295'
US60	Greenbrier, WV	37°46.393'	80°22.618'
US60	Kanawha, WV	38°21.614'	81°42.974'
US60	Kanawha, WV	38°20.506'	81°36.738'
US60	Kanawha, WV	38°19.792'	81°34.850'
US61	St. Louis, MO	38°38.117'	90°24.322'
US62	Scott, KY	38° 9.464'	84°36.719'
US119	Kanawha, WV	38°21.275'	81°39.097'
US127	Franklin, KY	38° 9.500'	84°53.620'
US150	Floyd, IN	38°18.189'	85°53.388'
US219	Greenbrier, WV	37°49.001'	80°25.684'
US231	Spencer, IN	38°11.622'	86°58.711'
US250	Albemarle, VA	38° 2.666'	78°43.550'
US250	Albemarle, VA	38° 1.229'	78°25.841'
US250	Augusta, VA	38° 1.941'	78°51.584'
US250	Henrico, VA	37°38.891'	77°35.654'
US250	Henrico, VA	37°36.313'	77°31.001'
US258	Hampton, VA	37° 2.423'	76°23.701'
US340	Waynesboro, VA	38° 3.663'	78°56.496'
US360	Richmond, VA	37°33.340'	77°24.620'
US460	Montgomery, KY	38° 4.676'	83°56.977'
US460	Norfolk, VA	36°55.279'	76°16.217'
US522	Louisa, VA	37°46.868'	77°53.326'

I65

I70	Marion, IN	39°46.918'	86° 8.474'
I70	Marion, IN	39°45.194'	86° 8.729'
I74	Marion, IN	39°42.212'	86° 6.502'
I80	Lake, IN	41°34.150'	87°18.029'
I85	Montgomery, AL	32°21.997'	86°19.330'
I90	Lake, IN	41°35.933'	87°18.370'
I165	Mobile, AL	30°45.143'	88° 5.717'
I264	Jefferson, KY	38°11.396'	85°43.798'
I265	Clark, IN	38°20.735'	85°45.260'
I265	Jefferson, KY	38° 6.901'	85°42.106'
I265	Davidson, TN	36°11.560'	86°46.540'
I440	Davidson, TN	36° 6.948'	86°46.411'
I459	Jefferson, AL	33°23.623'	86°47.098'
I465	Marion, IN	39°51.824'	86°16.463'
I565	Limestone, AL	34°39.454'	86°54.800'
US11	Jefferson, AL	33°30.583'	86°49.189'
US12	Lake, IN	41°35.888'	87°18.412'
US24	Jasper, IN	40°45.949'	87° 7.178'
US30	Lake, IN	41°28.270'	87°19.436'
US31	Autauga, AL	32°32.986'	86°27.469'
US31	Blount, AL	33°53.225'	86°50.915'
US31	Chilton, AL	32°48.110'	86°34.823'
US31	Jefferson, AL	33°47.333'	86°49.448'
US31	Jefferson, AL	33°24.737'	86°48.371'
US31	Limestone, AL	34°49.819'	86°56.328'
US31	Montgomery, AL	32°15.986'	86°21.289'
US31	Morgan, AL	34°18.999'	86°54.027'
US31	Shelby, AL	33°13.832'	86°48.461'
US31	Shelby, AL	33° 8.522'	86°45.000'
US31	Bartholomew, IN	39°18.272'	85°57.751'
US31	Clark, IN	38°23.623'	85°45.773'
US31	Clark, IN	38°17.441'	85°45.536'
US31	Clark, IN	38°17.361'	85°45.526'

US31	Clark, IN	38°16.505'	85°44.972'
US31	Jackson, IN	38°46.832'	85°49.775'
US31	Marion, IN	39°46.970'	86° 9.443'
US31	Giles, TN	35° 0.811'	86°52.763'
US31W	Hart, KY	37°17.447'	85°54.221'
US31W	Simpson, KY	36°39.917'	86°33.390'
US31W	Sumner, TN	36°20.825'	86°43.001'
US40	Marion, IN	39°46.013'	86° 8.582'
US41	Davidson, TN	36°10.289'	86°46.103'
US42	Jefferson, KY	38°15.293'	85°44.545'
US43	Mobile, AL	30°52.621'	88° 2.668'
US45	Mobile, AL	30°44.435'	88° 6.466'
US50	Jackson, IN	38°57.491'	85°50.603'
US52	Boone, IN	40° 4.178'	86°29.824'
US62	Hardin, KY	37°42.823'	85°49.782'
US64	Giles, TN	35°11.616'	86°52.251'
US68	Warren, KY	37° 1.883'	86°14.479'
US72	Limestone, AL	34°46.984'	86°56.386'
US80	Montgomery, AL	32°19.627'	86°20.087'
US80	Montgomery, AL	32°18.936'	86°20.205'
US84	Conecuh, AL	31°25.126'	87° 0.352'
US90	Mobile, AL	30°39.107'	88° 7.343'
US98	Mobile, AL	30°42.420'	88° 7.343'
US231	Jasper, IN	40°48.569'	87° 9.243'
US231	Lake, IN	41°23.603'	87°19.446'
US231	White, IN	40°40.046'	87° 2.446'
US231	Warren, KY	36°56.075'	86°25.091'
US278	Cullman, AL	34°10.214'	86°52.509'
US412	Maury, TN	35°38.567'	86°53.599'
US431	Williamson, TN	35°48.340'	86°51.011'

I66

I81	Frederick, VA	39° 0.559'	78°18.073'
I495	Fairfax, VA	38°53.194'	77°13.294'
US15	Prince William, VA	38°49.074'	77°38.380'
US17	Fauquier, VA	38°53.659'	77°54.719'
US17	Fauquier, VA	38°51.448'	77°50.558'
US29	District of Columbia, DC	38°54.142'	77° 3.492'
US29	Arlington, VA	38°53.944'	77° 4.572'
US29	Arlington, VA	38°53.937'	77° 4.269'
US29	Arlington, VA	38°53.757'	77° 5.940'
US29	Arlington, VA	38°53.258'	77° 9.722'
US29	Fairfax, VA	38°50.222'	77°26.855'
US29	Prince William, VA	38°47.982'	77°35.874'
US50	District of Columbia, DC	38°53.611'	77° 3.185'
US50	Fairfax, VA	38°51.715'	77°20.871'
US340	Warren, VA	38°57.644'	78°11.582'

I68

I70	Washington, MD	39°42.827'	78°11.330'
I79	Monongalia, WV	39°34.711'	79°58.552'
US119	Monongalia, WV	39°35.064'	79°57.229'
US219	Garrett, MD	39°41.398'	79°15.011'
US219	Garrett, MD	39°41.360'	79° 6.318'
US220	Allegany, MD	39°40.320'	78°43.925'
US220	Allegany, MD	39°38.714'	78°47.301'

I69

I69 B	Branch, MI	41°56.164'	84°58.399'
I69 B	Branch, MI	41°54.134'	84°59.437'
I69 B	Eaton, MI	42°34.645'	84°48.940'
I69 B	Eaton, MI	42°30.959'	84°50.156'
I75	Genesee, MI	42°59.088'	83°44.003'
I80	Steuben, IN	41°44.096'	85° 0.070'
I94	Calhoun, MI	42°17.836'	84°59.808'
I94	Calhoun, MI	42°17.774'	84°59.815'
I94	St. Clair, MI	42°58.525'	82°28.684'

I96	Clinton, MI	42°47.902'	84°42.062'
I96	Clinton, MI	42°47.361'	84°40.570'
I96	Clinton, MI	42°46.658'	84°40.207'
I96	Eaton, MI	42°41.476'	84°40.105'
I465	Marion, IN	39°53.688'	86° 3.244'
I475	Genesee, MI	43° 0.620'	83°40.747'
I496	Eaton, MI	42°43.172'	84°40.141'
US6	De Kalb, IN	41°26.377'	85° 3.289'
US20	Steuben, IN	41°38.146'	85° 2.882'
US20	Steuben, IN	41°38.090'	85° 2.891'
US24	Allen, IN	41° 2.032'	85°15.139'
US27	Clinton, MI	42°49.048'	84°32.584'
US27	Eaton, MI	42°39.463'	84°40.943'
US30	Allen, IN	41° 7.338'	85°11.199'
US35	Delaware, IN	40°16.607'	85°33.479'
US35	Grant, IN	40°28.672'	85°32.944'
US127	Clinton, MI	42°48.455'	84°30.706'
US224	Huntington, IN	40°49.653'	85°21.255'

I69 B

US12	Branch, MI	41°56.436'	85° 0.043'
US12	Branch, MI	41°56.164'	84°58.399'
US27	Eaton, MI	42°34.645'	84°48.940'

I70

I15	Millard, UT	38°34.627'	112°36.150'
I71	Franklin, OH	39°57.262'	82°59.074'
I71	Franklin, OH	39°57.052'	83° 1.021'
I74	Marion, IN	39°42.778'	86°15.871'
I75	Montgomery, OH	39°51.933'	84°11.339'
I76	Jefferson, CO	39°47.184'	105° 4.416'
I76	Bedford, PA	40° 2.962'	78°30.673'
I76	Bedford, PA	39°59.221'	78°15.416'
I76	Westmoreland, PA	40°13.159'	79°36.146'
I76	Westmoreland, PA	40° 6.649'	79°23.137'
I77	Guernsey, OH	39°59.972'	81°33.537'
I79	Washington, PA	40°11.273'	80°14.711'
I79	Washington, PA	40° 9.663'	80°11.723'
I81	Washington, MD	39°37.021'	77°47.147'
I135	Saline, KS	38°52.474'	97°38.719'
I170	St. Louis, MO	38°43.702'	90°19.899'
I270	Denver, CO	39°46.680'	104°53.706'
I270	Frederick, MD	39°23.864'	77°25.492'
I270	St. Louis, MO	38°44.915'	90°26.379'
I270	Franklin, OH	39°58.604'	83° 7.147'
I270	Franklin, OH	39°56.044'	82°51.124'
I435	Wyandotte, KS	39° 6.418'	94°48.618'
I435	Jackson, MO	39° 3.538'	94°29.426'
I465	Marion, IN	39°47.942'	86° 2.101'
I470	Shawnee, KS	39° 3.193'	95°46.612'
I470	Shawnee, KS	39° 1.631'	95°37.387'
I470	Jackson, MO	39° 2.515'	94°21.724'
I470	Belmont, OH	40° 4.058'	80°50.462'
I470	Ohio, WV	40° 2.943'	80°39.841'
I635	Wyandotte, KS	39° 6.248'	94°40.733'
I670	Wyandotte, KS	39° 6.043'	94°37.306'
I670	Wyandotte, KS	39° 5.514'	94°37.882'
I670	Jackson, MO	39° 5.766'	94°35.481'
I670	Franklin, OH	39°58.067'	83° 3.706'
I675	Clark, OH	39°51.893'	83°59.654'
I695	Baltimore, MD	39°18.351'	76°44.669'
US6	Clear Creek, CO	39°44.754'	105°26.298'
US6	Clear Creek, CO	39°41.027'	105°53.232'
US6	Eagle, CO	39°42.669'	106°42.438'
US6	Eagle, CO	39°39.150'	106°57.264'
US6	Garfield, CO	39°32.680'	107°39.198'
US6	Garfield, CO	39°30.604'	107°52.488'

US6	Jefferson, CO	39°43.499'	105°10.752'
US6	Mesa, CO	39°12.881'	108°51.948'
US6	Mesa, CO	39° 7.488'	108°19.296'
US6	Mesa, CO	39° 6.715'	108°38.592'
US6	Summit, CO	39°37.715'	106° 3.984'
US6	Emery, UT	38°58.887'	110°13.908'
US11	Washington, MD	39°36.751'	77°46.969'
US15	Frederick, MD	39°23.952'	77°26.455'
US19	Washington, PA	40°11.003'	80°13.669'
US22	Muskingum, OH	39°58.442'	81°50.086'
US23	Franklin, OH	39°57.212'	82°59.674'
US24	Eagle, CO	39°36.508'	106°26.844'
US24	Kit Carson, CO	39°18.075'	102°15.252'
US24	Kit Carson, CO	39°17.021'	102°55.878'
US24	Lincoln, CO	39°15.829'	103°40.098'
US24	Lincoln, CO	39°15.747'	103°38.796'
US24	Thomas, KS	39°21.976'	101°12.222'
US24	Wyandotte, KS	39° 6.877'	94°36.948'
US27	Wayne, IN	39°52.329'	84°53.299'
US29	Howard, MD	39°17.777'	76°49.555'
US30	Bedford, PA	39°59.962'	78°13.966'
US30	Bedford, PA	39°59.956'	78°14.350'
US31	Marion, IN	39°45.212'	86° 9.289'
US33	Franklin, OH	39°56.898'	82°56.649'
US33	Franklin, OH	39°55.924'	82°55.663'
US35	Wayne, IN	39°52.042'	84°55.576'
US35	Preble, OH	39°49.725'	84°46.775'
US36	Arapahoe, CO	39°42.954'	104°13.296'
US40	Clear Creek, CO	39°45.658'	105°38.946'
US40	Clear Creek, CO	39°45.514'	105°39.306'
US40	Jefferson, CO	39°43.856'	105°10.164'
US40	Fayette, IL	38°58.454'	89° 0.179'
US40	Fayette, IL	38°58.178'	89° 7.976'
US40	Madison, IL	38°47.161'	89°37.856'
US40	Wayne, IN	39°49.997'	84°49.021'
US40	Douglas, KS	38°59.573'	95°13.978'
US40	Gove, KS	39° 7.167'	100°48.474'
US40	Shawnee, KS	39° 2.081'	95°38.213'
US40	Wyandotte, KS	39° 6.351'	94°44.283'
US40	Frederick, MD	39°24.216'	77°22.903'
US40	Frederick, MD	39°23.864'	77°25.492'
US40	Howard, MD	39°18.196'	76°54.845'
US40	Washington, MD	39°39.311'	78° 3.110'
US40	Washington, MD	39°35.998'	77°40.972'
US40	Washington, MD	39°35.982'	77°42.178'
US40	Washington, MD	39°32.216'	77°36.391'
US40	Boone, MO	38°58.295'	92°25.851'
US40	Cooper, MO	38°56.141'	92°46.559'
US40	Jackson, MO	39° 4.144'	94°30.636'
US40	Jackson, MO	39° 2.836'	94°26.545'
US40	Jackson, MO	39° 1.293'	94°11.866'
US40	St. Charles, MO	38°48.380'	90°50.189'
US40	Belmont, OH	40° 4.589'	80°55.703'
US40	Belmont, OH	40° 4.321'	80°58.164'
US40	Belmont, OH	40° 3.533'	81° 7.389'
US40	Clark, OH	39°55.430'	83°41.290'
US40	Franklin, OH	39°57.427'	83° 2.704'
US40	Guernsey, OH	40° 2.166'	81°26.101'
US40	Muskingum, OH	39°56.872'	82° 2.801'
US40	Washington, PA	40° 9.839'	80°16.607'
US40	Ohio, WV	40° 4.453'	80°42.291'
US40	Ohio, WV	40° 4.324'	80°43.403'
US40	Ohio, WV	40° 4.318'	80°43.466'
US40	Ohio, WV	40° 2.676'	80°39.364'
US41	Vigo, IN	39°25.846'	87°24.861'
US42	Madison, OH	39°57.358'	83°22.504'
US50	Sevier, UT	38°55.984'	111°51.222'
US51	Fayette, IL	38°58.720'	89° 5.764'

I70 (cont)

US54	Callaway, MO	38°56.667'	91°56.458'
US62	Franklin, OH	39°56.907'	83° 2.187'
US63	Boone, MO	38°57.699'	92°17.491'
US65	Saline, MO	38°57.732'	93°12.487'
US65	Saline, MO	38°57.713'	93°12.424'
US67	St. Louis, MO	38°44.594'	90°23.790'
US68	Clark, OH	39°53.711'	83°51.208'
US69	Wyandotte, KS	39° 5.765'	94°38.941'
US75	Shawnee, KS	39° 4.004'	95°43.897'
US77	Geary, KS	38°59.966'	96°51.658'
US81	Saline, KS	38°52.474'	97°38.719'
US83	Thomas, KS	39°11.361'	100°52.170'
US89	Sevier, UT	38°52.690'	111°57.390'
US119	Westmoreland, PA	40°12.759'	79°35.444'
US127	Preble, OH	39°50.057'	84°37.751'
US169	Wyandotte, KS	39° 5.601'	94°37.547'
US183	Ellis, KS	38°53.905'	99°19.050'
US191	Grand, UT	38°56.557'	109°48.942'
US231	Putnam, IN	39°31.926'	86°48.157'
US250	Ohio, WV	40° 4.388'	80°42.808'
US281	Russell, KS	38°51.852'	98°51.262'
US283	Trego, KS	39° 0.872'	99°53.397'
US287	Denver, CO	39°47.047'	105° 1.470'
US385	Kit Carson, CO	39°17.650'	102°16.686'
US522	Washington, MD	39°42.455'	78°11.047'
US522	Fulton, PA	39°45.428'	78°11.389'

I71

I75	Boone, KY	38°52.615'	84°37.462'
I75	Hamilton, OH	39° 5.783'	84°31.273'
I76	Medina, OH	41° 1.828'	81°53.434'
I80	Cuyahoga, OH	41°19.960'	81°49.014'
I90	Cuyahoga, OH	41°28.447'	81°41.598'
I264	Jefferson, KY	38°17.408'	85°38.878'
I265	Jefferson, KY	38°18.889'	85°34.908'
I270	Franklin, OH	40° 6.622'	82°58.667'
I270	Franklin, OH	39°53.541'	83° 2.314'
I271	Medina, OH	41° 9.714'	81°47.145'
I275	Kenton, KY	39° 2.072'	84°35.959'
I275	Hamilton, OH	39°16.249'	84°21.070'
I471	Hamilton, OH	39° 6.381'	84°30.209'
I480	Cuyahoga, OH	41°25.244'	81°49.133'
I490	Cuyahoga, OH	41°28.447'	81°41.598'
I670	Franklin, OH	39°58.328'	82°59.033'
US22	Hamilton, OH	39°12.056'	84°22.472'
US22	Hamilton, OH	39° 8.591'	84°28.256'
US22	Hamilton, OH	39° 6.742'	84°30.035'
US27	Hamilton, OH	39° 5.833'	84°31.009'
US30	Richland, OH	40°46.940'	82°24.761'
US33	Franklin, OH	39°58.007'	82°59.027'
US35	Fayette, OH	39°37.157'	83°36.469'
US36	Delaware, OH	40°15.925'	82°55.649'
US40	Franklin, OH	39°57.853'	82°58.995'
US42	Jefferson, KY	38°17.740'	85°37.663'
US42	Cuyahoga, OH	41°27.399'	81°42.062'
US42	Cuyahoga, OH	41°21.273'	81°49.148'
US50	Hamilton, OH	39° 5.975'	84°30.271'
US50	Hamilton, OH	39° 5.829'	84°31.153'
US62	Franklin, OH	39°49.495'	83° 8.470'
US68	Clinton, OH	39°31.133'	83°50.761'
US127	Gallatin, KY	38°44.462'	84°50.000'
US127	Hamilton, OH	39° 5.829'	84°31.103'
US250	Ashland, OH	40°51.348'	82°15.549'
US421	Henry, KY	38°31.195'	85°14.066'

I72

I172	Pike, IL	39°42.983'	91°11.678'
US36	Macon, IL	39°50.205'	89° 3.150'
US51	Macon, IL	39°54.504'	88°57.316'
US51	Macon, IL	39°50.805'	89° 2.774'
US54	Pike, IL	39°40.697'	90°46.015'
US67	Morgan, IL	39°41.194'	90°13.703'
US67	Morgan, IL	39°40.819'	90°18.703'

I74

I75	Hamilton, OH	39° 9.011'	84°32.437'
I80	Henry, IL	41°26.426'	90°19.789'
I80	Scott, IA	41°35.774'	90°31.499'
I155	Tazewell, IL	40°37.237'	89°29.053'
I275	Hamilton, OH	39°13.206'	84°44.341'
I275	Hamilton, OH	39°12.854'	84°40.853'
I280	Rock Island, IL	41°27.469'	90°29.707'
I465	Marion, IN	39°48.324'	86°16.515'
I465	Marion, IN	39°43.925'	86° 2.685'
I474	Peoria, IL	40°44.547'	89°40.052'
I474	Tazewell, IL	40°37.980'	89°31.094'
US6	Rock Island, IL	41°27.469'	90°29.707'
US6	Scott, IA	41°33.289'	90°31.313'
US24	Peoria, IL	40°41.629'	89°35.191'
US27	Hamilton, OH	39° 9.218'	84°32.522'
US31	Marion, IN	39°41.966'	86° 8.930'
US34	Knox, IL	40°59.030'	90°20.174'
US36	Marion, IN	39°45.886'	86°16.012'
US40	Marion, IN	39°44.902'	86°15.869'
US41	Fountain, IN	40° 7.456'	87°14.575'
US45	Champaign, IL	40° 8.084'	88°14.601'
US45	Champaign, IL	40° 8.023'	88°11.726'
US52	Dearborn, IN	39°16.729'	84°51.709'
US67	Scott, IA	41°31.504'	90°30.815'
US136	McLean, IL	40°18.687'	88°43.623'
US136	Marion, IN	39°48.121'	86°16.197'
US136	Marion, IN	39°48.062'	86°16.515'
US150	Champaign, IL	40° 8.093'	88°15.477'
US150	Knox, IL	40°54.683'	90°14.890'
US150	McLean, IL	40°32.387'	89° 3.783'
US150	Tazewell, IL	40°40.211'	89°34.430'
US150	Vermilion, IL	40° 7.406'	87°42.703'
US150	Vermilion, IL	40° 6.294'	87°38.148'
US231	Montgomery, IN	40° 4.770'	86°54.236'
US421	Decatur, IN	39°21.736'	85°28.769'

I75

I80	Wood, OH	41°34.148'	83°34.877'
I85	Fulton, GA	33°47.737'	84°23.620'
I85	Fulton, GA	33°41.282'	84°24.011'
I94	Wayne, MI	42°22.101'	83° 3.479'
I96	Wayne, MI	42°19.240'	83° 4.958'
I275	Manatee, FL	27°35.139'	82°30.843'
I275	Monroe, MI	41°59.553'	83°19.610'
I275	Hamilton, OH	39°17.423'	84°26.509'
I280	Lucas, OH	41°41.424'	83°30.829'
I285	Clayton, GA	33°37.934'	84°24.072'
I285	Cobb, GA	33°53.362'	84°27.617'
I375	Wayne, MI	42°20.592'	83° 2.629'
I475	Bibb, GA	32°45.230'	83°42.719'
I475	Monroe, GA	32°57.490'	83°48.832'
I475	Genesee, MI	43° 5.774'	83°45.785'
I475	Genesee, MI	42°55.265'	83°40.843'
I475	Lucas, OH	41°40.657'	83°34.435'
I475	Wood, OH	41°31.732'	83°37.261'
I575	Cobb, GA	34° 0.050'	84°33.701'
I595	Broward, FL	26° 7.171'	80°20.794'

I640	Knox, TN	36° 0.008'	83°57.516'
I675	Henry, GA	33°32.446'	84°16.061'
I675	Saginaw, MI	43°29.857'	83°55.781'
I675	Saginaw, MI	43°26.018'	83°53.458'
I675	Montgomery, OH	39°36.861'	84°13.964'
I696	Oakland, MI	42°28.588'	83° 6.713'
US2	Mackinac, MI	45°51.449'	84°43.695'
US6	Wood, OH	41°21.062'	83°37.363'
US10	Bay, MI	43°35.760'	83°56.905'
US11	Hamilton, TN	35° 5.183'	85° 4.024'
US11	Hamilton, TN	35° 3.553'	85° 7.886'
US12	Wayne, MI	42°19.869'	83° 5.075'
US17	Charlotte, FL	26°56.395'	82° 1.091'
US19	Clayton, GA	33°35.129'	84°22.697'
US19	Fulton, GA	33°39.166'	84°23.772'
US20	Wood, OH	41°33.004'	83°36.216'
US23	Bibb, GA	32°55.131'	83°42.533'
US23	Bibb, GA	32°51.103'	83°38.519'
US23	Arenac, MI	43°56.842'	84° 0.850'
US23	Emmet, MI	45°46.339'	84°44.074'
US23	Genesee, MI	42°57.146'	83°43.399'
US24	Oakland, MI	42°44.432'	83°27.133'
US24	Lucas, OH	41°41.231'	83°33.338'
US24	Lucas, OH	41°40.036'	83°34.120'
US25	Madison, KY	37°52.573'	84°20.000'
US25	Madison, KY	37°46.412'	84°18.937'
US25	Rockcastle, KY	37°22.691'	84°19.841'
US25	Rockcastle, KY	37°20.516'	84°18.491'
US25E	Laurel, KY	36°58.623'	84° 6.659'
US25W	Whitley, KY	36°55.100'	84° 7.770'
US25W	Whitley, KY	36°47.569'	84°10.213'
US25W	Anderson, TN	36°13.999'	84° 9.640'
US25W	Campbell, TN	36°34.660'	84° 6.760'
US25W	Campbell, TN	36°17.853'	84°12.953'
US27	Broward, FL	26° 8.733'	80°26.544'
US27	Marion, FL	29°12.376'	82°11.081'
US27	Crawford, MI	44°35.401'	84°42.479'
US27	Hamilton, OH	39° 8.431'	84°32.091'
US27	Hamilton, OH	39° 8.289'	84°32.050'
US29	Fulton, GA	33°46.268'	84°23.418'
US31	Cheboygan, MI	45°43.976'	84°43.708'
US33	Auglaize, OH	40°33.282'	84°10.198'
US35	Montgomery, OH	39°45.464'	84°12.163'
US35	Montgomery, OH	39°44.864'	84°12.335'
US36	Miami, OH	40° 9.057'	84°13.222'
US40	Montgomery, OH	39°53.500'	84°11.276'
US41	Columbia, FL	29°59.978'	82°35.841'
US41	Bibb, GA	32°47.301'	83°40.097'
US41	Catoosa, GA	34°53.518'	85° 4.464'
US41	Dooly, GA	32°14.833'	83°44.597'
US41	Fulton, GA	33°51.758'	84°26.263'
US41	Fulton, GA	33°48.130'	84°24.473'
US41	Gordon, GA	34°33.417'	84°56.177'
US41	Houston, GA	32°26.778'	83°45.298'
US41	Lowndes, GA	30°59.519'	83°23.309'
US41	Lowndes, GA	30°53.694'	83°21.327'
US41	Tift, GA	31°28.700'	83°31.172'
US41	Whitfield, GA	34°47.600'	85° 0.070'
US41	Hamilton, TN	34°59.393'	85°12.232'
US50	Hamilton, OH	39° 5.977'	84°31.303'
US50	Hamilton, OH	39° 5.912'	84°31.269'
US60	Fayette, KY	38° 2.456'	84°25.189'
US62	Scott, KY	38°13.506'	84°32.305'
US68	Hancock, OH	41° 1.687'	83°40.384'
US80	Bibb, GA	32°48.858'	83°39.379'
US82	Tift, GA	31°27.009'	83°31.842'
US84	Lowndes, GA	30°49.085'	83°19.018'
US90	Columbia, FL	30°10.772'	82°41.327'

US92	Hillsborough, FL	27°59.814'	82°19.609'
US98	Hernando, FL	28°31.382'	82°14.230'
US127	Hamilton, OH	39° 9.267'	84°32.284'
US127	Hamilton, OH	39° 5.783'	84°31.273'
US129	Hamilton, FL	30°26.886'	82°55.987'
US224	Hancock, OH	41° 3.560'	83°40.099'
US280	Crisp, GA	31°57.586'	83°45.113'
US301	Hillsborough, FL	28° 2.231'	82°20.958'
US301	Hillsborough, FL	27°54.179'	82°20.634'
US301	Manatee, FL	27°31.745'	82°30.479'
US321	Loudon, TN	35°49.678'	84°16.699'
US341	Houston, GA	32°28.296'	83°44.652'
US411	Bartow, GA	34°14.713'	84°46.406'
US421	Fayette, KY	37°57.748'	84°23.325'
US441	Alachua, FL	29°48.077'	82°30.853'
US441	Anderson, TN	36°13.628'	84° 9.104'
US460	Scott, KY	38°12.965'	84°32.072'

I76

I77	Summit, OH	41° 3.714'	81°30.289'
I77	Summit, OH	41° 3.594'	81°33.983'
I79	Allegheny, PA	40°39.647'	80° 5.462'
I80	Deuel, NE	41° 1.582'	102° 9.264'
I80	Mahoning, OH	41° 6.558'	80°50.284'
I83	York, PA	40°12.698'	76°52.762'
I95	Philadelphia, PA	39°54.509'	75° 8.995'
I176	Berks, PA	40° 9.682'	75°53.923'
I270	Adams, CO	39°49.421'	104°57.822'
I276	Montgomery, PA	40° 5.444'	75°24.738'
I277	Summit, OH	41° 2.124'	81°33.948'
I283	Dauphin, PA	40°12.877'	76°47.218'
I295	Camden, NJ	39°52.481'	75° 6.151'
I295	Camden, NJ	39°52.038'	75° 6.129'
I376	Allegheny, PA	40°26.047'	79°44.928'
I476	Montgomery, PA	40° 3.888'	75°19.322'
I676	Camden, NJ	39°54.113'	75° 6.766'
I676	Philadelphia, PA	39°57.571'	75°10.942'
I680	Mahoning, OH	40°57.494'	80°38.583'
US1	Philadelphia, PA	40° 0.262'	75°11.699'
US6	Adams, CO	39°50.806'	104°55.368'
US6	Logan, CO	40°37.285'	103°10.332'
US6	Morgan, CO	40°16.293'	103°35.010'
US11	Cumberland, PA	40°13.679'	77° 9.026'
US15	Cumberland, PA	40°11.725'	76°58.534'
US19	Allegheny, PA	40°39.743'	80° 5.673'
US22	Allegheny, PA	40°26.321'	79°45.090'
US30	Philadelphia, PA	39°58.508'	75°11.681'
US30	Westmoreland, PA	40°18.932'	79°40.721'
US34	Morgan, CO	40°15.231'	103°52.854'
US34	Morgan, CO	40°14.800'	104° 3.324'
US62	Mahoning, OH	41° 2.551'	80°45.687'
US85	Adams, CO	39°52.841'	104°53.214'
US202	Montgomery, PA	40° 5.002'	75°23.698'
US222	Lancaster, PA	40°12.985'	76° 5.457'
US224	Mahoning, OH	41° 1.469'	80°43.391'
US224	Medina, OH	41° 1.828'	81°53.434'
US287	Adams, CO	39°47.977'	105° 1.470'
US385	Sedgwick, CO	40°58.070'	102°14.796'

I77

I79	Kanawha, WV	38°22.509'	81°36.406'
I80	Summit, OH	41°16.513'	81°38.203'
I81	Wythe, VA	36°57.648'	81° 3.891'
I81	Wythe, VA	36°56.749'	80°55.197'
I85	Mecklenburg, NC	35°16.374'	80°50.702'
I90	Cuyahoga, OH	41°29.751'	81°40.685'
I271	Summit, OH	41°13.714'	81°37.665'

I77 (cont)

I277	Mecklenburg, NC	35°14.638'	80°50.912'
I277	Summit, OH	41° 1.512'	81°30.116'
I480	Cuyahoga, OH	41°24.422'	81°38.833'
I490	Cuyahoga, OH	41°28.783'	81°39.702'
US1	Richland, SC	34° 4.922'	80°56.468'
US11	Wythe, VA	36°56.821'	81° 3.103'
US19	Mercer, WV	37°29.677'	81° 6.155'
US21	Iredell, NC	35°50.935'	80°51.566'
US21	Iredell, NC	35°40.438'	80°51.405'
US21	Iredell, NC	35°33.185'	80°51.485'
US21	Mecklenburg, NC	35°28.462'	80°52.512'
US21	Mecklenburg, NC	35°18.452'	80°50.917'
US21	Surry, NC	36°15.773'	80°49.489'
US21	Yadkin, NC	36°11.851'	80°48.699'
US21	Lexington, SC	33°55.643'	81° 4.622'
US21	Richland, SC	34°10.258'	80°58.304'
US21	York, SC	35° 5.525'	80°56.025'
US21	York, SC	34°58.412'	80°59.219'
US21	York, SC	34°54.796'	80°58.968'
US22	Guernsey, OH	40° 2.893'	81°33.769'
US29	Mecklenburg, NC	35°13.738'	80°51.665'
US30	Stark, OH	40°47.102'	81°23.094'
US33	Jackson, WV	38°49.202'	81°43.667'
US36	Tuscarawas, OH	40°17.478'	81°33.421'
US40	Guernsey, OH	40° 1.657'	81°33.697'
US50	Wood, WV	39°16.048'	81°29.967'
US52	Bland, VA	37°15.919'	81° 7.310'
US52	Bland, VA	37°14.359'	81° 6.414'
US52	Bland, VA	37° 6.062'	81° 7.749'
US52	Wythe, VA	36°55.955'	80°56.678'
US52	Mercer, WV	37°17.046'	81° 7.557'
US58	Carroll, VA	36°44.734'	80°46.363'
US60	Kanawha, WV	38°18.995'	81°33.723'
US60	Kanawha, WV	38°18.649'	81°33.467'
US62	Stark, OH	40°49.564'	81°23.828'
US70	Iredell, NC	35°46.487'	80°51.830'
US76	Richland, SC	33°58.413'	80°57.302'
US224	Summit, OH	41° 1.512'	81°30.116'
US250	Tuscarawas, OH	40°35.059'	81°31.352'
US250	Tuscarawas, OH	40°29.488'	81°28.687'
US421	Yadkin, NC	36° 7.300'	80°48.845'
US460	Mercer, WV	37°21.772'	81° 2.926'
US521	Mecklenburg, NC	35°10.813'	80°53.236'

I78

I81	Lebanon, PA	40°25.523'	76°31.294'
I95	Essex, NJ	40°42.386'	74° 9.125'
I287	Somerset, NJ	40°38.539'	74°38.743'
US1	Essex, NJ	40°42.566'	74° 9.669'
US22	Hunterdon, NJ	40°38.368'	74°52.762'
US22	Warren, NJ	40°40.235'	75° 8.108'
US22	Lebanon, PA	40°27.365'	76°22.774'
US22	Lehigh, PA	40°35.371'	75°35.408'
US202	Somerset, NJ	40°38.555'	74°38.299'
US222	Lehigh, PA	40°34.334'	75°32.402'

I79

I80	Mercer, PA	41°11.875'	80° 9.602'
I90	Erie, PA	42° 1.898'	80° 7.367'
I279	Allegheny, PA	40°35.186'	80° 6.008'
I279	Allegheny, PA	40°25.398'	80° 6.379'
US6	Crawford, PA	41°37.355'	80°10.939'
US6N	Erie, PA	41°52.775'	80°10.613'
US19	Allegheny, PA	40°39.512'	80° 5.494'
US19	Washington, PA	40° 6.481'	80°12.170'
US19	Braxton, WV	38°39.410'	80°44.406'

US19	Braxton, WV	38°37.084'	80°45.379'
US19	Lewis, WV	38°57.817'	80°30.931'
US19	Monongalia, WV	39°37.621'	79°59.309'
US20	Erie, PA	42° 5.647'	80° 7.322'
US20	Erie, PA	42° 5.594'	80° 7.283'
US22	Allegheny, PA	40°25.398'	80° 6.379'
US33	Lewis, WV	39° 1.299'	80°25.667'
US40	Washington, PA	40° 8.907'	80°12.404'
US50	Harrison, WV	39°16.711'	80°17.051'
US62	Mercer, PA	41°15.890'	80°10.001'
US119	Kanawha, WV	38°23.608'	81°35.392'
US250	Marion, WV	39°25.916'	80°11.300'
US422	Butler, PA	40°57.758'	80° 8.094'

I80

I81	Luzerne, PA	41° 2.788'	76° 0.809'
I84	Summit, UT	40°58.226'	111°26.280'
I88	Rock Island, IL	41°32.147'	90°20.471'
I90	Lake, IN	41°35.395'	87°13.447'
I90	Lorain, OH	41°23.344'	82° 9.823'
I94	Cook, IL	41°34.676'	87°34.914'
I95	Bergen, NJ	40°51.906'	74° 0.548'
I95	Bergen, NJ	40°51.500'	73°58.606'
I180	Bureau, IL	41°24.016'	89°22.973'
I180	Northumberland, PA	41° 2.961'	76°50.426'
I180	Laramie, WY	41° 7.132'	104°48.252'
I215	Salt Lake, UT	40°45.924'	111°57.012'
I215	Salt Lake, UT	40°42.840'	111°48.372'
I215	Salt Lake, UT	40°42.674'	111°47.436'
I271	Summit, OH	41°15.173'	81°35.168'
I280	Scott, IA	41°36.167'	90°40.625'
I280	Morris, NJ	40°51.528'	74°22.034'
I280	Wood, OH	41°31.550'	83°27.812'
I287	Morris, NJ	40°51.859'	74°25.071'
I294	Cook, IL	41°34.858'	87°40.710'
I305	Yolo, CA	38°34.527'	121°34.128'
I380	Johnson, IA	41°41.666'	91°38.291'
I380	Monroe, PA	41° 4.206'	75°23.689'
I475	Lucas, OH	41°35.510'	83°41.500'
I480	Douglas, NE	41°13.578'	95°57.128'
I480	Lorain, OH	41°22.718'	81°59.344'
I480	Portage, OH	41°15.350'	81°22.296'
I505	Solano, CA	38°22.411'	121°57.126'
I580	Alameda, CA	37°53.141'	122°18.468'
I580	Alameda, CA	37°49.542'	122°18.264'
I680	Solano, CA	38°13.001'	122° 8.208'
I680	Pottawattamie, IA	41°29.818'	95°35.107'
I680	Douglas, NE	41°13.480'	96° 5.211'
I680	Mahoning, OH	41° 7.495'	80°44.912'
I780	Solano, CA	38° 5.503'	122°13.758'
I880	Alameda, CA	37°49.801'	122°17.544'
US6	Cook, IL	41°34.675'	87°33.517'
US6	Henry, IL	41°27.296'	90°20.190'
US6	Will, IL	41°30.669'	88° 7.453'
US6	Lake, IN	41°34.990'	87°14.406'
US6	Cass, IA	41°29.831'	94°56.722'
US6	Cedar, IA	41°38.163'	91° 2.124'
US6	Dallas, IA	41°30.823'	94°11.748'
US6	Jasper, IA	41°41.002'	93° 4.614'
US6	Polk, IA	41°39.716'	93°29.683'
US6	Pottawattamie, IA	41°16.798'	95°47.040'
US6	Lancaster, NE	40°53.735'	96°34.006'
US6	Lancaster, NE	40°49.767'	96°42.712'
US11	Columbia, PA	41° 1.973'	76°20.110'
US15	Union, PA	41° 3.122'	76°52.322'
US19	Mercer, PA	41°11.560'	80°14.476'
US20	Lorain, OH	41°22.833'	82° 3.982'
US24	Lucas, OH	41°35.065'	83°37.098'

US26	Keith, NE	41° 6.906'	101°42.876'
US30	Will, IL	41°31.208'	87°59.512'
US30	Albany, WY	41°17.464'	105°31.680'
US30	Carbon, WY	41°47.336'	107°11.994'
US30	Carbon, WY	41°47.004'	107°15.930'
US30	Carbon, WY	41°44.480'	106°49.788'
US30	Laramie, WY	41°10.544'	104° 4.512'
US30	Laramie, WY	41° 9.429'	104°39.306'
US30	Laramie, WY	41° 6.895'	104°51.582'
US30	Sweetwater, WY	41°35.708'	109°11.856'
US30	Sweetwater, WY	41°34.752'	109°15.348'
US30	Sweetwater, WY	41°32.668'	109°54.402'
US30	Sweetwater, WY	41°32.484'	109°28.632'
US30	Sweetwater, WY	41°31.429'	109°26.694'
US31	St. Joseph, IN	41°43.823'	86°20.357'
US33	St. Joseph, IN	41°43.339'	86°15.005'
US34	Hall, NE	40°49.197'	98°22.698'
US34	Lancaster, NE	40°51.745'	96°42.947'
US34	Lancaster, NE	40°48.998'	96°42.409'
US40	Summit, UT	40°43.891'	111°29.826'
US41	Lake, IN	41°34.466'	87°28.759'
US41	Lake, IN	41°34.436'	87°30.519'
US42	Cuyahoga, OH	41°20.471'	81°49.678'
US45	Will, IL	41°33.182'	87°51.173'
US46	Morris, NJ	40°53.783'	74°29.276'
US46	Morris, NJ	40°53.626'	74°42.900'
US46	Morris, NJ	40°53.431'	74°40.811'
US46	Morris, NJ	40°51.620'	74°21.865'
US46	Warren, NJ	40°55.738'	75° 5.719'
US52	Will, IL	41°30.661'	88° 5.004'
US59	Pottawattamie, IA	41°29.869'	95°20.193'
US61	Scott, IA	41°35.777'	90°34.189'
US62	Trumbull, OH	41°10.571'	80°34.137'
US63	Poweshiek, IA	41°41.792'	92°33.098'
US67	Scott, IA	41°35.048'	90°22.024'
US75	Douglas, NE	41°13.785'	95°55.958'
US77	Lancaster, NE	40°53.809'	96°38.591'
US77	Lancaster, NE	40°49.081'	96°45.362'
US81	York, NE	40°49.268'	97°35.837'
US83	Lincoln, NE	41° 6.671'	100°45.810'
US85	Laramie, WY	41° 7.132'	104°48.252'
US89	Salt Lake, UT	40°43.087'	111°53.238'
US93	Elko, NV	41° 6.106'	114°57.336'
US95	Churchill, NV	39°56.516'	118°44.898'
US95	Humboldt, NV	40°57.271'	117°45.042'
US131	Elkhart, IN	41°44.837'	85°40.799'
US138	Deuel, NE	41° 1.837'	102°10.824'
US151	Iowa, IA	41°41.199'	91°54.648'
US169	Dallas, IA	41°32.413'	94° 0.736'
US183	Buffalo, NE	40°41.389'	99°22.782'
US189	Uinta, WY	41°18.490'	110°43.836'
US189	Uinta, WY	41°16.087'	110°56.268'
US189	Uinta, WY	41°15.662'	110°59.094'
US191	Sweetwater, WY	41°36.473'	109°13.734'
US191	Sweetwater, WY	41°33.474'	109°18.540'
US202	Morris, NJ	40°51.986'	74°26.402'
US202	Passaic, NJ	40°53.843'	74°14.999'
US206	Morris, NJ	40°54.367'	74°43.524'
US206	Morris, NJ	40°53.424'	74°41.905'
US209	Monroe, PA	40°59.888'	75° 9.314'
US209	Monroe, PA	40°59.115'	75°13.346'
US218	Johnson, IA	41°41.666'	91°38.291'
US219	Clearfield, PA	41° 8.826'	78°47.427'
US219	Clearfield, PA	41° 8.717'	78°47.230'
US220	Centre, PA	40°57.386'	77°46.232'
US220	Clinton, PA	41° 3.268'	77°26.221'
US250	Erie, OH	41°19.409'	82°36.992'
US275	Douglas, NE	41°12.711'	96° 5.475'

US283	Dawson, NE	40°44.507'	99°44.429'
US287	Albany, WY	41°17.864'	105°35.646'
US322	Clarion, PA	41°10.991'	79°14.639'
US395	Washoe, NV	39°32.244'	119°47.238'
US421	La Porte, IN	41°35.417'	86°53.840'
US422	Trumbull, OH	41° 8.891'	80°41.965'

I81

I83	Dauphin, PA	40°18.497'	76°50.126'
I84	Lackawanna, PA	41°25.488'	75°36.621'
I88	Broome, NY	42° 8.437'	75°54.100'
I90	Onondaga, NY	43° 5.588'	76° 9.863'
I181	Sullivan, TN	36°27.239'	82°31.388'
I381	Bristol, VA	36°37.571'	82°10.782'
I481	Onondaga, NY	43° 8.495'	76° 6.806'
I481	Onondaga, NY	43° 0.388'	76° 8.069'
I581	Roanoke, VA	37°20.489'	79°59.897'
I690	Onondaga, NY	43° 3.065'	76° 8.614'
I690	Onondaga, NY	43° 3.051'	76° 8.692'
US6	Lackawanna, PA	41°27.416'	75°39.668'
US11	Washington, MD	39°36.329'	77°48.203'
US11	Broome, NY	42°20.302'	75°58.745'
US11	Broome, NY	42°14.006'	75°54.910'
US11	Broome, NY	42° 9.884'	75°53.785'
US11	Broome, NY	42° 9.184'	75°53.882'
US11	Broome, NY	42° 7.442'	75°54.366'
US11	Broome, NY	42° 6.910'	75°54.532'
US11	Broome, NY	42° 6.157'	75°49.600'
US11	Jefferson, NY	43°40.779'	76° 4.418'
US11	Onondaga, NY	43° 6.676'	76° 8.789'
US11	Onondaga, NY	43° 3.108'	76° 8.890'
US11	Onondaga, NY	42°57.548'	76° 8.273'
US11	Cumberland, PA	40°18.997'	76°55.271'
US11	Cumberland, PA	40°14.055'	77° 7.676'
US11	Franklin, PA	39°45.391'	77°43.622'
US11	Botetourt, VA	37°32.735'	79°40.103'
US11	Botetourt, VA	37°30.028'	79°44.921'
US11	Frederick, VA	39°13.012'	78° 8.261'
US11	Montgomery, VA	37° 8.240'	80°21.395'
US11	Pulaski, VA	36°59.620'	80°47.571'
US11	Rockbridge, VA	37°40.115'	79°30.411'
US11	Rockbridge, VA	37°37.642'	79°34.520'
US11	Rockingham, VA	38°33.687'	78°44.730'
US11	Shenandoah, VA	39° 0.458'	78°20.073'
US11	Smyth, VA	36°48.461'	81°37.086'
US11	Washington, VA	36°46.982'	81°44.103'
US11	Washington, VA	36°42.833'	81°56.044'
US11	Bristol, VA	36°37.538'	82° 9.389'
US11	Berkeley, WV	39°34.769'	77°52.631'
US11E	Greene, TN	36°13.460'	83° 2.420'
US11W	Sullivan, TN	36°35.325'	82°15.496'
US20	Onondaga, NY	42°53.558'	76° 6.638'
US22	Dauphin, PA	40°18.133'	76°52.871'
US25E	Hamblen, TN	36° 8.188'	83°16.816'
US30	Franklin, PA	39°55.742'	77°38.186'
US33	Harrisonburg, VA	38°26.254'	78°51.066'
US40	Washington, MD	39°39.182'	77°44.992'
US52	Wythe, VA	36°57.605'	81° 5.929'
US60	Rockbridge, VA	37°45.412'	79°24.607'
US209	Schuylkill, PA	40°37.204'	76°26.283'
US211	Shenandoah, VA	38°38.881'	78°40.590'
US220	Botetourt, VA	37°23.270'	79°54.254'
US421	Bristol, VA	36°36.148'	82°13.682'

I82

I84	Umatilla, OR	45°47.521'	119°22.326'
I90	Kittitas, WA	46°58.236'	120°30.582'

I82 (cont)

I182	Benton, WA	46°14.945'	119°22.116'
US12	Yakima, WA	46°37.541'	120°30.342'
US97	Yakima, WA	46°32.261'	120°28.194'
US395	Umatilla, OR	45°55.094'	119°19.314'
US395	Benton, WA	46° 9.983'	119°11.952'

I83

I283	Dauphin, PA	40°15.188'	76°48.860'
I695	Baltimore, MD	39°25.201'	76°38.517'
I695	Baltimore, MD	39°24.684'	76°39.845'
US1	Baltimore city, MD	39°18.655'	76°37.418'
US22	Dauphin, PA	40°17.780'	76°49.554'
US30	York, PA	39°59.038'	76°43.805'
US40	Baltimore city, MD	39°17.681'	76°36.669'
US322	Dauphin, PA	40°15.168'	76°48.724'

I84

I86	Cassia, ID	42°34.241'	113°31.032'
I87	Orange, NY	41°30.887'	74° 4.445'
I90	Worcester, MA	42° 7.801'	72° 3.577'
I91	Hartford, CT	41°46.156'	72°40.097'
I184	Ada, ID	43°35.819'	116°17.724'
I205	Multnomah, OR	45°32.991'	122°33.642'
I205	Multnomah, OR	45°31.982'	122°33.798'
I380	Lackawanna, PA	41°22.376'	75°34.464'
I384	Hartford, CT	41°46.424'	72°35.138'
I684	Putnam, NY	41°23.435'	73°35.906'
I691	New Haven, CT	41°33.527'	72°55.085'
I691	New Haven, CT	41°32.580'	72°56.685'
US5	Hartford, CT	41°45.855'	72°38.774'
US5	Hartford, CT	41°45.818'	72°38.002'
US6	Fairfield, CT	41°25.028'	73°17.528'
US6	Hartford, CT	41°43.088'	72°47.807'
US6	New Haven, CT	41°28.603'	73°12.722'
US6	Orange, NY	41°24.911'	74°25.441'
US6	Putnam, NY	41°23.885'	73°36.076'
US6	Pike, PA	41°21.478'	74°42.803'
US6	Pike, PA	41°20.278'	74°50.293'
US7	Fairfield, CT	41°25.087'	73°25.326'
US7	Fairfield, CT	41°23.167'	73°28.670'
US9	Dutchess, NY	41°31.442'	73°53.434'
US9W	Orange, NY	41°31.163'	74° 1.219'
US20	Ada, ID	43°33.976'	116°11.742'
US20	Canyon, ID	43°41.402'	116°41.520'
US20	Canyon, ID	43°39.749'	116°39.546'
US20	Elmore, ID	43° 8.364'	115°39.774'
US20	Worcester, MA	42° 6.825'	72° 4.811'
US26	Gooding, ID	42°55.419'	114°55.944'
US30	Canyon, ID	43°40.222'	116°40.596'
US30	Gooding, ID	42°56.288'	115° 0.048'
US30	Minidoka, ID	42°34.135'	113°44.148'
US30	Payette, ID	43°54.413'	116°48.876'
US30	Baker, OR	44°44.833'	117°48.222'
US30	Hood River, OR	45°42.676'	121°32.940'
US30	Hood River, OR	45°42.610'	121°30.042'
US30	Hood River, OR	45°40.444'	121°52.296'
US30	Hood River, OR	45°39.591'	121°53.820'
US30	Malheur, OR	44° 1.480'	116°56.874'
US30	Umatilla, OR	45°40.553'	118°50.640'
US30	Umatilla, OR	45°39.539'	118°43.776'
US30	Union, OR	45°20.683'	118° 7.266'
US30	Union, OR	45°17.677'	118° 2.214'
US30	Union, OR	45° 1.542'	117°55.506'
US44	Hartford, CT	41°46.170'	72°40.387'
US89	Weber, UT	41° 8.238'	111°54.786'
US93	Jerome, ID	42°38.528'	114°26.694'

US95	Payette, ID	43°58.283'	116°54.786'
US97	Sherman, OR	45°40.285'	120°49.986'
US197	Wasco, OR	45°36.163'	121° 8.238'
US395	Umatilla, OR	45°45.778'	119°12.168'
US395	Umatilla, OR	45°39.793'	118°48.324'
US730	Morrow, OR	45°50.035'	119°37.344'

I85

I95	Petersburg, VA	37°13.136'	77°23.419'
I185	Muscogee, GA	32°24.308'	84°55.477'
I185	Troup, GA	33° 3.758'	84°56.522'
I185	Greenville, SC	34°47.386'	82°26.361'
I285	De Kalb, GA	33°53.499'	84°15.571'
I285	Fulton, GA	33°37.190'	84°27.721'
I285	Fulton, GA	33°37.078'	84°29.236'
I385	Greenville, SC	34°49.934'	82°17.836'
I985	Gwinnett, GA	34° 2.726'	84° 1.832'
US1	Vance, NC	36°23.561'	78°20.248'
US1	Warren, NC	36°32.074'	78°11.470'
US1	Brunswick, VA	36°51.050'	77°53.680'
US1	Dinwiddie, VA	37°11.941'	77°27.800'
US1	Mecklenburg, VA	36°45.028'	78° 5.686'
US15	Durham, NC	36° 1.469'	78°56.833'
US15	Granville, NC	36°16.254'	78°36.475'
US15	Granville, NC	36° 4.799'	78°46.008'
US19	Fulton, GA	33°47.924'	84°23.512'
US19	Fulton, GA	33°41.037'	84°24.490'
US25	Greenville, SC	34°47.473'	82°25.046'
US27	Muscogee, GA	32°24.308'	84°55.477'
US27	Troup, GA	33° 0.007'	85° 0.762'
US29	Chambers, AL	32°50.875'	85°11.140'
US29	Lee, AL	32°40.373'	85°19.896'
US29	Lee, AL	32°33.519'	85°30.381'
US29	Coweta, GA	33°14.483'	84°48.402'
US29	Cabarrus, NC	35°26.757'	80°36.563'
US29	Davidson, NC	35°46.252'	80°19.643'
US29	Davidson, NC	35°43.421'	80°23.248'
US29	Gaston, NC	35°15.009'	81°17.900'
US29	Mecklenburg, NC	35°17.084'	80°45.772'
US29	Anderson, SC	34°41.705'	82°30.223'
US29	Cherokee, SC	35° 9.824'	81°27.136'
US29	Spartanburg, SC	34°56.350'	82° 4.450'
US52	Rowan, NC	35°39.445'	80°27.575'
US58	Mecklenburg, VA	36°42.798'	78° 6.806'
US64	Davidson, NC	35°48.568'	80°10.950'
US70	Durham, NC	36° 1.971'	78°57.904'
US70	Durham, NC	36° 0.801'	78°52.298'
US70	Orange, NC	36° 2.320'	79° 0.773'
US76	Anderson, SC	34°34.396'	82°42.711'
US80	Montgomery, AL	32°22.087'	86° 8.002'
US80	Montgomery, AL	32°21.761'	86°12.827'
US129	Jackson, GA	34° 9.143'	83°38.734'
US158	Granville, NC	36°18.877'	78°32.648'
US158	Vance, NC	36°20.407'	78°24.662'
US178	Anderson, SC	34°34.761'	82°41.518'
US220	Guilford, NC	36° 1.097'	79°49.568'
US221	Spartanburg, SC	35° 0.984'	81°53.956'
US276	Greenville, SC	34°48.837'	82°20.215'
US280	Lee, AL	32°38.615'	85°21.145'
US311	Randolph, NC	35°54.225'	79°57.246'
US321	Gaston, NC	35°17.009'	81°11.290'
US441	Banks, GA	34°15.279'	83°27.781'
US460	Dinwiddie, VA	37°11.189'	77°29.465'
US501	Durham, NC	36° 1.202'	78°54.356'
US521	Mecklenburg, NC	35°14.300'	80°55.192'

I86

US30	Power, ID	42°54.747'	112°31.692'
US91	Bannock, ID	42°54.757'	112°27.912'

I87

I90	Albany, NY	42°42.020'	73°50.794'
I90	Albany, NY	42°41.707'	73°50.350'
I95	Bronx, NY	40°50.700'	73°55.645'
I278	Bronx, NY	40°48.182'	73°54.989'
I287	Rockland, NY	41° 7.387'	74° 9.894'
I287	Westchester, NY	41° 3.385'	73°50.144'
I587	Ulster, NY	41°56.732'	74° 1.839'
I787	Albany, NY	42°37.984'	73°46.934'
US9	Essex, NY	44° 4.576'	73°39.806'
US9	Saratoga, NY	43°14.139'	73°41.563'
US9	Saratoga, NY	43° 1.286'	73°47.525'
US9	Westchester, NY	41° 3.763'	73°51.754'
US9W	Albany, NY	42°37.217'	73°46.865'
US9W	Rockland, NY	41° 5.473'	73°55.775'
US11	Clinton, NY	44°58.862'	73°27.464'
US20	Albany, NY	42°41.045'	73°50.756'
US202	Rockland, NY	41° 7.169'	74° 8.923'

I88

I90	Schenectady, NY	42°47.463'	74° 1.003'
I294	Cook, IL	41°52.178'	87°55.028'
I355	DuPage, IL	41°48.612'	88° 3.205'
US20	Schenectady, NY	42°45.652'	74° 7.640'
US20	Schenectady, NY	42°45.616'	74° 7.187'
US30	Whiteside, IL	41°45.493'	89°38.218'

I89

I91	Windsor, VT	43°38.393'	72°20.329'
I93	Merrimack, NH	43°10.223'	71°31.839'
I189	Chittenden, VT	44°27.140'	73°10.956'
US2	Chittenden, VT	44°35.416'	73°10.232'
US2	Chittenden, VT	44°30.327'	73°10.884'
US2	Chittenden, VT	44°28.195'	73°11.081'
US2	Chittenden, VT	44°25.436'	73° 0.637'
US2	Washington, VT	44°21.667'	72°48.243'
US2	Washington, VT	44°15.968'	72°37.359'
US2	Washington, VT	44°15.451'	72°36.076'
US4	Grafton, NH	43°38.266'	72°16.890'
US4	Grafton, NH	43°38.106'	72°12.726'
US4	Windsor, VT	43°40.016'	72°23.167'
US4	Windsor, VT	43°39.966'	72°23.096'
US7	Franklin, VT	44°41.956'	73° 6.379'
US202	Merrimack, NH	43°10.834'	71°41.351'

I90

I91	Hampden, MA	42° 9.186'	72°38.911'
I93	Suffolk, MA	42°20.772'	71° 3.663'
I94	Cook, IL	41°57.665'	87°44.592'
I94	Cook, IL	41°46.508'	87°37.629'
I94	Lake, IN	41°35.395'	87°13.447'
I94	Yellowstone, MT	45°49.643'	108°23.616'
I94	Dane, WI	43° 9.229'	89°18.378'
I94	Dane, WI	43° 7.460'	89°17.422'
I94	Dane, WI	43° 6.234'	89°17.133'
I94	Monroe, WI	43°59.140'	90°26.840'
I95	Middlesex, MA	42°20.416'	71°15.740'
I190	Erie, NY	42°52.502'	78°47.288'
I190	Pennington, SD	44° 6.313'	103°13.914'
I229	Minnehaha, SD	43°36.391'	96°41.416'
I271	Lake, OH	41°35.451'	81°26.892'
I290	Cook, IL	42° 3.467'	88° 1.686'

I290	Cook, IL	41°52.545'	87°38.739'
I290	Erie, NY	42°56.975'	78°45.820'
I291	Hampden, MA	42° 9.712'	72°32.852'
I294	Cook, IL	41°59.425'	87°52.050'
I294	Cook, IL	41°58.984'	87°52.217'
I390	Monroe, NY	43° 2.863'	77°38.903'
I391	Hampden, MA	42° 9.476'	72°36.649'
I395	Worcester, MA	42°11.738'	71°50.768'
I405	King, WA	47°34.840'	122°10.350'
I481	Onondaga, NY	43° 5.683'	76° 3.236'
I490	Genesee, NY	43° 1.727'	77°57.900'
I490	Ontario, NY	43° 0.529'	77°26.373'
I690	Onondaga, NY	43° 6.688'	76°15.899'
I787	Albany, NY	42°40.038'	73°43.995'
I790	Oneida, NY	43° 6.710'	75°12.359'
I890	Albany, NY	42°45.247'	73°56.046'
I890	Schenectady, NY	42°50.433'	74° 0.891'
US2	Spokane, WA	47°38.035'	117°28.752'
US5	Hampden, MA	42° 9.236'	72°37.924'
US6	Cuyahoga, OH	41°30.601'	81°40.318'
US6N	Erie, PA	41°56.584'	80°27.808'
US7	Berkshire, MA	42°17.840'	73°17.682'
US9	Rensselaer, NY	42°33.549'	73°40.822'
US9	Rensselaer, NY	42°29.365'	73°40.694'
US11	Onondaga, NY	43° 5.524'	76° 8.932'
US12	Cook, IL	41°43.376'	87°32.957'
US12	Cook, IL	41°42.790'	87°32.116'
US12	Lake, IN	41°42.080'	87°31.375'
US12	Lake, IN	41°36.466'	87°23.609'
US12	Lake, IN	41°35.851'	87°18.316'
US12	Powell, MT	46°31.501'	112°47.970'
US12	Juneau, WI	43°38.972'	89°48.783'
US12	Monroe, WI	43°58.356'	90°28.367'
US12	Sauk, WI	43°34.180'	89°46.692'
US14	Winona, MN	43°54.662'	91°21.636'
US14	Winona, MN	43°51.464'	91°18.352'
US14	Pennington, SD	43°59.244'	102°12.882'
US14	Rock, WI	42°43.003'	88°59.037'
US14	Campbell, WY	44°17.399'	105°28.008'
US14	Crook, WY	44°24.898'	104°20.562'
US14	Crook, WY	44°23.515'	104°23.904'
US14	Crook, WY	44°16.345'	104°58.038'
US14	Sheridan, WY	44°55.117'	107° 8.880'
US14	Sheridan, WY	44°49.847'	106°57.462'
US14	Sheridan, WY	44°46.408'	106°56.160'
US16	Johnson, WY	44°21.497'	106°39.432'
US18	Dane, WI	43° 2.815'	89°16.644'
US19	Erie, PA	42° 2.966'	80° 4.889'
US20	Lake, IN	41°36.779'	87°28.826'
US20	Berkshire, MA	42°17.872'	73°14.457'
US20	Berkshire, MA	42°17.792'	73°11.160'
US20	Berkshire, MA	42°16.613'	73° 8.533'
US20	Berkshire, MA	42°15.693'	73° 7.660'
US20	Hampden, MA	42° 9.400'	72°48.942'
US20	Suffolk, MA	42°21.463'	71° 9.311'
US20	Worcester, MA	42°12.240'	71°48.859'
US20	Erie, NY	42°45.982'	78°49.091'
US20	Cuyahoga, OH	41°30.128'	81°40.216'
US20	Cuyahoga, OH	41°28.316'	81°50.178'
US20	Erie, PA	42°13.918'	79°46.851'
US41	Lake, IN	41°38.693'	87°30.505'
US51	Dane, WI	43°10.724'	89°19.460'
US51	Dane, WI	42°55.266'	89° 5.156'
US51	Dane, WI	42°52.392'	89° 3.340'
US52	Olmsted, MN	43°57.063'	92°21.460'
US53	La Crosse, WI	43°51.857'	91°14.207'
US59	Nobles, MN	43°38.264'	95°35.614'
US62	Erie, NY	42°45.610'	78°49.476'

I90 (cont)

US63	Olmsted, MN	43°53.111'	92°29.285'
US63	Olmsted, MN	43°53.066'	92°29.282'
US71	Jackson, MN	43°38.393'	94°59.681'
US75	Rock, MN	43°38.367'	96°12.759'
US81	McCook, SD	43°39.971'	97°23.291'
US83	Jones, SD	43°52.984'	100°42.330'
US83	Lyman, SD	43°54.745'	100°18.750'
US85	Lawrence, SD	44°31.184'	103°51.804'
US85	Lawrence, SD	44°28.713'	103°44.418'
US87	Johnson, WY	44°31.157'	106°48.000'
US89	Park, MT	45°42.427'	110°27.282'
US89	Park, MT	45°41.231'	110°30.042'
US89	Park, MT	45°38.649'	110°34.338'
US93	Missoula, MT	46°57.088'	114° 7.824'
US93	Missoula, MT	46°52.830'	113°59.490'
US95	Kootenai, ID	47°41.927'	116°47.448'
US97	Kittitas, WA	47° 0.367'	120°35.298'
US169	Faribault, MN	43°39.596'	94° 5.804'
US183	Lyman, SD	43°53.887'	100° 2.718'
US191	Gallatin, MT	45°41.834'	111° 2.712'
US191	Sweet Grass, MT	45°49.526'	109°58.536'
US195	Spokane, WA	47°38.809'	117°27.030'
US202	Hampden, MA	42° 8.657'	72°43.906'
US212	Big Horn, MT	45°34.722'	107°27.120'
US212	Yellowstone, MT	45°40.992'	108°42.324'
US212	Yellowstone, MT	45°39.769'	108°46.116'
US218	Mower, MN	43°40.844'	92°59.590'
US218	Mower, MN	43°40.430'	92°56.353'
US219	Erie, NY	42°48.905'	78°47.564'
US281	Aurora, SD	43°41.694'	98°26.631'
US287	Broadwater, MT	45°55.100'	111°35.778'
US322	Cuyahoga, OH	41°30.261'	81°40.229'
US395	Adams, WA	47° 6.684'	118°23.160'
US395	Spokane, WA	47°39.179'	117°24.690'
US395	Spokane, WA	47°39.179'	117°24.636'
US422	Cuyahoga, OH	41°29.613'	81°41.036'

I91

I93	Caledonia, VT	44°23.788'	72° 1.094'
I95	New Haven, CT	41°17.969'	72°54.871'
I291	Hampden, MA	42° 6.327'	72°36.046'
I391	Hampden, MA	42° 8.072'	72°36.598'
I391	Hampden, MA	42° 7.814'	72°36.527'
I691	New Haven, CT	41°32.269'	72°45.712'
US1	New Haven, CT	41°17.998'	72°54.871'
US2	Caledonia, VT	44°25.693'	72° 2.084'
US5	Hartford, CT	42° 1.256'	72°35.303'
US5	Hartford, CT	41°57.170'	72°36.088'
US5	Hartford, CT	41°45.074'	72°39.492'
US5	Hartford, CT	41°44.820'	72°39.674'
US5	Hartford, CT	41°44.047'	72°39.846'
US5	Franklin, MA	42°29.020'	72°37.001'
US5	Franklin, MA	42°28.012'	72°37.000'
US5	Hampden, MA	42° 8.167'	72°37.595'
US5	Hampden, MA	42° 4.912'	72°34.768'
US5	Hampden, MA	42° 4.594'	72°34.864'
US5	Hampden, MA	42° 4.537'	72°34.908'
US5	Hampden, MA	42° 4.485'	72°35.023'
US5	Hampshire, MA	42°18.406'	72°37.478'
US5	Caledonia, VT	44°30.980'	72° 0.447'
US5	Caledonia, VT	44°24.281'	72° 1.410'
US5	Orleans, VT	44°57.126'	72° 9.064'
US5	Orleans, VT	44°48.277'	72°12.770'
US5	Windham, VT	42°50.115'	72°34.050'
US5	Windsor, VT	43°38.711'	72°20.296'
US5	Windsor, VT	43°31.633'	72°24.134'

US5	Windsor, VT	43°15.998'	72°25.990'
US20	Hampden, MA	42° 6.206'	72°35.848'
US202	Hampden, MA	42°12.769'	72°38.024'
US202	Hampden, MA	42°11.994'	72°38.352'
US302	Orange, VT	44° 9.595'	72° 5.376'

I93

I95	Middlesex, MA	42°30.131'	71° 7.144'
I95	Norfolk, MA	42°12.444'	71° 8.440'
I293	Hillsborough, NH	42°57.701'	71°24.947'
I293	Merrimack, NH	43° 2.939'	71°28.330'
I393	Merrimack, NH	43°12.524'	71°32.001'
I495	Essex, MA	42°39.844'	71°11.681'
US1	Suffolk, MA	42°22.170'	71° 3.778'
US3	Grafton, NH	44°11.618'	71°40.882'
US3	Grafton, NH	44° 6.625'	71°40.990'
US3	Grafton, NH	44° 3.643'	71°41.225'
US3	Grafton, NH	43°57.527'	71°40.826'
US3	Grafton, NH	43°52.176'	71°40.087'
US3	Merrimack, NH	43°11.593'	71°31.579'
US3	Merrimack, NH	43° 1.385'	71°26.669'
US202	Merrimack, NH	43°12.524'	71°32.001'
US302	Grafton, NH	44°18.496'	71°47.917'
US302	Grafton, NH	44°17.063'	71°44.686'

I94

I96	Wayne, MI	42°20.993'	83° 5.964'
I194	Calhoun, MI	42°16.091'	85°10.723'
I194	Morton, ND	46°49.374'	100°50.610'
I196	Berrien, MI	42° 8.082'	86°22.079'
I275	Wayne, MI	42°13.307'	83°24.755'
I294	Cook, IL	42° 9.037'	87°52.462'
I394	Hennepin, MN	44°58.505'	93°17.212'
I494	Hennepin, MN	45° 5.498'	93°26.861'
I694	Hennepin, MN	45° 4.171'	93°17.137'
I694	Washington, MN	44°56.935'	92°57.515'
I696	Macomb, MI	42°29.711'	82°55.039'
I794	Milwaukee, WI	43° 2.145'	87°54.082'
I894	Milwaukee, WI	43° 1.592'	88° 2.169'
I894	Milwaukee, WI	42°57.685'	87°56.024'
US6	Cook, IL	41°36.061'	87°34.993'
US10	Ramsey, MN	44°57.149'	93° 2.434'
US10	Trempealeau, WI	44°34.756'	91°12.290'
US12	Cook, IL	41°43.301'	87°37.456'
US12	Berrien, MI	41°47.937'	86°42.368'
US12	Washtenaw, MI	42°13.889'	83°35.027'
US12	Washtenaw, MI	42°13.447'	83°39.115'
US12	Wayne, MI	42°19.586'	83° 9.628'
US12	Custer, MT	46°25.573'	105°47.136'
US12	Custer, MT	46°22.414'	105°52.272'
US12	Rosebud, MT	46°15.418'	106°41.586'
US12	Dunn, WI	44°54.434'	91°56.348'
US12	Dunn, WI	44°54.429'	91°55.977'
US12	Dunn, WI	44°53.146'	91°43.748'
US12	Eau Claire, WI	44°50.593'	91°36.244'
US12	Jackson, WI	44°18.569'	90°50.526'
US12	Monroe, WI	44° 4.234'	90°31.295'
US12	Monroe, WI	44° 1.273'	90°30.308'
US12	St. Croix, WI	44°57.813'	92°40.805'
US14	Cook, IL	41°59.421'	87°45.084'
US18	Milwaukee, WI	43° 2.150'	87°54.365'
US18	Waukesha, WI	43° 2.089'	88°10.307'
US20	La Porte, IN	41°41.612'	86°48.640'
US20	Porter, IN	41°36.456'	87° 6.431'
US20	Porter, IN	41°35.615'	87°13.084'
US23	Washtenaw, MI	42°13.522'	83°41.143'
US24	Wayne, MI	42°15.818'	83°16.235'

US31	Berrien, MI	42° 4.103'	86°26.191'
US41	Cook, IL	42° 8.725'	87°47.641'
US41	Cook, IL	42° 5.189'	87°45.500'
US41	Lake, IL	42°28.664'	87°57.005'
US52	Milwaukee, WI	43° 2.036'	87°56.861'
US52	Stutsman, ND	46°53.376'	98°40.560'
US53	Eau Claire, WI	44°46.046'	91°25.313'
US59	Otter Tail, MN	46°12.491'	96° 1.157'
US63	St. Croix, WI	44°56.255'	92°22.471'
US71	Stearns, MN	45°43.228'	94°57.133'
US75	Clay, MN	46°50.834'	96°46.066'
US83	Burleigh, ND	46°50.178'	100°17.274'
US83	Burleigh, ND	46°49.884'	100°46.374'
US85	Stark, ND	46°53.814'	103°11.370'
US127	Jackson, MI	42°16.617'	84°21.526'
US127	Jackson, MI	42°16.316'	84°25.616'
US131	Kalamazoo, MI	42°14.279'	85°38.256'
US151	Dane, WI	43° 8.206'	89°17.770'
US169	Hennepin, MN	45° 4.940'	93°24.090'
US281	Stutsman, ND	46°53.148'	98°43.062'
US421	La Porte, IN	41°39.509'	86°53.646'

I95

I195	Dade, FL	25°48.724'	80°12.394'
I195	York, ME	43°31.637'	70°27.195'
I195	Baltimore, MD	39°14.109'	76°42.626'
I195	Providence, RI	41°48.986'	71°24.903'
I195	Richmond, VA	37°35.389'	77°28.188'
I276	Bucks, PA	40° 7.744'	74°53.374'
I278	Union, NJ	40°38.459'	74°12.379'
I280	Hudson, NJ	40°45.277'	74° 7.115'
I287	Westchester, NY	40°59.239'	73°40.246'
I295	New Castle, DE	39°41.794'	75°37.015'
I295	Duval, FL	30°27.582'	81°38.957'
I295	Duval, FL	30°10.120'	81°33.380'
I295	Cumberland, ME	43°43.884'	70°13.894'
I295	Cumberland, ME	43°37.526'	70°21.093'
I295	Prince George's, MD	38°47.702'	77° 1.001'
I295	Bristol, MA	41°57.321'	71°18.283'
I295	Mercer, NJ	40°17.002'	74°41.786'
I295	Kent, RI	41°42.822'	71°28.381'
I295	Henrico, VA	37°39.450'	77°27.054'
I295	Prince George, VA	37° 9.526'	77°21.133'
I395	New London, CT	41°22.510'	72°11.594'
I395	Dade, FL	25°47.308'	80°12.250'
I395	Penobscot, ME	44°47.221'	68°48.538'
I395	Baltimore city, MD	39°16.069'	76°37.478'
I476	Delaware, PA	39°52.037'	75°20.582'
I495	New Castle, DE	39°42.854'	75°35.076'
I495	Cumberland, ME	43°43.286'	70°18.327'
I495	Kennebec, ME	44°13.018'	69°49.514'
I495	Prince George's, MD	39° 1.277'	76°57.168'
I495	Essex, MA	42°51.762'	70°53.613'
I495	Essex, MA	42°51.370'	70°53.833'
I495	Hudson, NJ	40°46.815'	74° 3.424'
I495	Fairfax, VA	38°47.500'	77°10.507'
I595	Broward, FL	26° 4.871'	80°10.120'
I595	Prince George's, M	38°56.694'	76°51.483'
I676	Philadelphia, PA	39°57.501'	75° 8.450'
I676	Philadelphia, PA	39°57.266'	75° 8.450'
I676	Philadelphia, PA	39°57.233'	75° 8.453'
I678	Bronx, NY	40°49.725'	73°50.258'
I695	Baltimore, MD	39°21.049'	76°29.751'
I695	Baltimore, MD	39°15.034'	76°40.834'
I695	Bronx, NY	40°50.175'	73°49.510'
I895	Baltimore city, MD	39°19.091'	76°32.063'
I895	Baltimore city, MD	39°16.387'	76°33.266'
I895	Bronx, NY	40°50.245'	73°52.882'

I895	Bronx, NY	40°50.200'	73°52.657'
US1	Fairfield, CT	41°12.047'	73° 6.995'
US1	Fairfield, CT	41° 9.920'	73°14.126'
US1	Fairfield, CT	41° 8.351'	73°17.223'
US1	Fairfield, CT	41° 4.352'	73°28.522'
US1	Fairfield, CT	41° 3.495'	73°30.844'
US1	Middlesex, CT	41°18.965'	72°21.563'
US1	New Haven, CT	41°17.994'	72°54.838'
US1	New Haven, CT	41°17.805'	72°42.261'
US1	New Haven, CT	41°17.760'	72°54.141'
US1	New Haven, CT	41°17.645'	72°47.068'
US1	New Haven, CT	41°17.135'	72°52.646'
US1	New Haven, CT	41°14.046'	73° 2.540'
US1	New London, CT	41°22.209'	72°12.074'
US1	New London, CT	41°19.238'	72°20.386'
US1	Dade, FL	25°44.926'	80°12.706'
US1	Duval, FL	30°21.358'	81°40.127'
US1	Duval, FL	30°18.833'	81°39.532'
US1	Duval, FL	30°18.463'	81°38.789'
US1	Duval, FL	30°11.063'	81°33.492'
US1	St. Johns, FL	29°39.743'	81°17.256'
US1	Volusia, FL	29°20.147'	81° 7.881'
US1	Aroostook, ME	46° 8.391'	67°50.427'
US1	Cumberland, ME	43°48.467'	70° 9.990'
US1	Cumberland, ME	43°47.078'	70°11.429'
US1	Prince George's, MD	39° 1.073'	76°55.600'
US1	Essex, MA	42°35.736'	70°57.874'
US1	Essex, MA	42°35.515'	70°57.764'
US1	Essex, MA	42°32.560'	70°59.189'
US1	Essex, MA	42°32.371'	70°59.283'
US1	Essex, MA	42°30.988'	71° 0.113'
US1	Norfolk, MA	42°13.692'	71°10.931'
US1	Norfolk, MA	42° 7.867'	71°13.384'
US1	Norfolk, MA	42° 7.538'	71°13.645'
US1	Bergen, NJ	40°51.500'	73°58.606'
US1	Essex, NJ	40°44.077'	74° 7.436'
US1	Mercer, NJ	40°17.002'	74°41.786'
US1	Bronx, NY	40°50.698'	73°54.178'
US1	Westchester, NY	40°59.236'	73°40.873'
US1	Westchester, NY	40°53.996'	73°47.785'
US1	Bucks, PA	40°11.578'	74°52.746'
US1	Providence, RI	41°52.384'	71°23.288'
US1	Providence, RI	41°49.033'	71°25.040'
US1	Providence, RI	41°47.242'	71°25.249'
US1	Henrico, VA	37°36.344'	77°27.319'
US1	Spotsylvania, VA	38°14.320'	77°29.974'
US1	Alexandria, VA	38°47.669'	77° 3.273'
US2	Aroostook, ME	46° 8.689'	68° 3.501'
US2	Aroostook, ME	46° 8.059'	67°47.783'
US3	Middlesex, MA	42°29.317'	71°11.519'
US3	Middlesex, MA	42°28.591'	71°13.231'
US7	Fairfield, CT	41° 6.386'	73°25.187'
US9	New York, NY	40°50.917'	73°56.267'
US9W	Bergen, NJ	40°51.482'	73°58.452'
US13	Cumberland, NC	35° 7.375'	78°45.292'
US13	Bucks, PA	40° 5.528'	74°55.250'
US13	Delaware, PA	39°52.051'	75°20.326'
US15	Orangeburg, SC	33°24.709'	80°29.963'
US17	Nassau, FL	30°42.682'	81°40.324'
US17	Bryan, GA	31°55.664'	81°19.871'
US17	Glynn, GA	31° 9.914'	81°33.311'
US17	Glynn, GA	31° 8.252'	81°34.534'
US17	Liberty, GA	31°39.225'	81°23.694'
US17	Jasper, SC	32°37.783'	80°52.859'
US17	Jasper, SC	32°30.142'	80°58.327'
US17	Jasper, SC	32°16.364'	81° 4.852'
US17	Stafford, VA	38°20.429'	77°29.537'
US20	Middlesex, MA	42°22.190'	71°16.188'

I95 (cont)

US21	Colleton, SC	32°45.050'	80°49.688'
US25	Glynn, GA	31°13.255'	81°31.364'
US40	Baltimore city, MD	39°18.542'	76°31.901'
US41	Dade, FL	25°46.007'	80°12.039'
US44	Providence, RI	41°49.917'	71°25.082'
US46	Bergen, NJ	40°50.776'	74° 1.045'
US52	Florence, SC	34°13.767'	79°47.966'
US58	Emporia, VA	36°42.143'	77°32.983'
US64	Nash, NC	35°58.908'	77°52.625'
US70	Johnston, NC	35°31.172'	78°17.381'
US74	Robeson, NC	34°36.043'	79° 6.203'
US76	Florence, SC	34° 9.314'	79°52.361'
US78	Dorchester, SC	33°11.734'	80°36.310'
US80	Chatham, GA	32° 6.745'	81°14.281'
US84	Liberty, GA	31°46.690'	81°22.723'
US90	Duval, FL	30°18.653'	81°38.980'
US92	Volusia, FL	29°10.304'	81° 5.091'
US98	Palm Beach, FL	26°40.538'	80° 4.218'
US158	Halifax, NC	36°25.846'	77°37.822'
US176	Orangeburg, SC	33°22.945'	80°31.146'
US178	Dorchester, SC	33°16.256'	80°34.160'
US192	Brevard, FL	28° 4.713'	80°42.382'
US201	Kennebec, ME	44°10.670'	69°50.065'
US201	Somerset, ME	44°36.097'	69°35.940'
US202	New Castle, DE	39°45.999'	75°32.599'
US202	Kennebec, ME	44°18.974'	69°48.757'
US206	Mercer, NJ	40°17.134'	74°43.965'
US222	Cecil, MD	39°35.594'	76° 3.969'
US264	Wilson, NC	35°45.785'	78° 0.260'
US301	Johnston, NC	35°35.539'	78° 8.045'
US301	Robeson, NC	34°50.014'	78°58.718'
US301	Robeson, NC	34°43.084'	78°59.868'
US301	Robeson, NC	34°40.190'	79° 0.370'
US301	Robeson, NC	34°30.132'	79°18.450'
US301	Clarendon, SC	33°39.043'	80°16.640'
US301	Greensville, VA	36°43.619'	77°31.596'
US301	Prince George, VA	37° 8.540'	77°21.376'
US301	Prince George, VA	37° 4.861'	77°21.464'
US301	Petersburg, VA	37°12.963'	77°23.059'
US302	Cumberland, ME	43°41.970'	70°19.019'
US322	Delaware, PA	39°50.815'	75°23.299'
US322	Delaware, PA	39°50.408'	75°24.329'
US378	Sumter, SC	33°54.018'	80° 5.629'
US421	Harnett, NC	35°17.926'	78°35.936'
US460	Petersburg, VA	37°13.738'	77°23.737'
US460	Petersburg, VA	37°13.651'	77°23.716'
US460	Petersburg, VA	37°12.782'	77°22.627'
US521	Clarendon, SC	33°44.361'	80°12.561'
US701	Johnston, NC	35°27.452'	78°23.372'

I96

I196	Kent, MI	42°58.597'	85°36.214'
I275	Wayne, MI	42°23.555'	83°26.041'
I275	Wayne, MI	42°23.159'	83°26.192'
I296	Kent, MI	43° 0.976'	85°40.852'
I496	Ingham, MI	42°40.489'	84°29.722'
I696	Oakland, MI	42°29.003'	83°26.096'
US12	Wayne, MI	42°19.869'	83° 5.235'
US23	Livingston, MI	42°31.540'	83°45.364'
US24	Wayne, MI	42°23.105'	83°16.574'
US31	Muskegon, MI	43°10.295'	86°12.399'
US127	Ingham, MI	42°40.489'	84°29.722'
US131	Kent, MI	43° 1.267'	85°40.104'

I97

I595	Anne Arundel, MD	38°59.070'	76°34.597'

I895	Anne Arundel, MD	39°12.159'	76°37.915'
US50	Anne Arundel, MD	38°59.070'	76°34.597'

I105

I110	Los Angeles, CA	33°55.719'	118°16.794'
I405	Los Angeles, CA	33°55.844'	118°22.050'
I605	Los Angeles, CA	33°54.821'	118° 6.246'
I710	Los Angeles, CA	33°54.707'	118°10.722'

I110

I405	Los Angeles, CA	33°51.403'	118°17.022'
US30	Escambia, FL	30°24.963'	87°12.406'
US54	El Paso, TX	31°46.884'	106°26.442'
US54	El Paso, TX	31°46.250'	106°26.772'
US61	East Baton Rouge, LA	30°32.268'	91°11.344'
US61	East Baton Rouge, LA	30°30.538'	91° 9.511'
US62	El Paso, TX	31°46.148'	106°27.018'
US90	Escambia, FL	30°25.336'	87°12.838'
US90	Harrison, MS	30°23.628'	88°53.628'

I124

US27	Hamilton, TN	35° 3.311'	85°18.934'

I126

US76	Richland, SC	34° 0.652'	81° 2.779'

I129

US20	Dakota, NE	42°26.960'	96°26.133'

I135

I235	Sedgwick, KS	37°45.706'	97°19.286'
I235	Sedgwick, KS	37°36.916'	97°19.708'
US50	Harvey, KS	38° 3.776'	97°19.325'
US50	Harvey, KS	38° 1.760'	97°19.657'
US50	Harvey, KS	38° 1.315'	97°19.667'
US54	Sedgwick, KS	37°40.759'	97°18.703'
US56	McPherson, KS	38°22.258'	97°37.222'
US81	Sedgwick, KS	37°36.478'	97°19.506'

I155

US51	Dyer, TN	36° 4.372'	89°20.879'
US136	Logan, IL	40°18.491'	89°27.173'
US412	Pemiscot, MO	36° 9.077'	89°39.811'
US412	Dyer, TN	36° 4.130'	89°23.793'

I164

US41	Vanderburgh, IN	37°56.567'	87°32.602'

I165

US43	Mobile, AL	30°41.966'	88° 2.798'

I170

I270	St. Louis, MO	38°46.547'	90°20.378'

I172

US24	Adams, IL	40° 0.437'	91°18.487'

I175

I275	Pinellas, FL	27°46.044'	82°39.486'

I176

US422	Berks, PA	40°18.400'	75°53.912'

I180

US6	Bureau, IL	41°22.279'	89°22.954'

US15	Lycoming, PA	41°14.351'	77° 0.005'		US79	Bossier, LA	32°32.827'	93°37.963'
US15	Lycoming, PA	41°13.907'	77° 2.404'		US80	Hinds, MS	32°18.016'	90°14.783'
US30	Laramie, WY	41° 8.018'	104°48.744'					
US30	Laramie, WY	41° 7.991'	104°48.828'		**I229**			
US220	Lycoming, PA	41°14.263'	76°48.580'		US36	Buchanan, MO	39°44.933'	94°51.187'
					US59	Buchanan, MO	39°46.220'	94°51.651'
I181								
US11E	Washington, TN	36°20.834'	82°22.716'		**I235**			
US11W	Sullivan, TN	36°33.384'	82°34.955'		US6	Polk, IA	41°37.663'	93°34.498'
US19W	Washington, TN	36°18.505'	82°20.317'		US54	Sedgwick, KS	37°40.394'	97°24.048'
					US62	Oklahoma, OK	35°29.594'	97°30.659'
I182					US65	Polk, IA	41°35.767'	93°35.917'
US12	Franklin, WA	46°14.974'	119° 4.302'		US254	Sedgwick, KS	37°45.706'	97°19.286'
US395	Franklin, WA	46°15.109'	119° 4.932'					
US395	Franklin, WA	46°14.909'	119° 7.512'		**I238**			
					I580	Alameda, CA	37°41.440'	122° 5.886'
I184					I880	Alameda, CA	37°41.414'	122° 8.178'
US20	Ada, ID	43°37.091'	116°13.938'					
					I240			
I185					US19	Buncombe, NC	35°35.536'	82°34.054'
US25	Greenville, SC	34°48.109'	82°25.696'		US19	Buncombe, NC	35°35.357'	82°34.711'
US27	Muscogee, GA	32°31.696'	84°57.570'		US25	Buncombe, NC	35°35.964'	82°33.243'
US27	Troup, GA	32°57.680'	84°57.162'		US64	Shelby, TN	35° 8.255'	90° 1.438'
US29	Greenville, SC	34°49.253'	82°24.988'		US70	Buncombe, NC	35°35.110'	82°31.370'
US80	Muscogee, GA	32°32.681'	84°57.667'		US72	Shelby, TN	35° 6.220'	89°52.197'
					US74	Buncombe, NC	35°33.893'	82°30.033'
I189					US78	Shelby, TN	35° 7.800'	90° 1.426'
US7	Chittenden, VT	44°26.823'	73°12.583'		US78	Shelby, TN	35° 4.807'	89°57.338'
I190					**I244**			
I290	Worcester, MA	42°17.231'	71°47.870'		I444	Tulsa, OK	36° 9.562'	95°58.794'
I290	Erie, NY	42°59.215'	78°54.878'		I444	Tulsa, OK	36° 8.669'	96° 0.216'
US16	Pennington, SD	44° 5.059'	103°14.010'		US64	Tulsa, OK	36° 9.530'	96° 0.104'
US62	Erie, NY	42°52.151'	78°49.327'		US75	Tulsa, OK	36° 6.723'	96° 0.715'
US62	Niagara, NY	43° 5.365'	78°59.438'		US169	Tulsa, OK	36° 9.955'	95°51.634'
I195					**I255**			
I295	Mercer, NJ	40°10.959'	74°43.333'		I270	Madison, IL	38°45.448'	90° 2.716'
I495	Plymouth, MA	41°47.017'	70°43.948'		I270	St. Louis, MO	38°30.227'	90°20.361'
US1	Dade, FL	25°48.658'	80°11.371'		US50	St. Louis, MO	38°30.048'	90°19.037'
US1	York, ME	43°30.712'	70°25.957'		US61	St. Louis, MO	38°30.125'	90°19.840'
US6	Bristol, MA	41°39.511'	70°53.308'					
US6	Bristol, MA	41°39.286'	70°59.307'		**I264**			
US9	Monmouth, NJ	40° 9.889'	74°14.161'		I464	Norfolk, VA	36°50.144'	76°17.294'
US44	Providence, RI	41°49.116'	71°22.951'		US13	Norfolk, VA	36°50.585'	76°12.641'
US130	Mercer, NJ	40°12.121'	74°38.148'		US17	Portsmouth, VA	36°49.291'	76°20.007'
US206	Mercer, NJ	40°11.120'	74°42.353'		US31E	Jefferson, KY	38°12.677'	85°40.285'
					US31W	Jefferson, KY	38°11.085'	85°48.796'
I196					US42	Jefferson, KY	38°16.782'	85°38.176'
I296	Kent, MI	42°58.376'	85°40.693'		US60	Jefferson, KY	38°14.991'	85°37.167'
					US460	Norfolk, VA	36°50.677'	76°16.088'
I205								
I580	Alameda, CA	37°44.565'	121°33.636'		**I265**			
US26	Multnomah, OR	45°29.845'	122°33.876'		US31E	Jefferson, KY	38° 8.422'	85°34.954'
					US60	Jefferson, KY	38°14.519'	85°30.228'
I210								
I605	Los Angeles, CA	34° 7.981'	117°57.114'		**I270**			
US90	Calcasieu, LA	30°14.123'	93° 9.946'		I370	Montgomery, MD	39° 7.317'	77°11.953'
					I495	Montgomery, MD	39° 1.166'	77° 6.248'
I215					I495	Montgomery, MD	39° 0.586'	77° 9.100'
US89	Salt Lake, UT	40°38.001'	111°53.334'		I670	Franklin, OH	40° 0.672'	82°54.041'
					US6	Adams, CO	39°48.001'	104°55.974'
I220					US23	Franklin, OH	39°52.502'	83° 0.223'
US49	Hinds, MS	32°21.564'	90°14.118'		US33	Franklin, OH	40° 5.945'	83° 8.080'
US71	Caddo, LA	32°33.244'	93°46.874'		US33	Franklin, OH	39°54.113'	82°53.897'
					US40	Franklin, OH	39°57.269'	82°50.660'

I270 (cont)

US40	Franklin, OH	39°57.169'	83° 7.142'
US62	Franklin, OH	40° 0.916'	82°54.215'
US62	Franklin, OH	39°54.241'	83° 4.548'
US67	St. Louis, MO	38°46.698'	90°21.610'

I271

I480	Cuyahoga, OH	41°25.781'	81°30.335'
I480	Cuyahoga, OH	41°23.923'	81°30.518'
US322	Cuyahoga, OH	41°31.211'	81°26.714'

I275

I375	Pinellas, FL	27°46.567'	82°39.565'
I471	Campbell, KY	39° 2.788'	84°27.448'
I471	Campbell, KY	39° 2.737'	84°27.645'
I640	Knox, TN	36° .008'	83°57.516'
US12	Wayne, MI	42°16.774'	83°26.510'
US19	Manatee, FL	27°34.753'	82°34.691'
US19	Pinellas, FL	27°42.995'	82°40.775'
US22	Hamilton, OH	39°15.682'	84°20.294'
US24	Monroe, MI	42° 1.072'	83°20.807'
US25W	Knox, TN	35°59.918'	83°57.359'
US27	Campbell, KY	39° 2.998'	84°26.797'
US27	Hamilton, OH	39°15.385'	84°36.057'
US41	Hillsborough, FL	28° 5.782'	82°27.117'
US41	Manatee, FL	27°35.095'	82°32.422'
US42	Hamilton, OH	39°17.345'	84°23.715'
US50	Clermont, OH	39° 9.568'	84°16.054'
US52	Hamilton, OH	39° 3.621'	84°25.271'
US52	Hamilton, OH	39° 3.307'	84°23.492'
US92	Hillsborough, FL	27°59.751'	82°27.234'
US92	Hillsborough, FL	27°57.290'	82°30.346'
US92	Pinellas, FL	27°51.140'	82°39.833'
US127	Hamilton, OH	39°17.119'	84°33.848'

I276

I476	Montgomery, PA	40° 6.780'	75°16.649'
US1	Bucks, PA	40° 7.870'	74°58.052'
US13	Bucks, PA	40° 7.228'	74°50.580'
US130	Burlington, NJ	40° 6.161'	74°47.540'
US202	Montgomery, PA	40° 5.404'	75°22.619'

I277

US29	Mecklenburg, NC	35°14.161'	80°50.379'
US74	Mecklenburg, NC	35°13.363'	80°49.793'
US74	Mecklenburg, NC	35°13.287'	80°49.835'

I278

I295	Bronx, NY	40°49.725'	73°50.258'
I478	Kings, NY	40°40.777'	74° 0.247'
I495	Queens, NY	40°44.075'	73°55.397'
I895	Bronx, NY	40°49.343'	73°53.264'
US1	Union, NJ	40°38.427'	74°13.842'

I279

I376	Allegheny, PA	40°26.396'	80° 0.562'
I579	Allegheny, PA	40°27.212'	79°59.932'
US19	Allegheny, PA	40°29.809'	80° 0.770'
US19	Allegheny, PA	40°26.957'	80° 1.547'
US19	Allegheny, PA	40°25.858'	80° 1.595'
US19	Allegheny, PA	40°25.474'	80° 1.839'

I280

I380	San Mateo, CA	37°37.633'	122°25.794'
I680	Santa Clara, CA	37°20.368'	121°51.048'
I880	Santa Clara, CA	37°19.028'	121°56.346'

US6	Scott, IA	41°35.493'	90°40.536'
US61	Scott, IA	41°30.545'	90°40.349'
US67	Rock Island, IL	41°26.767'	90°34.010'
US101	San Francisco, CA	37°44.138'	122°24.354'

I285

I675	De Kalb, GA	33°40.379'	84°19.706'
US19	Clayton, GA	33°37.914'	84°23.285'
US19	Fulton, GA	33°54.739'	84°22.754'
US19	Fulton, GA	33°54.692'	84°21.473'
US23	De Kalb, GA	33°54.177'	84°16.469'
US23	De Kalb, GA	33°40.052'	84°20.453'
US29	De Kalb, GA	33°49.619'	84°15.176'
US41	Cobb, GA	33°53.056'	84°28.180'
US78	De Kalb, GA	33°48.930'	84°15.119'
US78	Fulton, GA	33°47.210'	84°29.590'

I287

I684	Westchester, NY	41° 1.555'	73°43.934'
US1	Middlesex, NJ	40°31.682'	74°21.275'
US1	Westchester, NY	40°59.500'	73°40.654'
US22	Somerset, NJ	40°34.533'	74°34.054'
US46	Morris, NJ	40°52.215'	74°25.165'
US202	Somerset, NJ	40°39.463'	74°38.661'
US202	Somerset, NJ	40°35.779'	74°37.415'

I290

I294	Cook, IL	41°52.178'	87°55.028'
I355	DuPage, IL	41°57.547'	88° 1.595'
I395	Worcester, MA	42°11.738'	71°50.768'
I495	Middlesex, MA	42°21.781'	71°35.429'
I990	Erie, NY	42°59.838'	78°48.486'
US62	Erie, NY	43° 0.250'	78°49.363'

I291

US20	Hampden, MA	42° 8.700'	72°32.980'

I293

US3	Hillsborough, NH	42°58.489'	71°28.421'

I294

US6	Cook, IL	41°36.061'	87°40.855'
US12	Cook, IL	41°43.130'	87°48.377'
US34	Cook, IL	41°49.127'	87°54.850'

I295

I495	Queens, NY	40°44.673'	73°46.330'
I678	Bronx, NY	40°49.725'	73°50.258'
I695	District of Columbia, DC	38°52.648'	76°59.483'
I695	Bronx, NY	40°49.241'	73°48.932'
US1	Duval, FL	30°24.720'	81°44.850'
US1	Cumberland, ME	43°41.168'	70°15.148'
US1	Henrico, VA	37°39.514'	77°27.620'
US6	Providence, RI	41°49.703'	71°30.982'
US6	Providence, RI	41°49.208'	71°30.780'
US13	New Castle, DE	39°41.741'	75°34.615'
US17	Duval, FL	30°27.437'	81°38.168'
US17	Duval, FL	30°11.477'	81°42.331'
US30	Camden, NJ	39°52.488'	75° 2.934'
US33	Henrico, VA	37°40.846'	77°32.442'
US40	Salem, NJ	39°40.753'	75°29.081'
US44	Providence, RI	41°52.152'	71°30.947'
US60	Henrico, VA	37°30.561'	77°16.464'
US130	Burlington, NJ	40° 8.108'	74°42.966'
US130	Gloucester, NJ	39°48.233'	75°18.682'
US130	Salem, NJ	39°40.790'	75°29.590'

US301	Hanover, VA	37°38.677'	77°24.833'
US322	Gloucester, NJ	39°46.693'	75°20.383'
US360	Hanover, VA	37°36.439'	77°21.670'
US460	Prince George, VA	37°11.523'	77°19.655'

I296

US131	Kent, MI	43° 0.815'	85°40.554'
US131	Kent, MI	42°58.289'	85°40.687'

I305

US50	Sacramento, CA	38°33.527'	121°28.344'

I310

US61	St. Charles, LA	29°58.536'	90°19.264'
US90	St. Charles, LA	29°53.555'	90°24.283'

I335

I470	Shawnee, KS	38°59.497'	95°41.541'
US56	Lyon, KS	38°39.117'	96° 1.655'

I355

US20	DuPage, IL	41°57.077'	88° 2.074'
US34	DuPage, IL	41°48.185'	88° 3.443'

I359

US11	Tuscaloosa, AL	33°11.981'	87°34.016'

I376

I579	Allegheny, PA	40°26.056'	79°59.783'
US22	Allegheny, PA	40°26.329'	79°45.522'
US22	Allegheny, PA	40°26.323'	79°45.231'
US30	Allegheny, PA	40°26.056'	79°52.161'

I380

US6	Johnson, IA	41°42.322'	91°38.519'
US20	Black Hawk, IA	42°27.274'	92°18.728'
US20	Black Hawk, IA	42°26.966'	92°11.479'
US30	Linn, IA	41°55.604'	91°40.195'
US101	San Mateo, CA	37°37.991'	122°24.180'
US101	San Mateo, CA	37°36.865'	122°23.766'
US218	Black Hawk, IA	42°28.692'	92°19.339'

I384

I385	Hartford, CT	41°46.289'	72°28.258'
US44	Tolland, CT	41°47.372'	72°26.689'

I385

US221	Laurens, SC	34°33.173'	82° 0.355'
US221	Laurens, SC	34°33.166'	82° 0.300'
US276	Greenville, SC	34°51.247'	82°23.057'
US276	Greenville, SC	34°45.364'	82°17.320'

I390

I490	Monroe, NY	43° 9.454'	77°40.866'
I590	Monroe, NY	43° 6.611'	77°36.003'
US15	Monroe, NY	43° 6.721'	77°37.433'
US20	Livingston, NY	42°54.349'	77°41.734'

I394

I494	Hennepin, MN	44°58.271'	93°27.602'
US169	Hennepin, MN	44°58.406'	93°24.010'

I395

I495	Fairfax, VA	38°47.500'	77°10.507'
I695	District of Columbia, DC	38°52.930'	77° 0.717'

US1	District of Columbia, DC	38°52.742'	77° 2.164'
US1	Dade, FL	25°47.133'	80°11.354'
US1	Arlington, VA	38°52.001'	77° 3.100'
US6	Windham, CT	41°47.573'	71°52.625'
US20	Worcester, MA	42°11.038'	71°50.877'
US41	Dade, FL	25°47.206'	80°11.141'
US44	Windham, CT	41°55.448'	71°53.141'
US50	District of Columbia, DC	38°54.293'	77° 0.945'
US202	Penobscot, ME	44°47.203'	68°47.677'

I405

I605	Orange, CA	33°47.014'	118° 5.460'
I710	Los Angeles, CA	33°49.585'	118°12.390'
US26	Multnomah, OR	45°30.901'	122°41.268'
US30	Multnomah, OR	45°32.048'	122°41.148'
US101	Los Angeles, CA	34° 9.645'	118°28.092'

I410

US87	Bexar, TX	29°23.900'	98°23.338'
US90	Bexar, TX	29°23.822'	98°38.954'
US281	Bexar, TX	29°31.194'	98°28.767'
US281	Bexar, TX	29°19.296'	98°28.649'

I430

I630	Pulaski, AR	34°44.914'	92°23.482'

I435

I470	Jackson, MO	38°56.353'	94°32.539'
US24	Wyandotte, KS	39° 7.000'	94°48.664'
US24	Jackson, MO	39° 6.395'	94°29.151'
US40	Jackson, MO	39° 3.787'	94°29.308'
US69	Johnson, KS	38°56.112'	94°42.284'
US71	Jackson, MO	38°56.479'	94°32.141'
US169	Johnson, KS	38°55.922'	94°40.058'
US169	Clay, MO	39°18.594'	94°35.029'

I440

US1	Wake, NC	35°48.866'	78°36.338'
US1	Wake, NC	35°45.999'	78°44.159'
US64	Wake, NC	35°47.650'	78°34.972'
US64	Wake, NC	35°47.013'	78°42.043'
US65	Pulaski, AR	34°42.700'	92°16.216'
US70	Pulaski, AR	34°46.264'	92° 9.686'
US70	Wake, NC	35°50.099'	78°40.174'
US70	Davidson, TN	36° 8.205'	86°49.314'
US165	Pulaski, AR	34°44.138'	92°10.181'
US401	Wake, NC	35°45.176'	78°38.950'
US431	Davidson, TN	36° 7.359'	86°48.421'

I444

US64	Tulsa, OK	36° 8.581'	95°58.766'
US75	Tulsa, OK	36° 9.562'	95°58.794'

I459

US11	Jefferson, AL	33°35.617'	86°38.906'
US31	Jefferson, AL	33°23.069'	86°48.404'
US78	Jefferson, AL	33°32.918'	86°38.499'
US280	Jefferson, AL	33°26.531'	86°43.843'

I464

US13	Chesapeake, VA	36°46.465'	76°16.664'

I465

US31	Hamilton, IN	39°55.811'	86° 9.482'
US36	Marion, IN	39°49.925'	86° 2.156'
US40	Marion, IN	39°46.373'	86° 1.822'

I465 (cont)

US52	Marion, IN	39°45.080'	86° 2.008'
US421	Marion, IN	39°55.417'	86°13.715'

I470

US40	Jackson, MO	39° 1.997'	94°21.674'
US50	Jackson, MO	38°56.060'	94°24.358'
US71	Jackson, MO	38°56.000'	94°31.723'
US75	Shawnee, KS	38°59.651'	95°41.243'
US75	Shawnee, KS	38°59.509'	95°41.243'
US250	Ohio, WV	40° 3.074'	80°43.277'

I471

US27	Campbell, KY	39° 4.009'	84°27.932'
US27	Campbell, KY	39° 2.302'	84°27.256'
US50	Hamilton, OH	39° 6.197'	84°30.012'
US52	Hamilton, OH	39° 6.152'	84°29.925'

I474

US24	Peoria, IL	40°39.403'	89°38.644'

I475

US20	Lucas, OH	41°40.535'	83°41.645'
US23	Lucas, OH	41°41.078'	83°41.695'
US24	Lucas, OH	41°33.194'	83°41.188'
US41	Monroe, GA	32°57.197'	83°48.761'
US80	Bibb, GA	32°48.571'	83°43.555'

I476

US1	Delaware, PA	39°56.224'	75°21.926'
US30	Delaware, PA	40° 2.218'	75°21.371'

I480

US6	Pottawattamie, IA	41°15.709'	95°54.443'
US6	Douglas, NE	41°15.598'	95°55.321'
US6	Douglas, NE	41°15.592'	95°55.507'
US6	Douglas, NE	41°15.586'	95°57.227'
US6	Douglas, NE	41°15.524'	95°57.226'
US42	Cuyahoga, OH	41°25.103'	81°43.692'
US75	Douglas, NE	41°15.780'	95°57.112'
US75	Douglas, NE	41°15.763'	95°55.965'

I481

I690	Onondaga, NY	43° 3.412'	76° 3.158'

I490

I590	Monroe, NY	43° 8.635'	77°33.091'

I494

I35E	Dakota, MN	44°51.770'	93° 8.687'
I694	Washington, MN	44°56.935'	92°57.515'
US10	Washington, MN	44°53.192'	93° 0.200'
US12	Hennepin, MN	44°58.271'	93°27.602'
US169	Hennepin, MN	44°51.747'	93°25.469'
US169	Hennepin, MN	44°51.562'	93°23.675'

I495

I678	Queens, NY	40°44.591'	73°50.288'
US1	Norfolk, MA	42° 2.221'	71°18.431'
US1	Hudson, NJ	40°46.539'	74° 2.449'
US3	Middlesex, MA	42°36.433'	71°19.568'
US13	New Castle, DE	39°43.006'	75°33.470'
US20	Middlesex, MA	42°20.473'	71°34.556'
US29	Montgomery, MD	39° 0.919'	77° 1.013'
US44	Plymouth, MA	41°54.150'	70°57.932'

US50	Fairfax, VA	38°51.946'	77°13.237'
US202	Androscoggin, ME	44° 2.348'	70°15.815'
US202	Androscoggin, ME	44° 2.328'	70°15.899'
US202	Cumberland, ME	43°53.030'	70°20.174'

I496

US127	Ingham, MI	42°43.438'	84°30.428'

I510

US90	Orleans, LA	30° 1.598'	89°56.358'

I515

US93	Clark, NV	36° 7.984'	115° 5.322'
US95	Clark, NV	36°10.461'	115° 9.222'

I516

US17	Chatham, GA	32° 5.848'	81° 8.480'
US17	Chatham, GA	32° 3.218'	81° 8.511'

I520

US1	Richmond, GA	33°25.390'	82° 3.550'
US25	Richmond, GA	33°24.430'	82° 1.644'
US78	Richmond, GA	33°27.016'	82° 4.438'

I526

US17	Charleston, SC	32°49.180'	79°50.573'
US17	Charleston, SC	32°47.384'	80° 1.924'
US17	Charleston, SC	32°46.807'	79°57.939'
US52	Charleston, SC	32°53.462'	80° 0.794'

I535

US53	Douglas, WI	46°44.127'	92° 5.854'

I540

US64	Crawford, AR	35°26.828'	94°19.226'
US71	Sebastian, AR	35°18.726'	94°23.938'
US271	Sebastian, AR	35°17.590'	94°25.423'

I564

US460	Norfolk, VA	36°55.103'	76°16.321'

I565

US72	Madison, AL	34°45.509'	86°33.838'
US72	Madison, AL	34°44.323'	86°35.191'
US231	Madison, AL	34°43.798'	86°35.794'

I580

I680	Alameda, CA	37°42.045'	121°55.290'
I880	Alameda, CA	37°49.706'	122°17.490'
I980	Alameda, CA	37°49.478'	122°16.020'
US101	Marin, CA	37°57.733'	122°30.528'

I581

US11	Roanoke, VA	37°16.596'	79°56.171'
US220	Roanoke, VA	37°15.996'	79°56.219'
US460	Roanoke, VA	37°16.934'	79°56.302'

I585

US176	Spartanburg, SC	34°59.347'	81°57.886'
US176	Spartanburg, SC	34°58.216'	81°56.195'
US221	Spartanburg, SC	34°58.364'	81°56.351'

I595

US1	Broward, FL	26° 4.816'	80° 8.092'
US50	Prince George's, MD	38°56.575'	76°52.909'

US301	Prince George's, MD	38°57.251'	76°43.055'
US441	Broward, FL	26° 5.082'	80°12.184'

I610

US59	Harris, TX	29°48.489'	95°20.150'
US59	Harris, TX	29°43.716'	95°27.608'
US90	Orleans, LA	29°59.406'	90° 3.978'
US90	Harris, TX	29°47.800'	95°16.284'
US290	Harris, TX	29°47.889'	95°26.978'

I630

US67	Pulaski, AR	34°44.375'	92°16.604'

I635

US24	Wyandotte, KS	39° 7.006'	94°40.883'
US69	Johnson, KS	39° 2.399'	94°40.375'
US69	Platte, MO	39° 9.875'	94°37.625'
US75	Dallas, TX	32°55.437'	96°45.827'
US80	Dallas, TX	32°47.545'	96°37.499'

I640

US11W	Knox, TN	36° 1.038'	83°51.677'

I664

US13	Chesapeake, VA	36°47.233'	76°25.339'
US60	Newport News, VA	36°58.802'	76°25.456'

I670

US23	Franklin, OH	39°58.541'	82°59.896'
US69	Wyandotte, KS	39° 5.747'	94°37.547'
US230	Franklin, OH	39°58.536'	82°59.993'

I675

US23	Clayton, GA	33°34.655'	84°16.607'
US35	Greene, OH	39°44.153'	84° 5.566'

I676

US30	Camden, NJ	39°56.776'	75° 6.868'

I680

I780	Solano, CA	38° 2.901'	122° 7.680'
US62D	Mahoning, OH	41° 5.357'	80°39.019'
US6	Douglas, NE	41°15.801'	96° 4.556'
US62	Mahoning, OH	41° 5.188'	80°39.017'
US75	Douglas, NE	41°20.798'	95°58.913'
US101	Santa Clara, CA	37°20.368'	121°51.048'
US224	Mahoning, OH	41° 1.436'	80°37.624'
US711	Mahoning, OH	41° 7.120'	80°41.567'

I690

US11	Onondaga, NY	43° 3.067'	76° 8.868'

I691

US5	New Haven, CT	41°32.566'	72°47.178'

I694

I35E	Ramsey, MN	45° 2.256'	93° 3.714'
I35E	Ramsey, MN	45° 1.949'	93° 5.348'
I35W	Ramsey, MN	45° 4.020'	93°11.135'

I695

I795	Baltimore, MD	39°22.381'	76°44.798'
I895	Anne Arundel, MD	39°12.159'	76°37.915'
I895	Baltimore, MD	39°13.975'	76°40.048'
US1	Baltimore, MD	39°22.182'	76°30.848'

US40	Baltimore, MD	39°17.173'	76°44.309'

I696

US24	Oakland, MI	42°29.388'	83°17.091'

I759

US411	Etowah, AL	33°59.514'	86° 0.266'

I787

US9	Albany, NY	42°38.636'	73°45.053'
US9W	Albany, NY	42°37.973'	73°46.544'
US9W	Albany, NY	42°37.967'	73°46.575'

I820

US80	Tarrant, TX	32°44.073'	97°13.487'
US287	Tarrant, TX	32°41.426'	97°14.426'
US377	Tarrant, TX	32°50.359'	97°15.829'

I880

I980	Alameda, CA	37°48.037'	122°16.704'
US101	Santa Clara, CA	37°21.850'	121°54.036'

I894

US18	Milwaukee, WI	43° 2.119'	88° 1.994'
US41	Milwaukee, WI	42°57.748'	87°56.930'

I895

US40	Baltimore city, MD	39°18.133'	76°32.758'

I985

US23	Gwinnett, GA	34° 5.228'	83°59.612'
US23	Hall, GA	34°18.958'	83°47.331'
US129	Hall, GA	34°17.103'	83°48.351'

IH1

IH2	Honolulu, HI	21°24.080'	157°59.316'
IH3	Honolulu, HI	21°22.563'	157°55.668'
IH201	Honolulu, HI	21°20.454'	157°53.184'
IH201	Honolulu, HI	21°19.048'	157°51.420'

IH3

IH201	Honolulu, HI	21°22.507'	157°55.326'

Appendix 4: Receiver Comparison

The following tables provide comparison information for handheld GPS receivers from five manufacturers. These receivers were in production as of early 1997. Four of these manufacturers are U.S. companies — Garmin, Lowrance (which also makes receivers under the "Eagle" and "SeaNav" brands), Magellan, and Trimble — and one is a foreign company — Silva of Sweden. These manufacturers account for the majority of handheld GPS receivers in use by recreational and backcountry land navigators. Be aware that the receivers included in the comparison do not represent the complete offering of handheld receivers from these five companies. The receivers included are the primary models targeted at the recreational and/or backcountry user.

There are a number of other manufacturers that also produce handheld GPS receivers, but their units are either targeted for marine, GIS, or aviation use, or they are not readily available in the United States. The active manufacturers of handheld GPS receivers intended for recreational users (as of early 1997) include:

GARMIN International
1200 E 151st St
Olathe KS 66062

Koden Electronics Co., Ltd
2-10-45 Kami-Osaki Shingawa-Ku
Tokyo 141 JAPAN

Lowrance Electronics (Eagle & SeaNav)
12000 East Skelly Drive
Tulsa OK 74128

Magellan Systems Corp
960 Overland Court
San Dimas CA 91773

Micrologic Inc
9174 Deering Ave
Chatsworth CA 91311

Silva Sweden AB
Kuskvägen 4
Sollentuna S191 62 SWEDEN

Trimble Navigation
645 North Mary Avenue
Sunnyvale CA 94088-3642

II Morrow Inc
2345 Turner Road SE
Salem OR 97309

Raytheon Marine Company (Apelco)
676 Island Pond Road
Manchester NH 03109-5420

The information in the comparison tables is primarily based upon product literature and manuals supplied by the manufacturers. Where possible, verification of features and functions was obtained from the actual receiver. If you are interested in a receiver that is not included in the comparison, this compilation should nonetheless be useful as a framework for considering the merits of that unit. Question marks in any cells indicate information that could not be obtained.

Handheld GPS Receivers: Features and Functions

	Eagle AccuNav Sport	Lowrance Global Map Sport	Lowrance Global Nav 200	Garmin GPS 38	Garmin GPS 40	Garmin GPS 45 XL	Garmin GPS II	Garmin GPS 12 XL
Physical:								
Weight (w/batteries)	20 oz	20 oz	12 oz	9 oz	9 oz	9 oz	9 oz	9.5 oz
Dimensions (in. WxHxD)	3.6 x 7.8 x 1.8	3.6 x 7.8 x 1.8	2.2 x 6.7 x 1.7	2 x 6.2 x 1.3	2 x 6.2 x 1.3	2 x 6.3 x 1.4	2.3 x 5 x 1.6	2 x 6.2 x 1.3
Screen Size (in. WxH)	2.3 x 2.3	2.3 x 2.3	1.4 x 2.1	1.5 x 2.2	1.5 x 2.2	1.5 x 2.2	1.5 x 2.2	1.5 x 2.2
Graphic Display	yes	yes	yes	yes	yes	yes	yes	yes
Screen Res. (pixels WxH)	160 x 160	160 x 160	65 x 100	65 x 102	65 x 102	65 x 102	65 x 102	64 x 100
Keyboard Backlight	yes	yes	no	no	no	no	no	yes
Keyboard Style	numbers	scroll	scroll	scroll	scroll	scroll	scroll	scroll
Antenna Type	ext. patch	ext. patch	patch	patch	patch	quad helix	quad helix	patch
Antenna Extension Avail.	yes	yes	no	no	no	yes	yes	no
External Antenna Plug	proprietary	proprietary	proprietary	none	proprietary	BNC	BNC	MCX
Operating Temperature	-20C to +70C	-20C to +70C	-20C to +70C	-15C to +70C	-15C to +70C	-15C to +70C	-15C to +70C	-15C to +70C
Storage Temparature	-20C to +75C	-20C to +75C	-20C to +75C	-40C to ???	-40C to ???	-40C to ???	-40C to ???	-40C to ???
Water Resistence	waterproof	waterproof	waterproof	waterproof	waterproof	waterproof	waterproof	waterproof
Electronics:								
No. Parallel Channels	5	5	12	1	1	1	1	12
Max No. Satellites	12	12	12	8	8	8	8	12
Chipset	Rockwell	Rockwell	Rockwell	Garmin	Garmin	Garmin	Garmin	Garmin
Power Consumption	1.5W	2.3W	.9W	.75W	.75W	.75W	.75W	1W
No. & Size Batteries	6 x AA	6 x AA	4 x AA	4 x AA	4 x AA	4 x AA	4 x AA	4 x AA
Battery Strength Indicator	volts	volts	graph	graph	graph	graph	graph	graph
Input Voltage	6-35 VDC	6-35 VDC	6-35 VDC	5-8 VDC	5-8 VDC	5-40 VDC	5-36 VDC	5-40 VDC
Lockable On Switch	no	no	no	no	no	no	no	no
Auto Shutoff	no	no	no	no	no	yes	no	no
Initial Coordinate Entry	yes	yes	yes	yes	yes	yes	yes	yes
Simulator Mode	no	no	yes	yes	yes	yes	yes	yes
Data Interface:								
Differential Capable	yes	yes	yes	yes	yes	yes	yes	yes
NMEA Interface	180/183	183	180/183	180/182/183	180/182/183	180/182/183	180/182/183	180/182/183
Waypoint I/O Software	yes	yes	yes	yes	yes	yes	yes	yes
Datums:								
Number Preprogammed	1	99	189	104	102	102	106	106
User Definable	no	no	no	no	no	no	no	yes
Coordinate Types:								
Latitude/Longitude	yes	yes	yes	yes	yes	yes	yes	yes
UTM	no	yes	yes	yes	yes	yes	yes	yes
UPS	no	no	no	yes	no	yes	yes	yes
MGRS	no	no	yes	no	no	no	no	no
Other	no	no	2	7	7	7	7	7
User Definable	no	no	no	no	no	no	no	yes
Declination Adj:								
Automatic Magnetic	yes	yes	yes	yes	yes	yes	yes	yes
Automatic Grid	no	no	no	yes	yes	yes	yes	yes
User Specified	no	no	no	yes	yes	yes	yes	yes
Position Resolution:								
Decimal Degrees	no	no	no	ddd.ddddd	ddd.ddddd	ddd.ddddd	ddd.ddddd	dd.ddddd
Decimal Minutes	mm.mmm	mm.mmm	mm.mmm	mm.mmm	mm.mmm	mm.mmm	mm.mmm	mm.mmm
Decimal Seconds	no	ss.s	ss.s	ss.s	ss.s	ss.s	ss.s	ss.s
UTM	no	1 meter	1 meter	1 meter	1 meter	1 meter	1 meter	1 meter

Garmin GPSMAP 175	Magellan GPS 2000 XL	Magellan GPS 3000 XL	Magellan GPS 4000 XL	Magellan Meridian XL	Magellan Trailblazer XL	Magellan NAV DLX 10	Magellan NAV 6000	Silva 1000 XL	Trimble Scoutmaster
22 oz	10 oz	10 oz	10 oz	14 oz	14 oz	28 oz	21 oz	16 oz	14 oz
2.9 x 7.6 x 2.1	2.3 x 6.6 x 1.3	2.3 x 6.6 x 1.3	2.3 x 6.6 x 1.3	4.2 x 6.1 x 1.3	4.2 x 6.1 x 1.3	5 x 8.8 x 2.1	3.2 x 7.5 x 1.7	3.2 x 7.6 x 1.5	3.2 x 6.6 x 1.7
2.3 x 3.5	1.4 x 1.8	1.4 x 1.8	1.4 x 1.8	2.2 x 1.7	2.2 x 1.7	2.5 x 1.7	2.2 x 1.7	1.9 x .9	2.2 x 1
yes	yes	yes	yes	yes	yes	yes	yes	no	no
160 x 240	65 x 102	65 x 102	65 x 102	80 x 64	80 x 64	108 x 64	320 x 240	n/a	n/a
yes	no	no	no	no	no	no	yes	yes	no
scroll	scroll	scroll	scroll	scroll	scroll	numbers	scroll	scroll	scroll
patch	patch	patch	patch	quad helix	quad helix	quad helix	patch	patch	patch
no	no	no	no	yes	yes	yes	no	no	no
MCX	none	proprietary	proprietary	BNC	BNC	BNC	proprietary	proprietary	proprietary
-15C to +70C	-10C to +60C	-10C to +60C	-10C to +60C	-10C to +60C	-10C to +60C	-10C to +60C	-10C to +60C	-25C to +70C	-10C to +60C
-40C to ???	-40C to +75C	-40C to +75C	-40C to +75C	-40C to +75C	-40C to +75C	-40C to +75C	-40C to +75C	-30C to +80C	-20C to +70C
waterproof	waterproof	waterproof	waterproof	waterproof	waterproof	waterproof	waterproof	water tight	water resistent
12	2	2	2	2	2	10	2	5	3
12	12	12	12	12	12	12	12	12	8
Garmin	Magellan	Magellan	Magellan	Magellan	Magellan	Magellan	Magellan	Rockwell	Trimble
1.5W	.6W	.6W	.6W	.65W	.65W	1.44W	1.44W	1W	1.4W
6 x AA	4 x AA	4 x AA	4 x AA	3 x AA	3 x AA	6 x AA	6 x AA	6 x AA	4 x AA
graph	30 min warning	30 min warning	30 min warning	30 min warning	30 min warning	30 min warning	30 min warning	volts	20 min warning
6-40VDC	10-16VDC	10-16VDC	10-16VDC	10-16VDC	10-35VDC	10-35VDC	10-35VDC	6-16.5VDC	9-32 VDC
no	no	no	no	yes	yes	no	no	no	yes
no	no	no	no	no	no	yes	no	no	yes
yes	yes	yes	yes	yes	yes	yes	yes	yes	no
yes	yes	yes	yes	yes	yes	yes	no	yes	no
yes	no	yes	yes	yes	yes	yes	yes	yes	yes
180/182/183	no	183	183	183	183	183	180/183	183	183
yes	no	yes	yes	yes	yes	yes	yes	yes	yes
100+	72	72	72	72	72	11	93	100+	123
no	yes	yes	yes	yes	yes	yes	yes	yes	yes
yes	yes	yes	yes	yes	yes	yes	yes	yes	yes
yes	yes	yes	yes	yes	yes	yes	no	yes	yes
yes	no	no	no	no	no	no	no	no	no
no	no	no	no	no	no	no	no	no	no
7	5	5	5	5	5	6	6	9	4
no	yes	yes	yes	yes	yes	no	yes	no	no
yes	yes	yes	yes	yes	yes	yes	yes	yes	yes
yes	no	no	no	no	no	no	no	no	no
yes	no	no	no	no	no	yes	no	yes	no
dd.ddddd	no	no	no	no	no	no	no	no	no
mm.mmm	mm.mmm	mm.mmm	mm.mmm	mm.mm	mm.mm	mm.mmm	mm.mmm	mm.mm	mm.mmm
ss.s	ss	ss	ss	ss	ss	ss	ss	ss.s	ss.s
1 meter	1 meter	1 meter	1 meter	1 meter	1 meter	1 meter	1 meter	10 meter	1 meter

Handheld GPS Receivers: Features and Functions	Eagle AccuNav Sport	Lowrance Global Map Sport	Lowrance Global Nav 200	Garmin GPS 38	Garmin GPS 40	Garmin GPS 45 XL	Garmin GPS II	Garmin GPS 12 XL
Operating Status:								
Satellite Lock Indicator	always shown	always shown	always shown	alarm only	alarm only	alarm only	alarm only	alarm only
2D/3D Operating Mode	no	no	no	lookup	lookup	lookup	lookup	lookup
Quality of Position Fix	PDOP	PDOP	index	feet	feet	feet	feet	feet
Satellite Positions	azim/elev	azim/elev	graph	graph	graph	graph	graph	graph
Satellite Signal Strength	S/N ratio	S/N ratio	graph	graph	graph	graph	graph	graph
Satellite IDs (PRNs)	yes	yes	yes	yes	yes	yes	yes	yes
Navigation Features:								
Nearest Waypoints	plot	plot	plot	plot/list	plot/list	plot/list	plot/list	plot/list
Waypoint Deg/Dist Meas.	no	yes	yes	yes	yes	yes	yes	yes
Auto Waypoint Recording	no	yes	no	yes	no	no	yes	yes
Reversible Routes	yes	yes	yes	yes	yes	yes	yes	yes
CDI Range (miles)	.1 to 9.99	.1 to 9.99	.01 to 9.75	.25 to 5	.25 to 5	.25 to 5	.25 to 5	.25 to 5
Built-in Map	no	yes	no	no	no	no	no	no
Map Cartridges	no	IMSA/C-Map	no	no	no	no	no	no
Navigation Display:								
Configurable Screen	yes	yes	yes	no	no	no	no	no
Measurement Unit Config	individual	individual	individual	group	group	group	group	group
Graphic Compass Dial	yes	yes	yes	yes	yes	yes	yes	yes
Velocity Made Good	yes	yes	yes	yes	yes	yes	yes	yes
Maximum Speed (mph)	999	999	999	104	104	104	104	999
Cross Track Error (CDI)	yes	yes	yes	yes	yes	yes	yes	yes
Estimated Time Of Arrival	yes	yes	yes	yes	yes	yes	yes	yes
Estimated Time Enroute	yes	yes	yes	yes	yes	yes	yes	yes
Trip Odometer	no	no	no	yes	no	yes	yes	yes
Waypoints & Routes:								
Max. No. Waypoints	200	250	250	250	250	250	250	500
Max. No. Routes	20	20	20	20	20	20	20	20
Max. Legs Per Route	10	250	250	29	29	29	29	29
Waypoint Name Characters	13	12	8	6	6	6	6	6
Waypoint Memo Char.	none	none	none	16	16	16	16	16
Waypoint Date/Time Stamp	no	yes	yes	yes	yes	yes	yes	yes
Waypoint Icons	15	15	15	none	none	none	none	none
Waypoint Projecting	no	no	no	yes	yes	yes	yes	yes
Plot Capabilities:								
No. Track Plot Points	500	1000	2,000	768	768	768	1,024	1,024
Plot Update Rate	1 sec to 10 min	time or dist.	time or dist.	auto, variable	auto, variable	auto, variable	auto, variable	auto, variable
Plot Scale Range (miles)	.1 to 1,000	.1 to 4,000	.1 to 2,000	.2 to 320	.2 to 320	.2 to 320	.2 to 320	.2 to 320
Auto Backtrack	no	no	no	yes	no	yes	yes	yes
Alarms:								
Audible Alarms	yes	yes	yes	no	yes	yes	no	yes
Arrival	yes	yes	yes	no	no	no	no	yes
Proximity	no	no	no	no	no	no	no	yes
Anchor Drift	no	yes	yes	no	no	no	no	no
XTE	yes	yes	yes	no	no	no	no	no
Misc Features:								
Sunrise/Sunset Time	no	no	no	yes	yes	yes	yes	yes
Sun/Moon Azm/Elev	no	no	no	no	no	no	no	no
Moon Phase	no	no	no	no	no	no	no	no

	Garmin GPSMAP 175	Magellan GPS 2000 XL	Magellan GPS 3000 XL	Magellan GPS 4000 XL	Magellan Meridian XL	Magellan Trailblazer XL	Magellan NAV DLX 10	Magellan NAV 6000	Silva 1000 XL	Trimble Scoutmaster
alarm only	always shown	always shown	always shown	always shown	always shown	always shown	always shown	always shown	always shown
look up	always shown	always shown	always shown	always shown	always shown	always shown	always shown	always shown	always shown
feet	warning icon	warning icon	warning icon	warning icon	warning icon	warning icon	warning icon	PDOP	PDOP
graph	graph	graph	graph	graph	graph	azim/elev	graph	none	azim/elev
graph	index	index	index	index	index	index	index	S/N ratio	index
yes	no	no	no	yes	yes	yes	yes	no	yes
plot/list	graph/list	graph/list	graph/list	graph/list	graph/list	graph/list	graph/list	no	list
yes	no	no	no	no	no	no	no	no	yes
yes	no	no	no	no	no	no	no	yes	no
yes	yes	yes	yes	yes	yes	yes	yes	n/a	yes
.25 to 5	.2 to 8	.2 to 8	.2 to 8	.2 to 8	.2 to 8	.2 to 8	.2 to 8	n/a	.2 to 12
yes	no	no	no	no	no	no	yes	no	no
G-chart	no	no	no	no	no	no	C-map NT	no	no
no	yes	yes	yes	yes	yes	yes	yes	no	no
group	individual	individual	individual	individual	individual	individual	individual	individual	individual
yes	yes	yes	yes	yes	yes	yes	yes	no	no
yes	yes	yes	yes	yes	yes	yes	yes	no	no
104	951	951	951	951	951	951	951	999	999
yes	yes	yes	yes	yes	yes	yes	yes	yes	no
yes	yes	yes	yes	yes	yes	yes	yes	yes	yes
yes	yes	yes	yes	yes	yes	yes	yes	no	no
yes	yes	yes	yes	yes	yes	no	yes	yes	yes
250	200	200	200	200	200	1,000	500	999	250
20	5	5	5	5	5	20	25	none	10
29	20	20	20	15	15	20	50	n/a	10
6	6	6	6	5	5	5	8	7	14
20	26	26	26	26	26	18	20	none	none
yes	yes	yes	yes	yes	yes	no	yes	yes	yes
35	none	none	none	9	11	4	9	n/a	n/a
yes	yes	yes	yes	yes	yes	yes	yes	yes	yes
1,048	48	48	48	48	48	48	2,000	n/a	n/a
auto, variable	.1 to 5 miles	.1 to 5 miles	.1 to 5 miles	.1 to 5 miles	.1 to 5 miles	10 min to 24hr	.1 to 5 miles	n/a	n/a
.125 to 4096	.2 to 100	.2 to 100	.2 to 100	.1 to 50	.1 to 50	.25 to 100	.1 to 50	n/a	n/a
yes	yes	yes	yes	yes	yes	no	yes	n/a	n/a
yes	no	no	no	no	no	yes	yes	no	no
yes	yes	yes	yes	yes	yes	yes	yes	no	no
yes	no	no	no	no	no	yes	yes	no	no
yes	no	no	no	no	no	yes	yes	no	no
yes	no	no	no	no	no	yes	yes	no	no
yes	yes	yes	yes	yes	yes	yes	yes	no	yes
no	no	no	no	no	no	no	no	no	yes
no	yes	yes	yes	yes	yes	yes	yes	no	no

Handheld GPS Receivers: Features and Functions	A Brief Explanation Of The Receiver Comparison
Physical:	
Weight (w/batteries)	Receiver weight with batteries installed (w/o case)
Dimensions (in. WxHxD)	Overall size of the receiver in inches
Screen Size (in. WxH)	Size of the display screen in inches
Graphic Display	Whether the receiver has a graphic display, or is text only
Screen Res. (pixels WxH)	For receivers that have graphic displays, the number of pixels of screen resolution
Keyboard Backlight	Whether or not the receiver has a backlight feature for its data entry keys
Keyboard Style	Whether the keyboard has numeric keys, alphabetic keys, or 4 scroll keys for data entry
Antenna Type	The type of antenna; either a patch-style (usually internal) or quadrifilar helix (usually external)
Antenna Extension Avail.	Whether the antenna can be extended with the use of a cable
External Antenna Plug	The type of external antenna connection that is available on the unit
Operating Temperature	The rated range of temperature in which the receiver can safely operate (degrees Celsius)
Storage Temparature	The rated range of temperature in which the receiver can be safely stored (degrees Celsius)
Water Resistence	The rated ability of the receiver to withstand exposure to moisture
Electronics:	
No. Parallel Channels	The number of separate parallel channels within the receiver
Max No. Satellites	The maximum number of satellites the receiver can track at one time
Chipset	The manufacturer of the chipset used in the receiver
Power Consumption	The rated power consumption of the receiver in watts
No. & Size Batteries	The number of batteries used by the receiver and their size
Battery Strength Indicator	The type of battery condition indicator; warnings only indicate the very end of battery life
Input Voltage	The rated range of voltage the receiver will accept at its external power plug
Lockable On Switch	Whether the on/off switch can be locked to prevent accidental activation
Auto Shutoff	Whether the receiver has a feature that shuts the unit off after a certain amount of time
Initial Coordinate Entry	Whether the receiver allows approximate location coordinates to be entered to speed up initialization
Simulator Mode	Whether the receiver has a simulation mode of operation for practice and less power drain for data entry
Data Interface:	
Differential Capable	Whether the receiver can be connected to a differential GPS beacon
NMEA Interface	The versions of NMEA data interchange the receiver can provide
Waypoint I/O Software	Whether the receiver has the capability to upload and download waypoints to a PC (RS232)
Datums:	
Number Preprogammed	The number of different datums programed into the receiver
User Definable	Whether the receiver is capable of accepting user-defined datums
Coordinate Types:	
Latitude/Longitude	Whether the receiver has latitude/longitude coordinate capability
UTM	Whether the receiver has Universal Transverse Mercator coordinate capability
UPS	Whether the receiver has Universal Polar Stereographic coordinate capability
MGRS	Whether the receiver has Military Grid Reference System coordinate capability
Other	How many other different coordinate systems are built into the receiver (Maidenhead, local grids, etc.)
User Definable	Whether the receiver is capable of accepting user-defined coordinate systems
Declination Adj:	
Automatic Magnetic	Whether the receiver can automatically report magnetic directions based on the location of the receiver
Automatic Grid	Whether the receiver can automatically report grid directions based on the location of the receiver
User Specified	Whether the receiver can report directions based on a user-supplied offset
Position Resolution:	
Decimal Degrees	The maximum number of decimal places for decimal degree coordinates
Decimal Minutes	The maximum number of decimal places for decimal minute coordinates
Decimal Seconds	The maximum number of decimal places for decimal second coordinates
UTM	The highest resolution (in meters) for UTM coordinates

Handheld GPS Receivers: Features and Functions	A Brief Explanation Of The Receiver Comparison
Operating Status:	
Satellite Lock Indicator	How satellite lock status is indicated; always shown means all nav & position screens indicate lock
2D/3D Operating Mode	If and how 2D or 3D operating mode is indicated; lookup requires scrolling to a specific screen
Quality of Position Fix	How the receiver reports satellite geometry; PDOP is industry standard, others are manufacturer specific
Satellite Positions	How the position of satellites is reported; azim/elev are precise numbers, graph is visual approximations
Satellite Signal Strength	How satellite signal strength is reported; S/N ratios are precise numbers, graph & index are visual approximations
Satellite IDs	Whether the receiver reports satellite identification numbers (usually as PRN or SVN numbers)
Navigation Features:	
Nearest Waypoints	Whether and how the receiver displays the closest waypoints to its current position
Waypoint Deg/Dist Meas.	Whether the receiver has a dedicated feature for giving the distance and direction between stored waypoints
Auto Waypoint Recording	Whether the receiver is capable of automatically storing waypoints at fixed time or distance intervals
Reversible Routes	Whether the receiver is capable of navigating an existing route in the reverse direction
CDI Range	The minimum and maximum selectable values for a course deviation indicator (or cross track error) display
Built-in Map	Whether the receiver has a built-in electronic map of water and land features
Map Cartridges	The type of plug-in map cartridges the receiver is capable of using
Navigation Display:	
Configurable Screen	Whether the elements shown on position or navigation screens can be configured by the user
Measurement Unit Config	Whether the various distance and speed measurement units can be individually configured, or only as a group
Graphic Compass Dial	Whether the display has the capability to emulate a compass dial
Velocity Made Good	Whether the receiver has the capability to display the rate at which it is closing on a target waypoint
Maximum Speed Reported	The maximum speed the receiver is capable of reporting
Cross Track Error (CDI)	Whether the receiver is capable of reporting the lateral distance it is off a previously set course
Estimated Time Of Arrival	Whether the receiver can provide an estimated time of arrival at a waypoint based on current progress
Estimated Time Enroute	Whether the receiver can provide an estimated time of travel to a waypoint based on current progress
Trip Odometer	Whether the receiver can report the accumulated distance traveled
Waypoints & Routes:	
Max. No. Waypoints	The maximum number of waypoints that can be stored in the receiver's memory
Max. No. Routes	The maximum number of routes that can be stored in the receiver's memory
Max. Legs Per Route	The maximum number of legs that can be included in a single route
Waypoint Name Characters	The maximum number of characters that can be used in a waypoint's name
Waypoint Memo Char.	The maximum number of characters that can be used in a memo field associated with a waypoint
Waypoint Date/Time Stamp	Whether the receiver is capable of automatically recording the date and time a waypoint is stored
Waypoint Icons	The number of different icons available for representing waypoints on graphic screens
Waypoint Projecting	Whether the receiver is capable of defining new waypoints by projecting distance and/or direction
Plot Capabilities:	
No. Track Plot Points	The maximum number of points that can be recorded on a graphic track plot screen
Plot Update Rate	The minimum and maximum rate at which track plot points can be recorded
Plot Scale Range	The minimum and maximum scale available on the track plot screen (in miles)
Auto Backtrack	Whether the receiver has the ability to automatically backtrack a track plot course
Alarms:	
Audible Alarms	Whether any of the following alarms, if available, have an audible signal capability
Arrival	An alarm that signals your arrival at a destination waypoint (in a route or a "GoTo")
Proximity	An alarm that signals your proximity to a specified waypoint (usually a hazard marker such as a reef)
Anchor Drift	An alarm that signals you have moved away from a specified waypoint by a certain distance
XTE	An alarm that signals that you have moved laterally away from a course by some specified distance
Misc Features:	
Sunrise/Sunset Time	Whether the receiver is capable of providing the time of sunrise and sunset for any date and location
Sun/Moon Azm/Elev	Whether the receiver is capable of providing the position of the sun and moon for any date, time, and location
Moon Phase	Whether the receiver is capable of indicating the phase of the moon for any date and location

Glossary of Terms

2D Mode . . . . . . .A GPS receiver operating mode where only 3 satellites are used for a position fix. Only horizontal position estimates are provided as outputs; the last calculated elevation is used as a part of the position solution. Any elevation error can lead to substantial horizontal position error.

3D Mode . . . . . . .A GPS receiver operating mode where at least 4 satellites are used for a position fix. Both horizontal and vertical position estimates are provided as outputs.

Agonic Line . . . . .An isogonic line of zero magnetic declination. *see Isogonic Line*

Almanac . . . . . . .General information on the orbits and conditions of all the GPS satellites. Information for the entire constellation is transmitted by each of the satellites. It takes about 12.5 minutes for the complete almanac to be transmitted. The almanac remains valid for about six months. *see also Ephemeris*

Altimeter . . . . . . .A device used to measure altitude or elevation relative to a reference point (such as mean sea level). Usually it is a barometer, meaning it actually measures air pressure.

Altitude . . . . .A measurement of height, usually expressed in feet or meters above mean sea level (msl). Altitude usually refers to objects that are above the ground - such as airplanes. *see also Elevation*

Anti-Spoofing . . . .Encryption of the P-code signal from the GPS satellites so only authorized users may have access to the signal, and to guard against fake transmissions.

Azimuth . . . . . . .Angular horizontal direction, measured clockwise around a circle, where the value indicates 1/360th of a circle (degrees) and 0° is North, 90° is East, 180° is South, 270° is West, and 360° is also North. *see also Bearing and Heading*

Base Line . . . . . . .The line of latitude that passes through the Initial Point in the Township and Range (USPLSS) grid system.

Bearing . . . . .Angular horizontal direction, measured either clockwise or counter clockwise around one fourth of a circle, where the value is in degrees relative to either north or south. Written as N30°E (Azimuth=30°), S25°E (Azimuth=165°), etc. It is commonly misused in place of the term "Azimuth" in which case the context (degrees without direction letters) renders the "misuse" harmless. In a GPS receiver, it usually refers to the direction to a waypoint. *see also Azimuth and Heading*

Bench Mark . . . . .A relatively permanent natural or man-made object (usually shown on a topo map) whose precise elevation is known.

C/A-Code . . . . . . .Coarse Acquisition Code. The basic positioning signal that GPS satellites transmit on the civilian access channel (L1). It contains binary data the receiver uses to fix its position, the time, etc. This is the basis of the Standard Positioning Service.

Cartesian . . . .Coordinates that are defined by their linear distance along two or three axes
Coordinates   that form right angles. Two axes are used for the familiar two-dimensional paper grid. Three axes are used for three-dimensional space.

Cartography . . . . .The art and science of making maps.

CDI . . . . .Course Deviation Indicator. A GPS receiver function that indicates the amount of lateral distance it is "off" a straight line course between two waypoints.

Chart . . . . .A term used for maps designed chiefly for nautical or aeronautical purposes

Clark 1866 . . . . . .The name of the ellipsoid that is used to model the shape of the earth in NAD27.

COG . . . . .Course Over Ground. The direction a GPS receiver is actually traveling (it doesn't matter which way it is facing).

Cold Start . . . . . . .The power-on sequence when a receiver must download almanac data before establishing a position fix. *see also Initialization*

Compass . . . . .A device used to indicate horizontal directions, usually (but not always) based on the earth's magnetic field.

Compass Rose . . .A term used for a compass card that dates back to the days when compasses were divided into 32 directional indicators, i.e., N, NE, NNE, etc.

Contour Interval . .The difference in elevation between two adjacent contour lines.

Contour Line . . . .A line on a topographic map that represents a constant elevation.

Control Segment . .The ground stations and their related functions that are used to control GPS satellites. One of the three "parts" of the GPS system.

Coordinates . . . . . .The numbers (and/or letters) that describe a location within a spatial reference system. Examples include latitude/longitude, UTM "easting" and "northing" values, etc.

Course . . . . .In a GPS receiver, the direction between two waypoints in a route, or when a "GoTo" function is executed.

Datum . . . . .The vertical or horizontal reference system associated with particular coordinates and elevations. A vertical datum is used when measuring relative height, and is usually related to "mean sea level." A horizontal datum is used when measuring horizontal coordinate. It consists of a model of the shape of the earth (an ellipsoid) and a physical location that is deemed to be the origin.

Declination . . . . . .The angular difference between true (geographic) north and some other version of north (such as grid or magnetic north).

DEM . . . . .Digital Elevation Model. A type of electronic map that is based on a combination of coordinates and their associated elevation values.

Differential GPS . . .A system that uses radio signals broadcast from ground stations to substantially improve the positioning accuracy of GPS, and overcome the effects of selective availability.

Dividers . . . . . . .A tool with two hinged arms that can be used to precisely transfer distances from a map to its bar scale.

DOP . . . . .Dilution of Precision. A family of measurements that indicate how GPS satellite geometry affects the accuracy of a time or position fix.

DRG . . . . .Digital Raster Graphic. A type of electronic map based on a bit-map graphic image that has had its pixel coordinate values converted to geographic coordinate values.

Easting . . . . .The distance of a point east of the origin in the UTM coordinate system.

ECEF . . . . .Earth Centered Earth Fixed. A cartesian coordinate system where the origin is the center of the earth, and the axes are tied to specific latitude/longitude coordinates.

Elevation . . . . . . .A measurement of height, usually expressed in feet or meters above mean sea level (msl). Elevation is usually applied to things that are on the ground - such as cities. Also used to describe a celestial body's angle above the horizon. *see also Altitude*

Ellipsoid . . . . .A flattened sphere that can be described with a mathematical formula. They are used to represent the approximate shape of the earth at sea level. *see also Geoid*

Ephemeris . . . . . . .Precise information about the orbital path of a particular GPS satellite measured in both space and time. This information is transmitted only by the satellite in question, and only remains valid for a short period of time (from about 30 minutes to over an hour, depending on the receiver's design). *see also Almanac*

ETA . . . . .Estimated Time of Arrival. The projected time that you will arrive at your destination waypoint based on your current rate of progress.

ETE . . . . .Estimated Time Enroute. The projected travel time remaining before you will arrive at your destination waypoint based on your current rate of progress.

Geoid . . . . .An imaginary surface of the earth that is characterized by constant gravity. It corresponds to the average level of the ocean (where there are oceans), and to the vertical location that has the same gravity as the level of the ocean (everywhere else).

GIS . . . . .Geographic Information System. A category of computer programs and applications that are used to organize, analyze, and display spatial (geographic) data.

GLONASS . . . . . .Global'naya Navigatsionnaya Sputnikovaya Sistema. The Russian GPS system (their counterpart to NAVSTAR).

GMT . . . . .Greenwich Mean Time. Mean solar time at the 0° (prime) meridian that runs through Greenwich, England. *see also UTC*

GPS . . . . .Global Positioning System. A generic term that refers to a satellite-based positioning system that gives a user's position anywhere on earth. Specific systems include NAVSTAR and GLONASS.

Graticule . . . . . . .The lines of latitude and longitude on a map that represent the angular coordinate system. *see also Grid*

Great Circle . . . . .A plane that slices through the Earth **and** passes through the center of the earth. Always a "shortest distance" route between two points. *see also Little Circle*

Grid . . . . .Parallel lines on a map that represent a rectangular coordinate system. *see also Graticule.*

Grid North . . . . . . .The direction that the top of a north-south grid line points in a rectangular coordinate system.

Grid Zone . . . . . . .One of 60 semi-rectangular areas covered by the global UTM grid system. Each zone extends from latitude 80° South to latitude 84° North, and is 6 degrees of longitude wide.

Hachure Lines . . . .A series of short lines used to indicate topographic relief.

Heading . . . . .The horizontal direction that you are facing or traveling. *see also Bearing and Azimuth*

HDOP . . . . .Horizontal Dilution of Precision. *see DOP*

Hot Start . . . . . . .The power-on sequence when a GPS receiver has valid almanac and ephemeris data.

Initialization . . . . .The power-on process a GPS receiver goes through to locate its position when either a) it has been moved more than a few hundred miles, b) more than half a year has passed since its last use, or c) it has lost the correct UTC time.

Isogonic Line . . . .A line of constant magnetic declination (as of a specific date).

L1/L2 . . . . .The two channels used by NAVSTAR satellites to transmit timing and ranging signals to GPS receivers. Civilian personal navigation receivers use only the L1 channel, more advanced receivers (such as those used by the military) use both the L1 and L2 channels.

Landmark . . . . . . .A distinctive natural or manmade feature found in the outdoors. Also a term used by some GPS manufacturers to denote a waypoint.

Latitude . . . . .The angular distance (in degrees) of a point north or south of the equator. If direction is not specified, a negative value indicates south of the equator.

Legend . . . . .The section of a map that describes the symbology used on the map.

Little Circle . . . . .A plane that slices through the Earth without passing through the center of the earth. Not a "shortest distance" route between two points. *see also Great Circle.*

Lock . . . . .An operating state wherein a GPS receiver is actively reading enough satellite signals to calculate a fix.

Longitude . . . . . . .The angular distance (in degrees) of a point east or west of the prime meridian. In the case of U.S. maps, the prime meridian runs through Greenwich, England. If direction is not specified, a negative value indicates west of the prime meridian.

Loxodromic . . . . . .The path that is traced on the globe whenever a constant compass heading (excluding
Curve   exactly east, west, north or south) is followed. Eventually converges on either the North or South Pole.

MGRS . . . . .Military Grid Referrence System. A metric based coordinate system that is a subset of the UTM system. It uses letter pairs to represent 10km by 10km squares.

Magnetic . . . . .The difference between true north and magnetic north at a specific location.
Declination

Magnetic North . . .The direction that the north needle on a compass needle points (in the absence of local magnetic interference).

Mean Sea Level . .The average level of the ocean. On land, the elevation of the imaginary surface whose gravitational potential is the same as the average on the surface of the ocean.

Meridian . . . . .A line of longitude. *see Longitude*

Mil . . . . .A unit of angular measurement that divides a circle into 6400 units.

MOB . . . . .Man Over Board. A function found on many GPS receivers that allows rapid way-point definition and automatically starts navigation to that waypoint.

Multipath . . . . . .GPS satellite signal degradation caused by the signal bouncing off some reflective
Interference   surface prior to reaching the receiver.

NAD27 . . . . .North American Datum of 1927. The datum used on virtually all large scale USGS topographic maps.

NAD83 . . . . .North American Datum of 1983. A newer datum used on some maps produced more recently in the U.S. Almost identical to WGS84.

NAVSTAR . . . . . .The name of the U.S. Department of Defense satellite navigation system that is discussed throughout this book.

Neatline . . . . .The lines that separate the face of a map from the margins. On quadrangle maps the neatlines correspond to lines of latitude and longitude (graticules).

NMEA . . . . .National Maritime Electronics Association. An organization that sets standards for electronic devices used in marine applications.

Northing . . . . .The distance of a point north of the origin in the UTM coordinate system.

Orientation . . . . . .Establishing directional alignment between the ground, a map, and/or a compass.

Orienteering . . . . .A sport that involves using a compass to find locations.

Parallel . . . . .A line of latitude. *see Latitude*

P-Code . . . . .Precision Code. A second positioning signal sent by GPS satellites over the L2 channel. It is used in the Precise Positioning Service (PPS) to reduce error due to atmospheric conditions and to avoid the effects of Selective Availability (SA). *see also Y-code*

PDOP . . . . .Position Dilution of Precision. A summary DOP indicator that reflects horizontal, vertical, and time related error all in one figure. *see DOP*

Planimetric . . . . . .A type of map that contains physical features and various political/cultural boundaries, but does not include contour lines or other elevation data.

Polaris . . . . .The North Star.

Position Fix . . . . .The coordinates calculated by a GPS receiver by using the signals from at least three satellites.

PPS . . . . .Precise Positioning Service. Full accuracy GPS services that are obtained by a receiver that has access to both the C/A-code and the P-code signals.

Prime Meridian . . .The line of longitude that is assigned a value of zero in a particular horizontal datum. U.S. maps are based on a prime meridian that passes through Greenwich, England.

Principal Meridian The meridian that passes through the Initial Point in the Township and Range (USPLSS) grid system.

Protractor . . . . . . .A device used to measure horizontal angles on a map.

Quadrangle . . . . . .A rectangle-like area bounded by lines of latitude and longitude.

Quadrifilar Helix . .A type of circular polarized antenna that is used on some handheld GPS receivers.

Ray . . . . .A straight line that begins at a point and extends to infinity.

Reacquisition . . . .When a GPS receiver temporarily loses one or more of the satellite signals used for a position fix and it must reestablish its satellite lock.

Representative . . .The unit-less scale of a map expressed as the ratio of 1 distance unit on the map
Fraction   to the corresponding number of distance units on the ground.

Rhumb Line . . . . .A path between two points on earth that has a constant direction.

Roamer . . . . .A map template that has appropriate distance scales printed at right angles so that both northing and easting measurements can be read at once.

Route . . . . .In a GPS receiver, a sequential series of waypoints that form a series of legs.

Satellite Geometry The position of GPS satellites relative to the GPS receiver.

Scale . . . . .The relationship between distance on a map and the ground it represents.

Section . . . . .An area of approximately 1 mile by 1 mile square (approximately 640 acres) used in the U.S. Public Land Survey System. *see USPLSS*

SA . . . . .Selective Availability. The intentional degradation of GPS signals available to civilian users so that their position fixes are less accurate.

SOG . . . . .Speed Over Ground. The speed at which a GPS receiver is traveling.

Space Segment . . .The satellite portion of the GPS system.

SPS . . . . .Standard Positioning Service. The GPS service that is available to civilian users, with accuracy degradation caused by Selective Availability. *see C/A code*

SPCS . . . . .State Plane Coordinate System. A coordinate system that covers all 50 states with a combination of Transverse Mercator and Lambert Conic projections.

Three-Dimension . . .*see 3D Mode*
Mode

Topographic Map .A map that presents both horizontal and vertical positions of the features shown.

Township . . . . . . .An area approximately 6 miles by 6 miles square (36 sections) used in the U.S. Public Lands Survey System. *see USPLSS*

True North . . . . . .The direction indicated by a line of longitude.

TTG . . . . .Time To Go. The remaining elapsed time to your destination waypoint based on your current progress.

Two-Dimension . . .*see 2D Mode*
Mode

UPS . . . . .Universal Polar Stereographic. A rectangular grid system that is used to cover the North and South poles (above 84°N and below 80°S). A compliment to the UTM system.

USGS . . . . .United States Geologic Survey. A part of the U.S. Department of Interior. The primary mapping agency for the U.S. government.

USPLSS . . . . . . .United States Public Land Survey System. A rectangular grid system that is centered on the intersection of baselines (latitude) and principal meridians (longitude).

UTC . . . . .Universal Time Coordinated. The time to which all GPS signals are synchronized, virtually identical to Greenwich Mean Time.

UTM . . . . .Universal Transverse Mercator. A rectangular grid system that covers the earth between latitude 80° South to latitude 84° North.

User Segment . . . .The part of the GPS system that is at the user end of the system, i.e. the GPS receiver.

VMG . . . . .Velocity Made Good. The rate at which a GPS receiver is closing on a destination (GoTo) waypoint.

Warm Start . . . . . .Power-on sequence when a receiver already has valid almanac data, but must download ephemeris data for each of the satellites used to establish a position fix.

Waypoint . . . . . . .A representation of a point on the earth that is stored in a GPS receiver in the form of precise geographic coordinates. See also page *xi* in the Preface.

WGS 84 . . . . .World Geodetic System 1984. The internal datum of the NAVSTAR GPS system.

XTE . . . . .Cross Track Error. The amount of perpendicular distance a receiver is away from a course between two waypoints.

Y-Code . . . . .An encrypted form of the P-Code signal that provides anti-spoofing (A-S).

Bibliography

Dixon, Conrad (1994): *Using GPS*, Sheridan House, Dobbs Ferry, New York.

Fleming, June (1994): *Staying Found*, The Mountaineers, Seattle, Washington

Greenhood, David (1964): *Mapping*, University of Chicago Press, Chicago.

Hagar, J., Fry, l., Jacks, S., and Hill, D. (1992): *Datums, Ellipsoids, Grids, and Grid Reference Systems*, Defense Mapping Agency, Washington, D.C.

Hofmann-Wellenhof, B., Lichtenegger, H., and Collins, J. (1993): *GPS Theory and Practice*, Springer-Verlag, Wein New York.

Kals, W.S. (1983): *Land Navigation Handbook*, Sierra Club Books, San Francisco

Kjellstrom, Bjorn (1967): *Be Expert With Map & Compass*, Scribner's, New York

Muehrcke, Phillip C. and Juliana O. (1992): *Map Use*, JP Publications, Madison, Wisconsin.

Raisz, Erwin (1962): *Principles of Cartography*, McGraw-Hill, New York.

Sebert, Louis (1984): *Map Reading*, Canada Map Company, Toronto.

Seidman, David (1995): *The Essential Wilderness Navigator*, Ragged Mountain Press, Camden, Maine

Thompson, Morris M. (1988): *Maps for America*, U.S. Government Printing Office, Washington, D.C.

U.S. Army (1969): *Field Manual No. 21-26 (Map Reading)*, U.S. Government Printing Office, Washington, D.C.

U.S. Naval Observatory (1996): *Nautical Almanac*, U.S. Government Printing Office, Washington, D.C.

Index

About the author...

Michael Ferguson

Outdoor recreation has been an important part of Mike's life since his childhood. From his early years of hunting and fishing with his father, to his later years of kayaking, mountain biking, and backcountry skiing, one thing has remained constant: Mike would rather be in the backcountry.

Although GPS is a relatively new addition to Mike's outdoor gear bag, it quickly captured his attention. It took him but a few minutes to see the tremendous benefits GPS offers backcountry enthusiasts. It took him a little longer to write this book.

One of the reasons Mike undertook this effort was the lack of information available about land-based use of GPS for personal navigation. Since he started this project the public awareness of GPS has exploded, and it's hard to imagine anyone not being at least vaguely familiar with satellite-based navigation. Yet the challenge of understanding the technology associated with GPS remains as daunting as ever. Mike's goal in writing **GPS Land Navigation** has been to remove the mystery surrounding this phenomenal technology, and allow anyone who owns a GPS receiver to become an expert in its use.

When Mike is not having fun in the great outdoors, he can often be found in his office in the Idaho State Capitol building, where he serves as the Chief Economist for the State of Idaho. There he gets a different kind of excitement, interacting with legislators, lobbyists, bureaucrats, and the media. It's fun in its own way, but the truth is: Mike would rather be in the backcountry.

Also Available From Glassford Publishing:

GPS Waypoints: Arizona	304p $17.95	ISBN 1-892182-04-1
GPS Waypoints: Colorado	256p $15.95	ISBN 1-892182-08-4
GPS Waypoints: Idaho	160p $12.95	ISBN 1-892182-16-5
GPS Waypoints: Oregon	288p $16.95	ISBN 1-892182-41-6
GPS Waypoints: Utah	208p $14.95	ISBN 1-892182-49-1
GPS Waypoints: Washington	208p $14.95	ISBN 1-892182-53-X

This series of books provide state-by-state collections of coordinates for summits, lakes, campgrounds, airstrips, highway intersections, and many other categories. They provide GPS users with instant access to thousands of precise waypoints. These books are an essential accessory for anyone who uses GPS for personal navigation, whether on the highways or in the backcountry. Prices range from $12.95 to $18.95, depending on the state. Titles available as of this printing are listed above. Call or write for an updated list.

GPS Land Navigation   272p $19.95   ISBN 0-9652202-5-7

This is the definitive book for land-based users of GPS for personal navigation. Besides its thorough and easy to understand coverage of GPS, this book also provides extensive sections on maps, compasses, altimeters, map-reading tools, and the traditional (pre-GPS) navigation methods. It contains over 150 illustrations and three waypoint appendices. If you want to become an expert GPS land navigator, *GPS Land Navigation* is the book for you.

Forthcoming Titles:

GPS: Easy Navigation For Everyone   ISBN 0-9652202-6-5

This book is scheduled for release in mid-2000. It is a basic primer on how to get the most from your GPS receiver with the least amount of effort. Weighing in at under 100 pages and priced less than $10, it is the "little brother" to *GPS Land Navigation*, the most complete book available on using GPS for personal navigation. Perfect for field use, anyone who uses GPS will want to keep *GPS: Easy Navigation For Everyone* handy. It fills in the many gaps left by your receiver's manual.

Ordering Instructions And Further Information:

U.S. residents may purchase books directly from Glassford Publishing. Be sure to indicate the title, ISBN number, price, and quantity of each book you wish to order. Add $2.00 per order (not per book) for shipping charges. Send a check or money order (no cash, please) to the address below. Credit card purchasers (Visa, M/C, Discover) may order using the toll-free order line. Write, call, or fax for an updated list of available titles.

Glassford Publishing   208-343-9205
P.O. Box 2895   208-344-2335 (fax)
Boise ID 83701-2895   **888-477-6379** (toll-free, credit card orders only)

Website: **www.gps-books.com**
E-mail: info@glassfordpublishing.com